ALSO BY THE AMERICAN LIBRARY ASSOCIATION:

BEST OF THE BEST FOR CHILDREN   *Denise Perry Donavin, Editor*

THE
AMERICAN
LIBRARY
ASSOCIATION
GUIDE TO
INFORMATION
ACCESS

THE
AMERICAN
LIBRARY
ASSOCIATION
GUIDE TO
INFORMATION
ACCESS

A Complete Research
Handbook and Directory

SANDY WHITELEY, Editor

RANDOM HOUSE

NEW YORK

Library of Congress Cataloging-in-Publication Data

American Library Association guide to information access : a complete research handbook and
  directory / Sandy Whiteley, editor.
     p. cm.
  Includes index.
  ISBN 0-679-43060-1
    1. Searching, Bibliographical—Handbooks, manuals, etc.
  2. Information retrieval—Handbooks, manuals, etc.
  3. Research—United States—Methodology—Handbooks, manuals, etc.
  I. Whiteley, Sandra, 1943- . II. American Library Association.
  Z711.A39 1994
  025.5′24—dc20   94-10861
           CIP

Manufactured in the United States of America

First Edition

New York   Toronto   London   Sydney   Auckland

10 9 8 7 6 5 4 3 2 1

Book design by Jo Anne Metsch

Editorial Personnel

Sandy Whiteley, Editor

Arthur Plotnik, Project Publisher

Jean T. Thompson, Contributing Editor

Michael Gorman, Associate Project Editor
Karen A. Schmidt, Research Associate
Caroline Paulison, Editorial Assistant

Advisers

Betsy Baker
Head of Reference, Northwestern
   University Library
Evanston, Illinois

George McKinley Martin
Art Librarian, District of Columbia
   Public Library
Washington, D.C.
(formerly Associate
   Librarian/Coordinator of Core
   Collection
   Howard University Libraries
   Washington, D.C.)

Maureen Pastine
Central University Librarian
Southern Methodist University
Dallas, Texas

James Rettig
Assistant Dean for Reference and
   Information Services

College of William and Mary in
   Virginia
Williamsburg, Virginia

Ron Rodriguez
Coordinator/Librarian
California State University
Fullerton, California

James H. Sweetland
Associate Professor
School of Library and Information
   Science
University of Wisconsin/Milwaukee

Jean T. Thompson
Reference Consultant
Troy, Alabama
(formerly Assistant Director for
   Reference and Information
   Services,
   University of
   Wisconsin/Madison Libraries)

About the Editor

Sandy Whiteley, editor of *The American Library Association Guide to Information Access* and author of several of its sections, is one of the foremost reference authorities in the library profession. As editor of *Reference Books Bulletin* at the American Library Association's *Booklist* magazine, she has overseen the evaluation of thousands of reference publications aimed at the nation's researchers. Editor of *Dictionaries for Adults and Children* and other publications, she was formerly head of reference at Northwestern University in Illinois. Earlier she served as reference librarian at Yale. She lives in Evanston, Illinois, with her husband, Russell Maylone, and daughter Cybele.

Contributors

Contributions from the following individuals ranged from recommendations of key resources to description of research trends and draft overviews of research in subject areas. Any flaws that might appear in this final, edited version of the *Guide to Information Access* should not reflect on the valued expertise of these research professionals or on the institutions with which they are affiliated.

Hampton M. "Skip" Auld (Jobs and Careers), Branch Librarian, Carroll County Public Library North Carroll Branch, Greenmount, Maryland

Marilyn A. Brooks (Education), Dean of Instructional Resources and University Librarian, National-Louis University Division of Learning Resources, Evanston, Illinois

John Corbin (Law), Emeritus Professor of Law, Dallas-Fort Worth School of Law, Irving, Texas

Brian Coutts (History), Head, Department of Library Public Services, Western Kentucky University Helm-Cravens Library, Bowling Green, Kentucky

Patrick Dewey (Electronic Sources of Information), Director, Maywood Public Library, Maywood, Illinois

Alice Dowd (Self-Help/Psychology), Assistant Chief, Microforms Division, and Bibliographer for Popular Culture, New York Public Library, New York, New York

Jane A. Engh (Consumer Information), Regional Reference Coordinator, Traverse des Sioux Library System, Mankato, Minnesota

Cynthia L. Etkin (History), Documents and Law Librarian, Public Services, Western Kentucky University Helm-Cravens Library, Bowling Green, Kentucky

Bruce E. Fleury (Gardening), Head, Science and Engineering Division, Tulane University Howard-Tilton Memorial Library, New Orleans, Louisiana

Robyn C. Frank (Agriculture), Head, Information Centers Branch, U.S. Department of Agriculture National Agricultural Library, assisted by Henry Gilbert, Wayne Olson, Susan Chapman, Jerry Rafats, Pat Krug, Evelyn Brownlee, Karl Schneider, and Sheldon Cheney

Jean Geil (Music), Reference Librarian, Music Library, University of Illinois, Urbana, Illinois

Rosemary C. Hanes (Film, Television), Reference Librarian, Motion Picture, Broadcasting, and Recorded Sound Division, Library of Congress, Washington, D.C.

Roland C. Hansen (Visual Arts), Readers Services Librarian, School of the Art Institute, Chicago, Illinois

Robert B. Harriman (Newspapers), Coordinator, United States Newspaper Program, Library of Congress, Washington, D.C.

Margaret H. Harter (Sexuality), Head, Information Services, The Kinsey Institute, Indiana University, Bloomington, Indiana

Stephen M. Hayes (Government Publications), Reference and Public Documents Librarian, University of Notre Dame Theodore M. Hesburgh Library, Notre Dame, Indiana

Bill Heinlein (Boating), Reference Librarian, Madden Library, California State University, Fresno, California

Eric A. Hinsdale (Environment), Reference Librarian, Trinity University, San Antonio, Texas

Maureen W. Hoffman (The Home), Librarian, Reviewer, Chicago, Illinois

Clara G. Hoover (The High School Researcher), Director of Administration, Multi Options Systems, Omaha, Nebraska (formerly Librarian, Millard South High School, Omaha, Nebraska)

Anthony Hoskins (Genealogy), Reference Librarian, Local and Family History, The Newberry Library, Chicago, Illinois

Charlie D. Hurt (Science and Technology), Director, University of Arizona School of Library Science, Tucson, Arizona

Betty L. Jenkins (Multiculturalism), Reference Librarian, City College of New York Library, New York, New York

Rashelle S. Karp (Small Business), Associate Professor, Clarion University of Pennsylvania Library Science Department, Clarion, Pennsylvania

Nancy Kassell (Independent Researchers), Independent Researcher, Marblehead, Massachusetts

Michael R. Lavin (Business and Finance), Business and Management Subject Specialist, Business and Government Documents Department, State University of New York Lockwood Memorial Library, Buffalo, New York

Pat McCandless (Sports), Assistant Director, Public Services, Ohio State University Libraries, Columbus, Ohio

H. Robert Malinowsky (Automobiles), Principal Bibliographer, University of Illinois, Chicago, Illinois

Susan M. Miko (The Home), Librarian and Supervisor, Eastwood Local School District, Pemberville, Ohio

Marilyn K. Moody (Government Agencies, Politics and Government), Head, Technical and Instructional Services, Rensselaer Polytechnic Institute, Troy, New York

Dennis A. Norlin (Religion), Library Director, South Dakota School of Mines and Technology, Rapid City, South Dakota

Alan R. Nourie (Literature), Associate University Librarian, Public Services/Collection Development, Illinois State University Milner Library, Normal, Illinois

Harold M. Otness (Travel), Acquisitions Librarian, Southern Oregon State College Library, Ashland, Oregon

Sara R. Pemberton (Parenting), Head of Children's Services, Downers Grove Public Library, Downers Grove, Illinois

Arthur Plotnik (Writing), Associate Publisher, American Library Association, Chicago, Illinois; Author, *Honk If You're a Writer* (Simon & Schuster)

Mary Ellen Quinn (Theater and Dance), Head, Chicago Public Library Uptown Branch, Chicago, Illinois

Sally M. Roberts (The Internet), Curriculum Integration Librarian, Northwestern University Library Reference Department, Evanston, Illinois

Carol Tenopir (Electronic Sources of Information), Professor, University of Tennessee School of Library and Information Science, Knoxville, Tennessee

Polly Thistlewaite (Women's Studies), Reference Librarian, Wexler Library, Hunter College, New York

Leslie A. Troutman (Music), Music User Services Coordinator, University of Illinois Library, Urbana, Illinois

Richard D. Walker (Patents, Standards and Specifications), Professor, University of Wisconsin School of Library and Information Studies, Madison, Wisconsin

Josephine W. Yeoh (Health and Medicine), Director, Donald J. Vincent Medical Library, Riverside Methodist Hospitals, Columbus, Ohio

Acknowledgments

Heartfelt thanks—and indemnity from any faults or errors—go to the many members of the library and book community who gave of their time and expertise in the development of this project. Among them are Janet Bancroft, Patricia W. Berger, the (ALA) *Booklist* editors, Brett Butler, Laurie Calkhoven, Donald E. Chatham, Andrew M. Hansen, Charles Harmon, Angel J. Jackson, Ellen Lichtenstein, Mary Jo Lynch, Elaine R. Lyon, Susan Mangini, Nancy McCray, Jane McKeever, Edgar S. McLarin, Carol S. Nielsen, the Madden Library staff at California State University/Fresno, the Northwestern University Library staff, the Evanston (Illinois) Public Library staff, Carol Parkhurst, Donald Sifuentes, Mary Frances Wilkens, and Irene Wood.

Our appreciation goes also to members of the Reference and Adult Services Division, the ALA unit dedicated to effective reference and information services for all library users. RASD members were generous in advising this project.

Finally, to Russell and Cybele Maylone, the editor's deepest gratitude for their moral support.

Contents

Prying with a Purpose

Every week, some 150,000 librarians in the United States work with more than 125 million people doing research, from school reports to background reports for national policy. The *American Library Association Guide to Information Access (GIA)* has been compiled to share the judgment and expertise of these library professionals. Here, in a guide prepared under the auspices of the American Library Association, are the printed and electronic sources librarians favor, the strategies they teach, and the pathways to the great networks of information they have helped create.

The term *research*, as it is used in this book, refers to a concept close to what writer and librarian Zora Neale Hurston described in her autobiography, *Dust Tracks on a Road:* "Research is formalized curiosity. It is poking and prying with a purpose. It is a seeking that he who wishes may know the cosmic secrets of the world and they that dwell therein."

The *GIA* will guide your poking and prying with a purpose, whether that purpose is short-range or long-, practical or scholarly, personal or work-related; whether it's to choose a new car, track your heritage, find a career, run a business, locate a musical composition, or explore the halo motif in religious paintings from the Middle Ages through the Renaissance.

Thirty-six chapters concentrate on popular research areas; seventeen special sections explain the latest tools and techniques for researching *any* fact or topic, from a piece of movie trivia to a new theory of the cosmos. We hope that browsing through the guide will yield one of the great delights of research: finding something stimulating and pertinent that you weren't looking for.

The *Guide to Information Access* serves the interests of the general public. Specifically, it addresses the research needs of students (high school, college, and others), independent scholars, educators, professionals, businesspeople, adult learners, self-improvers, creative artists, political activists, retired citizens, and many other groups and categories of information seekers.

The *GIA* will serve the reference librarian as well, since it is the first major resource guide to take full account of the electronic revolution in research. No longer a novelty limited to high-tech institutions, the electronic storage and distribution of data are now the forces driving the organization, packaging, handling, and even the content of a great deal of research information in a wide range of facilities.

THE COMPLEAT RESEARCHER IN THE INFORMATION AGE

Even in the narrowest subjects, the deluge of information is often relentless. The much-discussed information explosion, fueled by electronic data, is more a cataclysm, shocking us into what Richard Saul Wurman calls Information Anxiety. Any effort to be "complete" in terms of information in one's field is doomed to failure. How, then, can this guide lay claim to being complete?

It is a complete guide to the *aspects* of modern research, applied to a number of selected fields. For while research topics and data are unlimited, the key aspects of information seeking are finite. The Compleat Researcher is one who can find the pathways that lead to information in virtually any field: the general guides, bibliographies, catalogs, indexes, databases, government documents, special collections, and so on.

The *GIA* allows the researcher to plunge directly into a subject of interest such as music or health and go as far as possible along the pathways we have mapped. Then, as need or interest arises, the reader can turn to any of the seventeen chapters explaining aspects of contemporary research, such as online services or government publications.

Like knowledge, information is humbling. The more one acquires, the more one appreciates the vastness of the unattained. An antidote to information anxiety is to separate what you really need to know from the vast body of material that is available. You don't have to learn every information source and technique in this guide. Know simply that certain types of sources are there when you need them, and that librarians are also there to help you find and use them.

Librarians—both those who have organized the information in libraries and the "public service" staff who dispense information—have a favorite word: *access*. Access is the freedom or ability to obtain and make use of information. Access is central to the program of the 56,000-member American Library Association, which advocates the greatest possible access for all people to the empowering resources of information. The preparation of this guide for a general audience has been in the interests of access; editor Sandy Whiteley, a distinguished reference librarian, and the accomplished librarians who contributed their expertise were similarly motivated.

The Information Age, with its abundance of instant information, has its dark side as well, as numerous social critics have observed. Some fear we are on the brink of creating a new Information Elite, set above the masses like the few privileged book owners before the age of print. This elite would be made up only of those who could afford the costly new forms of electronic information, the CD-ROMs and online databases that are already driving out some of the printed research materials once available free in libraries.

The challenge of providing free or affordable access to these expensive services is daunting; but libraries have taken it up, and thus offer the best hope for researchers of modest means to connect with the electronic sources in this book. To continue meeting this challenge, libraries need the support of every citizen who believes in the equality of opportunity, lest researchers "prying with a purpose" be limited to a very few purposes, indeed.

—Arthur Plotnik, Project Publisher
American Library Association, Chicago

Editor's Preface

In this book we have tried to provide a directory that will speed access to information sources both in print and electronic form. Many of the tools of access will be found in libraries, but some electronic information can also be accessed from home or office.

HOW TO USE THIS BOOK

The main part of this book is made up of topical chapters, Agriculture through Writing. Introductory chapters explain research trends and the various types of resources to be found in the topical chapters. Taken together, these chapters provide a minicourse on the major electronic sources of information: online services, bulletin boards, the Internet, CD-ROM, the national catalogs (OCLC and RLIN), and online catalogs in libraries. Traditional sources, such as government publications and newspapers, are also reviewed as are places where information can be found—libraries, archives, and government agencies. Finally, the book offers special tips to high school and college students and independent researchers. If you have the time, consider reading the introductory chapters first. In practice, we know that researchers work under deadlines and may need to go straight to the appropriate topical chapter. These explanatory chapters, however, can be referred to when you come across something you want more information about in the rest of the book.

TOPICAL CHAPTERS

The following sections will be found in most of the topical chapters (Chapters 18–53):

General Sources of Information

Here you will find books that are useful for an introduction to the topic. Whenever possible, we have listed a "guide to the literature," a book that lists all the other reference books on the topic and that may describe periodicals, libraries, and other sources, too. Many disciplines have hundreds or even thousands of reference books which we obviously could not cover here. Therefore, if the printed sources we list do not provide the information you need, look for a guide to the literature at the beginning of the section to lead you to additional sources.

One problem you may encounter is that libraries tend not to lend reference books on interlibrary loan. You may be able to get another library to photocopy a section of a book if you are able to identify the specific material you need. For example, if your library doesn't own the *Hobbyist Sourcebook* (Chapter 30, Hobbies), you may be able to get another library to copy the pages on photography or bird-watching for you. To find additional reference books, see:

Guide to Reference Books. 10th ed. Compiled by Eugene P. Sheehy. American Library Association, 1986.
Guide to Reference Books: Covering Materials from 1985–1990. Edited by Robert Balay. American Library Association, 1992.

To keep up with new reference books, ask your librarian for recent issues of *Choice* or the Reference Books Bulletin section of *Booklist,* two book review journals published by the American Library Association. Recent years of both magazines are available on CD-ROM from SilverPlatter.

Electronic Sources

Here you will find the appropriate reference tools available on CD-ROM and online. In some disciplines, such as science and medicine, there are so many sources that only a selection was possible.

If an electronic source has a print equivalent, it is listed in the annotation. The coverage of electronic sources goes back only to the 1960s, at the earliest, and in many cases doesn't begin until the 1980s; many print indexes started publication years before. So, for example, if you need articles written in the 1930s on physical education, use the print form of *Education Index,* which started publication in 1929, not the online or CD-ROM form, which goes back only to 1983. Included under Electronic Sources are bulletin board systems that may have information on the topic as well as appropriate sources on the consumer online services. Whenever you see a telephone number in boldface, it is a number for an electronic bulletin board, *not* a voice number. For information on additional electronic sources, see:

Gale Directory of Databases. 2 vols. By Kathleen Young Marcaccio. Gale Research. Annual. Also online and on CD-ROM.

Here you will find listings for magazines on the topic. When appropriate, some scholarly journals are also noted. Unfortunately, a few of these periodicals may have ceased publication by the time you read this book. For additional listings of periodicals, see:

Magazines for Libraries. 7th ed. Edited by Bill Katz and Linda Sternberg Katz. Bowker, 1992.

These directories are comprehensive, listing more than 100,000 periodicals each:

Ulrichs International Periodicals Directory. Bowker. Annual. Also available online and on CD-ROM.
Serials Directory. EBSCO. Annual. Also available on CD-ROM.

This list is a selection of publications from the U.S. government. On some topics, such as the visual arts and music, the government publishes little. In other areas such as health, consumer information, education, and business, the government output amounts to thousands of items each year, of which we list only a sampling. See Chapter 16, Government Publications, to learn how to buy these documents or consult them in a library, as well as for information on documents catalogs.

The government employs experts in many fields. In this section, you will find the federal agencies that are most likely to have staff that can answer your questions. Chapter 17, Government Agencies, lists books that will help you to find the names and telephone numbers of the appropriate people to call in these agencies. It's usually more effective to do your initial research in printed sources. After you have used books, government documents, and other sources, you will be better prepared to call a government agency with a specific question.

This is a list of not-for-profit groups that offer many varieties of information. Trade associations may be able to provide statistics for their industry that you can't find in printed sources. Professional associations may have publications you can purchase. Some associations may even be appropriate for you to join. For example, if you get seriously involved in genealogical research, you may want to join one of the genealogical societies we have listed. To find additional associations, consult:

Encyclopedia of Associations. 3 vols. Gale Research. Annual. Also available online and on CD-ROM.

Of the more than 100,000 libraries in the United States, only a few selected ones could be listed here. Start your research at the local public library or your institution's library. If you send inquiries first to the research libraries we have listed, you will often get back a form notice recommending that you visit your local public library. If you are able to use either the OCLC or RLIN national catalogs, or if your state has a statewide catalog online or on CD-ROM (as, for example, Illinois and Pennsylvania do), you should be able to find most of what you need in libraries that are close enough to visit. After you have exhausted these sources, write to the appropriate research library and specify that you have done so. Queries should be narrowed to specific requests for particular sources. Don't simply ask, "Do you have any information on . . . ?" Your local librarian can advise you on this. For information on libraries, see:

Libraries

American Library Directory. 2 vols. Bowker. Annual. Also available online with Dialog and on CD-ROM as part of *Library Reference Plus.*
Directory of Special Libraries and Information Centers. 2 vols. Edited by Janice A. DeMaggio and Debra M. Kirby. Gale Research, 1993.
Subject Collections. 2 vols. 7th ed. Edited by Lee Ash and William G. Miller. Bowker, 1993.
     Describes subject strengths of collections in academic and large public libraries.

LC Subject Headings

We have listed a selection of Library of Congress subject headings appropriate to the topic. However, you should not conclude that these samplings are the only headings to be used in searching the catalog. Ask a librarian to help you use *Library of Congress Subject Headings (LCSH),* the printed guide to headings used in catalogs, to find other words to describe your topic. If you are using an online public access catalog, ask if you can search by keyword, too. In a high school or small public library, the catalog may use *Sear's List of Subject Headings,* which is an abridged and simplified form of *LCSH.* Again, the librarian can help.

Research Centers

This section describes institutions that do research on the topic. They may have libraries and issue publications or have experts on staff who might provide specialized information. Usually, these are places to turn to at an advanced stage in your research, when you have exhausted other sources and have a specific query. For additional centers, see:

Research Centers Directory. 2 vols. Bowker. Annual.

     Although we haven't said so explicitly in every chapter, the first information source to consult is the reference librarians. They can often save you time by highlighting the sources the library holds on your topic. Librarians have also been on the cutting edge of the revolution in information technology and should be able to advise you on using electronic sources of information. They are there to serve you, whatever your topic. As historian James Billington, who currently serves as the Librarian of Congress, writes, "Librarians are the human mediators of both knowledge and information for people. Librarians are the gatekeepers to the new technological possibilities of the electronic culture, but they are also the dreamkeepers. They are the custodians of the past."

—Sandy Whiteley

PART I

Advice to
Researchers

1

THE UNDERGRADUATE RESEARCHER

Data are raw facts, perhaps in written form or in a series of numbers on a piece of paper or on a computer disk. Information is data put in some sort of context. When a series of numbers is part of a table in the *Statistical Abstract* showing the number of foreign-born people in the United States, it is information. Knowledge is information that has been tested and synthesized into a system. Ideally, the outcome of research is not just information, but knowledge.

Learning to use the college library to find information is an important part of your undergraduate education. Beginning students often remark how confusing their college library is compared to the high school and public library they are used to. Indeed, you may be familiar with libraries that count their holdings in the tens of thousands; suddenly you are faced with collections of hundreds of thousands or even millions of volumes. The techniques you used in your high school library just aren't adequate in one of this size.

LEARNING THE LIBRARY

How to cope? The library will undoubtedly offer tours to freshmen; take one. Your high school library was probably all on one level. Your college library will be spread out over several levels. Tours will tell you how to navigate the stacks, where the current and back issues of periodicals and the back files of newspapers on microfilm are, and how to locate the copy machines. You will be shown how to use the catalog, and if your library has special branches, you'll be told about them as well.

The library staff may also offer lectures on library research, as a course you can take for credit, as an open workshop, or as one lecture in a course you are taking. Take advantage of these lectures, if possible before your first term paper.

How to Ask for Help in the Library

Make sure you go to the reference desk for help, not to some other service area that may be staffed by nonlibrarians. Try to define specifically what you are looking for. "I need to do a paper on the Whiskey Rebellion. How can I find books on the topic?" is better than "Where are your history books?" Also remember that requesting a specific tool, let's say a periodical index, doesn't tell the librarian what you need, only what you think you need. Don't start out with "Where's the *Readers' Guide?*" Instead ask for a suggestion of an index appropriate to your needs.

Although your library may be open until midnight or even later, it's unlikely that a reference librarian will be on duty at that hour. If there's anyone at all at the desk, it will probably be another undergraduate. Try to get to the library early enough to consult with professional staff. More librarians will be on duty during the day and they'll be less harried than in the evening. If you wait until the end of the quarter/semester to visit the reference desk, you'll find many of your classmates with the same idea. You may get only cursory help if there is a long line of students waiting at the reference desk.

Your library probably has handouts that answer frequently asked questions: How do I find a book review? How do I find biographical information? The library will also have other literature that explains library policies, hours, and special collections. Look for a display near the catalog or reference room.

Don't feel intimidated by the library's online catalog or CD-ROM indexes. These technologies are relatively new to everybody—your professors are learning how to use them, too.

If you have a computer in your dorm room or at home, find out if you can use it to dial up the library's catalog. This can be very helpful when you are trying to finish a bibliography late at night and need to check publication dates or other details.

Writing the College Paper

College research is different from high school research in several ways. Professors will expect you to use a wider variety of sources. High school teachers usually accept papers that are based entirely on secondary sources, that is, comments about or interpretations of an author or event. College professors often want you to use primary sources as well. These are the original works of an author or records created at the time of the event being studied. For example, instead of reading someone's later interpretation of an event, your professors will want you to read an eyewitness account of the event and to draw your own conclusions. Primary sources include manuscripts and other archival materials, newspapers from the period, or printed diaries and autobiographies. Finding these materials will mean venturing beyond the catalog to find all the resources the library has to offer.

Your approach to research should follow a series of steps similar to those that librarians usually recommend:

A RESEARCH STRATEGY

1. Select and set the limits of your topic. Read an overview article in an encyclopedia or an annual review to get a sense of the breadth of the topic. Take note of the books and journal articles cited at the end of the article. Consult a guide to the literature of the discipline to help identify an overview article.
2. Go to the catalog and look up the books you found listed in the bibliography of the overview article. At the bottom of each catalog record will be the subject headings applied to that book. (On some online public access catalogs you may have to call up the "full record" or the "long record.") Look under those subject headings to find additional books. If these headings don't lead to enough material, use *Library of Congress Subject Headings* to find appropriate terms or search by keyword.
3. Go to the stacks to find the books you have identified and browse in the general area for additional material. If you are working in an interdisciplinary field such as women's studies or the environment, don't depend on browsing to find everything. Appropriate materials may be in widely separated parts of the collection.
4. After skimming through these books, reevaluate and refine your topic once again. If the bibliographies list relevant books you want to consult and your library doesn't own them, ask a librarian to help you prepare an interlibrary loan request RIGHT AWAY. If there are books in your college library that you'd like to consult but they are charged out, ask the circulation department to recall them, if possible.
5. In order to find recent periodical articles, consult a periodical index. Don't gravitate to the *Readers' Guide* just because you are familiar with it from high school. For some topics it may be appropriate, but in most cases your professors expect you to consult scholarly journals, not the popular magazines indexed by the *Readers' Guide*. Use a guide to the literature or ask a reference librarian to suggest the appropriate index. Check whether there is an appropriate index on CD-ROM. It will allow you to search at least ten years of an electronic index all at once, instead of going through a print index year by year. If your library has an online catalog, it may also contain a periodical index.

Depending on the size of your paper, you may want to have an online database searched but for many term papers, students are not expected to do a comprehensive literature search. If you need only a dozen or so references, you should be able to find them without much trouble. However, a senior honors thesis may require a more comprehensive search, and an online search (if your library doesn't own an appropriate CD-ROM index) will be a good idea, though you may have to pay for it.

If you write a lot of papers or are doing a yearlong project and have the necessary equipment, you should consider subscribing to a service such as EasyNet or one of the after-hours services such as Knowledge Index so that you can search databases yourself. (See Chapter 8, Online Services.) When using electronic sources, don't print out more references than you are realistically going to read. If the subject you search yields 500 citations, reframe your question so as to narrow the number of citations. Perhaps limit the search to only the last two years or only materials in English.

6. Consult other library sources, such as government publications, maps, or newspapers. These materials may be housed in separate sections of the library and may have their own catalogs. Remember that not all collections in the library are open the same hours. The government documents department, for instance, may be closed on Sunday when the rest of the library is open, so plan ahead. Visit another library, if necessary, always checking first with your library staff to see if you will be admitted.

7. Contact sources outside the library—an association or government agency—for information you haven't been able to find.

8. As you read each new source, evaluate it for its authority. Not all sources of information are equal. Don't assume that because something is in your library, it is authoritative—libraries buy books for many different reasons. Does the author bring bias to the topic? Is the information out of date and superseded by other sources? As time allows, consult book reviews to see how the book was received. Look up the author's credentials. The publisher is also a measure of authority. A book from a university press, for example, is usually considered to be a legitimate source. Also be aware of whether the periodicals you are using contain articles written by scholars or articles written by journalists for a popular audience.

9. Every time you find a relevant source, check its bibliography or notes. After a while, you should start recognizing some items in a new bibliography as things you have already read or seen listed elsewhere. When that happens, you're getting a handle on the literature of the subject. If you have been reading for several weeks and aren't beginning to notice this kind of closure, perhaps you should place some additional limitations on your topic.

There is one exception to this search strategy. If you are researching an event that happened in the past year, you aren't likely to find any authoritative books on the topic. You shouldn't waste your time looking for an overview of the topic or for books in the catalog, but should go straight to periodical and newspaper indexes and other current sources. Choosing a topic that is so recent that it has just appeared in newspaper headlines will present special challenges.

Keep accurate citations and a research log. Whenever you photocopy something, be sure to write the source of the article on the copy. Not all journals have running heads or footers and you may find yourself at a later date with an article that you can't identify. At a scheduled time, stop researching and start writing. It is tempting to keep looking for just one more piece of information and procrastinate on actually writing.

Very often, your specific course will require a theme, or your professor will provide a selection of ideas. When that is not the case, the college National Debate topics are good potential term paper ideas because they address issues of current concern and are phrased in such a way that you must take a position or make an argument. Here are examples of topics from recent years that may be useful for social science courses:

TERM PAPER TOPICS FOR UNDERGRADUATES

- Resolved: That the United States should substantially change its development-assistance policies toward Afghanistan, Burma, Bhutan, China, India, Nepal, Pakistan, or Sri Lanka.
- Resolved: That the federal government should adopt an energy policy which substantially reduces the consumption of fossil fuels in the United States.
- Resolved: That the United States should reduce significantly its military commitments to NATO member states.
- Resolved: That more rigorous academic standards should be established for all elementary and/or secondary schools in the United States, in one or more of the following areas: language arts, mathematics, natural science.
- Resolved: That the U.S. federal government should significantly increase the exploration and/or development of space beyond earth's mesosphere.
- Resolved: That any and all injury resulting from the disposal of hazardous wastes in the United States should be the legal responsibility of the producer of that waste.

For additional ideas for term paper topics, see:

CQ Researcher (formerly *Editorial Research Reports*). Congressional Quarterly. 4 times/month.

These brief reports give an overview of topics of current interest (nuclear fusion, school censorship, violence against women, gay rights) and provide lengthy bibliographies that will get you started on your research.

STYLE MANUALS

The style manuals used most frequently in high schools and colleges are listed below. Each contains the information needed for documenting sources, preparing bibliographies, and formatting papers.

MLA Handbook for Writers of Research Papers. 3d ed. By Joseph Gibaldi and Walter S. Achtert. Modern Language Association, 1988.

Prepared for persons writing in the humanities at the college level, but often used in high schools, it advocates parenthetical documentation and recommends a "Works Cited" page rather than a bibliography. It also has chapters devoted to "Research and Writing," "The Mechanics of Writing," and "The Format of the Research Paper." It identifies other style manuals, provides lists of abbreviations, and includes many examples of specific rules and sample pages.

The Publication Manual of the American Psychological Association. 3d ed. American Psychological Association, 1983.

Used mostly at the college level in the social sciences, including education and psychology, and is the style followed by many journals. Divided into five chapters: "Content and Organization of a Manuscript," "Expression of Ideas," "APA Editorial Style," "Typing Instructions and Sample Paper," and "Submitting the Manuscript and Proofreading." APA uses a parenthetical author-date form of citation and recommends using a "Reference List" instead of a bibliography.

The Chicago Manual of Style. 14th ed. University of Chicago Press, 1993.

Used widely by authors, editors, and copywriters. It is divided into three parts: "Bookmaking," "Style," and "Production and Printing." More than half the manual focuses on style rules, with many examples of each. Recommends an author-date system of documentation and explains footnotes, endnotes, and various types of bibliographies.

Electronic Style: A Guide to Citing Electronic Information. By Xia Li and Nancy B. Crane. Meckler, 1993.

The fourteenth edition of *The Chicago Manual of Style* gives some guidance in citing electronic sources, but this book gives hundreds of examples of citation formats for online databases, the Internet, even e-mail.

A Manual for Writers of Term Papers, Theses, and Dissertations. 5th ed. By Kate L. Turabian. University of Chicago Press, 1987.
Student's Guide for Writing College Papers. 3d ed. By Kate L. Turabian. University of Chicago, 1977.

A Manual for Writers is for more advanced writers, *Student's Guide* for high school and college students. Both explain rules for style, spelling, punctuation, and abbreviations and provide examples of each rule.

Other handbooks frequently used at the high school and college level include *Harbrace College Handbook, Prentice-Hall Handbook for Writers, The Random House Handbook,* and *Writing Research Papers: A Norton Guide.* The first three are basically usage guides, but contain excellent sections on writing research papers. The Norton guide focuses entirely on the research process and, while it does not provide as many rules about style, includes sample papers, bibliographies, outlines, and notecards.

Harbrace College Handbook. 11th ed. By John C. Hodges and others. HBJ Publications, 1990.

Prentice-Hall Handbook for Writers. 11th ed. By Glenn H. Legget and others. Prentice-Hall, 1990.

The Random House Handbook. 5th ed. By Frederick Crews. McGraw-Hill, 1988.

Writing Research Papers: A Norton Guide. 3d ed. By Melissa Walker. W. W. Norton, 1993.

THE
HIGH SCHOOL
RESEARCHER

We are living in the Information Age. How you succeed in school and as an adult in the twenty-first century may depend on how well you find, analyze, and use information.

Most schools have a library media center, sometimes called an instructional materials center or information center. It provides materials and services that support your school's courses and it encourages students to read. Use the library media center frequently rather than waiting for an assignment. You'll pick up useful skills and information and have fun along the way.

HOW TO USE THE SCHOOL LIBRARY MEDIA CENTER

The library media specialists who run the library (with the help of library paraprofessionals, often called library media assistants or aides) help students locate information for class assignments, teach them how to use library tools, and can also suggest good books for leisure reading.

Students often preface their inquiries by saying, "This is a really dumb question." Library media specialists—also known as school librarians—don't pass judgment on the quality of your question. They try to answer it and their code of ethics prohibits them from divulging any personal information you might reveal. You might not know how to phrase your question, but librarians are trained to interview you to learn more about what you need. If you've tried on your own to locate information, be prepared to tell the staff where you've looked and what, if anything, you've already found.

Don't be discouraged if the librarian suggests that you look in the card or computer catalog, *Readers' Guide*, or a reference book, when you expected the information to be found for you. School librarians are first and foremost teachers, responsible for helping you to acquire the information skills you will need throughout your life. Facts and resources change, but the process of locating information can be adapted to any situation.

Library media centers contain three types of resources: print, nonprint, and electronic. Print resources include books, periodicals (magazines), newspapers, vertical files, and microforms. Nonprint resources include videotapes and audiotapes, laser discs, computer software, transparencies, and filmstrips. CD-ROM indexes and online databases are examples of electronic resources. Information about what the library owns can be found in the card or online catalog. You can look for books by author, title, or subject. For each book, the card or computer screen will give you important information: title, author, publisher, copyright date, edition, number of pages, subject headings assigned to that book, and the call number that is used to locate the book.

The Process

School library media centers use the Dewey Decimal System to classify books; most college and university libraries and many large public libraries use the Library of Congress System. You don't have to know how these systems work; you just need to record the call number and then find the section where that number is shelved. Nonprint sources are also listed in the library catalog, though they may not be shelved with the books. If your library media center has an online catalog, find out if it is accessible from classrooms or even from your home.

The subject you're looking for may not be listed in the catalog under the words that you are using. Consult the *Sears List of Subject Headings* to determine what heading is used for your topic. The librarian will explain how this list of subject headings works.

Magazine articles must be found through indexes such as the *Readers' Guide to Periodical Literature* or *Education Index,* where articles are listed by subject. When you've identified an article that looks promising, write down the citation: author and title of the article; title, date, and volume of the periodical; and the page numbers. If you are using a CD-ROM index such as *Wilsondisc Readers' Guide, Newsbank, ERIC,* or *Magazine Index Plus,* you may be able to print out citations with the computer.

Once you have determined the articles you'd like to see, find out if the magazines or journals are available in your library. Most libraries provide information about their periodical holdings on a printed list, a rotary or flip card file, or a computer or microfiche catalog. If the periodicals you want are not available, ask how copies can be obtained.

Your library media center may subscribe to an online service such as Dialog, Dow Jones News/Retrieval, or CompuServe. The library media specialist will work with you in using these services. A wide range of information is available online and you can also obtain the full text of current newspaper articles. Schools may offer this service to students at minimal or no charge.

The vertical file is an often overlooked resource. It contains pamphlets, newspaper clippings, government publications, maps, travel brochures, reprints, and a variety of unique information filed in drawers by subject.

Special research materials are often found in high school libraries. *Social Issues Resources Series (SIRS)* reprints are an invaluable resource. Each *SIRS* notebook contains reprints of articles that originally appeared in periodicals, newspapers, and pamphlets. *SIRS* is also available in some library media centers on CD-ROM. The library media center may have other sources, such as the *Consumer Health Information Service*, microfiche reprints of all kinds of pamphlets related to health, or *New York Times Critical Issues*, microfiche copies of *Times* articles on a variety of popular topics. The subject chapters in this guide will provide scores of other possibilities for you to check out with your library media specialist.

Does your library media center have photocopying machines? Can you make copies from microfiche or microfilm? Are computers available for students to use? Sometimes schools within a district will loan books or make photocopies for each other. Are there charges for this service? If you ask for an interlibrary loan, plan in advance because it may be several days before your request arrives. Ask the library media specialist about other libraries in your area. You may be able to use local public, college, and special libraries, although they may have borrowing restrictions. Before you visit these libraries, check on their hours and policies. It will save you time.

THE RESEARCH PAPER: ADVICE FOR STUDENTS

The best ongoing preparation for research is to develop a lifetime habit of reading—not only books but also newspapers and magazines. Reading will expose you to new ideas and different perspectives as well as to new words and styles of writing. Be more than a passive viewer or listener when you watch television or listen to the radio. Keep a folder of interesting articles you've clipped. Jot down notes about books you've read or ideas you've heard on television or the radio.

Think of the research project as a process that involves both locating and interpreting information, not just as an assignment with a fixed set of requirements and deadlines. As you go through the research process, your feelings may range from uncertainty to relief and from confusion to clarity.

Beginning the research paper means developing a plan—this can't be stressed enough. Your teacher may help you by providing deadlines for a thesis statement, outline, notecards, and first draft. Establish a realistic timeline that incorporates the teacher's deadlines. If all you've been given is a final due date, develop deadlines for yourself. Most people tend to procrastinate. Be realistic about your capabilities and your time. A paper that is begun at the eleventh hour can't be well thought out and revised. Careful planning will mean you can get library materials, reserve a computer or typewriter, make revisions, and deal with emergencies.

The first step is to select a topic. Brainstorm with your teacher, other students, your parents, or the library media specialist. If you've kept a folder of articles or notes, see if it contains anything you can use. Do you have to write papers for two classes? If a research paper for an English class can be on any topic you choose and you also have to write a paper for history, perhaps you could combine them. Be sure to consult both teachers before you begin, however. In choosing a topic, think about your personal interests, your teacher's requirements, the amount of time you have, and the information available. Consider the purpose of your project. Is it to trace the historical development of something? Is it to be persuasive? Is it to present one side of a controversial topic? Is it to come to a scientific conclusion?

Think about ways to focus on your topic. If you know little about it, first consult a general reference source like an encyclopedia. Here you will find an overview of the topic, learn how it could be subdivided or narrowed, locate related ideas, and find a bibliography of relevant materials. Even if you are not allowed to list an encyclopedia as a source, take notes on the information you've found. They will help in your research. Explore a wide variety of sources. Consider whether your project involves current information that might more likely be found in periodicals than books. Ask your library media specialist about resources you might not have considered.

As you explore, don't take detailed notes; however, do keep lists of sources consulted, and jot down terms and ideas. You can review these notes later when you are ready to collect specific information. As you read, you will begin to have a sense of how to focus your topic. You may be able to develop a preliminary thesis statement and organize major ideas into a preliminary outline. They will guide you as you do further research, organize ideas, and begin to write. However, don't let the outline restrict your research; at this point it should still be open-ended. This is a good time to discuss your research with your teacher or library media specialist.

With your topic refined, you can now collect information and take detailed notes. Try to locate information that supports and enhances your thesis. You may even discover a person who could be interviewed about your topic. The library media specialist may also suggest using an online periodical index. You may need to use materials in other libraries or ask about obtaining them through interlibrary loan.

Your research might provide background for a speech, a demonstration, a videotape, or some other form besides the research paper. Consult with your teacher if you intend to present your topic in one of these formats.

Research is never finished; however, at some point, you have to decide that you have enough information. Important new information may come to light or you may discover that there are holes in your research, but at this stage, going on with the search generally leads to procrastination. Organize your information into an outline for the paper. Don't worry about complete sentences or a specific number of sections, but try to maintain balance. You may have lots of information to support one specific idea, but very little for another. You may have completely ignored something else. The outline will reveal such problems and also serve as the framework for the first draft.

Note taking, whether on cards turned in to your teacher or written for yourself, is an extremely important part of the research process. Take notes during the exploration process and organize them to support your thesis. You will probably end up with far more notes than you actually use. Note taking can be of three types: summarizing, quoting, or paraphrasing. Whichever type you use, properly document sources, both on your note-cards and, later, in your paper. Photocopying from the book or article or microform is helpful because it ensures that you have the exact information. It also allows you to highlight sentences and make notes on the copy. It is advisable also to make photocopies of title pages of books and table of contents pages of periodicals to ensure that you have the correct information for your bibliography. It's frustrating and time-consuming not to have the exact information and, at the eleventh hour, to return to a library to obtain complete citations. Don't forget to note the volume and issue numbers of periodicals.

It is important to validate the authority of your sources. This may mean determining an author's credentials by using a source such as *Contemporary Authors* or *Who's Who in America* or locating information about an organization or a periodical. You should know whether your author or publication is an authority in the field and whether he or she has a liberal or conservative background. Does your author have a vested interest in the topic? Even though something may seem uncontroversial or may appear to be an indisputable fact, you may discover that there is more than one point of view.

You may begin to mentally compose your paper as you locate information and prepare an outline. Preparing the first draft can be hard, especially if you don't have a focus for the material. If at all possible, use a word processor. The copy is much easier to revise and the paper easier to read. Using a computer often provides the freedom of writing as the mind flows, with the luxury of easily deleting, rearranging, adding, and rewording. This makes a first draft easier to produce.

Revision is an important part of the writing process. Allow time to set your draft aside for a day or two before you revise. Time away from your project gives you the benefit of a different perspective. As you read, you'll see places where it needs improvement. Could you use better words? Does the material need to be rearranged? Does it flow smoothly? Is your conclusion logical and believable? Your teacher may want to read your first draft and discuss it with you. Many writers have trusted readers who read their drafts at various stages. Have a friend, parent, brother or sister, another teacher, or even the library media specialist read through your drafts. Don't be offended or discouraged by their suggestions. Make note of their comments and consider them—to accept or reject—as you reread your draft. After you have revised your paper, again set it aside for a day or two before rereading it. You may want a trusted reader to go over this draft too. If possible, revise one more time before typing the final paper. The best papers are often revised twice. Try to plan ahead and develop a realistic schedule to make this possible.

Documentation gives credit to the original sources and allows readers to consult them for further information. It is extremely important to document carefully all the sources you use, not just when you quote them directly but also when you take ideas from them and put them into your own words. If you have been making note of the source and page number as you write, documentation should not be difficult. Your teacher will tell you what format or "style" you should use. Documentation, whether footnotes, endnotes, or parenthetical documentation, directs readers to the bibliography.

Avoid plagiarism, representing as your own the ideas or words that you've taken from another source, whether you quote that source exactly or put it in your own words. Some students plagiarize deliberately; others are unaware that they are plagiarizing. The new electronic sources make it very easy to download words from an encyclopedia or periodical and integrate them directly into something you are writing. This is plagiarism. It is ethically wrong and can have serious consequences, including failing a course or being expelled. When a plagiarized work is published, it can result in a lawsuit. You can avoid plagiarism if you document all sources as you take notes and as you write. Highlight quotation marks in your notes and drafts. Consult your teacher whenever you have doubts.

The bibliography is an important part of any paper. It contains a complete list of the works you have drawn on and quoted. Ask your teacher what format you should use. The teacher may recommend that you consult a standard manual such as the *MLA Handbook* or *Chicago Manual of Style* (see Chapter 2). A format may be specified in your textbook, or even in a style manual prepared by your school. If locally prepared manuals exist, the library media specialist most likely has a copy.

Find out whether your bibliography is to include only the sources cited in your paper or every source you used in your research. If you include only the sources cited, the bibliography may be titled "Works Cited." If you include all sources you used, you may want to have two sections, "Works Cited" and "Other Works Consulted."

Keep copies of your final papers. You may want to expand on your research at a later date or draw on it for future research projects, even if at the end of this one you feel researched-out.

**TERM PAPER
TOPICS FOR HIGH
SCHOOL STUDENTS**

For suggestions of term paper topics, see:

The Reference Shelf. H. W. Wilson. 6 times/year.

A good source found in many high school libraries. Each of these paperbacks is devoted to a topic of current interest and includes excerpts from magazines, newspapers, books, and government documents plus a bibliography to get you started on your research. Topics covered in recent years include:

Abortion
Affirmative Action
AIDS
Animal Rights and Welfare
The Breakup of Communism
Censorship
Energy and Conservation
Ethics in Politics and Government
The Federal Deficit
Free Trade versus Protectionism
The Greenhouse Effect
Gun Control

Health Care Crisis
Immigration
Islamic Politics and the Modern
    World
The Palestinian Problem
Race and Politics
School Reform
Terrorism
Waste Disposal
The Welfare Debate
Women in Combat

INDEPENDENT RESEARCHERS

Amateur scholars dominated the intellectual life of the United States up until the Civil War, and the Ph.D. did not become a common academic credential until after World War I. Some of the best books are still written by researchers without an academic affiliation.

Most "independent scholars" hold doctorates but do not have faculty appointments. Their research needs, however, are generally the same as those of researchers on university faculties. Many such researchers are members of the

National Coalition of Independent Scholars
P. O. Box 5743
Berkeley, CA 94705
(415) 549-1922

Its publication, *The Independent Scholar* (1987–   , quarterly), describes grants and institutional resources, and profiles institutions. It also lists local groups of independent scholars.

Many people without formal training in research materials and methods also have interests they want to pursue. They may be genealogists, political activists, or biographers. The following three books may be helpful in such work:

The Independent Learners' Sourcebook: Resources and Materials for Selected Topics. By Robert M. Smith and Phyllis M. Cunningham. American Library Association, 1987.

Covers "Thirty-four Popular Subjects for Inquiry," including anthropology, astronomy, birds and birdwatching, cooking and nutrition, futurism, parapsychology, peace/arms reduction, photography, political action, and the Third World.

The Lifelong Learner. By Ronald Gross. Simon & Schuster, 1977.
Couples information about people who were self-taught with practical advice on developing new skills and interests.

The Independent Scholar's Handbook: How to Turn Your Interest in Any Subject into Expertise. 2d ed. By Ronald Gross. Ten Speed Press, 1993.
Covers topics such as entering a new field, finding fellow researchers with whom to form intellectual partnerships, and developing research skills. Case studies of successful independent scholars provide inspiration.

Libraries are essential to the independent researcher. Public libraries provide basic reference materials, books, and periodicals. They may also be able to obtain materials from libraries throughout the nation. A few public libraries are in a special category; the Library of Congress, the New York Public Library, and the Boston Public Library, for example, are major research facilities. Many state libraries, open to the public, are strong in special collections such as regional history. The regional branches of the National Archives also serve the public, as does the main facility in Washington, D.C.

If the public library can't fulfill your needs, a local college or university library may have the necessary resources. Admission to the collections of a state university library is often free to anyone, though nonaffiliated users probably will not be able to borrow books. Sometimes the privilege is extended only to state residents. Some states do not grant free access. In California, for example, there is a charge of fifty dollars, a driver's license is demanded as identification, and stacks passes are granted only upon separate application.

If a college or university is private, the library may be off limits to the general public. Some public libraries, however, can issue passes to nearby academic collections for materials they don't have. These passes usually do not entitle visitors to borrow materials, so be prepared to pay for photocopying.

Here are some ways to get library privileges at a local academic library:
- Check with your employer. Occasionally corporations can obtain library privileges for their employees.
- College students may find that their school has a cooperative agreement allowing them to use neighboring institutions.
- Local groups of independent scholars sometimes make arrangements with local universities for research library access.
- If the membership is reasonable, join a Friends of the Library group.

Alumni of a university can often buy a card at a discounted rate if access isn't free. At some private universities, you can pay for reference or borrowing privileges even if you have no affiliation. The charge may be steep: $275 for three months at Harvard's college libraries, for example. The University of Chicago charges nonaffiliated individuals $100 per quarter for circulation privileges, and only after ascertaining that the research project is appropriate to the university's collections. Library cards at other institutions range from $50 to $700.

- If a university library is a federal document depository, it must open the documents collection to the public without charge.

To use independent research libraries, such as the Newberry Library in Chicago, the Huntington Library in San Marino, California, or the Folger Shakespeare Library in Washington, D.C., be prepared to explain by letter or a telephone call what it is you need that is not available elsewhere in the area. Libraries in museums and historical organizations ordinarily welcome users. An advance call or letter is advised.

An independent researcher may need one or more of the following privileges:

Access to the library catalog
Admission to book stacks
Admission to branch libraries and special collections
Borrowing privileges
Interlibrary loans
Online searches

Specialized branch libraries, such as science, law, or medical, may have access policies that differ from that of the main library. Always call first and check. Admission to special collections at public and even at private universities is often possible to anyone who can show a specific need and who agrees to the conditions of use. An interview with a staff member may be necessary to verify need.

Since even the richest library cannot own everything, interlibrary loan is an essential service; yet most academic libraries do not extend interlibrary loan privileges to visitors. Try requesting items through your public library. In some states librarians can search a statewide electronic database showing what other libraries hold or they can search the national OCLC database. Document delivery services (see Chapter 10) make periodical articles and other documents available quickly to anyone who is willing to pay a fee.

Researchers with computers may be able to access some of these services without visiting the library. As independent scholar James Bennett has written, "The masses of information stored in libraries are beginning to flow, as if liquefied, through electronic media." The catalogs of more than 200 university libraries can now be reached by anyone who has a computer and a modem. An online search in an academic library usually must be paid for, but that service may not be available to nonaffiliated visitors. Researchers with a computer at home can conduct these searches themselves through services such as Knowledge Index, BRS/AfterDark, or CompuServe.

Although the serious independent researcher may encounter frustrating barriers to library collections, persistence and sincerity of purpose often will pay off. Most librarians welcome the good use of their collections. While they must consider their institution's legitimate concerns about costs, rights of primary clientele, and security, they will often arrange some accommodation for researchers who have exhausted other resources for advancing their projects.

For address and telephone numbers of academic and public libraries, see:
American Library Directory. 2 vols. Bowker. Annual.

For subject access to some of America's libraries, see:
Subject Collections. 7th ed. 2 vols. Edited by Lee Ash and William G. Miller. Bowker, 1993.

This edition describes more than 18,000 collections on all topics in over 11,000 academic, public, and special libraries and museums in the United States and Canada.

PART II

The Electronic Revolution in Research: New Tools, New Techniques

ONLINE PUBLIC ACCESS CATALOGS

Online public access catalogs, or OPACs, are library catalogs displayed on a computer terminal. In addition to books, they may list periodicals, recordings, films and videos, maps, and other materials. In the 1970s, many libraries began to close the card catalogs they had used for more than a century to identify their collections and to replace them with computer terminals. Today, most college and university libraries, many public libraries, and some school libraries use OPACs instead of card catalogs. Many very large libraries have not been able to convert all the records in their card catalogs and, therefore, use OPACs only for materials added to their collections since a specific date. The card catalog still identifies everything acquired before that date and must be consulted when you are looking for older materials.

OPACs are more than computerized card catalogs. They may also give information about what material is on order, which issues of a journal have been received, whether a particular item is available or circulating to another patron, and when a circulating item is due. They can place a recall or hold on a book that is charged out, and learn what a professor has placed on reserve for a specific class.

OPACS: WHAT ARE THEY AND WHAT WILL THEY TELL YOU?

Some libraries also mount databases such as periodical indexes or the full text of encyclopedias on the same computer that supports their OPAC. For example, at Northwestern University in Illinois, researchers can search the *Expanded Academic Index* (a large periodical index) and *MEDLINE* (an index to medical journals) on the same terminals used to search the library's catalog. Some OPACs are linked to university or community information networks. Academic libraries are often part of a campus network, and public libraries can be hooked to municipal bulletin board systems that provide information ranging from tourism to agricultural assistance.

Searching in research jargon means navigating through a series of instructions to find desired information. As the choices and complexity of electronic systems increase, more sophisticated skills are required.

OPAC search options differ from one system to another. In addition to the traditional author, title, and subject access points, they may feature:

- Keyword searching: The computer will search the entire catalog for every occurrence of a particular word.
- Boolean searching: The researcher can use **and, not,** or **or** to narrow or broaden searches.
- Multi-index searches: Two indexes can be searched simultaneously; for instance, researchers can combine partial author and subject information in one search.
- Limitation of a search by language, date, range of dates, place of publication, material type (recording, videotape, etc.), publisher, and a variety of other data elements.
- Retrieval of items with the same subject heading as something already found.
- Capacity for printing out search results or downloading them to a disk.
- Capacity for searches from "remote" terminals—another floor in the library, your home or office, or from across the country.

Many OPACs provide cross-references that link the terms you use for searching with the OPAC's controlled vocabulary. This is important because users' search terms often are not exact matches with the subject headings used in the catalog. For example, typing **Filmography** into an OPAC may get the response **Search under Motion Pictures—Catalogs.** Truncation (providing just a part of the term you are seeking) is helpful when you don't know exactly how to spell a name. For example, typing **Solz** into many OPACs will retrieve a list that includes **Solzhenitsyn.**

Most online catalogs offer guidance on their use. This information can take the form of printed handouts or help messages on the screen. College libraries frequently offer classes in the use of the online catalog. Spending an hour in such a session will pay off many times over during a college career.

Today, many libraries permit remote access to their OPACs so that users can look up items in the catalog without coming to the library. The two methods of access are directly via a telephone line using a modem, or through the Internet web of telecommunications networks.

Many public and academic libraries offer modem access to their OPACs. Calling a local library will be free of charge. (Access to files other than the library's catalog may be limited to those who have been issued a password.) Dialing up a distant library will mean long-distance telephone charges, but may be well worth the investment if it enables you to find what you need quickly. Some states have a statewide catalog that can be accessed free. In Illinois, for instance, access to ILLINET is available to all state residents. If you don't have a computer or modem, your local library may be able to access this file for you.

Internet is the world's largest computer network. In addition to myriad other connections, it makes over 200 library catalogs in the United States and several catalogs overseas accessible. Not only can you use the catalogs of Harvard and the University of California, for example, you can also dial up the catalogs at the Technion in Israel and the University of Konstanz in Germany. For instructions on searching some of these catalogs, see *Search Sheets for OPACs on the Internet* by Marcia Klinger Henry (Meckler, 1991). See Chapter 12, The Internet, for further information.

The reasons for wanting to search catalogs from the home or office are as varied as the individuals searching them. Some common motivations include:

Why Would You Want to Access a Library Catalog?

- To check a citation quickly without having to visit the library. Often you can access the catalog even when the library is closed.
- To determine library holdings or locate unique items at remote locations. A traveling researcher can check in advance if the library owns a particular item or has a collection that meets special interests. You may also be able to speed up the interlibrary loan procedure by locating the library that has what you need and including that information with your interlibrary loan request.
- To obtain information such as library hours and policies.
- To download records to a personal database. Once downloaded, records can be modified for individual use and records can be integrated into text or bibliographies.
- To renew or place a hold on library material. (This feature is not available on all OPACs.)

Researchers need to know what remote catalogs are available, and how they are searched, since different OPACs use different software.

Information About OPACs

To learn what catalogs are available, consult the following sources:

OPAC Directory; An Annual Guide to *Online Public Access Catalogs and Databases.* Compiled by Regina Page. Meckler, 1990.
Gives instructions on accessing and using more than 280 OPACs.

"Searching Library Catalogs on the Internet: A Survey." By Aggi W. Rader and Karen L. Andrews. In *Database Searcher,* September 1990.

Pages 23–31 of this article list mailing addresses and phone numbers for libraries that make their catalogs available. While Internet access is the focus of this article, dial-in information is also provided, often with a help number and log-on and log-out procedures.

If you have Internet access, you can get a list of catalogs (Internet-Accessible Library Catalogs & Databases) by sending a message on the Internet to **LISTSERV@UNMVM, Get Library Package.**

Although OPACs provide access to a wealth of resources, their ease of use varies greatly. Some OPACs offer a menu of choices and steps ("menu-driven") while others require specific commands. In a menu-driven environment, specialized instructions are unnecessary; these systems are generally easy to use. Command-driven systems require the searcher to know system commands in order to submit a request. If you encounter one of these catalogs, type "HELP" or "?" at the command prompt. In most cases, a brief list of commands required to use the system will be displayed.

Methods of gaining access to OPACs also vary. Searchers will need to know log-on and log-off procedures. When dialing in with a modem, you will need to know what bit and parity settings to use and what modem speeds are accommodated. This information is given in *OPAC Directory.* Handouts explaining access are available from many libraries. If you plan to search a catalog frequently from your home or office computer, it's a good idea to keep a copy of such handouts by the modem.

OPACs provide access to the records of what a library owns, not to the material itself. If you are searching the catalog of a distant library, you will either have to travel to consult the desired items or make an interlibrary loan request at your local library. Technological advances have made access to the full text of library materials possible, but most libraries have not yet been able to make this potential an actuality. (See Chapter 10, Document Delivery Services, for other sources of materials.)

A good starting point for trying a selection of OPACs is the online service CARL, from the Colorado Alliance of Research Libraries. CARL provides access to about 500 public and academic library catalogs all over the country. All the catalogs are searched in the same way, so you don't need to learn 500 different log-on procedures. (CARL also offers access to some commercially available databases for which you must pay a fee to get a password.) CARL can be accessed through your modem by dialing **(303) 758-1551.** Modem speeds of 300, 1200, and 2400 bps can be accommodated.

6

BIBLIOGRAPHIC
UTILITIES

At the heart of research is the ability to find library materials, wherever they are. Not long ago, researchers had to be satisfied with what was available in their own libraries or through the scant and outdated printed catalogs of other libraries.

Thanks to a massive bibliographic project begun in 1948, about 500 libraries around the country began reporting their holdings for listing in the printed *National Union Catalog*. A researcher could now look up a work and see which large libraries reported having it. But these catalogs were expensive, cumbersome to use, and quickly outdated.

The same "union" principle, however, gave rise to electronic catalogs that could instantly provide a snapshot of what cooperating libraries owned. These not-for-profit electronic networks were designed to help librarians share the work of cataloging, so that the same book would not have to be cataloged thousands of times over in American libraries. Now known as "bibliographic utilities," the electronic networks play a key role in the quiet revolution in research.

OCLC, the Online Computer Library Center, began in 1971 as a cataloging cooperative for Ohio libraries and has since grown to serve 17,000 academic, special, and public libraries in the United States and fifty-two foreign countries. Today the OCLC database contains records for 30 million unique items, including books, periodicals, recordings, scores, videotapes, archives and manuscripts, and computer tapes. Nearly 2 million records are added each year. Librarians search the OCLC database for cataloging information on materials their libraries have just purchased. (If OCLC has no record for the item, the librarian catalogs it and adds the record to the OCLC database.) Since the database also notes which libraries own particular items, it can be used to locate materials for interlibrary loan.

Until recently, there was no way to access this huge file by subject; nor could it be used by the public. In 1990, OCLC introduced EPIC, a service that allows librarians to do subject searches of the database. In 1991, FirstSearch, an easy-to-use, menu-driven version of EPIC, became available for use in libraries. A library does not have to do its cataloging through OCLC to sign up for the FirstSearch service.

FirstSearch also makes available more than forty periodical indexes, ranging from *Art Index* through the *Modern Language Association International Bibliography* to the Government Printing Office's *Monthly Catalog*. Throughout subsequent chapters in this book, we note when indexes are available on this service.

Other recently developed OCLC services are ContentsFirst and ArticleFirst, which list the tables of contents for recent issues (the past one to three years) of more than 11,000 periodicals. This file can be searched by subject, periodical name, date, and several other ways. OCLC is also entering into joint ventures with several companies to offer "document delivery," that is, delivery of the full text of these periodical articles via mail or fax.

RLG   The Research Libraries Group (RLG) was founded in 1974 to provide cooperative cataloging for America's research libraries. Today, RLG has 200 general members. Most of them are large university libraries. Another 1,000 libraries can tap into RLG's database. They include independent research and museum libraries such as the American Antiquarian Society, the Art Institute of Chicago, the Martin Luther King, Jr., Papers Project, the Oregon State Archives, and the YIVO Institute for Jewish Research.

RLG owns the Research Libraries Information Network (RLIN), an online catalog begun in 1978 that now contains records for more than 56 million items. RLIN lists books, periodicals, films and videotapes, recordings, photographs, maps, computer tapes, manuscripts and archives, oral histories, and even three-dimensional objects. A new RLG service, Eureka, offers a menu-driven version of the catalog that the public will be able to search in member libraries.

The Library of Congress's *National Union Catalog of Manuscript Collections* from 1987 to the present can be searched through RLIN. RLIN's Research in Progress Database lists books and articles accepted for publication by the Modern Language Association, material on women's studies from the National Council for Research on Women, a National Gallery of Art file called Sponsored Research in the History of Art, and a list of current research projects funded by the National Endowment for the Humanities.

Other files unique to RLIN include the Eighteenth-Century Short Title Catalogue (a catalog of English-language books printed between 1701 and 1800), the Incunable Short Title Catalogue (a list of materials printed before 1501), SCIPIO (a database of art sales and auction catalogs), and the Avery Index to Architectural Periodicals. RLIN's offerings are especially strong in manuscripts and archives. Fourteen government archives, ranging from the Alabama Department of Archives and History to the State Historical Society of Wisconsin, are currently entering records of their holdings in RLIN. Plans are being made to create an online catalog of records for American literary manuscripts. Over 1,300 computer files at the Inter-University Consortium for Political and Social Research at the University of Michigan are listed on RLIN. The Rutgers-Princeton Center for Machine-Readable Texts in the Humanities has listed its inventory here.

In addition, RLG, like OCLC, makes certain commercial databases available through RLIN as a service called CitaDel. At this writing, about a dozen files can be found on CitaDel, several not available online anywhere else: *ISIS Current Bibliography of the History of Science, Current Bibliography of the History of Technology,* and *Hispanic-American Periodicals Index.* Copies of the articles indexed are available for a fee. RLIN has also developed Ariel, a document transmission service that uses the Internet (see Chapter 12) to deliver copies of articles, photographs, and other documents from one member library to another.

RLG member libraries can issue passwords so that individuals can access RLIN from their home or office computers. Independent scholars without a university affiliation who wish to access RLIN for a fee can get information about personal access by calling (800) 537-RLIN or by sending a BITNET message to **bl.ric@rlg.bitnet.**

OCLC and RLG are important resources for the researcher. Whether you are using a public or a university library, ask a librarian if any of the services described here are offered and what training is available.

7

DESKTOP
ELECTRONIC
RESEARCH

The microcomputer or personal computer (often referred to as a PC, though that is the generic name for IBM microcomputers) has steadily increased in capability and decreased in price over the past decade. In fact, many operations that would have required a mainframe computer only ten years ago can now be performed on an inexpensive home computer. This increase in capability has been matched by the proliferation of electronic information sources that computers can connect to over telephone lines or on a CD-ROM drive. These advances provide tremendous opportunities for the researcher working at home.

PC BASICS How do you start? The conventional wisdom is to define what you want to do with a computer, find the software that does it, and then buy the hardware that runs that software. The two major types of computers are those that run under the MS-DOS operating system (IBM and IBM-compatible machines) and the Apple Macintosh. At this writing, software that runs on MS-DOS machines won't work on Macintoshes (and vice versa) without an investment in conversion equipment. If you use a computer regularly at work or school and want one for home use, buy a model that will run the same software.

Currently offered microprocessor speeds are expressed as 286, 386, 486, or 586. For communications and to do database research, you will want at least a 386 computer. All standalone computers come with at least one floppy diskette drive and a hard drive. You might consider a CD-ROM drive (*C*ompact *D*isc-*R*ead *O*nly *M*emory) as well. All computers use a keyboard for data entry. A "mouse" can be used for some functions in lieu of the keyboard. Monitors (sometimes called CRTs) are available with mono-chrome or color display capacity. A color monitor may be worth the extra cost for its vivid display or if you are interested in multimedia. Monitors come in two qualities: VGA and Super VGA. VGA is required for most multimedia applications. Super VGA offers better resolution and more colors. Printers range in quality (and price) from dot-matrix to laser. For safety's sake, you will want to use a surge protector, a small inexpensive electrical device that protects the computer against power line disturbances.

Good sources of information for the novice selecting a computer are *Friendly PCs* by Mary Campbell (Random House, 1993) and *Dr. Mandell's Personal Computer Desk Reference* by Steven L. Mandell (Rawhide Press, 1993). If you understand the basic terminology of computers, check newsstand magazines such as *Computer Shopper* or the computer section of your newspaper. You may also want to scan magazines devoted to particular hardware, such as *MacUser, Amiga World,* and *PC World.* Other periodicals, such as *PC Novice* and *Home Office Computing,* also cover the latest in hardware and software. Some magazines treat specific software programs, such as *WordPerfect: The Magazine.* When you're ready to put your system together, look for the *PC Configuration Handbook* by John Woram (Random House, 1993).

COMMUNICATIONS EQUIPMENT

All popular microcomputers provide some type of telecommunications capability. The basic components you need for dialing into remote computers are a computer, a modem, a phone line, and some type of software that turns your computer into a terminal. The software you use will depend on the type of computer and its operating system. Computer magazines and newspapers can be a good source of advice on what system to choose, as are colleagues and friends who are already using this technology.

A **modem** (**mo**dulator/**dem**odulator) takes digital signals from your computer and turns them into analog signals that can be sent over the telephone lines. A modem at the other end of the line converts them back into digital signals that can be interpreted by the computer that it's connected to. With a modem, otherwise incompatible types of computers can communicate with each other. For example, you can dial up a bulletin board running on a Mac with your PC because data will flow between the computers in a standard code.

There are two basic types of modems, internal and external. The internal model has the advantages of fitting inside your computer and not taking up desk space or requiring a cable or serial port on your computer. However, the external modem has several benefits:

- Indicator lights indicate what the modem is doing. If you are having problems, it is handy to have a visual picture of what is happening.
- When an external modem does not respond to your software, you can simply flip it off and on and be back in business (although you will have

to redial). To reset an internal modem you will have to turn your computer off and "re-boot."

- An external model can be attached to any computer you have.

Modems are rated by the maximum speed at which they can transfer data. This speed is measured in "bits per second" (bps), sometimes expressed as "baud." Early modems communicated at 300 bps; then most services upgraded to 1200 bps. Today, 2400 bps modems are available for less than $100. Do not get anything slower than 2400 bps and seriously consider a higher-speed modem, though it will be more expensive. Many online services now offer 9600 bps service.

Modems on both ends of the connection *must* support the same set of protocols or communications procedures. Modems are usually "downwards compatible," so that a 9600 bps modem can dial a service communicating at 2400 bps. The modems will "negotiate" for the lowest common denominator protocol. It doesn't work the other way, however; you cannot dial up a 2400 bps service with a 1200 bps modem.

Buy a modem that is "100 percent Hayes-compatible." This means that the modem supports the Hayes "AT" command set, standard commands that your software will use to control the modem. If your modem is not Hayes-compatible, you will have to read the modem's manual to learn the correct commands so that you can set up your software properly.

While your computer is communicating over the telephone lines, you will not be able to make or receive telephone calls. People who are online for hours at a time may want to have a separate phone line dedicated to the use of the modem. (The fiber optic cable installed in some parts of the country can carry more than one message at a time.)

Many modems now also offer fax capability. Remember that when you receive a fax on your computer, you are only receiving a picture of the message. You can read it or print it, but ordinarily you cannot edit it in any way. (A few expensive fax modems will scan a fax so that your computer can read it.) You can only use a fax modem to send what is in your computer. To fax an illustration or a clipping from the newspaper, you need a free-standing fax or an optical scanner such as the one described below.

You can use a modem with a laptop computer and a cellular phone in your car. It is recommended that you only do this when the car is parked, not only for safety's sake, but also because as you drive you may leave one cell and enter another and thereby lose data.

Once you have all the pieces, follow the manufacturer's instructions to install the software and connect the modem. This is pretty straightforward—if someone in your home can program a VCR you will have no trouble.

With a computer and a modem, you will be able not only to transmit text but also, with the right software, to send and receive pictures. Part-motion video (about ten frames a second) can also be sent over the phone lines.

When the fiber optic network is installed, full-motion video (twenty-four frames a second) will be transmittable that way too.

By this stage your computer is talking to your modem and you are all set to conduct your research. There are a great number of possibilities—some are free and some cost money. If you are new to using a modem, it makes good sense to learn on the free sites. In almost all area codes, there will be a number of bulletin board systems (BBS) you can call. (See Chapter 11 for more information on BBS.) Many university libraries offer access to their online public access catalogs (Chapter 5, OPACs). If you are affiliated with a college or university, inquire about access to the Internet (Chapter 12).

Modem users can pay their way onto a host of commercial dial-up services, ranging from consumer services such as Prodigy, America Online, and CompuServe to such services for scholars and corporate users as Dialog and HRIN. (See Chapter 8.)

Ever-evolving storage and retrieval devices enable the researcher to gather whole libraries of information in forms that can be manipulated on a personal computer. CD-ROM (Compact Disc-Read Only Memory) is a relatively new electronic format that is similar in concept to compact audio discs, but can store text, pictures, sound, and even video. (See Chapter 9, CD-ROM). CD-ROMS are played on a special drive that is hooked up to a computer. CD-ROM drives will even play audio CDs, though the reverse is not true. A basic drive is available for about $300, but if it has multimedia capability with color graphics and stereo sound, a CD-ROM drive may cost as much as $2,000. For the consumer market, drives are often sold bundled with discs, usually for less than $1,000. If you plan to use a CD-ROM drive, you should buy a 386 computer with at least a 30 megabyte hard drive and a VGA graphics display monitor.

Optical scanners are devices that "read" text and images from paper into a computer file. This technique can save thousands of keystrokes when you want to put a long document into your computer. You can also scan pictures and other graphics that could not be entered into the computer using a keyboard. Not every scan is perfect; some editing may be required.

There are many peripherals or accessories available to computer owners. For example, speech synthesizers enable the computer to talk to you. They are especially useful for the visually disabled. Music synthesizers are popular. Video digitizers convert video images into digital ones that your computer can store and manipulate. A digitizing tablet lets what you draw on a slate (sort of like an "etch-a-sketch") appear on your computer screen.

Depending on your needs, your desktop workstation may soon outgrow your desktop. However, the tendency is for computers and peripherals to shrink in size even as they increase in power.

COMMUNICATING

THE COMPLETE WORKSTATION

8

ONLINE
SERVICES

Databases are large files that may be created and produced by scholarly associations (e.g., American Chemical Society, Modern Language Association), government agencies (National Library of Medicine), and private companies (ABC-Clio). Companies that make these databases available online—via telecommunications between computers—are called vendors. Sometimes the database producer and the vendor are the same company. The H. W. Wilson Company, for example, makes its own databases available through its Wilsonline service. But most database producers lease their files to such vendors as Dialog, BRS, ORBIT, HRIN, and others.

Online databases face increasing competition from CD-ROM (Compact Disc-Read Only Memory) databases, which are used without phone connections. (CD-ROMs are discussed in Chapter 9.) In spite of this, there is a large and ever-growing body of databases available to the online searcher; more than 5,000 databases are presently offered by several hundred vendors. Initially, most databases were bibliographic; that is, they contained references to, or abstracts of, journal articles, books, reports, and other materials. In recent years, a number of databases have become full text; these contain the actual journal and newspaper articles, reports, and other content.

Database searching has become a central tool in modern research. Information can be searched for by the researcher at a home computer or at a library.

If you need an online search but prefer not to do it yourself, many libraries will do it for you—almost always for a fee. Prices range from about $5 to $100 per search depending on the topic, the databases to be searched, and the policies of the library. Still, for a one-time search it can be more economical to pay a fee than to spend the time to do the search in printed sources. Most libraries recover only online costs and do not charge you overhead or service fees.

College and university libraries may have a special department devoted to online searching. There is likely to be at least one knowledgeable librarian who can talk to you about what you need, which online systems will be best for you, and what to expect from databases.

Some public libraries do online searching, either in-house or through a regional or state library system. If you work for a company with library staff, the chances are excellent that they do online searching and may be prepared to teach employees the technique.

Many online databases are also available in print and on CD-ROM. Neither of these formats may be as up-to-date or convenient as online searching, but they are usually free for you to use in libraries.

Information brokers—companies or individuals selling information services—will do searches for a fee. They can be found in the Yellow Pages or in:

FISCAL Directory of Fee-Based Research and Information Services. Compiled by Steve Coffmann. American Library Association, 1993.

Directory of Fee-based Information Services. By Helen Burwell. Burwell Enterprises. Annual.

These vendors can be grouped according to category or level of expense, sophistication, training required, size of audience, and the type of information retrieved.

MAJOR ONLINE VENDORS

Level 1: Scholarly and professional services such as Dialog, NEXIS, and NewsNet.

Level 2: Evening and weekend services for lay users (end users) such as Knowledge Index and BRS/AfterDark.

Level 3: Consumer services such as CompuServe and Prodigy, which provide popular information and may also include access to databases.

Note that several of these services provide "gateways" or communication links to other services. You may find it easier and more cost-effective to subscribe to one service and then use it as a gateway to access another. Remember that some databases are also available through OCLC and RLIN (see Chapter 6) and that your library may include databases on its online public access catalog (see Chapter 5).

Level 1 systems are most often used in offices and libraries by professional searchers. In general, they are the most expensive, although costs among databases can vary dramatically. These services may require an annual

Level 1

subscription fee; in addition, they all charge by the hour for searching. The databases available from these vendors are often targeted to professionals, i.e., lawyers, journalists, or scientists. Level 1 systems are highly sophisticated and complex and require training and practice to use cost-effectively. They are command- rather than menu-driven systems and often you must know codes specific to the vendor to search them. For example, searching Dialog to find material on the question of equal pay for women would involve typing in the following statement:

(wom?n? OR **female?)/TI,DE AND (pay()equity** OR **equal()pay** OR **comparable()worth?/TI,DE**

Customers get considerable advisory support, such as toll-free "help" numbers, from most of these companies.

Annual or start-up fees among vendors are as of this writing. The major cost to customers is usually the hourly search fees, which vary by database and conditions of use. The following are Level 1 vendors:

- *BRS:* About 145 databases in all subject fields, but especially strong in medical-related databases. Wilsonline databases (see below) are also available from BRS. Annual password is $50.
  BRS, 8000 Westpark Drive, McLean, VA 22102; (800) 289-4277.
- *DataTimes:* About 100 full-text U.S. and foreign newspapers such as the *San Francisco Chronicle* and *Beijing Daily.* Also such features as *Congressional Quarterly Weekly Report.* Initiation fee is $85.
  DataTimes Corporation, Parkway Plaza, 1400 Quail Springs Parkway, Oklahoma City, OK 73134; (800) 642-2525.
- *Dialog:* The largest U.S. vendor of online databases, with more than 400 databases in all subject areas containing 270 million references. Dialog recently absorbed the VU/TEXT system of full-text newspapers. Annual fee is $35. Dialog's Classmate service allows high schools to search certain files at a special rate.
  Dialog Information Services, 3460 Hillview Avenue, Palo Alto, CA 94303; (800) 3-Dialog.
- *Dow Jones News/Retrieval:* About seventy databases, some of them produced by Dow Jones (Dow Jones Historical Quotes) and others leased (Disclosure, Dun's). Only online source of *The Wall Street Journal.* Annual service fee is $18.
  Dow Jones News/Retrieval, P. O. Box 300, Princeton, NJ 08543; (800) 522-3567, ext. 201
- *Human Resources Information Network:* A service of the National Standards Association. Offers more than 100 databases from the Bureau of National Affairs, government agencies, professional societies, and information companies. Emphasis is on personnel and employment issues. Start-up fee is $250.

HRIN, 1200 Quince Orchard Boulevard, Gaithersburg, MD 20878; (800) 638-8094.

- *Mead Data Central:* Through its three services (LEXIS/NEXIS/MEDIS) it offers more than 350 databases. NEXIS is a full-text news service with newspapers, magazines, wire services, and more. LEXIS is a full-text legal database. MEDIS is Mead's medical service. Annual subscription required.
  Mead Data Central, P. O. Box 933, Dayton, OH 45401; (800) 227-4908.
- *NewsNet:* Full text of more than 500 business newsletters, worldwide wire services, industry reports. According to NewsNet, to subscribe to all these newsletters in print would cost $60,000. Subscription required.
  NewsNet, 945 Haverford Road, Bryn Mawr, PA 19010; (800) 345-1301.
- *ORBIT:* 100 databases, mostly scientific and technical, with a special emphasis on patents. Annual fee is $45. ORBIT and BRS were founded as independent firms, but at this writing are owned by the same company.
  ORBIT, 8000 Westpark Drive, McLean, VA 22102; (800) 456-7248.
- *WESTLAW:* Several thousand full-text law databases. Over 300 Dialog databases can also be used on WESTLAW. In addition, it offers a gateway to other Dialog databases, Dow Jones News/Retrieval, PaperChase (a MEDLINE service), and a Canadian law service. Subscription required.
  West Publishing Company, 610 Opperman Drive, St. Paul, MN 55164; (800) WESTLAW.
- *Wilsonline:* About twenty-five files in a variety of fields, such as art, business, education, and general science. No start-up fee. Wilsearch software turns Wilsonline into a menu-driven system. A unique Wilson feature enables those searching CD-ROM versions of their files to go online at no additional cost and find the most recent citations on their topic.
  H. W. Wilson Co., 950 University Avenue, Bronx, NY 10452; (800) 367-6770.
- *Non-U.S. vendors:* STN International (Germany), Questel (France), Data-Star (United Kingdom), ESA/IRS (Italy), and I. P. Sharp (Canada) all offer unique European databases that can be accessed in this country through a domestic phone call.
- *EasyNet:* This "intelligent gateway" is used to reach other host online systems. EasyNet provides access to 850 databases from a dozen vendors, including BRS, Dialog, NewsNet, ORBIT, and Wilsonline. When you dial EasyNet, you reach a computer in Pennsylvania that helps you decide which database would be most appropriate to search for your topic and helps you input your search strategy. The EasyNet computer then dials the online system it selects, runs your search, and downloads up to ten citations for you for a flat fee. Additional citations can be retrieved for an additional fee. EasyNet also features an online SOS command; use it

at any time during your search and a staff person will get online with you to help. CompuServe (see below) provides access to the EasyNet service. EasyNet, Telebase Systems, 435 Devon Park Drive, Wayne, PA 19087; (800) 220-9553.

Level 2   Level 2 systems, subsets of three of the systems described above, are available at lower rates during low-use periods at night and on weekends when home PC users can conduct their research. Generally, the databases available are those that are the most popular on the parent systems. Menu-driven interfaces mean that users can teach themselves to search.

- *BRS/AfterDark:* Provides access to about ninety of BRS's databases. Charges an initiation fee of $80. BRS/Colleague is a special option for health care providers with menu-driven access to medical databases. BRS/AfterDark, 8000 Westpark Drive, McLean, VA 22102; (800) 955-0906.

- *Knowledge Index:* Provides access to about ninety of Dialog's 400-plus databases at night through CompuServe. Knowledge Index uses a simplified search language and the documentation is excellent. A manual provides detailed information on: how to log on and off; how to navigate the menus; how to search using commands, including advanced techniques; and how to order the full text of documents from the service. Knowledge Index has an excellent newsletter describing new features and how best to use the system. CompuServe, P. O. Box 20212, Columbus, OH 43220; (800) 368-3343, ext. 35.

Before making the decision about which of these two services to use, call or write for a list of the databases available from them. Some popular databases, such as ERIC, are available from both Knowledge Index and BRS/AfterDark.

- *Dow Jones News/Retrieval:* An After Hours Plan allows certain databases to be searched nights and weekends at a lower rate. Flat fee plans are as low as $25 a month. Dow Jones News/Retrieval, P. O. Box 300, Princeton, NJ 08543; (800) 522-3567.

Level 3   Services at Level 3 are often described as electronic utilities and provide a wider range of services. These include:
- Communication by electronic mail (e-mail)
- Access to public bulletin boards (BBS), where people with similar interests will exchange messages

- Search files containing news, reference tools, popular and scholarly magazines, consumer information, and many other types of information
- Software that can be downloaded into the subscriber's computer

Level 3 systems attract the largest number of users because they provide access to a greater range of information—professional, research, consumer, and entertainment. The systems are relatively easy to use, requiring little instruction. With most of them you use your own telecommunications software to log on, but two, Prodigy and America Online, use dedicated or specific software; such software can also be purchased for CompuServe. The charges for most services are a flat rate for a certain number of hours; they are relatively low compared to the services at Levels 1 and 2. Peak usage hours are in the evening, the opposite of Level 1 services.

These services are accessible from most parts of the country with a local call. The charges given are as of this writing; they change rapidly, so check before subscribing.

- *CompuServe:* CompuServe and The Source were founded more than ten years ago as the first consumer services. CompuServe absorbed The Source and now has over one million subscribers. Basic service is $8.95 a month, but optional services, such as participating in forums (BBS), carry an extra charge ($8 an hour at a modem communication speed of 2400 bps, $16 an hour at 9600). For an extra charge, you can search some of the scholarly and professional databases on Dialog through Knowledge Index or from BRS, NewsNet, and other vendors through IQuest (identical to the EasyNet service described above). CompuServe has an e-mail link to the Internet. There are several ways to access CompuServe. You can use the general-purpose telecommunications software on your modem or software specifically designed for CompuServe, such as CompuServe Information Manager or Navigator. The Information Manager provides a more efficient and attractive way to access the system. Navigator automates access to forums and e-mail functions, thereby cutting your hourly connect fees. Services on CompuServe include live chat, games, public domain software, and much more. A vital source of information on the service is *CompuServe Magazine,* included with a subscription.
  CompuServe, P. O. Box 20212, Columbus, OH 43220; (800) 368-3343, ext. 35.

CompuServe Almanac: An Offline Reference of Online Services. CompuServe. Look for the latest edition. It is a well-organized listing of services.

CompuServe from A to Z: The Complete Encyclopedia to CompuServe. By Charles Bowen. Random House, 1991.

How to Get the Most Out of CompuServe. 5th ed. By Charles Bowen and David Peyton. Random House, 1993.

Alfred Glossbrenner's Master Guide to CompuServe. By Alfred Glossbrenner. Prentice-Hall, 1987.

The Complete Guide to CompuServe. By Brad Schepp and Debra Schepp. McGraw-Hill, 1990.

Inside CompuServe. 2d ed. By Julie A. Arca and Richard T. Lindstrom. New Riders Publishing, 1990.

Up and Running with CompuServe. By Bob Campbell. Sybex, 1991.

- *Delphi Internet:* The second-oldest consumer service, with some 100,000 subscribers. Delphi Internet has two pricing plans for evening and weekend use. Under one plan, $10 a month includes four hours of use; additional use is $4 per hour. Under the second plan, $20 a month includes twenty hours of use, with additional hours costing $1.80 each. Access during business hours carries a surcharge of $9 per hour under both plans. In addition to news, weather, sports, business, and travel information, Delphi Internet provides a gateway to Dialog. It's the only one of the consumer services listed here that offers full Internet service, including the ability to FTP (File Transfer Protocol) and TELNET. (See Chapter 12, The Internet.) BIX (Byte Information Exchange), another online service from the same company, is strictly about computers. Delphi Internet Services Corp., 1030 Massachusetts Avenue, Cambridge, MA 02138; (800) 695-4005.

Delphi: The Official Guide. 2d ed. By Michael Banks. General Videotex, 1993.

- *GEnie:* Has 350,000 subscribers. Basic service is $4.95 a month, with no hourly charges for night/weekend use but a charge of $18 per hour during the day. Access to RoundTables (BBS) costs $6 an hour nights and weekends. Surcharges apply to special services such as a consumer medical database and a file of public opinion polls. Basic services include a personal loan calculator, news, sports, weather, and stock market closings. GEnie has a gateway to Dow Jones News/Retrieval Service and to e-mail on the Internet. GEnie, General Electric Information Services, P. O. Box 6403, Rockville, MD 20850; (800) 638-9636.

Glossbrenner's Master Guide to GEnie. By Alfred Glossbrenner. McGraw-Hill, 1990.

- America Online and Prodigy require software that runs on your own computer rather than on the "host computer," as is common with most other services. These graphics-based services rely on elaborate menus, and very little typing is involved—usually just a word or phrase. If you can type *install* at a DOS prompt, you can use these services.
- *America Online:* Has 600,000 subscribers. The basic fee is $9.95 a month for five hours of use; additional time is $3.50 an hour. The electronic mail gateway allows you to send mail to people on CompuServe, the Internet, AppleLink, AT&T Mail, and MCI Mail. In addition to texts that can be read online (an encyclopedia, for instance), there are also files that can be read only by downloading them to your computer. AOL has an amazing variety of services—something for every member of the family—and is especially good in the field of education.
  America Online, 8619 Westwood Center Drive, Vienna, VA 22182; (800) 827-6364.

America Online Membership Kit and Tour Guide. By Tom Lichty. Ventana, 1992. Available in DOS, Windows, and Macintosh editions.

- *Prodigy:* With almost 2 million subscribers, this is the largest online service. Prodigy originally had a flat-rate monthly fee of $14.95 that included unlimited connect time. It has since added charges for more than two hours per month use of bulletin boards, stock quotes, airline reservation services, and company news. The service makes heavy use of graphics, and most screens include advertising along the bottom (part of the reason the cost is low). Examples of services offered are an encyclopedia, weather forecasts for 235 U.S. and 100 foreign cities, *Consumer Reports,* and services for children. Prodigy is the easiest of all these systems to use, but the trade-off is that it lacks some features found on the others, such as live chat and free software files to download.
  Prodigy Services Company, 445 Hamilton Avenue, White Plains, NY 10601; (800) 776-3449.

Fifty Ways to Get Your Money's Worth from Prodigy. By Raymond Werner. Alpha Books, 1992.

Official Guide to Prodigy Service. By John Viescas. Microsoft, 1991.

Prodigy Made Easy. 2d ed. By Pamela Kane. McGraw-Hill, 1992.

Using Prodigy. By Stephen Nelson. Que Corp., 1990.

- *Community Link:* Telephone companies are now allowed to participate in the information services industry. U.S. West offers Community Link in the Omaha and Minneapolis-St. Paul areas in conjunction with a French company, Minitel. If residents don't own a computer, they can rent from the phone company a "dumb" terminal, one that can be used only for telecommunicating. Many of the services offered by Community Link appear to be Delphi services, but some are local and others are French.
- *Cable companies:* These are also interested in providing information services through television sets; we will undoubtedly see more services from regional phone companies and cable companies in the future.

SOURCES OF
INFORMATION
ABOUT ONLINE
SEARCHING

Books

Here are several good *general* guides to online searching:

The Complete Handbook of Personal Computer Communications. 3d ed. By Alfred Glossbrenner. St. Martin's Press, 1989.

Tells you all you need to know about modems, communications software, online systems at all levels, and going online with your home computer.

Cruising Online: Larry Magid's Guide to the New Digital Highways. By Lawrence J. Magid. Random House, 1994.

Helps readers choose the best online service for their needs. Advice on electronic mail, travel services, shopping, and more.

Net Guide. By Michael Wolff and Company. Random House, 1993.

Locates and rates bulletin boards and special interest groups on the major online services. Organized by type of information.

Mac Online! Making the Connection. By Carla Rose. Windcrest/McGraw-Hill, 1993.

Similar to Glossbrenner but specific to the Macintosh and more up-to-date. Clear instructions on using a modem, even on how to send a fax. Covers all the major consumer services plus the Internet, BBS, and other e-mail services.

The Modem Reference. 2d ed. By Michael A. Banks. Brady, 1991.

Instructions on buying and setting up a modem and going online. Good reference section with descriptions and phone numbers for all commercial services.

Online Information Hunting. By Nahum Goldman. Windcrest/McGraw-Hill, 1992.

Theoretical guide to searching the more technical/scholarly online databases. Explains how online files are structured and the mechanics of searching. Advice on formulating a search strategy and running a search.

How to Look It Up Online. By Alfred Glossbrenner. St. Martin's Press, 1987.

Intended for individual researchers, this is a highly readable (and sometimes irreverent) book. It discusses specifics of major online systems, including Dialog, BRS, NEXIS, and Wilsonline. Somewhat out-of-date now, but the best of its type, it will help you to learn to refine your search strategy.

Prime-Time Computing: A Senior's Guide to Home Computing. By Mark Mathosian. Inkwell Publishers, 1992.

A beginner's book for senior citizens. Chapters on buying a computer, software for seniors and their grandchildren, going online with a modem, and more.

Gale Directory of Databases. 2 vols. By Kathleen Young Marcaccio. Gale. Annual. Also online with ORBIT.

Directories

Lists thousands of online databases in Volume 1 and notes the vendor(s) for each. Volume 2 lists CD-ROMs, diskettes, and databases available on magnetic tape. Most academic and major public libraries will have this directory.

Federal Database Finder: Directory of Free and Fee-based Databases and Files Available from the Federal Government. 3d ed. By Matthew Lesko. Information USA, 1990.

Fulltext Sources Online. BiblioData. Semiannual.

Lists more than 4,000 periodicals, journals, newspapers, newsletters, and newswires available online in full text.

Newspapers Online. BiblioData. Annual with supplements.

Lists 150 newspapers available online in full text. A subfile of *Fulltext Sources Online,* with more detailed information about each newspaper.

Online Access. 1985–   . Quarterly.

Periodicals

This newsstand magazine with the subtitle "The magazine that makes modems work" features articles on theoretical issues such as privacy on electronic networks, evaluations of hardware, and reviews of individual services and databases. Issues have included articles on CD-ROMs and on the Internet. Also has a calendar of online events on America Online, CompuServe, Delphi Internet, and GEnie, schedules of free online training, and a directory of new databases. The ads too are helpful to the novice.

Link-Up. 1983–   . Bimonthly.

Subtitled "The newsmagazine for users of online services." Contributors are knowledgeable, information is brief and accurate. Articles cover what is new in online systems, especially from the point of view of the general user.

Information Today. 1983–   . Monthly.

With the subtitle "The Newspaper for Users and Producers of Electronic Information Systems," this sister newspaper to *Link-Up* is aimed at the information professional. It covers the online and CD-ROM world, or what is termed the "information industry."

Online. 1977–   . Bimonthly.

Principally aimed at professional searchers, mostly librarians, but it also contains many articles of wider interest. It includes "gray pages" with industry news and gossip and often has articles that review new systems or databases.

Database. 1978–   . Bimonthly.

Offers in-depth reviews of databases and of software for database creation. A sister publication to *Online.*

BYTE and *PC Magazine* occasionally have articles about online searching. If you do not subscribe to these magazines, it is a good idea to browse through them from time to time in the library or to pick one up at a newsstand.

Note: Most consumer online systems have monthly newsletters or magazines that come automatically with your subscription. They are must reading if you search their systems.

Other Sources of Information

In library catalogs, the following subject headings will help you find books with further information on online searching:

Computer networks	Information storage and retrieval
Database searching	systems
Information retrieval	On-line bibliographic searching
	On-line data processing

You can learn a lot about online searching and about specific databases by attending a conference on the subject. The best of these meetings is the yearly Online/CD-ROM Conference sponsored by Online, Inc., the company that publishes *Online* magazine. Most of the attendees are librarians and other information professionals, but the exhibits are a learning bazaar and there are always sessions aimed at the layperson and beginner.

Learned Information publishes two videotapes that introduce the concepts of online searching:

Going Online: An Introduction to the World of Online Information. 1986.

ONLINE
SERVICES

45

Going Online for Business Information. 1988.

Each provides basic overviews of the world of online searching. Either videotape can be previewed for ten days for a fee.

9

CD-ROM

As we have seen in previous chapters, CD-ROM (Compact Disc-Read Only Memory) is becoming as common in research as CD-audio is in music. Both, in fact, use laser technology to store large quantities of electronic data. They are both optical, rather than magnetic, discs; that is, information is encoded and later read by a laser beam. An audio CD can usually be played on a CD-ROM drive, but CD-ROMs can only be used with a special drive connected to and controlled by a computer.

The CD-ROM is searched not for music but for text, data, and images. You can usually search for any word on the disc or for some combination of words. Unlike the floppy disks that PC users fill with data, CD-ROMs are "read only"; it is impossible to write anything on them. However, text can be copied from a CD-ROM disc onto your computer, where you can work with it.

A typical CD-ROM holds as many as 1,500 floppy disks, or about 600 megabytes of data, enough for some 300,000 pages of text or 20,000 images. CD-ROM technology was introduced in 1985, and there are now more than 2.5 million drives (sometimes called "players") in use. Some computers now come equipped with built-in CD-ROM drives; portable drives are available as well.

A CD-ROM drive must be used with a computer with a large-capacity hard disk on which MS-DOS CD-ROM extensions are installed; this enables the computer to interact with the drive. Most CD-ROM drives used by individuals and in small libraries are stand-alone devices hooked up to an individual PC and used by one person at a time. But today drives can be networked to a server, or "jukebox," that holds multiple discs and enables researchers to pull in many of the library's databases to their workstations. Remote dial-up access to CD-ROM drives from home and office is also possible.

The latest CD-ROM technology is multimedia. It can include audio, graphics, and animation in addition to text. Multimedia technologies such as CD-ROM XA incorporate part-motion video (ten to twelve frames per second). Digital Video Interactive is the only compact disc format at this writing that is capable of full-motion video (twenty-four to thirty frames per second). Unfortunately, these different multimedia formats use incompatible standards (or "platforms," as they are called in the industry), so they can't all be played on the same type of drive. Current developments in this area are tracked in *NewMedia: Multimedia Technologies for Desktop Computer Users,* a newsstand magazine.

At present, there are more than 4,000 CD-ROM titles available. Originally, most CD-ROMs were for MS-DOS computers, but now there are titles for the Macintosh as well. Many are all text, such as the numerous periodical indexes described later in this book. Others are all images. For example, the *Permanent Collection of Notable Americans* contains 3,093 images of paintings in the National Portrait Gallery. Some CD-ROM reference works, such as encyclopedias, contain text, images, sound, and animation. To find out what CD-ROM titles are available in your field of interest, consult the topical chapters in this book or one of the following books:

CD-ROMS in Print. Meckler Publishing. Annual.

Gale Directory of Databases. Gale Research. Annual.

Many databases are available on both CD-ROM and online. With most online services, you are charged by the minute or by the search. But a database on CD-ROM can be used all day, seven days a week, at no extra cost. The main advantage of online searching is that databases are usually updated more frequently.

An estimated 80 percent of public libraries have CD-ROM drives, and more than 90 percent of college and university libraries own them. Forty percent of school districts have drives; in response to a 1990 survey, another 37 percent said that they planned to purchase one soon. But no library will have all the CD-ROM titles listed in this book, and some small libraries won't have any. For example, the University of Minnesota Libraries have more than 100 CD-ROMs, the Northwestern University Libraries own several dozen titles, and the Evanston (Illinois) Public Library, serving a suburban community of 75,000, subscribes to five. In some reference areas, such as general events and business, there is a great deal of overlap in coverage among CD-ROM titles. If your library doesn't own a CD-ROM listed here, ask if it has another title that does the same thing or see if your library (or another) will search an equivalent database online.

To keep up with what is going on with this technology, read *CD-ROM*

World. 1986– . Monthly. It has an extensive section of reviews of new titles.

COMPACT DISC PRODUCTS FOR CONSUMERS

The consumer electronics industry wants to make CD-ROM an extension of television sets rather than of computers. There are, after all, many more TV sets in American homes than there are PCs. Consumer compact discs all require a special drive that retails for less than $1,000. Usually, instead of a keyboard there is a controller like those used in video games. The discs for these systems range from encyclopedias, dictionaries, and children's books to how-to products and games. Philips has a product called CD-I (Compact Disc-Interactive), Commodore sells CDTV, and Tandy has VIS (Video Information System). You can't play a CD-I disc on a CDTV player or vice versa; nor will any of these products work on a CD-ROM drive.

Miniature compact discs have been developed for handheld players such as Sony's Data Discman. Kodak's Photo-CD technology allows photo images you create to be put on a compact disc. They can then be viewed on a TV hooked up to a CD-I or Kodak CD player, or on a computer connected to some models of CD-ROM drives.

10

DOCUMENT
DELIVERY
SERVICES

Electronic technologies have revolutionized the way researchers identify needed information. These technologies can also help you quickly obtain copies of journal articles or other documents that are not available in your library. When you can't wait to get a document on interlibrary loan, document delivery services will fax or mail paper copies of articles to you. They will charge a fee that includes a charge for the service plus a copyright fee to be paid to the publisher or other copyright proprietor of the item.

Here is a selection of such services with an overview of the types of materials they provide. Some services require a large minimum deposit and therefore are used only by corporations and libraries. The telephone numbers listed here are voice numbers, not fax or computer numbers. Call to check fees before ordering:

CARL UnCover
CARL Systems
3801 E. Florida Ave.
Denver, CO 80222
(303) 758-3030

Some libraries offer dial-up or Internet access to CARL's online table-of-contents database of 12,000 journals published since 1988. It is possible to search the database by author or keywords in the titles or to reconstruct the table of contents for an issue of a periodical. There is no true subject index, however. Articles can be ordered online. For a fee of about $10, CARL will fax a copy of most listed articles within twenty-four hours.

Faxon Xpress
Faxon Research Services
238 Main St.
Cambridge, MA 02142
(617) 354-7112

Faxon Finder, a table-of-contents database for more than 11,000 journals in science, engineering, business, and medicine, can be searched on OCLC's FirstSearch service. Articles can be ordered through OCLC, Dialog, fax, and e-mail. A deposit account is required. For $11 plus a royalty fee, Faxon will fax an article within twenty-four hours.

Information Express
3250 Ash St.
Palo Alto, CA 94306
(415) 494-8787

Offers document delivery in all subjects within twenty-four to forty-eight hours. Orders taken via Dialog, fax, e-mail, and phone and delivered by fax. Prices vary according to source.

Information on Demand
8000 Waterpark Dr.
McLean, VA 22102
(800) 999-4463

A pioneer in document delivery, IOD supplies journal articles in all fields and from all dates, U.S. and foreign patents, conference papers, technical reports, and government documents. Orders taken via Dialog, OCLC, ORBIT, BRS, RLIN, fax, e-mail, and phone. Delivery by fax for $20 plus fifty cents per page.

Information Store
500 Sansome St., Suite 400
San Francisco, CA 94111
(415) 433-5500

Offers documents on all subjects. Orders taken through OCLC, Dialog, CompuServe, fax, BRS, MCI Mail. Delivered via fax and MCI Mail. Rush service, twenty-four to forty-eight hours. Call for price information.

ISI Genuine Article
Institute for Scientific Information
3501 Market St.
Philadelphia, PA 19104
(800) 336-4474

Strong in academic journals in science, engineering, medicine, the humanities, and the social sciences. Orders taken by phone, OCLC, Dialog, BRS, fax, and e-mail. Delivery by fax. Deposit required to open an account. About $21 per article; $7.75 extra for pre-1988 titles.

LEXIS Document Services
Mead Data Central
2901 Normandy Rd.
Springfield, IL 62703
(800) 634-9738
Provides legal documents to LEXIS database subscribers. Orders taken by phone or fax and delivered by fax for $2 per page.

NewsBank/Readex Quick Doc
5020 N. Tamiami Trail
Naples, FL 33940
(800) 762-8182
Provides copies of articles from newspapers back to 1971, U.S. and United Nations documents, some periodicals. Orders taken by fax and phone; articles delivered by fax in twenty-four hours. Fee is about $15 for 20 pages; thirty cents for each page thereafter.

OCLC ArticleFirst
6565 Frantz Rd.
Dublin, OH 43017
(800) 848-5878
In libraries subscribing to the OCLC service, ContentsFirst, an article table-of-contents service, can be searched on FirstSearch and copies can be ordered online to be delivered by fax. OCLC uses other document delivery services to provide the articles, so prices vary.

Research Libraries Group
1200 Villa St.
Mountain View, CA 94041
(800) 537-RLIN
Libraries with a computer connection to RLIN can search its CitaDel service, a series of commercially available databases (*ABI/Inform, Newspaper Abstracts, PAIS*, etc.), and order copies of articles online. Articles are provided by other document delivery services, so prices vary.

Research Publications
12 Lunar Dr.
Woodbridge, CT 06525
(800) 444-0799

Supplies all patents from the United States and most other industrial nations. Orders taken via Dialog, fax, and phone; delivery by fax. Rush service takes two to twenty-four hours and costs $20 plus seventy-five cents a page after ten pages.

UMI Article Clearinghouse
300 N. Zeeb Rd.
Ann Arbor, MI 48106-1346
(800) 521-0600
Provides articles from more than 12,000 scholarly and popular periodicals, conference proceedings, newspapers, and government documents. Unlike many of the services here, which only provide articles from the past five to ten years, UMI can provide articles from very old journals and newspapers. Requires no deposit. Order by fax, Dialog, BRS, OCLC, or telephone. Delivery by fax or Internet. Quick service is twenty-four hours and costs $9 plus thirty cents per page.

Universal Serial and Book Exchange
2969 W. 25th St.
Cleveland, OH 44113
(216) 241-6960
This service provides the original issues of back-date journals to libraries that are members. Deposit account required. Orders taken via OCLC, fax, phone. Delivery by express mail for $10.

For a more comprehensive list of such services, see:
FISCAL Directory of Fee-Based Research and Document Supply Services. 4th ed. Compiled by Steve Coffman. American Library Association and County of Los Angeles Public Library, 1993.
An in-depth listing of some 550 information and document providers who charge fees. Entries describe the range of products and services, subject strengths, types of orders accepted, delivery options, charges, and other terms and conditions. Geographic and research-specialty indexes are among the finding aids. Includes selected overseas providers.

11

ELECTRONIC BULLETIN BOARDS

An electronic bulletin board system (BBS) is a software communications program running on a PC or other small computer that allows people to dial up over the telephone lines and post and read messages. Some 10 million people use an estimated 45,000 BBSs in the United States. Boards can be public or private and can be used as a research source. Some are run by computer hardware and software companies as a way of providing customer support. Local groups of computer users often have bulletin boards. Many government agencies maintain BBSs. Some are highly specialized and not of much interest to the layperson; others disseminate information to the general public. Many BBSs are run by an individual system operator (sysop) as a labor of love. People start bulletin boards out of the same passion that used to inspire ham radio operators—they like to communicate with others.

Though some boards have been around for ten years, the life span of a BBS can be short. Some of those listed in this guide will undoubtedly have gone out of business by the time you try to dial them. The early bulletin boards used software that required a lot of human intervention and thus were available only at night and on weekends, when their sysops were home from work. Today, the software to run a BBS is much improved, and most boards are available twenty-four hours a day. While some are still rather primitive and hard to use if you're not a true computer hacker, most have menus that are easy to follow.

The typical BBS charges $15 to $75 for an annual membership. It is estimated that 80 percent of all bulletin boards are nonprofit and a third charge nothing at all. However, some BBSs have become big businesses, with more than a hundred telephone lines and thousands of calls coming in to their computers daily. The largest bulletin boards offer so many

FEDERAL GOVERNMENT BBS
List of 110 Bulletin Board Systems

ABLE INFORM (301)589-3536
  Nat Rehab Center & Data of Assist. Tech
ADAALS/Navy (202)342-4568
  Ada Language Sys/Navy Bulletin Board
ADA Tech Supp. BBS (804)444-7841
  Assist interested in ADA
ADAIC (703)614-0215
  ADA Information
ALF (301)504-6510
  National Agricultural Library BBS
ALIX (202)707-4888
  Automated Library Info eXchange
ASN (703)746-2645
ATTIC (EPA) (301)670-3813
  Alternative Treatment Tech Info Cent
BOM-BBN (202)501-0373
  Bureau of Mines-Bulletin Board Net
BRX Info Corner (703)756-6109
  BBS for IRS Employees
BULLDOG WEST (805)985-9527
  Harpoon support
BUPERS Access (703)614-8059
  Navy Personnel Information
CABB (202)647-9225
  Passport Info/Travel Alerts
CASUCOM (GSA) (202)653-7516
  Interagency Shared Serv/Resources
CERCNET (DARPA) (800)331-3808
  Concurrent Engineering Research Net
CIC-BBS (GSA) (202)208-7679
  Consumer Information Center
CLU-IN (EPA) (301)589-8366
  Superfund Data and Information
CPO-BBS (Census) (301)763-4574
  Jobs at the Census Dept
CRS-BBS (202)514-6193
  Amer. With Disabilities Act Info
Census-BEA (Census) (301)763-7554
  Census BEA Electronic Forum
Computer Sec. (NIST) (301)948-5140
  Nat Comp Sys Lab Comp Sec BBS
DASC-ZE (703)274-5863
  PC Info and files

DCBBS (DC Govt) (202)727-6668
  DC Government Information
DMIE (NIST/NCSL) (301)948-2048
  NIST/NCSL Data Manage Info
DRIPSS (EPA) (800)229-3737
  Drinking Water Info Process Support
EBB (202)482-3870
  Economic data and info
ELISA System (703)697-6109
  DoD Export License Tracking Sys
EOUSA-BBS (202)501-7521
  BBS for U.S. Attorneys
EPUB (202)586-2557
  Energy information and data
Energy Information (202)586-8658
  Petrol, Coal, Electric, Energy Stats
FAA Safety Exchange (800)462-3814
  Small Plane Safety Reports & info
FCC Public Access (301)725-1072
  Equip. authorization status advisory serv.
FCC-State Link (202)632-1361
  FCC daily digest & carrier stats/report
FDA's BBS (800)222-0185
  FDA info and policies
FDA/DMMS (301)443-7496
  PMA, IDE, 510k & guidance documents
FEDERAL BBS (202)512-1397
  GPO and Govt Data (Fee Based)
FEDIX (800)783-3349
  Links Fed Data to Higher Education
FERC-CIPS BBS (202)208-1781
  Fed Energy Regulatory Commission
FHA BBS (202)366-3764
  FHA staff and interested public
FMS-BBS (202)874-6817
  Inventory management data & programs
FRBBS (NIST) (301)921-6302
  FRBBS—Info on Fire Research
FREND #1 (Natl Arch.) (202)275-0920
  Fed. Reg. Elect. News Delivery
Fed Whistleblower (202)225-5527
  Report fraud, abuse, waste in U.S. Govt
Fort Benning (717)686-3037

Fort Drum (315)772-7836
Fort Leavenworth (913)684-7675
Fort Meyer (703)524-4149
    Officers' Club
Fort Richie (301)878-4573
GPSIC (703)866-3894
    GPS & Loran Info, Status & Data
GPSIC (703)866-3890
    Information on Global Positioning Sys
Gulfline (EPA&NOAA) (800)235-4662
    Gulf Coast Pollution Info
HSOL-BBS (HHS & UMd) (301)985-7936
    Head Start BBS (Region III)
HUD-N&E BB (HUD) (202)708-3563
    HUD News & Events BB. P R
IHS-BBS (HHS) (301)443-9517
    Indian Health Service BBS
IRSC BBS (GSA) (202)501-2014
    GSA information and lists
JAG-NET (703)325-0748
    Navy Judge Advocate General
Kelly AFB (512)925-9096
LC News Service (202)707-3854
    Library of Congress News Service
Labor News (202)219-4784
    Dept of Labor information and files
Langley AFB (804)764-3995
Malstrom AFB (406)731-2503
Megawatt 1 (202)586-0739
    Information on energy and DoE
Metro-Net (202)475-7543
    Army Morale, Welfare, and Rec.
NADAP (703)693-3831
    Navy Drug and Alcohol Abuse Prev.
NASA Spacelink (205)895-0028
    Education affairs, flight data, space history
NAVTASC (301)238-2131
    NAVCOMTELSTA Washington DC
NCJRS-BBS (301)738-8895
    National Criminal Justice Refer. Sys
NCTS BBS (202)475-7885
    Navy Computer & Telecom Station
NDB-BBS (301)436-5078
    Human Nutrition Information Service
NGWS BBS (703)602-1916
    Naval Gun Weapon System BBS
NIDR Online (NIH) (301)492-2221
    Nat. Institute of Dental Research

NIST ACTS (303)494-4775
    Auto Comp Tele Service, PC to NBS Time
NOAA Space Lab (303)497-5042
    Solar flare and geomagnetic data
NOAA-ESDD (NOAA) (202)606-4662
    NOAA Earth Sys Data Direct
NPS-BBS (EPA) (301)589-0205
    Nonpoint Source Program BBS
NRRC (518)370-0118
    Naval Reserve Readiness Center
NSSDC/NASA/Gd (301)286-9000
    The NASA NODIS Locator Sys.
NUPERS ACC BBS (703)614-8059
Naval Justice School (401)841-3990
OASH-BBS (NAPO) (202)690-5423
    AIDS Information & Reports
OEA BBS (202)208-7119
    Interior's Off of Environment Affairs
OERI BBS (202)219-2011
    Educational Research and Improvement
OIS (202)514-6102
    US Bureau of Prison employees
OPBO-BBS (202)482-1423
    Internal comm. for DOC employees
Offshore-BBS (703)787-1181
    Off Shore Oil & Gas Data
PIM BBS (EPA) (703)305-5919
    Pesticide Information Network
PPIC-BBS (EPA) (703)506-1025
    Pollu. Preven, Clean Product, Ozone
Patent Lic. BBS(NTIS) (703)487-4061
    Speeds acc. to Fed lab research
PayPerNet #1 (OPM) (202)606-2675
    Fed. Pay & Per. Management BBS
Port O'Call (504)947-8253
    Navy Computer & Telecomm. Command
QED-BBS (USGS) (800)358-2663
    Qk Epicenter Determ and EQ data
SALEMDUG-BBS (202)646-2887
    State and local FEMA user groups
SBA On Line (SBA) (800)859-4636
    SBA Information and data
SBAI-BBS (SBA) (202)205-6269
    Small Bus. Admin internal BBS
SESD-EBB (703)285-9637
    PC software & contract Info
SRS (202)634-1764
    Fed. R&D budget, Tech labor market stats

STIS (NSF) (202)357-0359
　　Science & Tech Information Sys.
SWICH BBS (301)585-0204
　　EPA—Solid Waste Management
S. Weath. Data (NWS) (301)899-1173
　　Sample data from Fee Based Sys.
Shaw AFB (803)668-4316
TEBBS (OGE) (202)523-1186
　　Office of Government Ethics BBS
TELENEWS (202)586-6496
　　Data and info on Fossil fuels
USA-GPCS BBS (703)285-9637
　　Army Info System Software
USCS-BBS (Customs) (202)376-7100
　　Cust. and Exchange Rate Data & Info

USGS QED (303)273-8672
　　Earthquake epicenter data, geomagnetism
USGS-BBS (USGS) (703)648-4168
　　Geological Survey BBS/CD-ROM Info
USNO ADS (202)653-1079
　　GPS data, sunrise/set/surveying data
USNO Time of Day (202)653-0351
　　USNO Atomic clock, trans. ASCII time string
VA-BBS (202)523-7399
　　VA info and PC programs
WSCA-BBS (800)735-7396
　　Board of Wage & Service Contract Appeal

services that they are sometimes compared to commercial consumer operations like CompuServe. In fact, those commercial services all offer bulletin boards as part of their package. Prodigy calls them bulletin boards, America Online calls them clubs, GEnie has RoundTables, CompuServe has forums, and on the Internet they are called news groups or listservs. (See Chapter 12.) In this chapter we focus on freestanding bulletin boards that are not part of some larger service.

What is on a typical BBS? It's possible to play games, participate in live chat, post or read messages, and download public domain software and shareware. Some boards claim to have more than 100,000 software programs, and they encourage you to upload software that you've developed. These may be text or computer programs. Files are sometimes compressed in order to save space. To "UNZIP" such files, you will need a special software program.

Software obtainable through a BBS can include language tutorials, business programs, and games. Some boards have thousands of files of photographs and drawings. Sysops can lease *USA Today* news and post it. Hundreds of bulletin boards feature "adult" material (Compu Erotica, Virtual Extasy). CUFON (Computer UFO Network), **(206) 776-0382,** is a free twenty-four-hour source of reliable, verifiable information about UFOs. There is no discussion, just documents to read and download. The National Amputee Connection, **(214) 238-0928,** is for amputees and those involved with them. Active message areas include spinal injury and chronic pain. The Meeting Works, **(212) 737-6932,** gives sales and association executives tips on running meetings. Some BBSs are part of a network. FidoNet, one of the largest, passes electronic mail from one board to another and also offers an e-mail link to the Internet.

Some bulletin boards may advertise that they are for Mac users, others that they are for PCs, indicating the kind of software available to download to your computer. However, telecommunication enables you to dial up a PC bulletin board with a Mac or vice versa and read what is on the board.

To access a board, call the BBS's telephone number using your modem and telecommunication software; the BBS's modem will answer the telephone and emit a tone that your modem will recognize and respond to. The modems will establish a connection and you will be able to communicate with the computer on the other end. You may need to hit the **< ENTER >** key a few times to get the other computer to respond. In modem language, the majority of BBSs communicate at 2400 bits per second, though there are increasingly more 9600 bps boards. Modem software prompts the user to set up certain communication parameters; the great majority of boards are set to "8 bits, no parity, 1 stop bit." You will need to register with the other computer by telling it who you are and where you live, your password, and other information. Some "adult" boards require proof of age sent through the mail. You will be presented with a "main menu," which allows you to choose from among the resources on the BBS. Many BBSs allow a free period of time to look around to see if the board interests you. After this period, free privileges are suspended.

Typically, people dial up local boards in their own area code. Within many area codes, there are dozens, even hundreds, of boards to choose from. Calling boards that aren't in your area code can be expensive, leading to astronomical phone bills for the addicted. If you make frequent use of BBSs outside your area code, you might want to subscribe to a packet-switching network that can lower your long-distance bills. Two of these are PC Pursuit (SprintNet), (800) 336-0437, and Star*Link, (505) 881-6980.

Some boards offer 800 numbers. For example, Hayes Microcomputer Products hosts a board with information about its products, **(800) 874-2937;** the National Education Association has a board for its members, **(800) 541-0816;** and the government's Small Business Administration offers SBA Online, **(800) 859-4636.**

Finding the right BBS can take some time. For a list of the BBSs in your local area, check with a computer store or a local computer magazine. A local computer club or user group may have additional information. Also, many boards maintain lists of other boards. BBSs that offer only entertainment can be found in every area code. Boards that are good sources of information on a special topic, however, are not duplicated in every area code and you may have to make some long-distance calls.

To find out about boards on the national scene, look for *Boardwatch Magazine* on the newsstand. This monthly, subtitled "Guide to Online Information Services and Electronic Bulletin Boards," has articles on hardware and software (including reviews of CD-ROMs), news about the Internet, and information for sysops. The most useful features for beginners are notes about interesting BBSs; a directory of bulletin boards in particular cities; a list of people who maintain lists of BBSs on a particular topic, like conservation, or for a particular area code; and a list of new BBSs.

Another place to look for lists of BBSs is on CompuServe (Chapter 8) or in the *National Directory of Bulletin Board Systems* by Patrick Dewey, an annual publication of Meckler Publishing, which lists some 10,000 BBSs. The *Computer Shopper,* an inexpensive monthly newsstand publication, also contains a list of numbers. Most lists do not provide descriptions or subject access, but they are a starting point. *Modem USA: Low Cost and Free Online Sources for Information, Databases, and Electronic Bulletin Boards via Computer and Modem in 50 States,* Second Edition by Lynne Motley (Allium Press, 1993) lists 1,000 bulletin boards in thirteen subject categories and gives brief descriptions.

BBSs can be large repositories of information on specialized topics, with as many potential sources of information as there are callers. They can be a useful way to tap into sources of expert information and advice. Generally, BBS users are eager to share their knowledge and are very sociable—electronically, at least. Many of the specialized BBSs enable you to talk with knowledgeable people in your field. Bear in mind, however, that although a sysop can control what is posted on a board, there is no formal refereeing. A book goes through an editing procedure that weeds out at least the most egregious errors, but anybody can post anything on a bulletin board. If you plan to quote information, try to get a referral to a printed source to support your quotation. Also get permission to use what you quote from any copyright holder if the material is not in the public domain.

You can set up your own BBS and thereby create an online source of information specially tailored to your interests. This is more practical if you have a spare computer and a dedicated telephone line to devote to the project, rather than using your workstation during off hours. Running your own BBS can be very time-consuming. You will have to troubleshoot both hardware and software problems and answer cascades of e-mail. Not everyone who calls will observe proper decorum.

If you want to make the best use of BBSs, consult:

Using Computer Bulletin Boards. Rev. ed. By John V. Hedtke. MIS Press, 1992.

Mac Online! Making the Connection. By Carla Rose. Windcrest/McGraw-Hill, 1993.
Several easy-to-read chapters cover using a modem to dial up BBSs. Covers the commercial services such as CompuServe as well.

Microcomputer Market Place. By Steven J. Bennett and Richard Freirman. Random House, 1992.

Includes an extensive list of bulletin boards along with technical information and phone numbers.

If you wish to create your own BBS, you will find these books on target:

Create a Computer Bulletin Board System. By L. Myers. TAB Books, 1993.

Essential Guide to Bulletin Board Systems. By Patrick R. Dewey. Meckler, 1987.

12

THE
INTERNET

The Internet is a worldwide network of networks that runs on many kinds of computers. The backbone of the system is a National Science Foundation network linking the regional supercomputer centers.

The Internet has evolved into a global network connecting millions of users through some 6,700 networks in more than fifty countries. The Internet is not owned by any one person or company, but is loosely organized and runs largely through the cooperation of its users. The efforts of volunteer members of the Internet Society (ISOC) have led to standard protocols that allow all these computers to communicate. There are various subgroups, such as the Internet Architecture Board, which maintain computer site addresses.

This vast network has been likened to a superhighway for information, enabling large amounts of data to travel from one place to another. Most of this information travels over phone lines; the advent of fiber optic cable has greatly increased the amount of data that can be sent at one time and the speed at which it goes. The Internet also functions like a highway system in that it connects to other computer networks such as BITNET, a large academic network, and numerous regional networks, such as NYSERNET.

The Internet also links up with such networks abroad as JANET (Joint Academic Network) in the United Kingdom and EARN (European Academic Research Network). Australia, Japan, Turkey, Russia—almost every country in the developed world can be accessed. Since many computers run continuously, time zones pose no problem for sending electronic mail or searching for information. In fact, because peak hours of use occur at different times in different countries, response time can be greatly improved when there is less traffic on the wires.

The Internet protocols (referred to as TCP/IP) allow different types of computers to communicate with one another, so that a university with an IBM VM system, for instance, can connect to a host UNIX computer. This doesn't mean it's always easy, but you can connect and look for information in a way that the host machine understands because, though the language may differ, the basic way of performing certain functions remains the same. Once you know how to use your own computer system, the barriers for remote systems are not that difficult to overcome.

Internet use and services were growing at the rate of about 10 percent a month in mid-1993; about 30 million people have access. National legislation has mandated the creation of NREN, the National Research and Education Network. Intended to supplant the Internet, NREN has been designed as a formal network with rules and a governing body to serve the needs of government, research institutions, and the general public. Plans are under way to have NREN operational as early as 1996.

The Internet, which started out as a way for scholars to exchange information, has expanded to the point that it can provide virtually any type or format of information. In addition to textual information, it offers archives of graphic materials—astronomical maps and data, exhibits of documents, chemical formulae, among other things—as well as computer software and the catalogs of more than 200 libraries. Multimedia, with sound and video, is soon expected on the Internet.

You can do a lot of things on the Internet, for instance:

THE USES OF THE INTERNET

- Send and receive electronic mail (e-mail), private correspondence that can be read only by the addressee.
- Send and retrieve files—both text files and software—in exchanges with a remote (distant) computer, a process called File Transfer Protocol, or FTP.
- Connect to a remote computer simply to look at information it contains (TELNET). This connection might be with the online public access catalog of a library.
- Subscribe to electronic group discussions (listservs), the Internet's version of bulletin boards.

Electronic mail, or e-mail, is a very heavily used utility on the Internet. It is a way of sending messages using a modem to link your computer via the phone lines to a larger computer, which will then send the message on to someone else. The advantages of an electronic message, sent computer to computer, are that it is fast; the message can be printed, if desired; it doesn't require a paper copy or another machine for transmittal, as do most faxes; and it is relatively inexpensive.

Electronic Mail

Many people today send electronic mail through such commercial systems as MCI Mail, SprintMail, CompuServe, Prodigy, or America Online.

Obviously both the sender and the recipient of e-mail must be subscribers to the same system in order to communicate. The Internet broadens access to electronic mail, allowing you to reach others who may not be subscribers to your system, as long as their system provides Internet access. So, as a customer of CompuServe, for instance, you could contact someone at a university with an Internet address, and that person could also respond to you via the Internet connection to CompuServe.

The Internet provides a standard form of addressing, so that it is generally clear from the address where the person you are contacting is located. (Information on how to read an address is provided at the end of this chapter.) What isn't always easy is finding an address; as of this writing, there is no one global—or even national—directory of e-mail addresses. This situation results partly from the security concerns of system administrators or individuals, and partly from the staggering number of addresses for which no one agency has responsibility. The easiest way to get people's e-mail addresses is to telephone them and ask.

File Transfer Protocol

FTP (File Transfer Protocol) is both the software and the command used on the Internet to transfer a file from one computer to another. If you log in to your own computer, then generate the command FTP followed by an address, the host computer you reach will understand that you are connecting via the Internet, and that the reason you are connecting is that you wish to receive (GET) or send (PUT) some sort of file.

Files can be strictly textual or they can be in some sort of compressed form, indicated by the way they are named. Files can be graphics or software programs as well, and how they are designated usually tells you that. For instance, from a number of sources you can get weather maps that are updated hourly but that vary in format depending on the sources from which you obtain them.

Project Gutenberg is one of the more fascinating collections on the Internet that can be accessed by FTP. It is an effort, carried out entirely by volunteers, to convert literature into machine-readable form. It contains texts ranging from *Alice in Wonderland* to *The CIA World Factbook* in simple untagged text form. For more information, contact Project Gutenberg, National Clearinghouse for Machine-Readable Texts, Illinois Benedictine College, 5700 College Road, Lisle, IL 60532 or **hart@vmd.cso.uiuc.edu.**

TELNET

TELNET is the command that you use to connect to another computer for the purpose of looking at information on it. When you use the TELNET command with the Internet address of the host computer, that host accepts your request to log on (connect) and then lets you look at data, just as any local user would. You become, in effect, just another terminal on the host computer's system. TELNET is used to connect to bulletin boards, to library catalogs, and, increasingly, to a number of commercial sites that have databases available for a fee, such as Dialog and LEXIS/NEXIS. Telnetting is free to most systems, but to use commercial services you must have an account and your own password. For commercial services, the Internet just takes over the telecommunications function, replacing packet-switching networks such as Sprintnet and Tymnet.

To "telnet," or log on to another computer, you need to know the machine name or the numeric address, something you will have found in a directory. After connecting to the host computer, you must pay special attention to instructions on how to use the host system and how to exit when you are through. Some systems are better than others at giving you this information.

Increasingly, the Internet is becoming a place where scholars and researchers "publish" their work, in the form of electronic journals. Besides saving the time and expense of traditional printing, paper, and postage, electronic publishing may eliminate many intervening levels of editing and review. This is not viewed in many circles as an entirely good thing, as peer review has traditionally been a way to ensure the quality of research published. However, some electronic journals are peer-reviewed. *The Online Journal of Current Clinical Trials,* for example, publishes refereed articles. A good, regularly updated list of available journals can be found electronically at **listserv@acadvm1.uottawa.ca,** or in published form: *Directory of Electronic Journals, Newsletters, and Academic Discussion Lists.* 3d ed. By Michael Strangelove and Diane Kovacs. Association of Research Libraries, 1993.

**Electronic
Journals**

Electronic conferences, newsgroups, or "listservs" have become a very popular way of communicating via the Internet. Imagine attending a conference organized around a topic of interest to you. You will hear various papers, comments and questions, and a lively discussion and exchange of ideas. This is very much how an electronic conference, or newsgroup, works; the major difference is that the communication is done via the computer. Listserv has become a common name for these groups, although, technically, "Listserv" is the BITNET software that provides conferencing and archiving of the conference material.

Bulletin Boards

The more than 2,000 listservs appeal to every conceivable kind of interest, from the serious and esoteric to the amusing and weird. As you might imagine, many conferences exist for computer software and hardware interests, and a good number for finding out about or furthering the Internet. But if, for example, you're an avid gardener, Gardens-L can lead to tips for growing peonies or where to find antique roses. There are lists for golden retriever enthusiasts, origami makers, Peace Corps volunteers, Amnesty International members, and Sinead O'Connor followers. If you're a

Star Trek or an *L.A. Law* fan, you will find groups just for talking about these programs in the alt (for alternative) group of lists on BITNET. The alt and soc (social) groups are wonderful places in which to find kindred spirits—and sometimes research sources—on everything from politics to religion to weather.

As a subscriber to a list, you may send out a message, a question, or an item for discussion to the entire membership list just by sending one electronic message. Participants will respond, generally to the whole membership. Everyone benefits from the answer to your question or from the discussion you have launched. Occasionally discussions become heated or go off on tangents, and the list owner or administrator will intervene to get everyone back on track. Some lists are moderated, with an administrator who decides what gets posted. Some are "digestified," which means that the owner digests messages on the same topic so that there won't be so much to read. On very active lists, the messages can pile up in your electronic mailbox unless you read and/or delete them regularly. This is the major drawback to such listservs. And sometimes the topic at hand is no longer interesting or is too specialized for you. There is, however, a way to be a part of such discussion groups without actually subscribing to them. USENET is a worldwide network whose UNIX-based program distributes electronic messages. The difference between it and similar software systems is that the messages go to your local network computer, not your individual mail box. You can log on to the system, peruse the news, and log out without having to delete a stack of messages. The housekeeping is done periodically by the system.

Other newsreading software allows those with electronic mail accounts to view active messages on the listservs merely by looking at a newsreader utility. You simply log into the newsreader and scan for items of particular interest. Messages don't collect in your mail account, though you can save them if you wish, just as you can in regular e-mail. And you can still join a discussion by sending a message to the discussion group. The primary drawback to the newsreaders is that they are updated and purged regularly, so that unless you make a point of logging on fairly often you may miss something useful.

FINDING TOOLS Using the amount of information flowing from the Internet has been compared to "drinking from a firehose." Individuals must find a way to channel the deluge of information. Finding exactly what you are looking for requires using some specialized tools.

Archie, which comes from the word *archive,* is such a system. Developed at McGill University, Archie is software mounted on various server computers around the world. It can be accessed in different ways, but one of the easiest is to telnet to the nearest server, log on as Archie, and ask it to look for the address of a file you want. The catch here is that you must already know what file you want, which might not be obvious in certain situations. Every Archie server periodically scans about 900 sites on the Internet and adds names of files to its data store, so it is constantly being updated. One Archie server is **archie.rutgers.edu.**

Gopher is a finding tool for the Internet that was developed at the University of Minnesota (whose team mascot is a gopher or go-fer). Gopher was the first real attempt to help searchers navigate the maze of computers on the Internet. It looks into the menus of all the computers it knows about and finds information to match the key words you ask it to find. Accessed by the command **Gopher,** it is available in widely varying versions for different operating systems.

Another method for retrieving information is WAIS, the Wide Area Information Servers. Developed at Thinking Machines Corporation, it attempts to find what you want within the files or databases it knows about by looking for a term or terms. There are simple WAISes (and more advanced ones) which will try to refine your search by finding other documents that are most like the ones you chose from an initial search.

For researchers, one of the most useful things on the Internet is the large and growing number of library catalogs. If you are seeking a particular book, you can electronically check the nearest large university library to see if it has it. If you are working in a particular subject area, you can use printed guides to see which libraries have good collections in that field, and, if they are on the Internet, search through their collections. Most large university libraries, along with some college libraries and research institute libraries, now have a part or all of their collections in electronic form available through the Internet.

Library electronic catalogs increasingly offer more than a record of the books and periodicals housed in the library. Some also offer access to the full text of specific works, such as Shakespeare's plays (Dartmouth) or the *Concise Oxford Dictionary* (Rutgers). (See Chapter 5, Online Public Access Catalogs.)

Much of the research community already has access to the Internet's bounty. Most university and college computer centers have mounted the necessary software and created a link through high-speed dedicated phone lines. Large corporations and other commercial users can become a "node" for about $10,000 a year. The best way to find out if your college or company has Internet access is to ask the library, computing, or data processing staff. Even if your own organization doesn't have Internet capability, such people generally will know who in the area provides it for the public.

If you are not linked to the Internet, you must use a computer and modem to dial up a computer that is. Some communities—Cleveland was the first—provide "freenets," both to offer community-based information and to help members of the community connect with the Internet. You can become a freenet member by logging into the system and giving some basic personal information. You don't even have to live in the community that sponsors the freenet, although it may mean long-distance calls if you don't. Freenets serve as a gateway service to much that is available on the Internet.

Freenets are not all alike, but tend to reflect their communities, offering a variety of services, from access to the area libraries to weather information to local sports and cultural schedules. For more information on freenets, contact the National Public Telecomputing Network, Box 1987, Cleveland, OH 44106, or **aa622@cleveland.freenet.edu.** Also check listings in books about the Internet; call your local public library; use Gopher on the Internet.

Local bulletin board systems may offer access to the Internet through FidoNet (see Chapter 11, Electronic Bulletin Boards), but these systems are often very busy and service is limited. Many of the commercial online services have access, though often only for electronic mail. America Online, CompuServe, Prodigy, and GEnie offer this kind of service. Delphi offers full Internet service, including the ability to ftp and telnet. (See Chapter 8, Online Services, for more information about these companies.) A new service, Worldlink (call (703) 709-9890), also offers full service. Performance Systems International (call (800) 82-PSI-82), HoloNet (call (510) 704-0160), and the California Education and Research Federation (call (800) 876-CERF) are three of the better known providers of fee-based access to the public, but the number is in the dozens and growing. A good list of Internet access providers, compiled by SRI International Network Information Systems Center, is available in the book *Internet: Getting Started* (see below).

BIBLIOGRAPHY

The period 1991–93 saw a remarkable number of publications about the Internet. Of the recent materials available on finding and using resources on the Internet, the following are especially helpful to the novice user:

"Communication, Computers and Networks." *Scientific American,* September 1991.
This special issue is an interesting and wide-ranging introduction to computer networks.

Internet Basics: Your Online Access to the Global Electronic Superhighway. By Steve Lambert and Walter Howe. Random House, 1993.
Accessing the Internet through Delphi. Thorough instructions and hints and tips. Updates available online.

The Internet Companion: A Beginner's Guide to Global Networking. By Tracy LaQuey with Jeanne C. Ryer; foreword by Al Gore. Addison-Wesley, 1993.

Perhaps the most basic introduction to the Internet. Clear and nontechnical, it provides copious information on how to use the many available resources.

The Whole Internet: User's Guide & Catalog. By Ed Krol. O'Reilly & Associates, 1992.

A comprehensive guide to the hows and whys of Internet networking, recommended for every Internet user from the beginner to the experienced user. Especially useful is the directory of interesting Internet services and the list of Internet access providers.

Net Guide: What's on in Cyberspace. Michael Wolf and Company. Random House, 1993.

An entertaining guide to information online, arranged by category across several services.

Internet: Getting Started. Updated ed. By April Marine and others. PTR Prentice-Hall, 1993.

Another good book for the beginner.

Zen and the Art of the Internet: A Beginner's Guide to the Internet. 2d ed. By Brendan P. Kehoe. PTR Prentice-Hall, 1993.

First published electronically on the Internet, this guide has been expanded and revised. Some of the more technical explanations may be hard to grasp without hands-on experience.

Crossing the Internet Threshold: An Instructional Handbook. By Roy Tennant and others. Library Solutions Press, 1993.

A workbook approach to learning the ins and outs of Internetworking, and very complete in its definitions. The command summaries and glossaries are particularly helpful.

NetPower: The Educator's Resource Guide to Online Computer Services. National Education and Technology Alliance, Postal Drawer 6051, Lancaster, PA 17603.

Though not limited to the Internet (it also covers CompuServe, Dialog, etc.), the section on the Internet is specifically geared to its use in K-12 education.

Internet: Mailing Lists. Rev. ed. Edited by Edward T. L. Hardie and Vivian Neou. PTR Prentice-Hall, 1993.

A directory of more than 800 Internet, BITNET, and USENET mailing lists and interest groups with instructions on subscribing. Subject index is not detailed enough.

Directory of Directories on the Internet. By Gregory Newby. Meckler, 1993.

Internet World. 1990–   . 9 times/year.
Subtitled "The Newsletter for Non-Commercial and Commercial Uses of the Internet and the National Research and Education Network."

READING AN INTERNET ADDRESS

The name to the left of the symbol @ is the name assigned to you by your local host computer—the computer that serves as your link to the Internet. Depending on local policy, it may be based on your real name or formed from a series of numbers, sometimes combined with letters.

To the right of the @ is the "domain" or name of the computer where your mailbox resides, followed by a three-letter code designating the kind of Internet membership. The codes are:

.edu—educational institutions
.com—commercial companies
.gov—government agencies
.mil—military installations
.org—nonprofit organizations

Here are some examples:

U53559@uicvm.edu	Someone at the University of Illinois at Chicago
MaryJ@aol.com	An America Online address
12345.678@compuserve.com	A CompuServe address
johnson@apple.com	Someone who works for Apple Computer
acuff@simtel20.army.mil	Army address (the computer is at White Sands Missile Range, but the person isn't necessarily there)
jsmith@carl.pac.org	Colorado Alliance of Research Libraries, an organization

Foreign addresses need a code for the country:

Heverlee@ccl.kuleuven.ac.be	Someone at the University of Leuven in Belgium
sjones@vm1.mcgill.ca	Someone at McGill University in Canada

PART III

Understanding the Sources: Five Treasuries of Information

13

LIBRARIES

A library is a collection of informational and cultural materials organized for use. The distinguishing part of this definition is "organized for use." A warehouse full of books is not a library. The cataloging, indexing, and arranging that librarians do transform an inventory of books, periodicals, microforms, sound recordings, manuscripts, computer tapes, and other materials into a library. While the word *library* is based on the Latin word for book, today's libraries collect materials in many different forms.

America's more than 100,000 libraries are run by about 150,000 professional librarians and an equal number of support staff members. Librarians usually have a master's degree in library science; school librarians may have degrees in education and school library media. The work of these librarians is augmented by that of paraprofessional and clerical staff, including student workers. In addition to library staff at public service desks, people behind the scenes administer the library's operations, manage automated functions, acquire and catalog materials, and perform the scores of duties necessary to maintaining services and collections.

With a membership of some 56,000, the American Library Association is the largest as well as the oldest library organization in the world. Founded in 1876, ALA is the chief advocate for high-quality library and information services for the American people. ALA protects the public's right to read without censorship, supports the continuing education of librarians, and helps to improve library services. Library associations in every state are affiliates of ALA.

Libraries in the United States fall into eight general categories:

TYPES OF LIBRARIES

1. *Public libraries* are tax-supported institutions that are by definition open to the public. There are more than 9,000 public libraries in the United

States, and, if each branch is counted, more than 15,000 buildings in which library services are provided.

Public libraries serve the community's interests by providing reading materials, recordings, videotapes, public programs, and much more. Most public libraries have basic reference and research collections, and a few metropolitan institutions, such as those in New York, Boston, and Philadelphia, boast research collections comparable or superior to those of the best university libraries in certain subject areas.

Cooperative lending agreements with surrounding communities often increase the number of titles libraries have available. A few states provide a borrowing card that is good throughout the state's public library system.

2. *State libraries,* found in all fifty states, are set up to serve state government, but they also administer state funding to public libraries and the sharing of materials between libraries, and, in addition, help to develop statewide catalogs in electronic formats. Often, state libraries have special research collections that the public can use.

3. *The Library of Congress (LC),* as the name implies, serves as the library for members of Congress. However, it is the de facto national library of the United States. With over 100 million items, 20 million of them books, it is also the world's largest library. LC's collections are noncirculating; they must be used in the building. However, the Library of Congress will lend books on interlibrary loan if no other American library owns them.

Because a copy of every book must be deposited with the library as part of the copyright process, LC has vast collections of American books, films, and recordings. The Library of Congress also maintains offices in many foreign countries to purchase books, and there is no region of the world not represented in its collections.

One of LC's great contributions to American libraries is the cataloging it provides for library materials, the basis of many of the catalog records in local libraries. It provides catalog records to services that distribute them electronically as well as to individual libraries.

4. *Academic libraries* are found in both tax-supported and private colleges and universities. Some 4,600 community college, college, and university libraries together own more than 514 million books; the collections range from under 50,000 volumes to the 12 million volumes owned by Harvard University. Academic collections support undergraduate and graduate education and faculty research. Large universities may have branch libraries for departments and professional schools. About 100 of the largest university libraries describe themselves as "research" libraries and have formed the Association of Research Libraries.

Academic libraries differ in the services they offer to the general public. Talk to your public librarian or telephone the college or university library staff before scheduling a visit. (See also Chapter 4, Independent Researchers.)

5. *Independent research libraries* are privately endowed libraries that are usually autonomous. Fifteen such institutions have joined together to form the Independent Research Libraries Association. Some of these libraries were formed on the basis of a great private collection (Folger, Huntington, Pierpont Morgan) while others were gifts to a community from a wealthy donor (the Newberry Library in Chicago). Many of these libraries have fellowship programs that enable researchers to spend time in residence.

6. *School libraries* (or school library media centers, as they are often called) are found at all levels, from kindergarten through high school. There are about 92,000 of them. School librarians are often educated as teachers and work in an instructional partnership with the school faculty. Services can range from storytelling in an elementary school library to teaching students computer database searching skills in the higher grades. (See also Chapter 3, The High School Researcher.)

7. *Special libraries* include almost 10,000 corporate, association, museum, hospital, and other specialized libraries. Their collections are often very narrow in scope, but have great depth within that specialty, reflecting the needs of the host institution. They vary greatly in their restrictions on use by outsiders. Again, your public library or the libraries themselves can advise you. The Special Libraries Association is chief among organizations for special librarians, though several groups, such as the American Association of Law Libraries, serve narrower constituencies.

8. *Government libraries.* There are almost 2,000 libraries serving the federal government. Two of them are termed national libraries—the National Agricultural Library and the National Library of Medicine. Military libraries and Veterans Administration hospital libraries are other examples of government libraries.

The Library in America: A Celebration in Words and Pictures. By Paul Dickson. Facts On File, 1986.

BOOKS ABOUT LIBRARIES

A lively, illustrated history of public libraries.

Treasures of the Library of Congress. 2d ed. By Charles A. Goodrum. H. N. Abrams, 1991.

A lavishly illustrated sample of important LC collections: rare books, photographs and prints, maps, music and musical instruments, Oriental materials, and manuscripts.

Treasures of the New York Public Library. Abrams, 1988.

Color photographs highlight the outstanding collections of this library.

The Whole Library Handbook: Current Data, Professional Advice, and Curiosa about Libraries and Library Services. Compiled by George M. Eberhart. American Library Association, 1991.

A librarian's miscellany filled with interesting facts.

Bowker Annual Library and Book Trade Almanac. Bowker. Annual.

Statistical and directory information on librarianship and the publishing industry.

THE FUTURE OF LIBRARIES

Libraries have experienced tremendous growth in their collections since the 1960s and have long been looking for solutions to their space problems. Microforms were once seen as a panacea ("the library in a shoe box"), but while they have proved useful for back files of newspapers and periodicals, people really don't like to read books on microform readers.

Electronic technology, either online or CD-ROM (see Chapters 8 and 9), is now seen not only as the answer to space shortages but as a way of providing research materials to people wherever they are. The term "virtual library" is being used as a metaphor for the networked library, the library without walls. In the future, researchers may not need to come to the physical library to use its resources; with desktop workstations, they will be able to draw on collections at great distances.

However, our great research libraries contain most of the country's cultural and intellectual heritage and will continue to have a role in its preservation and dissemination. Paul Saffo, research fellow at the Institute for the Future, says we are living in a "moment between two revolutions—one of print, not quite spent, and another of electronics, not quite underway." Librarians have the twin challenges of trying "to maintain and sustain the paper medium, while at the same time exploring new, paperless media." Researchers, also caught in the transition, must learn new sources and new skills for getting at them.

14

ARCHIVES

The researcher will find it easier to move between libraries and archives than to understand the subtle differences that librarians and archivists draw between the two types of repositories. If it's called an archives, it will contain documents and papers of historic value. The *ALA Glossary of Library and Information Science* defines archives as: "The organized body of noncurrent records made or received in connection with the transaction of its affairs by a government, or a government agency, an institution, organization, or other corporate body, and the personal papers of a family or individual, which are preserved because of their continuing value."

Archives can include notes, minutes, manuscripts such as correspondence, photographs, and other materials. They are administered by archivists, who are usually history professionals with special archival training. Archival collections are usually of two types:

1. *General or cultural archives, in which the documents are preserved for their own sake rather than as the records of the host institution.* Such archives tend to be built around a subject. Examples would be the archival collections in historical societies or in independent research libraries such as the Huntington Library or the Folger Shakespeare Library.

2. *Institutional archives maintained in order to preserve the records of the host institution.* They include public records in government archives, and the archives of religious denominations, corporations, associations, colleges and universities, health care institutions, and labor unions. Sometimes these institutions are unable to maintain their own archival records, so they will deposit them with another institutional archive or a general or cultural archive. The archives of many corporations, for example, are found in university archives and historical societies.

Unlike most library materials, archival records are not usually analyzed for an item-by-item catalog; instead they are arranged, usually in the order established by their creator, and described. A descriptive inventory includes:

- A sketch that describes the context in which the papers were created.
- A narrative description of the collection.
- A container list that summarizes what is in each box and folder of the collection.

Because of the great bulk of records, most archives do not describe individual items. In a few collections, such as the papers of George Washington, every letter may be listed and described; but this approach would take too much work for most collections.

For some collections, a printed catalog serves as a guide to the contents. But in many cases, the only guide is the descriptive inventory in typescript form at the archives. Certain descriptive inventories are also commercially available in microfiche.

Most archival records are unique materials and are therefore not subjected to the risks of interlibrary loan. Researchers who need such materials usually must travel to the archival site. You may be able to order photocopies or microfilm copies of records, but unless you can identify exactly what you need, this can be expensive. The National Archives and Records Administration has established regional centers to facilitate access to records (see Chapter 27, Genealogy).

At this writing, the Library of Congress has placed archival materials from two of its special exhibits, the Russian Archives and the Vatican, online with America Online and the Internet in order to make materials from its exhibits available to a wider audience, especially to those who may not be able to visit Washington.

HOW TO FIND OUT ABOUT ARCHIVAL COLLECTIONS

Libraries: If libraries hold archival collections, the library catalog may list them. Otherwise, ask the reference librarian about collections and finding aids.

Local archives: Visit the archives or telephone and consult with an archivist on how the collections are indexed. Archivists can guide researchers to other pertinent collections.

Beyond local archives: The following catalogs and directories describe collections at three levels of detail: general descriptions of archives, general descriptions of individual collections within archives, and descriptive inventories of specific collections. Before making your visit, be sure to write or telephone to confirm the information you've gathered about collections and accessibility:

Directory of Archives and Manuscript Repositories in the United States. National Historical Publications and Records Commission. 2d ed. Oryx Press, 1988.

Provides general descriptions of archival repositories and information on hours, copying facilities, and any published guides that describe the collections. Arranged by state with a subject index.

National Union Catalog of Manuscript Collections. Library of Congress, 1959–   . Annual.

Index to Personal Names in the National Union Catalog of Manuscript Collections, 1959–1984. Chadwyck-Healey, 1988.

Index to Subjects and Corporate Names in the National Union Catalog of Manuscript Collections, 1959–1984. Chadwyck-Healey, 1993.

Descriptions of individual collections in U.S. archives. Descriptions are published as collections are processed. Each volume has a subject index. Also available online on RLIN, 1987–   .

The two national online catalogs, RLIN and OCLC (see Chapter 6), also contain many descriptions of manuscript collections. RLIN introduced the Archives and Manuscripts Control format in 1984 and is now the largest and richest online catalog of unique archival materials anywhere. Examples of collections described on RLIN include records from the Burroughs Corporation (a computer manufacturer) at the University of Minnesota, records showing the development of Old Sturbridge Village in Massachusetts, and the personal papers of John Steinbeck at Stanford University.

National Inventory of the Documentary Sources in the United States. Chadwyck-Healey, 1990–   . Microfiche.

This ongoing project reproduces on microfiche the descriptive inventories of many archives. It is published in three parts: federal records; the Manuscript Division of the Library of Congress; and state archives, university archives, historical societies, academic libraries, and other repositories. There is a cumulative CD-ROM index to the whole set.

A number of catalogs describe archives devoted to a specific topic or located in a particular place, for example:

Women's History Sources: A Guide to Archives and Manuscript Collections in the United States. 2 vols. By Andrea Hinding. Bowker, 1979.

A Guide to Archives and Manuscript Collections in the History of Chemistry and Chemical Technology. Compiled by George D. Tselos and Colleen Wickey. The Center for History of Chemistry, 1987.

Resources for the History of Computing: A Guide to U.S. and Canadian Records. By Bruce H. Bruemmer. Charles Babbage Institute, University of Minnesota, 1987.

A Guide to Manuscripts and Archives in the Whitney Library of the New Haven Colony Historical Society. By Ottilia Koel. The Society, 1988.

Directory of Archives and Manuscript Collections in the St. Louis Area. Association of St. Louis Area Archivists/Washington University Libraries, 1985.

For additional archives guides, consult *Guides to Archives and Manuscript Collections in the United States: An Annotated Bibliography.* By Donald L. DeWitt. Greenwood, 1994.

Also, look in your library's catalog under the subject, person, or place you are researching and the subheading Archives or Manuscripts. For example:

Harvard University—Archives—Catalogs
Jefferson, Thomas 1743–1826—Archives
Douglass, Frederick, 1817–1895—Manuscripts—Catalogs

Notes on collections appear in the journals published by professional archival associations. For example:

The American Archivist. Published by the Society of American Archivists.

Provenance. From the Society of Georgia Archivists.

Archival Issues. From the Midwest Archives Conference.

Historical journals also publish descriptions of archival collections (see Chapter 29).

15

NEWSPAPERS

Most people perceive newspapers as ephemeral, to be read for the day's news and then discarded. For the researcher, however, the news and the way it is reported may be a major source for facts, trends, attitudes, and much more.

Long aware of the research value of newspapers, the library community has helped promote both the preservation and the indexing of this resource. The acid content of newsprint means that in a short time the pages will yellow and often crumble when handled. Newspapers have been stored in every conceivable condition, torn, mildewed, yellowed, and disintegrating. Microfilm thus became the standard medium for preserving newspapers. More and more newspaper files are now available electronically as well. Electronic searching makes it possible for the researcher to extract specific information from the millions of words generated every day in newspapers. A national project (see Historical Newspapers, below) is making available to researchers the records and texts of some quarter of a million local and regional newspapers published throughout the nation's history.

All the editorial matter in more than 100 major American newspapers can be searched online, and about thirty newspapers are available in full text on CD-ROM. Many foreign newspapers also are available electronically. Coverage usually extends back only a decade or so.

CURRENT NEWSPAPERS

Full Text

Online: Most online services update files daily, though often there is a twenty-four time lag.

- NEXIS. Covering more than fifty general U.S. newspapers, NEXIS is the only online service that carries *The New York Times* in full text. It also covers foreign newspapers and news services such as AP and UPI. Coverage of the *Washington Post* begins in 1977, the *Times* in 1980; other newspapers are covered from the mid-to-late 1980s.

- Dialog. With a service formerly called VU/TEXT, Dialog offers the full text of more than forty general newspapers. Coverage varies, from early to late 1980s. Dialog also has wire services, both domestic and foreign.
- DataTimes. Contains more than fifty U.S. newspapers online as well as some foreign newspapers, such as the *Jerusalem Post.*
- CompuServe. Gives access to various news services and is also a gateway to Dialog's newspaper files. Executive News Service, an extra-fee service, scans the news from five sources daily for stories that match a search profile you have created. Consumer online services such as Prodigy and America Online provide headline news, updated several times a day, but do not maintain back files.

CD-ROM: More than thirty individual newspapers are available full text on CD-ROM from several different companies. Coverage usually starts in the late 1980s and the discs are updated monthly or quarterly, as compared with the daily updating of the online versions. Generally a library will have, at best, the local newspaper and/or a national newspaper such as *The New York Times* or *The Wall Street Journal* in this format.

Indexes

These products, available both in electronic form and in print, enable the user to find the date a subject was discussed in a newspaper. They do not supply the text of the article. Users must go to microfilm to read the actual article.

Electronic Indexes

Newspaper Abstracts OnDisc. (CD-ROM) UMI, 1985–   . Monthly.

Allows free-text searching of abstracts of articles from as many as eight newspapers. All libraries that subscribe get *The New York Times* (1987–   ) and can choose from among the following newspapers: *Atlanta Constitution, Boston Globe, Chicago Tribune, The Christian Science Monitor, Los Angeles Times, Wall Street Journal,* and *Washington Post* (1989–   ). Also available online as *Newspaper and Periodical Abstracts* with Dialog (File 484) and on OCLC FirstSearch and RLIN's CitaDel.

National Newspaper Index. (CD-ROM) Information Access. Updated monthly.

Indexes the last four years of *The New York Times, The Wall Street Journal, The Christian Science Monitor,* the *Los Angeles Times,* and *The Washington Post.* Also available online with Dialog (File 111) and Knowledge Index (NEWS2), updated daily, and on microfilm, updated monthly.

NewsBank. (CD-ROM) NewsBank, 1980–   . Monthly.

Indexes articles from more than 450 U.S. newspapers. This index is also available in print. Either format is accompanied by microfiche copies of all the articles indexed. While generally useful, this product is especially popular in libraries that subscribe to only a few newspapers.

Large electronic periodical indexes such as *Magazine Index Plus* or *Resource/One Ondisc,* described in Chapter 18, General Reference Sources, also index some newspapers, most often *The New York Times, The Wall Street Journal,* and *The Christian Science Monitor.*

New York Times Index. The Times, 1851–   . Semimonthly.
   Oldest continuously indexed U.S. newspaper.

UMI (University Microfilms International) publishes most of the other printed indexes to U.S. newspapers. The following indexes are updated quarterly: *Wall Street Journal* (1958–   ), *Washington Post* (1971–   ), *Atlanta Journal* and *Atlanta Constitution* (1989–   ), *Chicago Tribune* (1988–   ), *Boston Globe* (1980–   ), *Denver Post* (1976–   ), *Detroit Free Press* (1988–   ), *Houston Post* 1988–   ), *St. Louis Post-Dispatch* (1988–   ), *San Francisco Chronicle* (1988–   ), *Los Angeles Times* (1985–   ), New Orleans *Times-Picayune* (1989–   ), and the *Christian Science Monitor* (1989–   ). Also publishes *The Index to Black Newspapers* (1977–   ).

The Times (London) *Index.* Research Publications, 1785–   . Monthly.
   This is the oldest continuously published newspaper index.

Canadian News Index. Micromedia, 1977–   . Monthly.

Among research resources, no publication captures the day-to-day life of a community and its citizens better than the local newspaper. Even when the editorial content of a paper represents journalism at its worst, the ordinary details of daily life can still be found in the advertisements, legal notices, obituaries, and illustrations. For those searching beyond mere events to discover a sense of time and place, newspapers are often the only source available. Academic and large public libraries usually own historical files of important papers such as *The New York Times* on microfilm. Until recently, however, finding back files of smaller newspapers was a hit-or-miss affair.

The Library of Congress and the National Endowment for the Humanities have been directing a massive effort to preserve the rich mix of detail, opinion, fact, and folly that survives in the pages of newspapers throughout the country. The United States Newspaper Program (USNP) is a cooperative national effort to locate, catalog, preserve on microfilm, and make available to researchers newspapers published in the United States from the eighteenth century to the present. Projects in the states and the U.S. Trust

Territories are seeking out and surveying newspaper collections, cataloging the newspapers, and organizing and selecting appropriate files for microfilming.

USNP projects are organized as cooperative efforts within each state. Project staff members survey libraries, courthouses, newspaper offices, historical agencies, archives, and private collections to locate and inventory the newspapers they find. The survey data help to bring scattered files together and to fill gaps in the collections assembled prior to microfilming. Library of Congress personnel train and assist state project staffs in their work to ensure that all cataloging and preservation work meets national standards.

As of this writing, participants include forty-three states and two territories plus eight institutions with large national newspaper collections. NEH expects to continue funding the projects through this decade, at the end of which time an estimated 250,000 newspapers will have been cataloged. Each state will continue preserving and providing access to the newspaper files.

The cataloging records for newspapers compiled by the project are accessible through two online catalogs, OCLC and WLN (the Western Library Network).

For information about the USNP and how to use the records and microfilmed newspapers, contact:

Program Coordinator
Serial Record Division—LM 5151
Library of Congress
Washington, DC 20540
(202) 707-5946

16

GOVERNMENT
PUBLICATIONS

In the course of their work, government agencies compile and disseminate mountains of information in various formats that cover a range as broad as human activity. Although researchers generally think of government publications for such items as census data and legislative records, they are also a source of unique, "official," or current information. Most large libraries have a government documents specialist or documents librarian.

Government publications are issued by local, regional, state, national, and international agencies. Searching aids exist for each type, though their quality varies. This chapter concentrates on U.S. or federal government publications.

DEPOSITORY LIBRARY PROGRAM

The government distributes a great deal of information to libraries around the country on the premise that the public has a right to be informed. A system of U.S. government documents depository libraries has been in existence for more than 100 years. Depositories are libraries that, in return for housing, organizing, and providing reference services, receive copies of government publications at no cost. The 1,400 U.S. depository libraries are in a variety of institutions, including public libraries, large university libraries, law schools, and college libraries. A list is available from the Superintendent of Documents, Government Printing Office, North Capitol and H Sts. NW, Washington, DC 20401; (202) 783-3238. Your congressional office also can direct you to local depositories.

Not every depository library receives everything published by the U.S. government. Regional libraries receive all publications distributed by the U.S. Government Printing Office (GPO) in all formats. Selective depositories can request only the material that is of interest to their clientele. Some selective depositories request very few publications, while others receive

almost all available publications. Researchers must locate the best depository for their research needs and, if necessary, ask the depository to request
publications via interlibrary loan.

Just as collection content and size vary from depository to depository, the
organization and arrangement of government publications may vary too.
Some libraries integrate government publications into their main collection and include them in the library catalog. Many, however, maintain
separate government publications collections and catalog them using the
Superintendent of Documents (SuDoc) classification scheme designed specifically to arrange government publications.

Researchers will need to learn the arrangement of the depository they
choose to use and whether government publications are represented in the
library catalog or if they must consult special catalogs. The standard and
most comprehensive finding aid for current government publications is:

Monthly Catalog of United States Government Publications. Government Printing Office. 1885–   .

The cumulative subject index is most helpful. Coverage of publications
issued since 1976 is available on CD-ROM from several publishers:

> *Government Documents Catalog Service.* AutoGraphics, 1976–   .
> *Government Publications Index.* Information Access, 1976–   .
> *GPO CAT/PAC.* MARCIVE, 1976–   .
> *GPO Monthly Catalog.* OCLC, 1976–   .
> *GPO on SilverPlatter.* 1976–   .

Online access to the *Monthly Catalog* from 1976 is available through
DIALOG (File 66), BRS and BRS/AfterDark (GPOM), and OCLC's First-
Search service.

Another finding aid for government documents is:

GPO Sales Publications Reference File. Microfiche. Updated monthly.

While the *Monthly Catalog* lists new documents as they are published, the
Publications Reference File lists documents that are currently available from
the Government Printing Office, regardless of when they were published.
Also available online as *GPO Publications Reference File,* 1971–   , updated
every two weeks from Dialog (File 166) and Knowledge Index (GOVE1).

The government issues several free lists of new publications that are of
interest to the general public:

Consumer Information Catalog. Quarterly. Order from: Consumer Information Center, Pueblo, CO 81009.

A pamphlet listing free and inexpensive publications on consumer topics.

Index to the Subject Bibliographies. Irregular series. Order from: U.S. Government Printing Office, Superintendent of Documents, Stop: SSOP, Washington, DC 20013.

Indexes more than 230 *Subject Bibliographies* that list government publications on diverse topics.

New Books. Bimonthly. Order from: New Books, U.S. Government Printing Office, Superintendent of Documents, Washington, DC 20402-9325.

Listing of new government publications for sale.

U.S. Government Books. Quarterly. Order from: FREE CATALOG, Box 37000, Washington, DC 20013.

Highlights the most popular items for sale by the Government Printing Office, most of which will also be available in depository libraries.

Prior to 1978, most government publications were in paper format. Later, microfiche was common. Today, electronic diskettes, CD-ROM, and online databases are also used for depository distribution.

By law, government agencies must distribute most of their publications to depository libraries. The Government Printing Office handles the physical distribution. However, since individual agencies decide what to issue to the GPO, libraries may not have as complete a collection as researchers need.

Try to develop a relationship with a government publications/information librarian who can help you plan your research strategy. The government information librarian may have to work with several agencies and individuals in order to locate the information you need. Here are five questions to help researchers frame their strategies:

1. Specifically, what do you need (e.g., monthly statistics; national-level or local MSA data; ten years of data or latest year only; data by age, race, or sex)?
2. What will you settle for (for instance, if statistics are not available by MSA, then by county or state)?
3. What formats can you use (print, computer printout, raw data on floppy disk, magnetic tape)?
4. When do you need it (is your research timetable short-term or long-term)?
5. What costs are you willing to assume? (Government information is not necessarily free. Agencies may charge "appropriate fees" to cover such costs of information transfer as photoreproduction and staff processing.)

Depository libraries are only one key to government information. There are several other distribution channels, including the National Technical Information Service (NTIS); the Educational Resources Information Center (ERIC); the Defense Technical Information Center (DTIC); and the Department of Energy's Technical Information Center.

NTIS (main telephone: (301) 975-3058) was developed to collect and house technical information produced within the United States. It also establishes cooperative exchange programs with foreign countries to acquire their technical information. In reality, NTIS has become a repository for a wide range of government information *not* technical in nature. For example, the Federal Election Commission reports are housed at NTIS. Perhaps most significant for the researcher is that NTIS is *the* source for electronic data files and software produced for and by the government. They can be found in the following indexes to NTIS publications:

Government Reports Announcements & Index. NTIS, 1946–   . Biweekly. Available on CD-ROM and online with Dialog (File 6) and Knowledge Index (GOVE2), 1964–

Directory of Computer Data Files. NTIS

Directory of Computer Software. NTIS

The Defense Technical Information Center (DTIC) contains reports from the defense agencies and their contractors. Documents are grouped as either classified or nonclassified, and use of classified reports will require clearance. There is some cooperation between NTIS and DTIC, and a portion of DTIC's reports are represented in *Government Reports Announcements & Index.* A university or other institution that is a "contractor" with a defense agency may register with DTIC and gain access to DTIC material. Check with the librarian.

ERIC is the Education Department's comprehensive collection of reports and information; *Resources in Education* indexes this resource. (See Chapter 23, Education, for further information about this agency.)

The Department of Energy's National Energy Information Center and the National Aeronautics and Space Administration Information Center both cooperate with NTIS, but not all their publications are listed in *Government Reports Announcements & Index.* The index to Department of Energy publications is *Energy Research Abstracts. Scientific, Technical & Aerospace Reports* indexes the NASA materials.

Do not overlook the National Archives and Records Administration for electronic information transferred from government agencies (e.g., the Nixon tapes). The Archives also has census records, war records, historic letters, files, and other unpublished materials. A preliminary telephone call can give you a staff contact and save time and effort. *Information about the National Archives for Prospective Researchers* (General Information Leaflet No. 30, GPO, 1990) and NARA's quarterly magazine *Prologue* are useful in explaining the resources and programs of the National Archives, the regional archives, and the twelve presidential libraries.

It can be helpful to develop a working relationship with the government information librarian in local and regional government agencies. The librarian knows the sources of government information that may facilitate research.

One splendid local resource in major metropolitan areas is the system of bookstores operated by the Government Printing Office to sell popular GPO publications. The stores, located in the cities listed below, will also help customers order items from the GPO catalogs.

Government publications can also be ordered from the Government Printing Office by mail (Superintendent of Documents, Government Printing Office, Washington, DC 20402) or by phone ((202)783-3238) or fax ((202)512-2250) using a MasterCard or Visa.

Atlanta, GA: Rm. 100, 275 Peachtree St. NE	(404)331-6947
Birmingham, AL: 2021 3rd Ave. N	(205)731-1056
Boston, MA: Rm. 179, 10 Causeway St.	(617)720-4180
Chicago, IL: Rm. 1365, 219 S. Dearborn St.	(312)353-5133
Cleveland, OH: Rm. 1653, 1240 E. 9th St.	(216)522-4922
Columbus, OH: Rm 207, 200 N. High St.	(614)469-6956
Dallas, TX: Rm. 1C50, 1100 Commerce St.	(214)767-0076
Denver, CO: Rm. 117, 1961 Stout St.	(303)844-3964
Detroit, MI: Ste. 160, 477 Michigan Ave.	(313)226-7816
Houston, TX: 801 Travis St.	(713)228-1187
Jacksonville, FL: Rm. 158, 400 W. Bay St.	(904)353-0472
Kansas City, MO: 120 Bannister Mall	(816)767-8225
Los Angeles, CA: C-Level, ARCO Plaza	(213)239-9844
Milwaukee, WI: Rm. 190, 517 E. Wisconsin Ave.	(414)297-1304
New York, NY: Rm. 110, 26 Federal Plaza	(212)264-3825
Philadelphia, PA: 100 N. 17th St.	(215)597-0677
Pittsburgh, PA: Rm. 118, 1000 Liberty Ave.	(412)644-2721
Portland, OR: 1305 SW 1st Ave.	(503)221-6217
Pueblo, CO: 720 N. Main St.	(719)544-3142
San Francisco, CA: Rm. 1023, 450 Golden Gate Ave.	(415)252-5334
Seattle, WA: Rm. 194, 915 2nd Ave.	(206)553-4271
Washington, DC: 710 N. Capitol St. NW	(202)275-2091
1510 H. St. NW	(202)653-5075

FREEDOM OF
INFORMATION ACT

Intended to allow the general public to gain access to government records while at the same time protecting the privacy of the individual, the Freedom of Information Act (FOIA) has proved useful to many researchers.

Each government agency must establish a FOIA office or officer to handle its FOIA requests. *A Citizen's Guide on Using the Freedom of Information Act and the Privacy Act of 1974 to Request Government Records* (H. Rpt 101–193 or H. Rpt 100–199) is published during the first session of each congress. One free copy may be requested from the House Document Room, Washington DC 20515, or from your local legislator.

A researcher may simply send an FOIA request addressed to the attention of the appropriate FOIA office; however, this blind method is not recommended. It is better to call the agency's FOIA office and discuss what you need with the FOIA officer. Two useful sources of phone numbers for FOIA offices are the *Federal Yellowbook* (Washington Monitor) and the *United States Government Manual* (Government Printing Office).

The FOIA process can be frustrating. In answer to one query you may get what you want. At other times you may be required to initiate a FOIA request. Very often there will be some editing or censorship of documents before they are released to a researcher. In some cases, very little may be expunged; in another, almost all the text may be deleted. There also may be significant costs involved, but when you talk to the FOIA officer, ask how to apply for a fee waiver and what criteria are used in granting the waiver. Many times the fee will be waived for nonprofit research institutions, scholarly journals, or members of the press. There is an appeal procedure should the waiver be declined.

Finally, be prepared to wait a significant period of time. Here is a typical scenario: In May 1990, a letter requesting FBI files on Mr. John Q. Public is mailed. In June a letter from the FBI FOIA office is received asking for further information (i.e., if Mr. Public is alive, his written permission is needed for the researcher to receive the files; if deceased, a copy of the obituary is required). In December, an acknowledgment of the receipt of the obituary is received with notification that the request has been approved. In January, a report is received indicating that 600 pages of information have been found and that charges will be greater than $25. Therefore permission and approval to proceed must be received before processing. In February, receipt of permission is acknowledged. In May a letter states that the FBI FOIA office presently has 8,200 requests and it is estimated that it will take several months to process materials. This processing will include reviewing, declassifying, editing, and photocopying the information. This request, initiated in May 1990, is completed in July 1991.

The following sample FOIA request letter may help expedite the procedure:

Name of Government Agency
Address

To the FOIA officer:

This request is made under the Federal Freedom of Information Act, 5 U.S.C. 552.

Please send me copies of *(Describe documents, photos, etc. Include identifying material, such as names, places, and dates)*.

As you know, the FOIA provides that if portions of a document are exempt from release, the remainder must be disclosed. Therefore, I will expect you to send me all nonexempt portions of the records I have requested and ask that you justify any deletions by reference to specific exemptions of the FOI Act. I reserve the right to appeal your decision to withhold any materials.

I promise to pay reasonable search and duplication fees in connection with this request. However, if you estimate that the total fees will exceed $———, please notify me so that I may authorize expenditure of a greater amount.

Thank you for your assistance. I look forward to receiving your reply within ten business days, as required by law.

Sincerely,

Information is available at all levels of government, and building a relationship with librarians familiar with this material may be helpful.

RECORDS FROM OTHER LEVELS OF GOVERNMENT

A system of depository libraries disseminates United Nations documents. Consult the catalog:

UNDOC: Current Index; United Nations Documents Index. United Nations, 1979–   . 10 times/year.

Earlier indexes to UN documents were issued under the series name *UNDEX.* Also available as *Index to United Nations Documents & Publications on CD-ROM.* NewsBank, 1946–

PAIS International. (CD-ROM) SilverPlatter, 1972–   . Quarterly. Also available as *PAIS on CD-ROM.* Public Affairs Information Service, 1972–   . Quarterly.

Subject index to selected U.S. government publications and UN documents and to more than 1,200 periodicals. Also available online on BRS (PAIS), BRS/AfterDark, Dialog (File 49), Knowledge Index (SOCS2), FirstSearch (PAIS Decade), 1976–   , and from 1980–   , on RLIN's CitaDel. Contains records from the print source *PAIS International in Print,* 1991–   (formerly called *PAIS Bulletin,* 1976–90, *Public Affairs Information Service Bulletin,* 1915–76, and *PAIS Foreign Language Index,* 1972–90).

Most university and public libraries collect state documents for their state. Consult:

Monthly Checklist of State Publications. Library of Congress, 1910–   .
Monthly.

A catalog of documents sent to the Library of Congress. Arranged by state and issuing agency with an index by subject.

ACCESS TO GOVERNMENT INFORMATION

Perhaps the most significant change in the ability of researchers to do their work is the introduction of electronic data processing into federal agencies.

The Paperwork Reduction Act of 1980 encouraged the use of technology to collect, store, organize, and analyze information—but not to disseminate it. Agencies have been modernizing and automating their information functions. This has an enormous potential for increasing the usefulness of data. Yet, because the law calls for the distribution of "publications," some agencies feel that electronic data need not necessarily be distributed to depository libraries. Some information producers, such as the Census Bureau, are voluntarily including their electronic products in the Depository Library Program. Other agencies, assuming a more restrictive definition of the word *publication*, are not. Thus, many paper-based publications, converted to the more economical and efficient electronic format, may disappear from the depository library.

A parallel trend has been the privatization of some government information functions. This means that information that was formerly distributed free of charge may now be available only if the library is able to pay for it.

Must an agency disseminate its information or merely provide access to it? The issue is now under debate, and its resolution will have an impact on researchers. The near future may bring an interesting trade-off: an ever-increasing menu of fee-based information products, but diminishing access to nonprofitable areas of the public record.

17

GOVERNMENT AGENCIES

See also: Government Publications, Politics and Government

According to information expert Matthew Lesko, some 700,000 government employees are information experts. Within the federal bureaucracy there are people with extremely specialized jobs. For example, the Bureau of Industrial Economics of the Commerce Department has experts who monitor the ball and roller bearing industry. Taxpayers pay the salaries of these people and fund their research. Some of this research finds its way into government publications. Your local library can help to determine which government agency might have the information you need and can sometimes provide the publications of that agency. But what if you need more customized or more up-to-date information than can be found in a printed source?

The telephone is one of the most productive ways to track down information from a government agency, but you must be persistent. Armed with some of the resources described in this chapter, telephone the government official who is most knowledgeable about the topic. If the first person with whom you speak doesn't have the information you need, ask to be transferred to someone else who might be able to help. Expect at least six transfers before you reach the right person. *Someone* in the government is an expert in the area you are researching or has the information you need and that person, once located, is probably more than willing to share the information.

Sometimes the expert you locate will explain that the information you want is not collected by any public or private agency. While this will be disappointing, it is useful to know and will spare you additional fruitless searching.

Use your legislators' staff members as a resource. In both federal and state government, representatives' staff may be quite helpful in negotiating with an agency office, researching a particular piece of information, or obtaining copies of government publications. Serving constituents is a priority for many of these staffers.

The guides to federal and state government agencies listed below should provide the names and telephone numbers you need. Some of them are available from the Government Printing Office; others are issued by commercial publishers. If you have trouble locating the appropriate government agency, contact the closest Federal Information Center. These centers serve as clearinghouses for information about the federal government and can eliminate the necessity of having to make your way through a maze of referrals. If your state or metropolitan area is not listed below, call (301) 722-9098 for assistance.

A useful guide to agencies and experts at both the federal and state level is:

Lesko's Info-Power II. By Matthew Lesko. Visible Ink Press, 1994.
Lists 8,000 government specialists, plus hotlines, electronic bulletin boards, recorded messages, and publications. This paperback is an excellent source for home or office use. Also available on diskette. Updated quarterly on CompuServe.

Information USA. (CD-ROM) Compton's NewMedia.
Type in a keyword and gain access to government resources for giveaways, databases, and more. Based on Matthew Lesko's *Information USA* (Viking, 1986).

FEDERAL GOVERNMENT DIRECTORIES

The United States Government Manual. U.S. National Archives and Records Administration. Annual.
Most libraries own this basic reference tool, which gives addresses, telephone numbers, and general information about government agencies. It does not always go into enough detail for the researcher, however, in that it lists only about a dozen or two top officials for each agency and is updated only once a year. See agency telephone directories or other sources below for fuller, and often more up-to-date, listings of staff.

Federal Executive Directory. Carroll, 1980–   . Bimonthly.
Lists names, addresses, and telephone numbers for staff working in federal agencies.

Federal Regional Executive Directory. Carroll, 1984–   . Bimonthly.
Provides names, addresses, and telephone numbers for staff in the regional offices of federal agencies.

Alabama		**Missouri**	
Birmingham, Mobile	(800)366-2998	St. Louis	(800)366-2998
Alaska		Elsewhere	(800)735-8004
Anchorage	(800)729-8003	**Nebraska**	
Arizona		Omaha	(800)366-2998
Phoenix	(800)359-3997	Elsewhere	(800)735-8004
Arkansas		**New Jersey**	
Little Rock	(800)366-2998	Newark, Trenton	(800)347-1997
California		**New Mexico**	
Los Angeles, San Diego	(800)726-4995	Albuquerque	(800)359-3997
San Francisco, Santa Ana,		**New York**	
Sacramento	(916)973-1695	Albany, Buffalo,	
Colorado		New York City,	
Colorado Springs, Denver,		Rochester, Syracuse	(800)347-1997
Pueblo	(800)359-3997	**North Carolina**	
Connecticut		Charlotte	(800)347-1997
Hartford, New Haven	(800)347-1997	**Ohio**	
Florida		Akron, Cincinnati,	
Ft. Lauderdale, Miami,		Cleveland, Columbus,	
Jacksonville, Orlando,		Dayton, Toledo	(800)347-1997
St. Petersburg, Tampa,		**Oklahoma**	
West Palm Beach	(800)347-1997	Oklahoma City, Tulsa	(800)366-2998
Georgia		**Oregon**	
Atlanta	(800)347-1997	Portland	(800)726-4995
Hawaii		**Pennsylvania**	
Honolulu	(800)733-5996	Philadelphia, Pittsburgh	(800)347-1997
Illinois		**Rhode Island**	
Chicago	(800)366-2998	Providence	(800)347-1997
Indiana		**Tennessee**	
Gary	(800)366-2998	Chattanooga	(800)347-1997
Indianapolis	(800)347-1997	Memphis, Nashville	(800)366-2998
Iowa	(800)735-8004	**Texas**	
Kansas	(800)735-8004	Austin, Dallas, Ft. Worth,	
Kentucky		Houston, San Antonio	(800)366-2998
Louisville	(800)347-1997	**Utah**	
Louisiana		Salt Lake City	(800)359-3997
New Orleans	(800)366-2998	**Virginia**	
Maryland		Norfolk, Richmond,	
Baltimore	(800)347-1997	Roanoke	(800)347-1997
Massachusetts		**Washington**	
Boston	(800)347-1997	Seattle, Tacoma	(800)726-4995
Michigan		**Wisconsin**	
Detroit, Grand Rapids	(800)347-1997	Milwaukee	(800)366-2998
Minnesota			
Minneapolis	(800)366-2998		

Federal   Regulatory   Directory. Congressional   Information   Service.
1979–   . Annual.

Gives a comprehensive look at the responsibilities and powers of fifteen
agencies with regulatory functions as well as more abbreviated information
on an additional sixty-three agencies. Also lists ample telephone contacts.

Official Congressional Directory. U.S. Congress Joint Committee on Printing.
Annual.

The basic source for locating information about members of Congress,
including how to contact them. While it emphasizes the legislative branch,
it also has considerable coverage of the executive and judicial branches.

The following three print titles are also available in electronic form as
Staff Directories on CD-ROM. Staff Directories. Semiannual.

Federal Staff Directory. Staff Directories. Semiannual.

Provides addresses and phone numbers for more than 20,000 employees
of the executive branch of government.

Congressional Staff Directory. Staff Directories. Semiannual.

Provides a detailed list of the staff who work for each member of Congress along with their telephone numbers. Useful for pinpointing the most
appropriate staffer to contact.

Judicial Staff Directory. Staff Directories. Annual.

Lists more than 1,300 federal judges and their staffs.

Federal Yellow Book: A Directory of Federal Departments and Agencies. Washington Monitor, 1976–   . Quarterly.

*Congressional Yellow Book: A Directory of Members of Congress, Including their
Committees and Key Staff Aides.* Washington Monitor, 1976–   . Quarterly.

These two Yellow Books are similar to the directories listed above, but are
updated more frequently.

Washington Information Directory. Congressional Quarterly. Annual.

Describes both governmental and nongovernmental organizations, with
addresses and phone numbers. It is especially useful for locating lobbying
groups and special-interest organizations.

Who Knows: A Guide to Washington Experts. Washington Researchers,
1977–   . Irregular.

Lists more than 11,000 experts in the federal government along with
their addresses and telephone numbers. Arranged by agency with a subject
index.

At least a dozen departments, including the Departments of State, Transportation, Labor, and Commerce, distribute their staff telephone directories through the Government Printing Office. Check with your local depository library (see Chapter 16, Government Publications) for copies.

Book of the States. Council of State Governments. Biennial.

Provides information on the agencies and functioning of individual state governments. Heavy on facts and figures, including lists of state officials, it also provides an overview and analysis of current issues and trends in state government. The compiler, the Council of State Governments, is an organization with representation from all fifty state governments. It issues three supplements in odd-numbered years: *State Elective Officials and Legislators, Administrative Officials Classified by Function,* and *State Legislative Leadership, Committees, and Staff.*

National Directory of State Agencies. Cambridge Information Group. Annual.

Provides a state-by-state listing of state agencies, classified by their function, such as "motor vehicles" or "natural resources," with their administrators, addresses, and telephone numbers.

State Executive Directory. Carroll, 1980–   . Bimonthly.
County Executive Directory. Carroll, 1984–   . Bimonthly.
Municipal Executive Directory. Carroll, 1984–   . Bimonthly.

These directories list names, addresses, and telephone numbers of officials in all state agencies, all counties, and towns with populations larger than 15,000.

Municipal Yearbook. International City Management Association, 1934–   . Annual

Most useful for its comparative statistical data on city government, it also includes a directory of officials.

Every state publishes a "blue book," a reference guide to state government that lists major officials. The titles vary from state to state. In order to find them in a library catalog, try these subject headings:

[state name]—Politics and government—Handbooks and manuals
[state name]—Registers
[state name]—Officials and employees

Or, for a comprehensive list of "blue books," see *State Legislative Sourcebook: A Resource Guide to Legislative Information in the 50 States.* By Lynn Hellebust. Government Research Service. Annual.

Describes each state legislature and its publications.

PART IV

Research Sources
by Topic

18

GENERAL
REFERENCE
SOURCES

General reference works are wide-ranging information sources; the great ones may also be sources of delight. Even the more mundane general sources, statistical abstracts or periodical indexes, for example, can be stunning in their organization of data and in the information they reveal.

This chapter highlights library resources—print and electronic—that are used across all areas of research, in the humanities, social sciences, and natural sciences. They may be first-stop sources for one's research or provide specific answers.

Usually, researchers will do best to plunge directly into the sources designed for their specialty. An index to film reviews will provide more depth, certainly, than a general periodicals index would. A women's studies encyclopedia will explore more specific areas, offer more extensive bibliographies, and bring sharper focus to general topics concerning women than would a general encyclopedia. However, because not every library will hold or even have access to the ideal specialized reference sources, the more general sources will often be your starting point.

Books in Print. 10 vols. Bowker, 1948–   . Annual with midyear supplement. **GUIDES**

Lists by author and title more than one million books currently available from U.S. publishers with their prices. Also available on microfiche, online, and CD-ROM.

Subject Guide to Books in Print. 5 vols. Bowker, 1957–   . Annual.

Lists the 750,000 nonfiction titles from *Books in Print* by subject.

Books in Print (BIP) and *Subject Guide to Books in Print* are updated by *Forthcoming Books.* 1966–   . Bimonthly.

Books in Print Plus. (CD-ROM) Bowker, 1990–   . Monthly.

   Accesses the *BIP* database by author, title, subject, keyword, publisher, ISBN, price, publication date, or grade level (for children's books). Also available online with Dialog (File 470) and BRS (BBIP). *Books in Print with Book Reviews Plus* is a version enhanced with book reviews from ten journals.

Guide to Reference Books. Compiled by Eugene P. Sheehy. 10th ed. American Library Association, 1986.

Guide to Reference Books: Covering Materials from 1985-1990. Edited by Robert Balay. American Library Association, 1992.

   This standard guide, the "librarian's bible," lists some 10,000 reference works, including foreign-language publications, with descriptions of each source. The emphasis is on reference materials for scholarly research, but works for general readers are also included. The supplement lists more than 4,500 reference works published in the six years since the 10th edition was prepared. Electronic sources are listed by subject along with printed works. A valuable resource when specialized reference tools are needed.

COLLECTED REFERENCE BOOKS ON DISC

The following CD-ROMs contain a collection of reference books on a disc. For the researcher, this is the equivalent of having a whole shelf of reference books on your computer.

Microsoft Bookshelf. (CD-ROM) Microsoft.

   This compact disc contains the full text of seven standard reference books: *The Concise Columbia Encyclopedia, American Heritage Dictionary, Roget's II Thesaurus, Bartlett's Familiar Quotations, Concise Columbia Dictionary of Quotations, Hammond Atlas of the World,* and the *World Almanac.*

The Toolworks Reference Library. (CD-ROM) Software Toolworks.

   Contains the text of *The New York Public Library Desk Reference, The Dictionary of 20th Century History, Webster's New World Dictionary, Webster's New World Thesaurus, The Guide to Concise Writing, Webster's New World Dictionary of Quotable Definitions,* and *The National Directory of Telephone Numbers.*

ENCYCLOPEDIAS

General encyclopedias attempt to cover systematically all of human knowledge. They provide an overview of many topics and are also useful for locating facts. Much of the information in encyclopedias does not change dramatically over time, but population and socioeconomic statistics, scientific information, sports records, and other data are constantly changing. Several American encyclopedias are revised every year, but this does not mean that all articles are rewritten or that all facts are updated. To check on the currency of the set being used, look at the copyright date of the encyclopedia as a whole and the most recent publication dates in the bibliography for the article you are reading. Examining an article on a topic about which you are well informed will also help you judge the currency of the encyclopedia. Electronic encyclopedias on CD-ROM offer access to the text and may incorporate sound and video. CD-ROM encyclopedias as well as the print versions are listed below.

Academic American Encyclopedia. 21 vols. Grolier. Annual.

Emphasizes information useful for middle school, high school, and college students. Subject strengths include pop culture, international affairs, and current technology. The concise, factual entries, many less than 500 words, provide a good starting point for further research. At least half of the articles end with a short, up-to-date bibliography. Illustrations, graphics, and maps are exceptionally well done. A substantial proportion of the articles are revised each year. Also available online on BRS, CompuServe, Dialog, Prodigy, and other services, revised four times a year. Also see *The Grolier Master Encyclopedia Index on CD-ROM* below.

The New Grolier Multimedia Encyclopedia. (CD-ROM) Grolier. Along with the text of the *Academic American Encyclopedia,* this easy-to-use CD-ROM encyclopedia provides pictures, color maps, sound, and animated sequences. The software encourages exploration of additional topics by links between a timeline or the "knowledge tree" and related articles. *Knowledge Disc,* a 12-inch videodisc version to be used with a laser videodisc player, is also available.

Collier's Encyclopedia. 24 vols. P. F. Collier. Annual.

Designed for the adult reader as well as junior and senior high school students. Authoritative articles are by scholars in the field, and coverage of biography, the arts, humanities, and social sciences is particularly good. Graphics, diagrams, and drawings are included, and the use of color photographs has been expanded in the latest revisions. Rather than appending bibliographies to each article, *Collier's* places most reading lists in Volume 24. Although *Collier's* has many short entries, it is known for its broad, topical articles. It is essential to use the detailed index in Volume 24 to find specific information.

Compton's Encyclopedia and Fact-Index. 26 vols. Compton's Learning. Annual.

Compton's emphasizes curriculum-related information for students in the upper elementary grades through high school. In 1992, the set was completely redesigned and extensively reillustrated. The fact-index in the final volume of the set includes brief biographical sketches, statistics, and short treatments of topics not covered in the main text. The set is attractively illustrated; two-thirds of its many pictures are in color. Fact-finder boxes refer readers to related topics, and preview boxes serve as a table of contents for longer articles. Many articles provide reading lists appropriate for children and young adults. Also available online with America Online.

Compton's Multimedia Encyclopedia. (CD-ROM) Compton's New Media.

Designed for upper elementary and high school students, this attractive product contains the full text of all the articles in *Compton's Encyclopedia,* as well as *Webster's Intermediate Dictionary.* Audio, visual images, and animation are included. The "idea search" allows users to enter a phrase or question. Search results can then be modified by using menus or icons. Photographs and drawings can also be searched by caption or concept or browsed. Updated annually.

Also available as *Compton's Family Encyclopedia,* with the same text and illustrations but no animation and less sound; and as *Compton's Concise Encyclopedia* for use with Data Discman, Sony's handheld CD player. A CD-I version is being developed.

Encarta Multimedia Encyclopedia. (CD-ROM) Microsoft. Annual.

Microsoft's electronic encyclopedia is based on the twenty-nine-volume *Funk & Wagnalls New Encyclopedia* but has additional articles written just for *Encarta.* It also contains the concise edition of *Webster's Electronic Dictionary* and 40,000 entries from *Webster's College Thesaurus.* The text is supplemented by sound, animation, photographs, and maps. Users can create custom charts and graphs from statistics in *Encarta.*

Encyclopedia Americana. 30 vols. Grolier. Annual.

A readable adult encyclopedia, suitable also for students from junior high through college. Contributors are authorities in their fields. Material on the sciences, mathematics, American history, and the social sciences is particularly good. A traditional strength of *Americana* is the inclusion of a large number of articles on U.S. and Canadian places and persons. Bibliographies at the end of major articles list recent titles, and the final volume contains a detailed index.

The Grolier Master Encyclopedia Index on CD-ROM. Grolier, 1993.

This single CD allows the searching of the indexes to all three of Grolier's encyclopedias at once: *Encyclopedia Americana, Academic American Encyclopedia,* and *The New Book of Knowledge,* a children's set.

The New Encyclopaedia Britannica. 15th ed. 32 vols. Encyclopaedia Britannica. Annual.

First published in Scotland in 1768, the *Britannica* is the most scholarly of the English-language encyclopedias, covering a wide range of topics in more depth than other sets. *Britannica* is intended for adults but is also useful for high school and college students. It consists of three parts: the *Propaedia*, a one-volume outline of knowledge; the *Micropaedia*, a twelve-volume set with more than 60,000 short entries; and the *Macropaedia*, seventeen volumes containing lengthy signed articles with bibliographies. A detailed index provides thorough access to the contents of the entire set. More photographs, drawings, and maps have been added in recent printings, but illustrations are not a strong point. New entries are added to the *Micropaedia* frequently. Revision of the longer articles in the *Macropaedia* is done as needed, but it is often necessary to use the *Britannica's Book of the Year/ Britannica World Data* for up-to-date statistics, recent political developments, and other current material.

Also available is the *Britannica Electronic Index on CD-ROM*, which includes a version of *Webster's Ninth New Collegiate Dictionary*. The CD-ROM must be used in conjunction with the printed encyclopedia, but it provides the ability to do keyword searches of the index and to print out citations. For example, it is possible to print a list of all French artists discussed in the set.

World Book Encyclopedia. 22 vols. World Book. Annual.

World Book gives a broad view of a multitude of topics in an easy-to-read format. It aims to provide information for elementary and secondary school students on world events, natural and physical sciences, the social sciences, and the arts, but it is also useful for adults. The encyclopedia is extensively revised every year, and all statistics are updated on a regular basis. The bibliographies that accompany many articles are arranged by reading level.

The Information Finder. (CD-ROM) World Book.

Provides the full text of *World Book Encyclopedia* and *World Book Dictionary*. Users can search by topic or keyword. Special features include a notepad, "bookmarks" to let users move around in the text and return to the same spot, and quick fact tables. An article's outline is always visible on the screen.

A one-volume encyclopedia may be a useful home or office reference tool.

The Columbia Encyclopedia. 5th ed. Columbia University Press/Houghton Mifflin, 1993.

With 50,000 entries, it is especially strong in place names and biography. Has many maps; other illustrations limited to line drawings.

The Random House Encyclopedia. Rev. ed. Random House, 1990.

In two parts: the *Colorpedia,* which has lengthy articles arranged topically with color illustrations; and the *Alphapedia,* which has concise entries on specific topics, arranged alphabetically. Also available on CD-ROM for the Sony Multimedia CD-ROM player (PIX-100) with *The Random House Webster's Electronic Dictionary* as *The Random House Electronic Desk Reference.*

DICTIONARIES

According to a recent Gallup poll, most American homes own at least one general English-language dictionary. Dictionaries are pressed into use regularly to check spelling, meaning, pronunciation, and syllable division, or to determine a word's history and usage. Not everyone needs a large, unabridged dictionary. A good collegiate or desk dictionary generally costs no more than a hardcover novel and is a worthwhile investment.

With dictionaries in electronic form, users can easily look for words when they are uncertain of the spelling, do not know an appropriate word, or need a rhyming word. Electronic dictionaries often work well in conjunction with a word processing program. Several of the dictionaries listed here are available on floppy disk to be loaded onto the hard drive of a computer or on CD-ROM. These electronic editions are listed immediately following their print editions.

When choosing a dictionary, keep in mind that the word *Webster* is in the public domain and can be used by any publisher. While many good dictionaries carry the name Webster, its presence in a title is not a guarantee of quality.

Unabridged Dictionaries

Random House Unabridged Dictionary. Rev. 2d ed. Random House, 1993.

This recently revised volume is the most up to date of the unabridged dictionaries. It incorporates new terminology—scientific and technical terms, idioms, and slang—and reflects changes in definitions and usage over the past twenty years. For each entry, the most commonly used meaning of a word is given first, and definitions are frequently supplemented by illustrative phrases or sentences. The date of a term's entry into the language is given. Coverage of regional usage is included, and words of American origin are so labeled. Many usage notes as well as restrictive labels ("slang," "informal," etc.) are provided. Names of persons, places, and works of art, music, and literature are included in the main alphabetical listing.

At the end of the volume, the *Random House Unabridged* includes a list of signs and symbols, a directory of colleges and universities in the United States and Canada, and a basic style manual. The appendixes also include concise foreign-language/English, English/foreign-language dictionaries for French, Spanish, Italian, and German.

The *Random House Unabridged Dictionary, CD-ROM Version* is available separately or packaged with the printed dictionary. It includes the complete text of the printed book, plus some material that was cut from that volume to conserve space.

Webster's Third New International Dictionary of the English Language. Merriam-Webster, 1961, 1986.

Webster's Third covers the English language in use since 1755, the date of Dr. Johnson's *Dictionary of the English Language.* In revisions since the original publication of *Webster's Third* in 1961, new words have been included in the main word list or listed in an addendum at the end of the volume. Biographical and geographical names and most foreign words and phrases are not included in the dictionary. Definitions are given in historical order, with the oldest first, and are often illustrated by quotations, many from contemporary sources. The emphasis is on language as it is used; the dictionary assigns few restrictive labels. Word histories are authoritative.

The Oxford English Dictionary. 2d ed. 20 vols. Oxford University Press, 1989.

This monumental work includes definitions of some half a million words in the English vocabulary from Chaucer's time to the present day, with information on their form, pronunciation, etymology, and changes in meaning over time. It emphasizes British usage and spelling. More than 2 million quotations illustrate the definitions. This edition integrates the text of the first edition, published in 1933, with the supplements issued between 1972 and 1986, and includes additional new words and new meanings of existing words.

The Oxford English Dictionary Second Edition on Compact Disc. Oxford University Press, 1992.

A single disc contains the complete text of the new edition of the Oxford dictionary. The software makes it possible to locate any of the 2.4 million illustrative quotations by date, author, or title, or textual content using standard English, the international phonetic alphabet, Old English, or Greek. Searches by word history or definition are also possible; for example, the user can find all words in English that derive from Turkish.

The IBM edition runs under Windows; a Macintosh version is also available. An excellent manual is provided with the compact disc.

Desk Dictionaries

The American Heritage Dictionary of the English Language. 3d ed. Houghton Mifflin, 1992.

The 1992 volume is less conservative than previous editions and includes 11,000 new words and meanings. Abbreviations, acronyms, people, and places are listed alphabetically in the main text and prescriptive usage labels, such as "slang" or "obscene," are provided. Coverage of American regionalisms has been expanded. Definitions are concise and clear. Expanded word histories and usage notes as well as photographs and line drawings appear throughout the text. A somewhat abbreviated desk version is available as *The American Heritage College Dictionary,* 3d ed. Houghton Mifflin, 1993.

American Heritage Dictionary. (Floppy disk) 2d college ed. Writing Tools Group, 1992.

Paired with *Roget's II Electronic Thesaurus,* this software enables users to search for words with common letters (terms ending in *-ist,* for instance) and to search for words in definitions, among other features. The software is available in DOS, Windows, and Mac versions.

Merriam-Webster's Collegiate Dictionary. 10th ed. Merriam-Webster, 1993.

Based on the unabridged *Webster's Third New International Dictionary,* this collegiate edition is limited to English words in current use. It provides up-to-date definitions and etymologies for almost every entry, including the date of the first recorded use of a word. Meanings are arranged historically, and many definitions are illustrated with quotations. Biographical entries, place names, a style guide, and foreign words and phrases are included in the appendix, though many commonly used foreign words and phrases are defined in the main part of the dictionary.

Webster's Ninth New Collegiate Dictionary on CD-ROM. Highlighted Data, 1989.

Provides the complete text, including illustrations, of *Webster's Ninth New Collegiate Dictionary.* The unique feature of this CD-ROM dictionary is that every word is pronounced aloud, a big advantage for those who have trouble deciphering the pronunciation key in the typical dictionary. This product will run on Macintosh or IBM-compatible equipment. It is easy to install and use. A CD-ROM version of *Merriam-Webster's Collegiate Dictionary* (10th ed.) is under development.

Random House Webster's College Dictionary. Rev. ed. Random House, 1992.

This desk dictionary provides usage notes, synonym studies, word histories, and illustrative phrases or sentences to clarify definitions. The most frequently used definition is given first. Commonly used foreign words and phrases, biographical names, and geographic names are incorporated in the main alphabetical list. The volume includes a guide for writers, with rules on punctuation and manuscript preparation, and an essay on avoiding sexist language.

Random House Webster's Electronic Dictionary. (Floppy disk) Reference Software International.

Gives the full definitions contained in *Random House Webster's* and the complete text of the *Random House Thesaurus*. Users can toggle back and forth between the spell checker and thesaurus in their word processors and in this product. The software offers wild card, anagram, and definition searches. DOS, Windows, and Macintosh versions are available.

Webster's New World Dictionary of American English. 3d college ed. Webster's New World, 1988.

New World emphasizes American vocabulary and usage. Words, phrases, and meanings that entered the English language in the United States are marked with a star. Definitions are concise and readable and are given in historical order. Etymologies as well as extensive usage explanations and examples are provided, with restrictive labels for nonstandard vocabulary and usage. Biographical and geographical names, abbreviations, and foreign words and phrases are included in the main alphabetical arrangement of the text. A section on signs and symbols, a style guide, and a family tree of Indo-European languages conclude the volume.

Languages of the World. (CD-ROM) NTC Publishing Group.

This dictionary enables users to find definitions, translations, and synonyms among twelve languages: Chinese, Danish, Dutch, English, Finnish, French, German, Italian, Japanese, Norwegian, Spanish, and Swedish.

Multilingual Dictionaries

Facts On File: A Weekly World News Digest with Cumulative Index. Facts On File, 1940–   . Weekly; cumulated annual volume.

Summarizes news events, national and international, and also covers theater openings, film releases, television ratings, best-selling books and records, and obituaries. The information is gathered from more than seventy-five international newspapers and periodicals. Since many newspapers are not indexed, *Facts On File* is particularly useful for determining the dates during which an event might have broad newspaper coverage. A detailed cumulative index is published twice a month, and there is an annual index.

NEWS
(See also Chapter 15, Newspapers)

Facts On File News Digest CD-ROM. Facts On File, 1980–   .

Contains the complete text of the printed *Facts On File News Digest*, cumulated from 1980 to date. Updated annually. *Facts On File* is also available online from 1980 to date on Dialog (File 264), Knowledge Index (NEWS5), and NEXIS (FACTS).

Current Biography. H. W. Wilson, 1940–   . 11 times/year. Yearbook, 1940–   .

This useful source publishes biographies of newsworthy individuals from around the world. A photograph and bibliography are included with each

BIOGRAPHY

article. The yearbooks cumulate the articles in one volume and incorporate additional information when necessary. A fifty-year index, *Current Biography: Cumulated Index 1940–1990,* makes it possible to locate almost 20,000 biographies with ease.

Biography Index: A Cumulative Index to Biographical Material in Books and Magazines. (CD-ROM) H. W. Wilson, 1984–   . Quarterly.

Indexes biographical articles in nearly 1,700 periodicals, as well as biographical material in books, published letters and diaries, and memoirs. Includes an index by occupation and profession. Available online on Wilsonline and FirstSearch, 1984–   , and in print, 1946–   .

Biography and Genealogy Master Index CD-ROM. Gale, 1993. Updated annually.

Enables the user to search 8.25 million references to biographical information in 700 published sources. Also online with Dialog (File 654), updated annually. Based on the print product *Biography and Genealogy Master Index.* 2d ed. 8 vols. Gale, 1980. *BGMI 1981–85 Cumulation.* Gale, 1986. *BGMI 1985–90 Cumulation.* 3 vols. Gale, 1991. Annual updates, 1991–   . Also available on microfiche as *Bio-Base.*

Dictionary of American Biography. 20 vols. Charles Scribner's and Sons, 1928–37. Supplements 1–8, 1944–88.

This scholarly American biographical dictionary has lengthy signed articles with bibliographies on 18,000 notable people who died before 1971. A separate volume published in 1990 contains indexes by birthplace, schools and colleges attended, occupation, and topics. Small libraries may own the *Concise Dictionary of American Biography* (4th ed., 1990).

Who's Who in America. 2 vols. Marquis, 1889–   . Annual.

This standard biographical work listing living Americans from all walks of life is published annually; it was issued biennially until 1993. A separate volume indexes biographees by place of residence and occupation. Sketches removed from *Who's Who in America* because of death are listed in *Who Was Who in America.*

The following titles are designed to supplement *Who's Who in America.* A few people deemed especially noteworthy are duplicated in *Who's Who in America* and a regional volume.

Who's Who in the East. Marquis, 1943–   .
Who's Who in the Midwest. Marquis, 1949.
Who Who in the South and Southwest. Marquis, 1950–   .
Who's Who in the West. Marquis, 1949–   .

Who's Who in the World. Marquis, 1970–   . Biennial.

Biographical information on more than 30,000 living people worldwide.

Complete Marquis Who's Who Plus. (CD-ROM) Reed Publishing. 1994–   .
Annual.

Biographical profiles on more than 400,000 living people from *Who's Who in America,* the regional *Who's Whos, Who's Who in the World,* and the *Directory of Medical Specialists. Who's Who in America* is also available online through Dialog (File 234), Knowledge Index (REFR2), and CompuServe.

The cartographic publishers represented here produce a wide range of atlases. Only atlases commonly found in libraries are listed. Several of them are appropriate for home use and some are available in smaller versions. (See Chapter 29, History, for historical atlases and Chapter 21, Business and Finance, for a commercial atlas.)

ATLASES

Hammond Atlas of the World. 6th rev. ed. Hammond, 1992.

An unusually attractive atlas, the 1992 *Hammond* reflects recent changes in the former Soviet Union, Czechoslovakia, and Yugoslavia. This atlas was generated completely by computer, using a form of map projection that reduces distortion. The atlas includes thematic maps and graphics on the environment, population, and other topics, as well as two sections of tabular information.

National Geographic Atlas. Rev. 6th ed. National Geographic, 1992.

Maps include major topographical features, but are particularly good for political information. As in all the newer atlases, the reunification of Germany as well as the political changes in the former Soviet Union and Eastern Europe are incorporated in this revision of the sixth edition. Thematic maps include "environmental stress" maps. The index lists cities by country with plate number and coordinates.

The New Cosmopolitan World Atlas. Rand McNally, 1992.

Covers the world in regional maps, though one page is devoted to each state of the United States. Topographical, hydrological, and political information are shown together. Maps have been updated to show reunified Germany and the Baltic states as independent countries. After the index to the maps is a table giving populations for all cities and ZIP codes for U.S. cities.

Times Atlas of the World. 9th comprehensive ed. Random House, 1992.

This very large atlas begins with many pages of geographic information as well as thematic maps. Political information on all maps has been updated to reflect current realities as of the date of publication. The index-gazetteer is extremely detailed. References to latitude and longitude coordinates are given along with plate number and grid.

PC Globe (Floppy disk) and *PC USA* (Floppy disk). Broderbund Software.

The latest version of this electronic atlas software package incorporates current political realities, including the Baltic states, the Commonwealth of Independent States, Croatia, Slovenia, and the Yugoslav Federation. *PC Globe* can display maps of the whole world as well as maps of regions, continents, and 177 individual countries. The software can also compute statistics by predefined or user-defined country groups or in text or graphic format. There is audio for 175 national anthems. A companion product with similar features, *PC USA* covers the United States. In addition to statistical information, *PC USA* includes a screen of historical facts and climate information for major cities. *PC Globe* and *PC USA* are DOS-based.

The Software Toolworks World Atlas (CD-ROM) and *The Software Toolworks U.S. Atlas.* (CD-ROM) Software Toolworks.

In addition to almost 300 color road and relief maps, these discs contain a wealth of statistical data. City data include tourist information, area codes, and weather maps. The program allows users to print reports with maps and text or to export maps to graphics programs. A multimedia version will play state songs. Also available on diskette.

DIRECTORIES   *Directories in Print.* 10th ed. 2 vols. Gale, 1992.

Describes nearly 14,000 directories. A detailed subject index gives access. Also available online with Dialog (File 469).

Encyclopedia of Associations. 3 parts. Gale. Annual.

This directory of national associations and other nonprofit membership groups furnishes address, chief executive officer, size of membership, date of founding, and a description of purposes and publications of each organization. Entries are arranged by subject interest, but the detailed keyword index is even more useful for locating organizations by subject or by name. Not all libraries purchase the second and third parts of the set, which index organizations by location and names of officials, and provide updates on new associations and recent information on the groups listed in Part 1.

Also available online on Dialog (File 114) and on CD-ROM.

Encyclopedia of Associations: International Organizations. Gale.

Describes multinational and binational organizations and national organizations based outside the United States.

Regional, State, and Local Organizations. 5 vols. Gale.

Provides information about organizations that are not national in scope. In regional volumes (Great Lakes States, Northeastern States, etc.); many libraries buy only the volume for their region.

Encyclopedia of Associations CD-ROM. SilverPlatter.

This CD-ROM product provides access to information on all the organizations included in Gale's directories: national; regional, state, and local, and international. The CD-ROM is updated every six months. Also available online with Dialog (File 114).

National Five-Digit ZIP Code and Post Office Directory. Postal Service. Annual.

This handy tool provides detailed listings of every ZIP code in the United States. The first and most extensive section of the publication lists ZIP codes by state and post office (i.e., place name). For places with more than one ZIP code, there is an alphabetical guide to street names and their accompanying ZIP codes. The second section of the *Directory* arranges all ZIP codes in numerical order, together with corresponding post offices.

Official Museum Directory. American Association of Museums, 1961–   . Annual.

Covers all types of museums (art, history, natural history, science) in the United States and Canada. Includes addresses, hours, major collections.

ALMANACS

An almanac is a compendium of miscellaneous facts and statistics, usually published annually and organized for quick reference. Both recent and retrospective information are provided. The titles listed here share many characteristics, but each covers some topics not found in the others. Some libraries will also have almanacs from other countries, such as *Whitaker's Almanack* from Great Britain.

Information Please Almanac. Houghton Mifflin, 1947–   . Annual.

In addition to statistics on numerous topics, the almanac features articles such as "The Year in Religion." Of the almanacs, *Information Please* is the most comprehensive on fine arts and on the labor force.

Statesman's Year-Book. St. Martin's, 1864–   . Annual.

Provides information about government, commerce, agriculture, population, religion, etc., for countries of the world. Compiled in Great Britain, coverage is especially good for Commonwealth nations.

World Almanac and Book of Facts. Funk & Wagnalls, 1989–   . Annual.

Contains statistical data for the current and preceding years, a list of important events of the year, and many other items. *World Almanac* is particularly strong on consumer economics and television. Its long publication history makes it especially useful when comparative statistics are needed.

Universal Almanac. Andrews and McMeel, 1989–   . Annual.
    The design and layout of this almanac are attractive, with effective charts and graphs throughout. *Universal Almanac* excels in coverage of business and the economy, U.S. cities, and information about the media.

STATISTICAL SOURCES

Statistical Abstract of the United States. Government Printing Office, 1879–   . Annual.
    Widely available and indispensable source of statistical information collected by U.S. government agencies and some private organizations. Social, political, and economic data are included. The volume is also useful as a guide to the original, more detailed sources from which the information has been abstracted.

American Statistics Index (ASI). Congressional Information Service, 1973–   . Monthly.
    An index of the statistical publications of more than 500 federal agencies. Data cover economics, international trade, education, and more. Also available online through Dialog (File 102) and on CD-ROM as part of *Statistical Masterfile,* updated quarterly.

Statistical Reference Index. Congressional Information Service, 1980–   . Monthly.
    Indexes statistical reports produced by nongovernmental bodies: research centers, trade and professional associations, and other sources. Also on CD-ROM as part of *Statistical Masterfile.*

Index to International Statistics. Congressional Information Service, 1983–   . Monthly
    Indexes major publications from organizations such as the United Nations. Also on CD-ROM as part of *Statistical Masterfile.*

World Factbook. Central Intelligence Agency, 1982–   . Annual.
    This volume provides statistical information for each country in the world on such topics as land, population, government, economy, communications, and defense. There are many subdivisions under each topic. Also available on CD-ROM from several different publishers.

The Economist Book of Vital World Statistics. By the Editors of the *Economist.* Times Books, 1990.

Provides social and economic statistics for 146 countries with populations greater than 1 million or a gross national product of more than $1 billion. Abundant charts, tables, and graphs.

U.S. Census of Population and Housing on CD-ROM.
The Census Bureau began to issue volumes of the 1990 Census in 1992. For the first time, census data are being provided to the nation's government document depository libraries on CD-ROM as well as in print. (See Chapter 16, Government Publications.) With the electronic version, the user can search by specific area and look at selected characteristics or at a general profile. The data are in dBASE format and can be downloaded into a user's database. *Census Catalog and Guide, 1992,* Bureau of the Census, is a guide to this data. It lists census products in all formats (print, online, computer tapes, floppy disks, CD-ROM). Also lists more than 1,400 State and Business/Industry Data Center Organizations, 200 Census Bureau specialists, National Clearinghouse for Census Data Services, population estimates contacts, and federal statistical reports by agency.

County and City Data Book; Statistical Abstract Supplement 1993. Bureau of the Census, 1993.
A convenient reference source published every five years with recent statistics from the various U.S. government censuses for counties, cities, and towns of 2,500 or more. Also available on CD-ROM.

State and Metropolitan Area Data Book 1991. 4th ed. Bureau of the Census, 1991.
Provides statistics on population, education, employment, income, crime, housing, manufacturing, etc., for states and standard metropolitan statistical areas of the United States. Also available on diskettes.

QUOTATION BOOKS

There are many books to help you locate the source or accurate form of a quotation. A number of these books are also enjoyable for browsing. In addition to the titles listed here, specialized sources cover every type of utterance from quips by boxers to last words. To find a subject-related quotation book in the library catalog, look for QUOTATIONS as a subheading under your subject interest; for example, SPORTS—QUOTATIONS. You can also consult *The Quote Sleuth: A Manual for the Tracer of Lost Quotations* by Anthony W. Shipps (University of Illinois Press, 1990).

Familiar Quotations: A Collection of Passages, Phrases, and Proverbs Traced to Their Sources in Ancient and Modern Literature. Compiled by John Bartlett and edited by Justin Kaplan. 16th ed. Little Brown, 1992.
The famous "Bartlett's," this comprehensive collection of quotations, primarily literary, is arranged chronologically by author. The extensively

revised 1992 edition includes 340 new sources, many corrections of dates, and additions of attribution. Bartlett's provides exact references and many interesting notes. Indexed by author and keyword.

The Home Book of Quotations, Classical and Modern. By Burton Stevenson. 10th ed. Dodd, 1967.

This useful collection of more than 50,000 quotations is organized by subject and indexed by author and key words. Usually provides exact citation for source of quote.

Oxford Dictionary of Quotations. Edited by Angela Partington. 4th ed. Oxford University Press, 1992.

Quotations are arranged alphabetically by author and exhaustively indexed by keyword. Quotations from foreign languages appear in the original language as well as in English. Contributions from contemporary and international authors and from women are more adequately represented than in earlier editions. The third edition of this book is online as *Quotations Database* with Dialog (File 175) and Knowledge Index (REFR1).

PERIODICAL INDEXES

Subject indexes to periodicals are important tools that enable researchers to find magazine and journal articles on particular topics. *The Readers' Guide to Periodical Literature,* for example, has been published since 1900.

In the 1970s, some periodical indexes became available for online searching. In the 1980s, these indexes, along with several new ones, were issued on CD-ROM. The market for general periodical indexes on CD-ROM is very competitive. Some database producers do several general-interest indexes—often expanded or otherwise modified versions of their original electronic product. Coverage, software features, and even titles change frequently. Some of the electronic indexes correspond to paper or microfiche publications; others exist only as electronic databases. All offer more varied means of searching for information than are available in a printed index. They also enable the user to print out a list of citations.

Some publishers also offer the actual periodical articles themselves on CD-ROM. Usually they are "full text," providing the complete article, without illustrations. Some companies are making periodical articles available on CD-ROM in "full image," with the screen exactly reproducing the magazine page, with illustrations intact. The advantage of the full-text format is that you can search on every word in the article; this is not possible with the full-image format.

Most libraries offer only one general periodical index in CD-ROM format, though other comparable databases may be available online. Indexes vary as to the number and type of periodicals covered, quality of the indexing, availability of abstracts or full-text articles, ease of use, and cost.

Most indexes are also available on magnetic tape, and some academic and large public libraries have mounted a periodical index on their computer along with the library's online public access catalog. If your library has an online catalog, be sure to ask if a periodical index is available as an additional file. Periodical indexes, whether online locally or on CD-ROM, may sometimes indicate whether the local library owns a given magazine and may also display the local call number and/or location.

Magazine Article Summaries. (CD-ROM) EBSCO, 1984–   .

Provides indexing with abstracts for more than 340 general-interest periodicals and includes book reviews for current literature and about 500 classic literary works. EBSCO also produces *Academic Abstracts*, which indexes over 500 periodicals. Available online with BRS. No print equivalent.

Magazine Index Plus. (CD-ROM) Information Access, 1980–   .

Information Access (IAC) has several periodical indexes in its popular InfoTrac series. Corresponding in part to *Magazine Index* on microfilm, *Magazine Index Plus* covers 400 magazines plus current issues of *The New York Times* and *The Wall Street Journal.*

- *Magazine Index Select* is a smaller version, indexing 200 periodicals.
- *Magazine ASAP Plus* provides the full text for over 100 of the popular general-interest titles indexed in *Magazine Index Plus.*
- IAC also produces on CD-ROM public library and academic library versions of *General Periodicals Index,* which provides five years' worth of indexing of 1,100 periodicals and three major newspapers, *The New York Times, The Christian Science Monitor,* and *The Wall Street Journal.* Versions include: *Academic Index* (400 journals), *Expanded Academic Index* (1,500 journals), and *Expanded Academic Index ASAP* (full text of 400 of the magazines).
- High school libraries may own *TOM,* which indexes 140 periodicals from 1985 to date. Thirty of the magazines are available in full text on CD-ROM; some high school libraries will have them on microfiche.

IAC databases are available online on Dialog, which offers *Academic Index,* 1976–   (File 88); and *Magazine Index* (File 47), 1959–70, 1973–   . BRS and BRS/AfterDark offer *Magazine Index* (MAGS, 1959–70, 1973–   ) and *Academic Index* (ACAD, 1985–   ).

All of the IAC products are updated monthly. There is no print equivalent of these indexes.

Readers' Guide to Periodical Literature. (CD-ROM) H. W. Wilson, 1983–   . Updated monthly.

An author and subject index to more than 230 general-interest magazines and *The New York Times. Readers' Guide Abstracts* adds well-written summaries for 60,000 articles a year since 1984; *Readers' Guide Abstracts Select Edition* abstracts 25,000 selected articles since 1988. *Readers' Guide Abstracts* is also available on microfiche; there is no print edition of this version. The online version, available on Wilsonline and FirstSearch, is updated twice a week.

Available in print as *Readers' Guide to Periodical Literature.* H. W. Wilson, 1900–   . School and small public libraries may have the *Abridged Readers' Guide to Periodical Literature,* which indexes eighty-two magazines from 1966 to date. H. W. Wilson also publishes indexes to scholarly periodicals in many disciplines, e.g., *Art Index, Education Index, Social Sciences Index.* They are listed in the appropriate subject chapters that follow this one.

Resource/ One Ondisc. University Microfilms, 1986–   .

University Microfilms (UMI) has several periodical indexes in its ProQuest series. *Resource/ One Ondisc* indexes 140 general-interest periodicals plus *USA Today* and *The New York Times Current Events Edition.*

- *Magazine Express* contains the *Resource/ One* index plus full-image coverage of eighty-five of the most popular of the indexed periodicals beginning with 1988.
- UMI also produces *Periodical Abstracts Ondisc,* which is available in three editions: a Library Edition that covers 500 periodicals plus recent issues of *The New York Times* and *USA Today;* PA Research I, which indexes 950 periodicals; and PA Research II, which covers 1,500 periodicals plus recent issues of *The New York Times* and *The Wall Street Journal.*
- UMI's *General Periodicals Ondisc* offers indexing from one of the versions of *Periodicals Abstracts Ondisc* plus the full image of 350 of the periodicals, beginning in 1988.

UMI's general periodical indexing is available online on Dialog (File 484) as Newspaper & Periodical Abstracts. On OCLC's FirstSearch and on RLIN's CitaDel this database is available online as two files, one covering periodicals and one covering newspapers. There is no print equivalent of this index.

Also see Chapter 10, Document Delivery Services, for table of contents services such as CARL UnCover and OCLC's ContentsFirst that offer delivery of articles.

Cumulative Contents Index. (CD-ROM and magnetic tape) Chadwyck-Healey, 1996–   .

Planned for 1996, this ambitious indexing project is designed to provide bibliographic access to back volumes of scholarly periodicals. The publisher plans to include the table of contents for each issue of more than 3,000 journals published in the nineteenth and twentieth centuries. Users will be able to search by author or by keywords in titles and to scan the table of contents of issues of periodicals. There will be no subject access, however. Current plans call for the publication of two segments per year on CD-ROM and magnetic tape, with each segment including approximately one million citations.

19

AGRICULTURE

See also: *General Reference Sources, The Environment, Gardening*

Agriculture is both a business and a science, and the range of reference materials reflects that fact. Many books and articles have been published on the subject and it is an important topic for national and international research and debate. Farmers are increasingly using computers to keep farm records and to gather agricultural data. There are schools of agriculture in every state and there is increasing research on such matters as a genetically engineered food supply, environmental issues, food safety, and food distribution.

The sources of agricultural research listed here can be used by the researcher to find both popular and technical information.

Agriculture: Illustrated Search Strategy and Sources. By John N. Koch and Jean A. Gilbertson. Pierian Press, 1992.

A step-by-step guide to using major tools in agricultural research, such as *AGRICOLA* and *Biological & Agricultural Index.*

Guide to Sources for Agriculture and Biological Research. By J. Richard Blanchard and Lois Farrell. University of California Press, 1981.

Though now dated, this extensive guide to 5,700 sources can still be useful to the serious researcher in agriculture.

Directory of American Agriculture. Agricultural Resources & Communications, 1988– . Annual.

Lists national and state agricultural organizations, regional offices of

STATE COOPERATIVE EXTENSION OFFICES

Alabama:
80 Extension Hall
Auburn University
Auburn, AL 36830

Alaska:
Cooperative Extension
  Service
University of Alaska
Fairbanks, AK 99775

GENERAL SOURCES OF INFORMATION

Arizona:
Dept. of Agricultural
  Economics
University of Arizona
Tucson, AZ 85721

Arkansas:
Cooperative Extension
  Service
P. O. Box 391
Little Rock, AR 72203

government agencies dealing with agriculture, Cooperative Extension offices in each state, land grant universities, and periodicals.

Agriculture in the United States: A Documentary History. 4 vols. Edited by David W. Rasmussen. Greenwood, 1977.

Reprints historical documents relating to agriculture from the colonial period through 1973. Includes maps, charts, and tables.

Bibliography of Agriculture. Oryx, 1942–   . Monthly with annual cumulations.

Compiled by the National Agricultural Library, this indexes journals, reports, and publications of the U.S. Department of Agriculture, state agricultural experiment stations, state extension services, and the United Nations Food and Agriculture Organization. Available online and on CD-ROM as part of *AGRICOLA,* below.

See also government publications listed in this chapter.

AGRICOLA. (CD-ROM) SilverPlatter, 1972–   . Updated monthly. Also OCLC, 1979–92.

This database from the National Agricultural Library offers comprehensive coverage of worldwide literature on agriculture, animal studies, fertilizers, hydroponics, soils, and more. Available online with BRS and BRS/AfterDark (CAIN), Dialog (File 10), Knowledge Index (AGRI1), and OCLC FirstSearch, 1970–   . Corresponds in part to the print product *Bibliography of Agriculture,* 1942–   .

Biological & Agricultural Index. (CD-ROM) H. W. Wilson, 1983–   . Monthly.

Indexes 255 key periodicals in life sciences and agriculture. Covers such topics as agricultural chemicals, animal husbandry, fishery sciences, food sciences, forestry, horticulture, plant pathology, social science, and veterinary medicine. Also online from Wilsonline and OCLC FirstSearch, 1983–   , and in print, 1964–   . Preceded by *Agricultural Index,* 1919–64.

CAB Abstracts. (CD-ROM) SilverPlatter, 1984–   . Updated monthly.

Comprehensive database of information from the Commonwealth Agricultural Bureaux in the United Kingdom. Especially good for agriculture in the Third World. Available online with Dialog (File 50), Knowledge Index (AGRI3, AGRI4), BRS and BRS/AfterDark, 1972–   . Also available in print in a series of forty-six abstracting services: *Dairy Science Abstracts, Rice Abstracts, Sugar Industry Abstracts,* etc. Some

California:
Dept. of Agricultural Economics
University of California
Davis, CA 95616

Colorado:
Dept. of Economics
Colorado State University
Fort Collins, CO 80521

Connecticut:
Dept. of Agricultural Economics
University of Connecticut
Storrs, CT 06268

ELECTRONIC SOURCES

Delaware:
232 Townsend Hall
Dept. of Agricultural Economics
University of Delaware
Newark, DE 19717

Florida:
Room 1157, McCarty Hall
University of Florida
Gainesville, FL 32611

Georgia:
Agricultural Economics Dept.
Colliseum
University of Georgia
Athens, GA 30602

Hawaii:
Dept. of Agricultural & Resource Economics
875 Komohana Street
Hilo, HI 96720

titles have been published since the 1920s; others began publication in the 1970s.

CRIS/ICAR. (CD-ROM) SilverPlatter, 1975–   . Annual.

Provides access to current government-supported research in agriculture, food and nutrition, forestry, and related fields in the United States and Canada. The U.S. research from the USDA is online with Dialog (File 60) for the two most current years.

Food Science and Technology Abstracts. (CD-ROM) SilverPlatter, 1969–   . Updated monthly.

Worldwide literature dealing with all human food commodities and food processing. Online with Dialog (File 51), Knowledge Index, and ORBIT. Print version published by C.A.B., 1969–   .

Bulletin Boards

"ALF," Agricultural Library Forum. National Agricultural Library. **(301) 504-5496.**

Includes bulletins, conferences, messages, and files on many agricultural topics. Bullet25 is a list of other agriculture-related bulletin board systems in the United States. Products, projects, policies, and procedures of the National Agricultural Library (NAL), the AGRICOLA database, and NAL Information Centers are especially well covered. Contact Information Systems Division, National Agricultural Library, 10301 Baltimore Blvd., Beltsville, MD 20705; (301) 504-5113, for further details.

Human Nutrition Information Service. Department of Agriculture. **(301) 436-5078.**

Topics related to food and nutrition research.

Internet

- News Group–**misc.rural.**
- Advanced Technology Information Network offers market prices, news, weather, job listings, and safety information. Because it is offered by the California Agricultural Technology Institute, some material has a West Coast slant. Access via **telnet caticsuf.csufresno.edu;** log in **super.**
- Commodity Market Reports contains reports on 1,200 commodities from the USDA, updated daily. Access via **WAIS agricultural-market-news.src.**
- Pen Pages offers a complete information server on all aspects of rural life, with some bias toward Pennsylvania. Contains commodity prices, news, and information on family farm life and seniors on the farm. Access via **telnet psupen.psu.edu.** Use your two-letter state postal abbreviation as your log-in name.
- USDA Research Results summarizes research findings of the Department of Agriculture. Access via **WAIS usda-rrdb.src.**

Agricultural Research. 1953–   . Monthly.

Published for the layperson by the Agricultural Research Service of the U.S. Department of Agriculture, this magazine contains brief articles by government scientists highlighting USDA research projects of interest to farmers.

Farm Journal. 1877–   . 14 times/year.

For farm families, with information on livestock, poultry, and crop production. Covers the agricultural economic outlook, price forecasts, legislation affecting farmers, farm credit, and personnel issues in farming.

Farmer's Digest. 1937–   . 10 times/year

Similar in concept to *Reader's Digest,* selects and reprints articles from 300 farm and technical periodicals as well as USDA sources.

The New Farm: Magazine of Regenerative Agriculture. 1979–   . 7 times/year.

Information on alternative forms of agriculture, such as weed and pest control without the use of chemicals.

Successful Farming: For Families that Make Farming Their Business. 1902–   . Monthly.

Published in several regional editions, this magazine provides business, production, and family information along with practical help for decision-making. Special features evaluate farm machinery.

The federal government is a prolific publisher in the area of agriculture. In addition to the general publications listed here, there are titles on very specific topics. For example, the Agricultural Statistics Board Reports series contains a monthly publication entitled *Celery.*

Census of Agriculture, 1987. Bureau of the Census, 1989–   .

Issued as part of the decennial census of population from 1840 to 1920, an independent mid-decennial census began in 1925. Since 1950, the agriculture census has been on a five-year cycle, most recently collecting data for years ending in two and seven. The next edition is scheduled to be published in 1994. Also available on CD-ROM from the Census Bureau.

Fact Book of U.S. Agriculture. Department of Agriculture, Office of Public Affairs, 1950–   . Irregular.

An overview of American agriculture for reporters, students, and others who write and speak about agriculture. Lists telephone numbers for contacts at various USDA offices and related government agencies.

PERIODICALS

Louisiana:
Cooperative Extension
    Service
Louisiana State
    University
Baton Rouge, LA 70803

Maine:
Dept. of Agricultural
    Economics
302 Winslow Hall
University of Maine
Orono, ME 04469

Maryland:
Dept. of Agricultural &
    Resource Economics
Symons Hall
University of Maryland
College Park, MD 20742

GOVERNMENT PUBLICATIONS

Massachusetts:
Hampshire County
    Extension Office
15 Straw Avenue
Northampton, MA
        01060

Michigan:
Dept. of Agricultural
    Economics
Michigan State
    University
East Lansing, MI
        48824-1039

Yearbook of Agriculture. (Title varies: *United States Department of Agriculture Yearbook.*) Department of Agriculture, 1895– . Annual.

Volumes published before 1936 include statistical data (now published in *Agriculture Statistics*) and annual summaries. Since 1936, each volume has been devoted to a particular topic. For example: *New Crops, New Uses, New Markets: Industrial and Commercial Products from U.S. Agriculture* (1992); *Agriculture and the Environment* (1991); *Americans in Agriculture: Portraits of Diversity* (1990); *Farm Management: How to Achieve Your Farm Business Goals* (1989). This last title contains several chapters on selecting computer software for farm management.

Agricultural Handbooks. Department of Agriculture, 1950– . Irregular.

A series of more than 600 titles that provide scientific information for farmers. For example, number 674, *Atmospheric Environment* (Volume 3 in *The Container Tree Nursery Manual*), discusses growing tree seedlings in greenhouses.

Agriculture Statistics. Department of Agriculture, 1936– . Annual.

Data on production, supplies, consumption, facilities, costs, and returns.

See also the following *Subject Bibliographies* from the Government Printing Office:

#162—*Agricultural Research, Statistics and Economic Reports*
#31—*Agricultural Yearbooks*
#277—*Census of Agriculture*
#161—*Farms and Farming*
#10—*Livestock and Poultry*
#7—*Soil and Soil Management*

GOVERNMENT AGENCIES

Department of Agriculture
14th Street and Independence Avenue SW
Washington, DC 20250
(202) 447-2791

An excellent source of agricultural information on foreign markets as well as environmental issues in farming. Rural development, credit, conservation programs, and food inspection are also part of its program. If USDA publications do not satisfy your special research needs, consult the *Fact Book of U.S. Agriculture* for the name of the staff member with the expertise you are looking for.

Department of Commerce
14th Street between Constitution Ave. and E Street NW
Washington, DC 20230
(202) 377-2000

Many agencies within this department relate directly to agriculture: The Bureau of Census publishes the Census of Agriculture; the National Technical Information Service publishes technical documents relating to agriculture; and the National Oceanic and Atmospheric Administration deals with weather data.

Department of Health and Human Services
200 Independence Avenue SW
Washington, DC 20201
(202) 619-0257

Its Food and Drug Administration and National Institutes of Health are concerned with food delivery and other agricultural issues.

Environmental Protection Agency
401 M Street SW
Washington, DC 20460
(202) 382-2096

Its activities have a direct bearing on pesticides, fertilizers, and chemicals used in agriculture.

Valuable information on local farming conditions is available from your County Extension Agent, who provides a direct link to the land grant university in your state. Land grant universities have schools of agriculture and can advise you on the latest research. Call your County Extension Agent or check the attached list or the *Directory of Agriculture* (above) for the address of the Extension Specialist for your state.

American Farm Bureau Federation
225 Touhy Avenue
Park Ridge, IL 60068
(708) 399-5700

Federation of forty-nine state farm bureaus with a membership of over 3 million. Analyzes problems of its members and formulates action to improve their education, economic opportunity, and social advancement.

American Society of Agronomy
677 S. Segoe Rd.
Madison, WI 53711
(608) 273-8080

Professional society of agronomists, plant breeders, physiologists, soil scientists, chemists, educators, technicians, and others concerned with crop production and soil management.

New Jersey:
Dept. of Agricultural Economics & Marketing
P. O. Box 231, Cook College
Rutgers University
New Brunswick, NJ 08903

New Mexico:
Dept. of Agricultural Economics
New Mexico State University
Las Cruces, NM 88001

New York:
Dept. of Agricultural Economics
Cornell University
442 Warren Hall
Ithaca, NY 14853

ASSOCIATIONS

North Carolina:
Cooperative Extension Service
Box 8109
North Carolina State University
Raleigh, NC 27659-8109

North Dakota:
Cooperative Extension Service
North Dakota State University
Fargo, ND 58102

Chicago Mercantile Exchange
30 S. Wacker Dr.
Chicago, IL 60606
(312) 930-1000
Commodity futures exchange for many agricultural products.

National Farmers Union
10065 E. Harvard Ave.
Denver, CO 80231
(303) 337-5500
Membership of 250,000 farm families interested in the welfare of agriculture. Educational and legislative activities. Assists farm families in forming cooperatives.

National Grange
1616 H St. NW
Washington, DC 20006
(202) 628-3507
This fraternal organization of rural families was founded in 1867. Offers members a credit union, insurance, and educational and legislative programs.

A number of associations specialize in narrower areas. Among the largest groups are the American Dairy Association, the National Cattleman's Association, and the American Poultry Association. Others deal with farmland, fertilizers, pollution, real estate, equipment, trade, and banking. See the keyword index to the *Encyclopedia of Associations* to find such specialized organizations.

The United Nations, and, in particular, the Food and Agricultural Organization (FAO) of the UN, is a source for international commodity statistics.

SPECIAL LIBRARIES/ LIBRARY COLLECTIONS

National Agricultural Library
10301 Baltimore Blvd.
Beltsville, MD 20705-2351
(301) 504-5755
The nation's largest library on agriculture, the NAL is divided into twelve specialized information centers: Agricultural Trade and Marketing; Alternative Farming Systems; Animal Welfare; Aquaculture; Biotechnology; Food and Nutrition; Global Change; Plant Genome Data; Rural Information; Technology Transfer; Water Quality; and Youth Development.

Publications include *Bibliographic Series, Current Titles Listing,* which lists currently available titles in the series Quick Bibliographies, Special Reference Briefs, Agri-Topics, Pathfinders, Aqua-Topics, and Nutri-topics. Copies are available from Reference Unit, Room 111n NAL-USDA, 10301 Baltimore Blvd., Beltsville, MD 20705-2351.

The land grant university in every state has an agriculture library. Here are two examples:

Albert R. Mann Library
Cornell University
Ithaca, NY 14853-4301
(607) 255-2285

An important library serving, among other clientele, Cornell's School of Agriculture, New York State's land grant university.

University of California at Davis, General Library
Biological and Sciences Department
Davis, CA 95616
(916) 752-2110

Another land grant university library, with especially strong collections on viniculture and wine making.

Use these headings in library catalogs:

Agricultural chemicals	Farm produce
Agricultural credit	Fertilizer equipment
Agricultural exhibitions	Food—Preservation
Agricultural extension work	Food additives
Agricultural implements	Food crops
Agricultural industries	Food industry and trade
Agricultural pests	Food supply
Agricultural price supports	Frozen foods
Agricultural subsidies	Fruit grading machinery
Agriculture—Accidents	Green revolution
Agriculture—Economic aspects	Plant breeding
Agriculture—Statistics	Plant pathologists
Agriculture, Cooperative	Poultry as food
Corn—Forecasting	Seed technology
Dairy processing	Soil conservation
Dairy products industry	Sustainable agriculture
Farm management	

Agricultural Research Institute
9650 Rockville Pike
Bethesda, MD 20814
(301) 530-7122

South Carolina:
Dept. of Agricultural Economics
Clemson University
Clemson, SC 29631

South Dakota:
Dept. of Economics
South Dakota State University
Brookings, SD 57007

Tennessee:
Dept. of Agricultural Economics
University of Tennessee
P. O. Box 1071a
Knoxville, TN 37901

LC SUBJECT HEADINGS

Texas:
Dept. of Agricultural Economics
Texas A&M University
College Station, TX 77843-2124

Utah:
Dept. of Agricultural Economics
Utah State University
Logan, UT 84321

Vermont:
Dept. of Agricultural & Resource Economics
University of Vermont
178 South Prospect
Burlington, VT 05401

OTHER SOURCES OF EXPERT ADVICE

Originally part of National Academy of Sciences. Organizes conferences and workshops on agricultural research issues.

International Alliance for Sustainable Agriculture
Newman Center, University of Minnesota
1701 University Avenue SE
Minneapolis, MN 55414
(612) 331-1099
Promotes the establishment of agricultural systems that are economically viable, ecologically sound, and socially just and humane. Maintains resource center, publishes books and journals.

When searching for agricultural information online or on CD-ROM, remember to search for synonyms and scientific names. For example, if you are searching for information on corn, remember to search also maize, maiz, maise, and zea mays. When searching for sources on soybeans, search soy beans, soyabeans, soya beans, soja beans, all in both singular and plural, and the scientific name, *glycine max*. Use alternative spellings, such as estrus and oestrus, and alternative plurals. For example, in addition to searching larva and larvas, make sure to look under larvae as well. Even with a more ordinary topic like chickens or poultry, don't overlook broilers, or you'll miss a lot of material.

Virginia:
Dept. of Agricultural
   Economics
Virginia Polytechnic
   Institute & State
   University
Blacksburg, VA 24061

Washington:
Dept. of Agricultural
   Economics
Washington State
   University
Pullman, WA 99163

West Virginia:
2088 Agricultural
   Sciences Bldg.
West Virginia University
Morgantown, WV
            26506-6108

Wisconsin:
Extension Farm
   Management
University of Wisconsin
427 Lorch Street
Madison, WI 53706

Wyoming:
P. O. Box 3354
University of Wyoming
Laramie, WY 82071

At the national level,
contact:
Program Manager
Farm Management
   Extension Service
Room 3340-S
U. S. Department of
   Agriculture
Washington, DC 20250

20

AUTOMOBILES

See also: General Reference Sources, Consumer Information

Henry Ford II said in 1975, "This country developed in a particular way because of the automobile, and you can't just push a button and change it." The motor vehicle industry is the largest in the United States, with an unparalleled impact on our economy. The auto phenomenon touches virtually every other aspect of our culture as well, from suburban growth and environmental conditions to the freedom and romance of the motorized life as represented in our arts and entertainment.

Consistent with our national passion for automobiles is our thirst for information about their design, technology, performance, prices, history, trends, and so on. Publishers, software producers, and magazine editors provide a constant flow of new data to meet that demand.

GENERAL REFERENCE SOURCES

The Automobile Industry, 1896–1920. By George S. May. Facts On File, 1990.
The Automobile Industry, 1920–1980. By George S. May. Facts On File, 1989.
Part of the Encyclopedia of American Business History series, these two volumes give the history of manufacturers, models, inventors, and company executives.

Complete Car Cost Guide. Intelligent Choice Information. Annual.
Information on the total costs of owning and operating more than 1,000 different new and used cars. Includes the cost of fuel, repairs, regular maintenance, depreciation, insurance, and financing costs.

Gale's Auto Sourcebook. 2d ed. Edited by Karen Hill. Gale, 1992.
Provides facts, figures, and published evaluations on more than 300 cars

and light trucks sold from 1987 to 1992. Includes price history, dimensions, engines, recall notices, safety and repair citations, and model-specific associations and information sources. Other sections list car clubs, industry directories, buyers guides, customer service contacts at manufacturers, and model rankings by major automotive reviewers.

Standard Catalog of American Cars. 2d ed. 3 vols. Krause Publications, 1989–92.

Standard Catalog of Imported Cars, 1946–1986. By James M. Flammang. Krause Publications, 1992.

Extensive technical information on every model of car sold in the United States since 1905, plus thousands of photographs.

Buying Guides/Car Prices

AutoIntelligence New Car Decision Maker. 2 vols. By Paul Katzka and Bill Yankus. Random House, 1993.

More than 100 cars are profiled, with comparisons to similar models and prices given. Volume 1 covers small cars, sporty cars, and midsize sedans; Volume 2, large, luxury, and high-performance cars, station wagons, and compact vans.

Buyer's Guide Reports. Pace Publications. Bimonthly.

There are separate volumes for new cars, used cars, foreign cars, and new and used trucks and vans. They cite dealer cost and list price for new vehicles and average wholesale and retail prices for used ones. Extensive lists of costs for options and option packages are also provided.

Consumer Guide. 36 times/year.

About a dozen of these periodical issues each year make up the Auto Series, providing current price and buying information.

Edmund's New Car Prices. Edmund Publications. 3 times/year.

Guides note standard invoice, dealer cost, and average retail price for vehicles and most options. Separate volumes cover imports, used cars, vans and pickups.

Kelley Blue Book New Car Price Manual. Kelley Blue Book. Bimonthly.

Provides original list price and used wholesale and retail prices for approximately seven years of vehicles. Mileage charts show price variations for high and low mileage. Additional volumes cover older cars, motorcycles and ATVs, motor homes and campers, and trailers.

N.A.D.A. Official Used Car Guide. National Automobile Dealers Association. Monthly.

The "blue book" lists used car values for the past seven years. Includes average trade-in, loan, and used retail prices. Individual options are listed for each car. Additional volumes cover RVs and motorcycles, snowmobiles, and ATVs.

New Car Cost Guide. H. M. Gousha. 6 times/year.
    Price information for many models with specific accessories and equipment.

Chilton's Auto Repair Manual. Chilton. Annual.
Chilton's Import Car Repair Manual. Chilton. Annual.
    This popular series is designed for the do-it-yourselfer with some experience. Other volumes cover motorcycles and trucks and vans. There is also a series on specific cars for mechanics.

Repairs

The automobile industry was one of the earliest to use CD-ROM for automotive parts catalogs.

ELECTRONIC SOURCES

Automotive News. 1988–   . Weekly.
    Full text of this industry newspaper is available on NEXIS and Dow Jones News/Retrieval.

AutoWeek. 1988–   . Weekly.
    This magazine for auto enthusiasts is available online with NEXIS.

Electronic Blue Book. (CD-ROM) DISC Information Services. 8 times/year.
    Provides regionalized valuation data for cars and light trucks. Also available on diskette as *Electronic Automobile Red Book.*

AutoVantage: Descriptions and prices for new and used cars. Order reports online. Available from Dow Jones News/Retrieval, GEnie, Delphi, America Online. Or telephone (800) 324-9261 to order reports.

Consumer Online Services

Prodigy: In the Autos section are reports on sixty models of the current year's cars plus articles from *Consumer Reports* and "Last Chance Garage" (a column on repairs from WGBH), a calendar of auto shows, and a bulletin board.

CompuServe: New Car Showroom is a database of features and specifications for cars, vans, and trucks.

Department of Transportation: Federal Highway Administration Electronic BBS **(202) 366-3764.**

Bulletin Boards

The Internet: HONDA is a discussion group on Honda and Acura automobiles. Access via: **HONDA@MSCRC.SUNYSB.EDU.**

INDEXES

Auto Index. 1973– . Bimonthly.
   Indexes fourteen magazines for road tests, owner surveys, and manufacturers. Covers popular titles such as *Hot Rod* and *Popular Mechanics* plus *Cars and Parts* and other more specialized publications.

Popular car magazines are also indexed in the general periodical indexes listed in Chapter 18, General Reference Sources.

PERIODICALS

AutoWeek. 1958– . Weekly.
   Devoted to worldwide auto racing, provides dates of races, information about cars and drivers, and other related facts. Also online with NEXIS.

Car and Driver. 1955– . Monthly.
   A general-interest magazine that evaluates cars in all price ranges. Tests on individual new cars are excellent.

Hot Rod. 1948– . Monthly.
   The favored publication of enthusiasts who rebuild cars into high-performance machines.

Motor Trend. 1949– . Monthly.
   This general-interest magazine reports on road tests of all makes, classes, and prices of cars.

Road and Track. 1947– . Monthly.
   Another magazine that provides detailed write-ups of road tests of all makes of cars.

Truckin'. 1974– . Monthly.
   Covers pickups, minitrucks, and vans.

GOVERNMENT AGENCIES

Department of Transportation
400 Seventh St. SW
Washington, DC 20590
(202) 366-4000
   Its National Highway Traffic Safety Administration does lab testing and research on equipment and driving safety. See under Libraries below.

Environmental Protection Agency
401 M St. SW
Washington, DC 20460
(202) 382-2096
Sets standards for automobile emissions and air quality.

The Back-Yard Mechanic. 3 vols. 1976–81.
   Articles reprinted from *Drivers* magazine explain simple auto repair and maintenance jobs.

Consumer Tire Guide. Department of Transportation. 1990.

Cost of Owning and Operating Automobiles and Vans. Department of Transportation. 1991.

Gas Mileage Guide. Department of Transportation/Environmental Protection Agency. Annual.

Nine Ways to Lower Your Auto Insurance Cost. Office of Consumer Affairs. 1990.

See also *Subject Bibliography* #49—Motor Vehicles, and #3—Highway Construction, Safety and Traffic from the Government Printing Office.

American Automobile Association
1000 AAA Dr.
Heathrow, FL 32746-5063
(404) 444-7000
   This federation of automobile clubs provides domestic and foreign travel services and emergency road services. Has affiliates in every state.

Motor Vehicle Manufacturers Association
7430 Second Ave.
Detroit, MI 48202
(313) 872-4311
   Trade association of the automotive industry. Publishes *Motor Vehicle Facts and Figures* (annual), *World Motor Vehicle Data Book,* and other books, pamphlets, and technical reports.

Society of Automotive Historians
c/o National Automotive History Collection
Detroit Public Library
5201 Woodward Ave.
Detroit, MI 48202
(313) 833-1000
Members study the history of the automobile, the industry, and its people. Publishes *Automotive History Review*.

Society of Automotive Engineers (SAE)
400 Commonwealth Drive
Warrendale, PA 15096
(412) 776-4841
Engineers and scientists in the field of self-propelled vehicles.

Clubs exist for almost every make and model of car; for example, the BMW Automobile Club of America, Classic Car Club of America, Oldsmobile Club of America, and Thunderbirds of America. For a complete list, see *Gale's Auto Sourcebook*.

LIBRARIES   Libraries with special automobile or transportation collections:

National Automobile History Collection
Detroit Public Library
5201 Woodward Ave.
Detroit, MI 48202
(313) 833-1000
More than 300,000 photographs and other materials.

Automobile Reference Collection
Free Library of Philadelphia
Logan Square
Philadelphia, PA 19103
(215) 686-5300
Back issues of shop manuals, sales catalogs, parts books.

Transportation Library
Northwestern University
Evanston, IL 60208
(708) 491-5273

Transportation Research Institute
University of Michigan
Ann Arbor, MI 48109
(313) 764-7494

Institute of Transportation Studies Library
University of California
McLaughlin Hall
Berkeley, CA 94720
(510) 642-3604

U.S. Department of Transportation Library
400 Seventh St. SW
Washington, DC 20590
(202) 366-2565

Use these headings in library catalogs:

LC SUBJECT HEADINGS

Advertising—Automobile industry and trade
Air bag restraint systems
Antique and classic cars
Automobile drivers
Automobile industry and trade
Automobile industry workers
Automobile racing
Automobile theft
Automobiles
Automobiles—Bumpers
Automobiles—Crashworthiness
Automobiles—Design and construction
Automobiles—Maintenance and repair
Automobiles—Pollution control devices
Automobiles—Purchasing
Automobiles—Seat belts
Automobiles—U.S.—Safety measures
Automobiles, Compact
Car pools
Insurance, Automobile
Specific car names; e.g., Ford automobile, Jaguar automobile, etc.

21

BUSINESS
AND FINANCE

See also: *General Reference Sources, Jobs and Careers, Patents, Small Business*

For the economist, the planner, entrepreneur, investor, consumer, job seeker, or student, the ability to find and use business information can be enormously important. For that reason there is a wealth of business information, including online databases, CD-ROMs, business magazines and newsletters, books, loose-leaf services, and other specialized packages.

Several general characteristics of business publications are worth noting. Because business information must be revised constantly, most major publications are issued at regular intervals, with continuing updates. For the same reason, a great deal of business data appears in electronic form. Many business publications tend to focus on narrow topics, and competing publishers often produce similar information using different arrangements and formats.

When you approach a business research project, the following guidelines may be helpful:

1. Use a variety of tools when conducting research. A financial newsletter, for example, will have a different take on an industry than a Department of Commerce bulletin.
2. Ask "Who knows what I need to know?" In business research you may have to be creative in finding the source of information you seek. A general reference librarian is less likely to be able to help than a business librarian or other specialist in business information.
3. Identify the most current source of information. Events in the business world change rapidly, so older information may no longer be valid. Newspapers, newsletters, electronic bulletin boards, and online databases are among the most rapidly updated resources.

4. Try to determine the schedule on which the information you seek is released. Certain government statistics are updated monthly or even weekly, while others are revised only every ten years.

5. Evaluate whether published information is accurate, reliable, and unbiased. Is the publisher respected for this type of research? Do people in the field use the material? How was the information gathered?

6. Wherever possible, verify information in at least one other source. Publications containing addresses, personnel listings, sales data, financial statements, or statistics may provide partial or outdated information, make mistakes, or use definitions other than those that are common.

7. Try to use a special business or economics library that focuses on the type of materials you need. Corporate libraries, for instance, may have detailed information on the industry you are studying. Librarians of such collections are particularly knowledgeable.

8. Use unpublished resources. A telephone call to an appropriate subject specialist can save time and set your research on the proper path, often at little cost. Libraries are an excellent source of referral to other organizations. The librarian can help you locate relevant government agencies, trade and professional associations, specialized libraries, research centers, and other sources of expert information.

The following sources provide an overview of business research. Few libraries will own every title on the list, but the librarian can probably suggest a similar source.

GUIDES TO THE LITERATURE

Business Information: How to Find It, How to Use It. 2d ed. By Michael R. Lavin. Oryx Press, 1992.

A step-by-step introduction to business research methods. Individual chapters are devoted to specific areas, from company finance to marketing. Each chapter explains basic concepts, discusses research strategies and methods, and provides detailed descriptions of important reference tools. Sources are evaluated and compared and tips are offered on how to use them.

Handbook of Business Information: A Guide for Librarians, Students, and Researchers. By Diane Wheeler Strauss. Libraries Unlimited, 1988.

Similar to Lavin, though not as up to date, this book also covers a few fields of business that Lavin doesn't: insurance and real estate, for example.

Business Information Sources. 3d ed. By Lorna Daniells. University of California Press, 1993.

The latest edition of this standard reference work lists many more titles than Lavin does, but doesn't give as much instruction in using them.

The Directory of Business Information Sources: Associations, Newsletters, Magazines, Trade Shows. 2d ed. Edited by Leslie Mackenzie. Grey House, 1994.

Lists the items named in the subtitle for ninety-five industries, from amusement/entertainment to water supply.

Encyclopedia of Business Information Sources. Gale Research. Biennial.

This essential tool lists 24,000 business publications and related sources of information. Listings are arranged alphabetically by subject, then subdivided into type of resource, such as periodicals, directories, databases, and yearbooks. Over 1,000 topics are covered.

Business Organizations and Agencies Directory. Gale Research. Biennial.

Focuses on major organizations of interest to business researchers. Information comes from other Gale publications and staff research as well as from listings in government directories. Among the organizations described are trade associations, chambers of commerce, regional planning and development agencies, labor unions, business schools, major newspapers, and business libraries. Also available online with OCLC FirstSearch.

Statistical Reference Index. Congressional Information Service, 1980–   .
Monthly.

Detailed abstracts of statistical reports produced by business journals, commercial publishers, research centers, trade and professional associations, and other nongovernment sources. Part 1 is an index by subject, title, and issuing agency; Part 2 describes each report and how it can be obtained. Two companion publications, arranged in similar fashion, are also available: *American Statistics Index* provides comprehensive coverage of statistical reports issued by the federal government; the *Index to International Statistics* describes major publications from organizations such as the United Nations. All three of these titles are available on CD-ROM as *Statistical Masterfile,* updated quarterly.

**GENERAL SOURCES
OF INFORMATION**

Business Rankings Annual. Gale Research. Annual.

Each day, Brooklyn Business Library workers scan incoming business magazines, government documents, and reference publications in search of ranked business lists. The 4,000 resulting lists are arranged by topic, and the top five to ten candidates are reported for each category—the ten largest fast-food chains, the most respected CEOs. Also cites the source of the original information. *European Business Rankings* is a companion publication.

Market Share Reporter. Gale Research. Annual.

Similar in purpose to the *Business Rankings Annual, Market Share Reporter* examines comparative market share for products, brands, companies, or geographic areas. Data are arranged by Standard Industrial Classification (SIC) number, with a subject and name index. Information is gathered primarily from newspaper and journal articles and from the *Investext* database of financial analysts' reports. Original sources are cited for further research. Online with NEXIS.

Rand McNally Commercial Atlas and Marketing Guide. Rand McNally. Annual.

The most current, comprehensive, and detailed atlas of the United States. Thousands of currently revised place names are listed for each state. But the *Atlas* also provides a wealth of market data for business researchers, including local population estimates, ranked comparisons of major cities, thematic maps, transportation information, and directories of military bases and colleges.

Periodicals are among the most current, accessible, and specific sources of business information. Because thousands of specialized periodicals are published, researchers need a variety of indexing tools to locate what they need. Many indexing systems provide immediate access to the text of articles, either online, on CD-ROM, or via microform.

PERIODICAL INDEXES

Wilson Business Abstracts. (CD-ROM) H. W. Wilson, 1982–   . Monthly.

Provides comprehensive indexing and detailed abstracts of 350 leading business magazines and trade and academic journals plus selected articles from *The Wall Street Journal* and *The New York Times.* Indexing is by subject, SIC (Standard Industrial Classification) code, and company name. Records can also be searched by author, title, journal, or keyword. Online access is available through FirstSearch and Wilsonline. A printed version of the index, minus the abstracts, is published as *Business Periodicals Index,* 1958–   .

Business Index. (CD-ROM) Information Access. Current 4 years. Monthly.

Covers more than 300 business journals, over fifty regional business publications, and hundreds of general-interest and computing magazines, *The Wall Street Journal,* and *The New York Times.* It provides subject and author indexing, with limited keyword access.

Business Index coverage is partially duplicated by other of the publisher's "InfoTrac" databases, most notably the *General Periodicals Index,* but many of the business journals are found only on the *Business Index.* Subscribers can also lease a more comprehensive CD-ROM system called *Business and Company ProFile.* This service includes the complete *Business Index,* extensive listings from *Ward's Business Directory,* plus the full text of recent corporate press releases and financial analysts' reports. Another CD-ROM product, *Business ASAP*, carries the full text of the articles listed in *Business Index*.

The periodical file is available as two online databases: *Trade and Industry Index* (index only) from Dialog (File 148) and Knowledge Index, 1981–   ; and *Trade and Industry ASAP* (full-text articles) from BRS, Dialog (File 648), and NEXIS. Full text can also be accessed through a self-contained microfilm system called the *Business Connection*. There is no print equivalent of this index.

ABI/INFORM OnDisc. (CD-ROM) UMI/Data Courier, 1971–   . Monthly.

The hallmarks of this respected index are its lengthy, well-written abstracts and its sophisticated search system. Compared with the other general-purpose business periodical indexes, *ABI* provides the best coverage of scholarly journals, but it also indexes popular magazines and trade journals—approximately 800 in all. *ABI/INFORM Express Edition* is a smaller version covering 110 journals, 1987–   . *ABI* is also produced as an online file, available through BRS, BRS/AfterDark, Dialog (File 15), Knowledge Index, HRIN, ORBIT, and NEXIS, 1971–   . The online version includes the full text for many articles. There is no print equivalent of this index.

Predicasts F&S Index United States Plus Text.
Predicasts F&S Index International Plus Text. (CD-ROM) SilverPlatter. Most recent two years. Monthly.

This major CD-ROM source includes the complete text of many articles. Both indexes cover more than 1,000 magazines and newspapers, and both focus on news relating to products, markets, companies, and technology. Articles are indexed by Predicasts' product codes, country codes, event codes, and company name. The databases are also searchable by keyword. The United States version focuses on business activities that take place in this country, whether or not the company is American. The international edition covers events outside the United States, regardless of the headquarters location of the company involved. Both indexes are available in print minus the full text or abstracts, and as two online products: *PTS F&S Indexes* (without text) from BRS (1972–   ) and Dialog (File 18, 1980–   ), and *PTS PROMT* (with text or abstracts) from BRS, Dialog (File 16), and NEXIS, 1972–   .

Business Dateline OnDisc. (CD-ROM) UMI/Data Courier, 1985–   . Monthly.
Business NewsBank. (Microfiche) NewsBank, Inc. Monthly.

On CD-ROM, *Business Dateline* provides the full text of selected articles from 165 regional business newspapers and magazines, an excellent source of individual company news. Articles are well indexed, and keywords in the text are searchable. *Business Dateline* is also offered as an online database through Dialog (File 635), Dow Jones News/Retrieval, HRIN, and NEXIS, 1985– .

Business NewsBank reproduces selected business articles from 450 daily newspapers and 150 weeklies. Because the articles are on microfiche, words in the text are not searchable, but the *NewsBank Electronic Information System* on CD-ROM provides a comprehensive index to the microfiche collection, with keyword-searchable abstracts. Although the microfiche is not as convenient as full-text CD-ROMs or online alternatives, the system covers more regional periodicals than any other single source does. By the end of 1994, all current articles on microfiche should be available on disc.

Across the Board. 1939– . 10 times/year.
Published by the Conference Board, a nonprofit research center that monitors economic conditions and management trends, this general-interest magazine focuses on public policy issues as they relate to the business world.

Barron's National Business and Financial Weekly. 1921– . Weekly.
This newspaper for investors from the publisher of *The Wall Street Journal* analyzes companies and tracks market conditions. Good source for investment statistics. Listings for major stock exchanges are also given.

Business Week. 1929– . Weekly.
The leading business weekly in America contains short articles on the economy, business and financial trends, and corporate and investment news. A cover story provides an in-depth look at a current business issue. Online with NEXIS and Dow Jones News/Retrieval.

Forbes. 1917– . Biweekly.
This slightly irreverent news magazine focuses on financial and economic news, but coverage is wide-ranging. Although written for business executives, *Forbes* is appropriate for the general business audience. Online with NEXIS.

Fortune. 1930– . Biweekly.
Noted for excellent profiles of companies and executives and thorough exploration of current management trends, *Fortune* is perhaps best-known for its annual rankings, including the "Fortune Five Hundred" companies, the largest private fortunes, highest-paid executives, etc. Online with NEXIS.

Harvard Business Review. 1922–   . Bimonthly.

This influential journal offers articles by leading business and academic writers. The emphasis is on management strategies and techniques, with topics ranging from production management to boardroom policies. Online with BRS, BRS/AfterDark, Dialog (File 122), Knowledge Index, NEXIS, HRIN.

Money. 1972–   . Monthly.

This consumer magazine helps readers in all income brackets to manage their money. Hints on saving for a home, a college fund, or retirement, advice on all types of investments, and tax savings plans are presented in an easy-to-read style.

The Wall Street Journal. 1889–   . Weekdays, except holidays.

This widely read, almost indispensable national paper provides far-ranging coverage of business, economic, and political news as well as special features. The *Journal* is famous for the high caliber of its investigative reporting. Also available on CD-ROM from Dow Jones and online with Dow Jones News/Retrieval and NEXIS.

STATISTICAL PUBLICATIONS

Business Statistics. U.S. Bureau of Economic Analysis. Biennial.

The Bureau of Economic Analysis calculates the country's gross domestic product (GDP), and this compendium of economic and industrial statistics provides twenty years of retrospective coverage. Also provides historical information on the nearly 2,000 subject areas used in calculating the GDP. The biennial cumulation is updated monthly by the *Survey of Current Business.*

Predicasts Basebook. Predicasts. Annual.

Focuses on historical data, providing fifteen years of coverage in each annual volume. Statistics are gathered from trade journals, government reports, and other sources, and nearly 30,000 data series are provided. The publication is arranged by Predicasts' unique product codes, a modified version of the government's SIC system. The emphasis is on specific products and industries, but general economic indicators, such as unemployment data and inflation rates, can also be found.

Survey of Buying Power: Demographics USA. Market Statistics. Annual.

Published since 1929, this is one of the oldest and most widely used sources of market demographics. Data are provided for states, counties, major cities, metropolitan areas, and areas of dominant influence (i.e., television markets). The publisher calculates annual estimates for total population, number of households, median age, effective buying income, and household distribution by age of householder, size of household, and income. Estimates of local retail sales are provided for nine sales categories. Comparative tables rank local areas by various characteristics including buying power. Also includes five-year projections for key variables.

American Business Disk. (CD-ROM) American Business Information. Annual.

With 9.6 million company listings, this is one of the most comprehensive business directories in the United States. Gathered from 4,700 phone books across the country, listings indicate address, SIC codes, and phone book Yellow Pages classifications. The file can be searched by company name, SIC code, or subject, and searches can be limited geographically. An online version, called *American Business Directory,* is offered through Dialog (File 531). The *American Business Phonebook,* a scaled-down version of the CD-ROM, lists the same number of companies, but shows only name, partial address, and phone number, and has more limited search capabilities.

Dun's Million Dollar Disc.
Dun's Middle Market Disc. (CD-ROM) Dun's Marketing Services. Quarterly.

These two directories provide background information on nearly 400,-000 of the largest companies in the United States, over 90 percent of which are privately held. The *Million Dollar Disc* describes companies with more than 250 employees and more than $25 million in annual sales; the *Middle Market Disc* covers midsize companies with 100 to 250 employees and annual sales between $4 million and $25 million. Records include company address, phone number, executive officers, business description, SIC numbers, sales volume, and employee size. Biographical information is also provided for nearly 700,000 key executives. The *Million Dollar Disc* is also available online with Dialog (File 517) and in print as two separate publications: the *Million Dollar Directory* and *Dun's Reference Book of Corporate Managements.* The *Middle Market Disc* has no online or printed equivalent.

Standard Directory of Advertisers. National Register Publishing. Annual, with updates.

Known as the "Advertiser Red Book," this source covers 25,000 companies and nonprofit organizations with large advertising budgets. For each company, general background information is provided, including annual sales volume, year founded, and brand names used. A separate volume indexes more than 60,000 brand names alphabetically so that the researcher can identify the company offering a product. Available on CD-ROM as part of *Advertising Red Books Plus* from Reed Reference Publishing, updated quarterly. This disc also contains the *Standard Directory of Advertising Agencies* and *International Advertisers and Agencies.*

Hoover's Handbook of American Business.
Hoover's Handbook of World Business.
Hoover's Handbook of Emerging Companies.
Hoover's MasterList of Major U.S. Companies.
Reference Press. Annual.

Compact, easy-to-use, affordable guides to company information. The first three volumes provide well-designed, informative, single-page profiles of leading public and private corporations. The American edition covers more than 500 U.S. firms; the second volume describes approximately 150 companies outside the country; the third volume describes 250 rapidly growing enterprises. Because inclusion is based on a company's "influence in our daily lives," selections are somewhat subjective. Also available as *Hoover's Handbook* on disc for Data Discman and online with America Online. *Hoover's MasterList* provides limited directory information on nearly 6,000 companies.

Thomas Register of American Manufacturers. Thomas Publishing Company. Annual.

Published since 1907, this twenty-six-volume buyers' guide identifies the manufacturers of everything from burial vaults to fish ponds. Both industrial and consumer products are listed. Two volumes in the set provide an alphabetical directory of more than 120,000 companies, with a separate trade name index. Another sixteen volumes provide classified listings of products and the companies that make them. The remaining eight volumes reproduce the actual product catalogs for many of the companies appearing in the set. The *Thomas Register* is also available on CD-ROM and as an online database, both from Dialog, updated semiannually.

INVESTMENT SOURCES

Compact D/ SEC. (CD-ROM) Disclosure, 1985–   . Monthly.

Extensive information on every company required to file reports with the U.S. Securities and Exchange Commission can be found on this sophisticated, yet easy-to-use database. Each company record contains a brief profile; lists of subsidiaries, executives, directors, and major shareholders; five years of financial statements; financial footnotes; stock information; and, in most cases, the president's annual letter to shareholders and the comptroller's management discussion.

Approximately 12,000 companies are covered, and an average record is about ten pages in length. Users can request information on a particular company, but the real value of *Compact D* is its ability to locate companies that have specified characteristics, including product type, geographic area, size, net worth, or other financial attributes. Characteristics can be searched in combination to create extremely specific lists. Users can also generate their own customized reports, ranked lists, or comparative tables. A version of this database is available online with FirstSearch and Dialog. Another CD-ROM version, *SEC Online on SilverPlatter,* provides similar information for 4,000 companies.

Moody's Bank & Finance Disc.
Moody's Industrial Disc.
Moody's OTC Industrial Disc.
Moody's OTC Unlisted Disc.
Moody's Public Utility Disc.
Moody's Transportation Disc.
(CD-ROM) Moody's Investors Service. Quarterly,

Contains business and financial information on U.S. companies, including detailed financial statements, capital structure, long-term debt, and company history and description. Also partially available online with Dialog as *Moody's Corporate Profiles* and *Moody's Corporate News,* updated weekly. Corresponds to the print *Moody's Manuals.*

Standard & Poor's Stock Reports. Standard & Poor's Corporation. Quarterly.

One of the fastest ways to find a succinct, authoritative summary of a public stock company, this series covers every company listed on the New York or American Stock Exchange, plus 1,600 over-the-counter firms. A two-page report describes the business, summarizes recent news events, cites key financial and stock performance figures, and offers an outlook for investment purposes. Subscribers can receive the set either in paperback form (mailed quarterly) or in loose-leaf form (mailed weekly on a rotating schedule). Each company report is updated four times per year. Reports are also available on CD-ROM as part of COMPMARK, updated quarterly.

Value Line Investment Survey. Value Line. Weekly.

The best-known stock advisory service in America, providing detailed reports for 1,700 of the most widely followed U.S. stocks. Each single-page report contains current and historical stock and financial data, the Value Line performance chart, commentary on the company and its outlook, and several Value Line ratings. Companies are grouped by industry category, and brief analyses of industry performance are also provided. Reports are updated quarterly, on a weekly rotation. Each weekly mailing includes a newsletter with an overview of the market and timely stock recommendations, and a variety of stock screening lists. Value Line data are also available online through CompuServe, on floppy diskette under the name *Value/*

Screen II, and on CD-ROM as part of the Lotus One Source *CD/Investment* disk.

Morningstar Mutual Funds. Morningstar. Biweekly.

Of the many mutual fund advisory publications on the market, Morningstar products have emerged as the most popular. The Morningstar service includes a biweekly newsletter with articles and screening lists, plus single-page reports on individual funds, each of which is updated on a twenty-week cycle (i.e., about twice per year). All NASDAQ-listed funds are covered. Reports describe the fund's investment criteria, offer a narrative analysis of its performance, list the top twenty-five securities in its current portfolio, show twelve years of comparative data, and rate the fund. An annual version of the service is also published in two hardcover volumes as *Mutual Fund Sourcebook.* Reports in the annual edition are similar to the biweekly version, but in place of the narrative performance analysis, biographical information on the fund's manager can be found. A CD-ROM product, with monthly updates, is called *Morningstar Mutual Funds Ondisc.*

The Hulbert Guide to Financial Newsletters. 5th ed. By Mark Hulbert. Dearborn, 1993.

Hundreds of investment newsletters offer advice to individual investors on managing their own portfolios. This book provides a directory and statistical analysis of the past performance of 120 of the top newsletters.

Other investment services are listed under Other Electronic Sources below.

OTHER ELECTRONIC SOURCES

There are more than 100 online databases on business and investments. NewsNet contains the full text of many investment newsletters. Dow Jones News/Retrieval has such files as the Mutual Funds Performance Report. See the *Gale Directory of Databases* for a comprehensive list. Many of the consumer services provide stock quotes (usually with a fifteen-minute delay), and some have a service whereby, for an extra fee, you can track your investments.

- CompuServe has many services for the investor, including the Money Magazine Financial Information Center, Investor's Guide and Mutual Fund Directory, News-a-tron Market Reports, and S & P MarketScope, plus the Investors Forum.
- GEnie has Schwab's Investors RoundTable, Wall Street SOS (recommendations on stocks to sell or buy), and the GEnie Quotes Securities Database.
- Delphi Internet offers Wall Street SOS, News-a-tron Market Reports, and others.

- America Online provides the Independent Investors Forum, USA Today Personal Investing, Stock Link (stock prices), market news, stock market timing and charts, and columns such as "Your Money."
- Prodigy has business headlines, and company news that can be searched by name, ticker symbol, or industry. It also offers a Trade Resources Directory prepared by the Trade Promotion Resources Commission with an overview of federal government export assistance programs. There are columns on investing from *Consumer Reports* and *Kiplinger's* and economic indicators in Prodigy's graphics. Bulletin boards include Money Talk and International Business.

Many government agencies, including the Energy Information Administration, the Internal Revenue Service, the Office of Personnel Management, and the Customs Service, support business-oriented electronic bulletin boards. The Commerce Department's Economic Bulletin Board provides the latest statistical releases from several government agencies and gives access to regular government reports, such as *Treasury Auction Results* and *Economic Indicators*. Annual subscriptions are $35 a year (2400 bps) plus connect time charges. Free limited-access service is available for those who would like to try the board before subscribing. Call **202-377-3870** and type **GUEST** when asked for an ID.

As of this writing, Internet offerings for business users focus primarily on academic subjects; many universities and libraries have loaded specialized databases for Internet access. Economic and demographic statistics are among the most prevalent Internet files, especially those using data in the public domain.

GOVERNMENT PUBLICATIONS

Economic Report of the President. Council of Economic Advisers. Annual.

The annual report of the President to Congress on the state of the economy, the progress of the administration's economic program, and the short-term economic outlook. The narrative section is devoted to major issues. Approximately one-third of the report consists of extensive statistical tables of current and retrospective economic indicators. The statistical section is updated by a monthly periodical entitled *Economic Indicators*.

National Trade Data Bank. (CD-ROM) Department of Commerce. Monthly. *National Economic, Social, and Environmental Data Bank.* (CD-ROM) Department of Commerce. Quarterly.

NTDB is a remarkable database containing the complete text of more than 90,000 government reports and statistical tables of interest to the import-export trade. Reports are provided by more than fifteen federal agencies, including the Census Bureau, the CIA, and the Federal Reserve Board. Among the information to be found: individual country reports;

market research on foreign demand for American products; current and retrospective foreign exchange rates; and import and export statistics. A separate disk contains the Commerce Department's *Foreign Trader's Index*, a monthly guide to foreign companies seeking to buy American products.

In the same format as *NTDB*, the *National Economic, Social, and Environmental Data Bank* provides full-text reports and statistical tables on domestic business and social conditions. Data supplied by many agencies gives it wide-ranging coverage. Documents include the *Economic Report of the President*, the *Digest of Educational Statistics*, the federal budget analysis and outlook from the Congressional Budget Office, summary data from the 1990 Census, regional economic projections from the Bureau of Economic Analysis, and the EPA's toxic release data for counties and businesses.

It can be difficult to search for and choose reports. The software can be slow and clumsy, partly because of the enormous size and diversity of the data on each disk. However, these limitations are easily outweighed by the comprehensiveness and affordability of these massive files.

Standard Industrial Classification Manual. Office of Management and Budget. 1987.

The official guide to the government's definitions of industry categories. The SIC system groups similar business activities using four-digit codes. The *Manual* lists the codes in numerical order, provides an alphabetical index for locating the appropriate SIC number for a given industry, and describes the scope of each industry grouping. The *Manual* is a basic research tool because a great many publications and databases are organized by SIC number. The *Manual* is also useful as a conceptual framework of the structure of American industry.

U.S. Industrial Outlook. International Trade Administration. Annual.

An encyclopedic overview of 350 major industry groups, containing readable narrative reports plus statistical tables. Each report supplies the government's analysis of that industry's outlook for the next five years. Among the most useful features are statistics on industry production and revenues, import/export summaries, and a list of sources for further research.

See also the Government Printing Office's *Subject Bibliography #4*—Business and Management, #152—Census of Business, and #100—Federal Trade Commission Decisions and Publications.

GOVERNMENT AGENCIES

Bureau of the Census
Department of Commerce
Washington, DC 20233
(301) 763-4100

Best known for the decennial *Census of Population and Housing,* a gold mine of information on the characteristics of U.S. residents. The Census Bureau also compiles current population estimates and projections, conducts ongoing household surveys, mounts nine major censuses of economic activity, publishes a variety of current business and housing reports, and collects monthly foreign trade statistics. Subject specialists at the Census Bureau are helpful and accessible as are employees at the twelve regional offices. For information about the Census Bureau's electronic bulletin board, call (301) 763-1580.

Bureau of Labor Statistics
441 G Street NW
Washington, DC 20212
(202) 523-1327

Collects and reports data on such topics as employment, occupational outlook, productivity, union membership, inflation, and consumer expenditures. Data are produced as monthly statistical releases, detailed periodicals, and an extensive series of specialized *BLS Bulletins.* The *Monthly Labor Review,* the bureau's flagship publication, is a widely read magazine containing articles on labor force trends as well as summary labor statistics. The bureau maintains eight regional offices. For information about its electronic bulletin board, call (202) 523-7343.

Securities and Exchange Commission
450 Fifth Street NW
Washington, DC 20549
(202) 272-2650

The SEC, charged with regulating securities markets in the United States, publishes little of the information it collects on publicly traded corporations. Filing documents are, however, available for inspection at each of the agency's ten public reference rooms. SEC filings can also be ordered through commercial document-delivery services, obtained on microfiche or CD-ROM at larger business libraries (see *Compact D/SEC* above), or accessed electronically via a commercial online service called *SEC Online,* available with Dialog, WESTLAW, and LEXIS. To contact the SEC's Public Reference Room in Washington, call (202) 272-7450.

Academy of Management
P. O. Box 209
Ada, OH 45810
(419) 772-1953

Members are professors of management in business schools. Issues several research journals.

ASSOCIATIONS

American Association of Individual Investors
625 N. Michigan Avenue
Chicago, IL 60611
(312) 280-0170
Assists individuals in becoming effective managers of their own assets. Offers home-study courses on investment topics, sponsors seminars. Publishes several journals, and provides an electronic bulletin board.

American Bankers Association
1120 Connecticut Ave. NW
Washington, DC 20036
(202) 467-4000

American Management Association
135 W. 50th Street
New York, NY 10020
(212) 586-8100
Organization of managers in industry, commerce, government, and non-profits, and of university teachers of management. Maintains an extensive library, bookstore, and Management Information Service, which includes films and cassettes. Offers courses and workshops and publishes many books under the name AMACOM.

American Marketing Association
250 S. Wacker Dr.
Chicago, IL 60606
(312) 648-0536

Chamber of Commerce of the United States
1615 H St. NW
Washington, DC 20062
(202) 659-6000
Regarded as a major advocate for business, particularly small businesses. Publishes *Nation's Business* and other magazines. Has 2,800 state and local affiliates.

The Conference Board
845 Third Ave.
New York, NY 10022
(212) 759-0900
Conducts research and publishes studies on business economics and management. Operates Work and Family Life Center, Consumer Research Center. Publishes several journals and newsletters.

Insurance Information Institute
110 William St.
New York, NY 10038
(800) 942-4242 consumer hotline
Provides information to the public about insurance issues.

National Association of Investors
1515 E. 11 Mile Rd.
Royal Oak, MI 48067
(313) 543-0612
Helps people set up investment clubs and monitors their performance.

National Association of Manufacturers
1331 Pennsylvania Avenue NW
Washington, DC 20004
(202) 637-3000
Lobbying group that represents industry's view to government. Member
companies produce 80 percent of the nation's manufactured goods. Affiliated with 150 local and state trade associations of manufacturers.

National Association of Realtors
430 N. Michigan Ave.
Chicago, IL 60611
(312) 329-8200

National Association of Securities Dealers
1735 K St. NW
Washington, DC 20006
(202) 728-8000
Regulates the sale of over-the-counter securities and operates the
NASDAQ automated quotations system.

For additional trade associations, see:

National Trade and Professional Associations of the U.S. Columbia Books.
Annual.
Lists 7,000 associations, ranging from the American Zinc Association
and the National Golf Course Owners Association to the Processed Apples
Institute. Trade associations are among the best sources of business information. While some associations provide services to their members only,
others can be extremely generous to outside researchers.

Business Library
Brooklyn Public Library
280 Cadman Plaza W.
Brooklyn, NY 11201
(718) 780-7800
Most big-city public libraries have large business collections, but this is one of the strongest.

Business, Economics, and Labor Department
Cleveland Public Library
325 Superior Ave.
Cleveland, OH 44414
(216) 623-2800

Perkins Library
Duke University
Durham, NC 27706
(919) 660-5800
Has archives of the J. Walter Thompson Co., the single most complete record of the history of advertising.

Baker Library
Graduate School of Business Administration
Harvard University
Soldiers Field Road
Boston, MA 02163
(617) 495-6405
One of the largest business collections, with important historical materials.

Business and Economics Department
Los Angeles Public Library
630 W. Fifth St.
Los Angeles, CA 90071
(213) 612-3280
Strong collections dealing with international trade, especially trade with Mexico and the Pacific Rim.

Northwestern University Library
1935 Sheridan Rd.
Evanston, IL 60208
(708) 491-7656
Business collection is integrated into main library collections.

Kresge Business Administration Library
University of Michigan
Ann Arbor, MI 48109
(313) 764-7356

Lippincott Library
The Wharton School
University of Pennsylvania
3420 Walnut St.
Philadelphia, PA 19104
(215) 898-5924

U.S. Department of Commerce Library
HCHB, Rm. 8060
14th and Constitution Ave.
Washington, DC 20230
(202) 482-3611

The 263 business schools accredited by the American Assembly of Collegiate Schools of Business have good business libraries. Corporate libraries are an excellent source of information on specific businesses and industries. For a list, see:

Directory of Special Libraries and Information Centers. 2 vols. Edited by Janice A. DeMaggio and Debra M. Kirby. Gale Research, 1993.
This directory describes more than 20,000 special libraries, many of them corporate libraries, and notes if they are open to the public. A subject index leads to libraries on advertising, banks and banking, insurance, the media, and more.

Use these headings in library catalogs:

**LC SUBJECT
HEADINGS**

Business enterprises (use instead of Companies or Firms)
Business enterprises—Finance
Business enterprises—Purchasing
Business failures
Business incubators
Business relocation
Commerce
Consolidation and merger of corporations (use instead of Mergers and
   acquisitions)
Corporate planning
Corporations

Family-owned business enterprises
Industrial management
Industrial organization
Management
Finance, Personal
Investments

For most topics, useful subheadings to consult when beginning a research project are:

—Handbooks, Manuals, etc.
—Information Services

Also consult terms for specific topics or activities, such as Accounting; Marketing; Production management; Real estate business.

For materials on types of business, use phrases ending with "industry" or "industry and trade" (e.g., Automobile industry and trade; Frozen foods industry).

OTHER SOURCES OF INFORMATION

Commercial sources of business information can be expensive, but a wide range of help is available by telephone. Consult your telephone book under state listings and contact the appropriate agencies dealing with such topics as economic development, banking, insurance, securities regulation, or corporate registration. At the local level, a regional, county, or municipal planning agency is often a good place to start. The U.S. Bureau of the Census has established a national network of state and local data organizations that provide marketing and business data on their areas. The statewide coordinating agencies for this network, called either State Data Centers or Business and Industry Data Centers, are listed in the bureau's annual *Census Catalog & Guide.* Services offered by local Chambers of Commerce vary from one community to another, but they too can be important information resources.

22

CONSUMER INFORMATION

See also: *General Reference Sources, Automobiles, The Home*

To make informed decisions on major purchases, consumers need objective evaluations of products, ratings of specific features, and price information. Consumer magazines and consumer buying guides are the best sources of this information. Comparisons of products and their features may also be found in periodicals that cater to special-interest groups; for example, *Stereo Review* publishes evaluations of stereo equipment.

If there are no published evaluations of a category of products you need, contact the appropriate trade association and ask for brochures on purchasing considerations. Ratings of energy efficiency, safety, and other features also may be available from governmental agencies such as the Environmental Protection Agency.

The reputation of a company is often a good indicator of the quality of its products. Recent reports on the firm may have appeared in newspapers or magazines (see Chapter 21, Business and Finance). Call the Better Business Bureau or the Chamber of Commerce in the city where the company is based. Phone numbers for Better Business Bureaus are listed in the *Consumer Resource Handbook,* a free publication of the federal government, listed below. This handbook has many other useful numbers for patrons who want to make their complaints known. Note, however, that the Better Business Bureau and Chambers can only reveal whether there are outstanding, unsettled formal complaints about a company. The absence of such information about the company does not necessarily mean the company is reputable.

Consumer Product Manufacturer Ratings, 1961–1990. 2 vols. Edited by David J. Faulds. Gale, 1993. Annual updates.

Provides ratings from the past thirty years for about 2,000 consumer-product manufacturers in the United States, Europe, and Japan. Products have been rated on quality, price, and value by independent testing organizations, associations, and government agencies. Ratings are provided for categories of products, such as refrigerators, not for individual models. This is a useful source for determining the reputation of a manufacturer, but it will not help the consumer select a particular model for purchase.

Consumer Sourcebook. 7th ed. Edited by Shawn Brennan. Gale, 1991.

Describes some 8,000 programs and services available to the consumer at little or no cost. They are arranged by subject; for example, food and drug safety, funerals, legal services, travel, utilities, and veterans services. Some are state or federal government programs; others are from associations or other organizations. Consumer affairs departments of corporations are also listed.

Consumers Reference Disc. (CD-ROM) National Information Services Corp. 1985–   . Quarterly.

Contains two databases: *Consumer Health and Nutrition Index* (available in print from Oryx), indexing articles from eighty magazines, and *Consumers Index* (available in print from Pierian Press), indexing 126 periodicals. *Consumers Index* lists articles evaluating items purchased for the home, office, and educational community. It is also available online with OCLC's FirstSearch.

Consumer Reports. (CD-ROM) Dialog. Quarterly. (See below.)

Full text of all articles from 1982 to the present, plus *Consumer Reports Health Letter* and *Consumer Reports Travel Letter* (1989–   ). Also available online on Dialog (File 646) and Knowledge Index (REFR6). Available on NEXIS, Prodigy, America Online, and CompuServe, 1988–   .

Available in full text on Dialog and CompuServe are magazines such as *Consumer's Research Magazine* (File 647) and *Consumers Digest* (File 647) and titles such as *High Fidelity* and *Stereo Review* that have product information.

Computer Database. (Online) Information Access, 1983–   . Weekly.

Available on Dialog (File 275), Knowledge Index, BRS, BRS/AfterDark, and CompuServe.

Microcomputer Index. (Online) Learned Information, 1981–   . Monthly.

Available on Dialog (File 233) and Knowledge Index. Also available in print.

These two databases index reviews of hardware and software in computer magazines.

For indexes to periodicals, see *Consumers Reference Disc/Consumers Index* (above) or the general periodicals indexes in Chapter 18, General Reference Sources.

PERIODICALS

Consumer Reports. 1936–   . Monthly.

The best-known and most extensive publisher of product evaluations, the magazine includes major test reports, ratings for brand and models, and general buying information for selected products. The December issue, the Buying Guide, indexes articles that have appeared during the last five years and reprints condensed versions of selected product comparisons. (See electronic version above.)

Consumer's Research Magazine. 1927–   . Monthly.

Independent investigations of consumer products. It often summarizes studies done by the U.S. government. Regular columns on gardening, food, and movies. (See electronic version above.)

Consumer Guide. 36 times/year.

Each issue, the size of a small paperback book, covers a specific topic, such as prescription drugs, appliances, investments, electronic equipment, and social security.

Consumers Digest. 1959–   . Bimonthly.

Emphasizes products for an upscale audience for whom price is not the most important consideration. Lists brand names. (See electronic version above.)

What to Buy for Business. 1987–   . Monthly.

Each issue is devoted to detailed comparisons of individual brands and models of office equipment: fax machines, photocopiers, and more.

An annual buying guide appears in many magazines including:
 Audio: October issue
 Video Review: April and October issues
 Skiing: September issue
 World Tennis: shoe guide in April issue
 Runner's World: shoe guide in April and October issues
 Bicycling: March issue
 Inc. Office Guide: separate buying guide with annual subscription
 Motor Boating and Sailing: January boat show issue

**SELECTED GUIDES
FOR SPECIFIC
PRODUCTS**

Consumer's Directory of Certified Efficiency Ratings for Residential Heating and Water Heating Equipment. Gas Appliance Manufacturers Association. Semiannual.

Covers oil-fired and electric equipment in addition to gas.

ABOS Blue Book series. Intertec. Annual.

Volumes on boat trailers, boats with inboard and outboard motors (both new and trade-in price guides), pontoon and houseboats, snowmobiles.

Orion Blue Book series. Orion Research. Annual.

Trade-in guides give new list price, retail used price, and several wholesale prices. There are volumes for audio equipment, car stereos, musical instruments, video and television, computers, cameras.

. . . Buyer's Guide. Harris Publications. Annual.

Guides to computers, fishing tackle, audio/video.

Stereo Review Presents . . . Diamandis Communications. Annual.

Buyer's guides for compact discs, stereo, and video.

Best's Insurance Reports. A. M. Best Co. Annual.

Evaluates the financial position of insurance companies. In two editions: Life-Health and Property-Casualty.

Kovel's Antiques & Collectibles Price List. By Ralph Kovel and Terry Kovel. Crown, 1993.

Appraiser-approved prices for 50,000 items. Many photographs.

McBroom's Camera Bluebook. By Michael McBroom. Amherst Media, 1993.

Sybex Computer Blue Book: The Official New and Used Computer Price Guide. Sybex. Semiannual.

Notes new and used prices for a wide range of computers, peripherals, and software.

Blue Book of Gun Values. Investment Rarities. Annual.

Average new and used prices for a wide variety of firearms, both modern and antique.

Purchaser's Guide to the Musical Industries. Music Trades Corporation. Annual.

Provides information about distributors and retailers of all types of musical instruments, equipment, and auxiliary services.

The Piano Book: Buying & Owning a New or Used Piano. 2d ed. By Larry Fine.
Brookside Press, 1990.

Covers purchase of both new and used instruments. Includes a consumer guide to new and recently made pianos and also addresses the topics of piano moving and servicing.

Many government agencies have a consumer affairs office. See the *U.S. Government Manual* for details.

Office of Consumer Affairs
Department of Health and Human Services
200 Independence Ave.
Washington, DC 20201
(202) 619-0257
Coordinates all federal activity in the area of consumer affairs.

Consumer Product Safety Commission
5401 Westbard Ave.
Bethesda, MD 20207
(301) 492-6580
Protects the public against risks of injury from consumer products. Assists consumers in evaluating safety, develops uniform safety standards, and promotes research into causes and prevention of product-related injuries.

Federal Trade Commission
Pennsylvania Ave. at Sixth St. NW
Washington, DC 20580
(202) 326-2222
Safeguards the public by preventing false or deceptive advertising, price discrimination, and the circulation of incorrect credit reports. Promotes truthful labeling of products and disclosure of accurate credit costs for consumer purchases.

Consumer's Resource Handbook. Office of Consumer Affairs, 1992.

Lists corporate consumer representatives, private resolution programs, federal, state, and local government agencies with consumer responsibilities. Tells how to write an effective complaint letter and much more.

Consumer Information Catalog. Consumer Information Center. General Services Administration. Quarterly.

Lists several hundred free and low-cost government publications, similar to the following titles:

Choosing and Using Credit Cards. Federal Trade Commission, 1991.

A Consumer's Guide to Life Insurance. Department of Agriculture, 1992.

Consumers Should Know About Service Contracts and Repair Services. Federal Trade Commission, 1989.

Family Economics Review. U.S. Department of Agriculture.
   A quarterly periodical with articles on family budgeting, living costs in various areas, home buying, and more.

Financial Institutions: Consumer Rights. Federal Financial Institutions Examination Council, 1990.

Fraud by Phone. Federal Trade Commission, 1991.
   How to protect yourself from fraudulent telemarketing.

How to Choose, Use and Care for Audio and Video Tape. Federal Trade Commission, 1990.

Protecting Your Privacy. Office of Consumer Affairs, 1990.
   How to check your credit file, medical records, have your name removed from mailing lists.

See also the Government Printing Office's *Subject Bibliography* # 2—Consumer Information.

ASSOCIATIONS

Center for Science in the Public Interest
1875 Connecticut Ave. NW
Washington, DC 20009
(202) 332-9110
Concerned with the effects of science and technology on society in the areas of food safety, nutrition issues, and alcohol advertising.

Consumer Federation of America
1424 16th St. NW
Washington, DC 20036
(202) 387-6121
A federation of national, regional, state, and local consumer groups that advocates consumer issues before Congress, regulatory agencies, and the courts.

Consumers Union of the United States
256 Washington St.
Mt. Vernon, NY 10553
(914) 667-9400
Tests and rates competing brands of products and publishes results in *Consumer Reports.*

Public Citizen
P. O. Box 19404
Washington, DC 20036
(202) 833-3000
Founded by Ralph Nader, this group lobbies, litigates, and monitors government agencies. Concerned with consumer rights, safe products, a healthful environment, safe energy, and corporate and governmental accountability.

LIBRARIES

Public libraries all have information for consumers. State university libraries supporting study in home economics and agriculture will also have good collections.

LC SUBJECT HEADINGS

Consumer materials are not to be found in only one part of the classification scheme in a library. Books are classified according to the product covered. Unless the library has set up a special consumer section, it is usually impossible to browse in just one shelf area; you will need to use the catalog. Here are some suggested headings:

Brand name products—Evaluation
Consumer goods—Evaluation
Consumer credit—Law and legislation
Consumer goods—U.S.—Testing
Consumer protection
Consumer protection—Law and legislation—U.S.
Household appliances
Household electronics
Product recall
Product safety
Quality of products

Purchasing can be a subheading under many products; e.g., Compact disc players—Purchasing, Computers—Purchasing, and Household electronics—Purchasing.

23

EDUCATION

See also: General Reference Sources

A daunting body of information awaits the parent, the teacher, the student, or the researcher interested in education. With the proliferation of computers in schools has come another tide of electronic sources of information for teachers and educational researchers.

GENERAL SOURCES OF INFORMATION

Core List of Books and Journals in Education. By Nancy Patricia O'Brien and Emily Fabiano. Oryx, 1991.

Lists 1,000 recent books and journals under such topics as Educational Reform, Higher and Continuing Education, and Multicultural Education. The books are described briefly but not the journals.

Education: A Guide to Reference and Information Sources. By Lois J. Buttlar. Libraries Unlimited, 1989.

Describes more than 900 reference books, online databases, research centers and organizations, and core periodicals. Does not note the availability of reference tools on CD-ROM. Helpful for students beginning research.

The Educator's Desk Reference: A Sourcebook of Educational Information and Research. By Melvyn N. Freed. American Council on Education and Macmillan, 1989.

Aimed at the professional educator and graduate student, this guide provides authors with lists of journals, book and software publishers. It also lists suggested software for research, standardized tests, and educational organizations. Most useful is the question-and-answer section: "Where Should I Go to Find . . ." suggesting specific reference books that will answer queries.

Encyclopedia of Educational Research. 4 vols. 6th ed. Edited by Marvin C. Alkin. Macmillan, 1992.

Articles summarizing research in various areas of education are followed by extensive bibliographies of further reading. Recent research on topics as varied as *Class Size, Critical Thinking, AIDS Education,* and *Teen Mothers, Education for* can be found here.

Places Rated Almanac: Your Guide to Finding the Best Places to Live in America. 4th ed. By David Savageau and Rick Boyer. Prentice-Hall, 1993.

Ranks 333 metropolitan areas on nine factors, one of which is schools.

ABOUT ELEMENTARY AND SECONDARY SCHOOLS

Patterson's American Education. 1904– . Educational Directories. Annual.

This directory lists state departments of education with their administrators; public, private, and Catholic secondary schools with their principals; superintendents of parochial school systems; and colleges and universities with their presidents. *Patterson's Elementary Education* (1989–) does the same thing for primary schools.

Public Schools USA: A Comparative Guide to School Districts. 2d ed. By Charles Harrison. Peterson's Guides, 1991.

This guide evaluates 404 school districts in major metropolitan areas in twenty-six states. Because the number of school districts covered is small relative to the total number in the United States, introductory material tells how to get comparable information on a local school district from a state agency. Another section gives hints on evaluating a school.

SchoolMatch. (CD-ROM) OCLC. Annual.

Evaluates public, private, and parochial schools according to twenty-two criteria, including student/teacher ratio and student performance on standardized tests. Also online as *SchoolMatch* through HRIN. Available in print as *SchoolMatch Guide to Public Schools.* Arco, 1990– (title varies: *Arco's SchoolMatch Guide to Public Schools*). You can request a search of the SchoolMatch database by calling (800) 992-5323. A SchoolMatch report card that tells how a local school rates is about $50. A search for fifteen school systems that most closely meet some defined criteria is about $100.

American Universities and Colleges. 14th ed. By the American Council on Education. De Gruyter, 1992.

In three sections: topical essays on higher education; a list of professional education programs and institutions from architecture to veterinary medicine; and descriptions of colleges with admissions and degree requirements, distinctive educational programs, student-life information, and more. More than 1,900 institutions granting baccalaureate or higher degrees are described here.

Beacon. (CD-ROM) Macmillan New Media, 1992.

This interactive program includes information on two- and four-year colleges, graduate schools, and careers. It helps students choose a college using as many as 200 criteria. An audio feature provides advice on topics such as preparing an application and visiting a school.

The College Blue Book. (CD-ROM) Macmillan, 1991.

Identifies degree-granting colleges as well as institutions offering skill training in nondegree programs. Includes information on scholarships and loans. Search "templates" (fill-in forms) allow searching by region, state, major, degree, and other criteria. Also available in print as *The College Blue Book.* 5 volumes. Macmillan. Biennial.

The College Handbook. (CD-ROM) Macmillan, 1992.

Based on the College Board's *College Handbook,* this CD-ROM has facts on 2,700 undergraduate schools and includes information for potential transfer students. Users can search over 600 options, including location, setting, field of study, and tuition. *The College Handbook* can also be searched on America Online, either by college name or by keyword. The print version of *The College Handbook* is published annually by Macmillan.

Lovejoy's College Counselor. (CD-ROM) Intermedia, 1993.

About 2,500 colleges are covered in this interactive guide, with audio and video features. The print version, *Lovejoy's College Guide,* is published by Prentice-Hall. It has an index of 500 majors and the colleges offering them, full descriptions of the colleges, and detailed information on intercollegiate sports.

Peterson's College Database. (CD-ROM) SilverPlatter.

The detailed profiles of colleges here are taken from *Peterson's Guide to Four-Year Colleges* and *Peterson's Guide to Two-Year Colleges* (Peterson's Guides, annual). The database can be searched in more than a dozen categories with hundreds of institutional characteristics. Also available online as *Peterson's College Database* on Dialog (File 214), BRS, BRS/After-

Dark, BRS Colleague, Knowledge Index (EDUC2), CompuServe, and Dow Jones News/Retrieval. *Peterson's College Selection Service* is a software version (for Apple IIs, Macintoshes, or IBM PCs) that guides students through the search and application process.

Peterson's GRADLINE. (CD-ROM) SilverPlatter, 1992.
   Based on the five-volume *Peterson's Guide to Graduate Schools* (Peterson's Guides, annual), this database is also available online on Dialog (File 273) and Knowledge Index (EDUC3).

Profiles of American Colleges on CD-ROM. Laser Resources, 1992.
   This electronic version of *Barron's Profiles of American Colleges* (Barron's, biennial) has a multimedia supplement with maps, color photographs, sound, and animation.

Graduate Scholarship Book. 2d ed. By Daniel Cassidy. Prentice-Hall, 1990.

How and Where to Get Scholarships and Financial Aid for College. By Robert L. Bailey. Arco. Annual.

The Scholarship Book. 3d ed. By Daniel J. Cassidy and Michael J. Alves. Prentice-Hall, 1991.

Scholarships, Fellowships and Loans. 9th ed. Edited by Debra M. Kirby. Gale, 1992.

ABOUT SCHOLARSHIPS AND FINANCIAL AID

A-V Online. (CD-ROM) SilverPlatter, 1964–   . Semiannual.
   Over 300,000 citations to nonprint educational materials for all levels, from preschool through graduate school. Lists films, filmstrips, audio and videotapes, slides, phonograph records, software, and CD-ROMs. Also online as *A-V Online,* 1964–   , updated quarterly from Dialog (File 46), Knowledge Index (EDUC4), and Human Resources Information Network. Partially based upon the print titles *NICEM Film & Video Finder* and *NICEM Audiocasette Finder.*

OTHER ELECTRONIC SOURCES

   ERIC (Educational Resources Information Center) is a service of the U.S. Department of Education. The two ERIC databases are available on CD-ROM, online, and in print form with more than 750,000 citations to journal and report literature. They cover all fields in education: adult, vocational, teacher education, handicapped, disadvantaged, gifted, higher education, early childhood, counseling, tests and measurements, and all academic disciplines (reading, math, etc.). The two databases are:

Current Index to Journals in Education (CIJE).
Abstracts of articles from 750 education journals.

Resources in Education (RIE).
Abstracts of hundreds of thousands of research reports, including conference papers, curriculum materials, other unpublished documents of interest to educators.
These two files are available on CD-ROM from two companies and updated quarterly: *DIALOG OnDisc: ERIC.* UMI. 1966–   , and *ERIC on SilverPlatter,* 1966–   . These files are also online through CompuServe, Dialog (File 1), Knowledge Index (EDUC1), BRS, BRS/AfterDark, BRS Colleague, OCLC FirstSearch from 1966–   . Updated monthly. The print versions of *CIJE* (Oryx, 1969–   ) and *RIE* (U.S. Government Printing Office, 1966–   ) are updated monthly.

To search ERIC most efficiently, whether on CD-ROM, online, or in print, use the *Thesaurus of ERIC Descriptors* (12th ed., Oryx, 1990) to find the appropriate subject headings.

ERIC Microfiche Collection contains the full text of more than 300,000 educational documents indexed in *Resources in Education* (NOT the journal articles indexed in *CIJE*). Collections are located at approximately 825 libraries and agencies and are open to the public. Call ACCESS ERIC for locations (800/USE-ERIC).

Education Index. (CD-ROM) H. W. Wilson, 1983–   . Updated quarterly.
Indexes approximately 350 English-language periodicals and yearbooks. As with all Wilsondisc products, you can dial up for the most recently added citations at no extra charge. Online 1983–   through Wilsonline (updated twice a week), and OCLC's FirstSearch (updated monthly). In print, 1929–   , updated monthly.

Exceptional Child Education Resources. (Online) 1966–   . Updated monthly.
Compiled by the Council for Exceptional Children, this index contains more than 170,000 citations to published and unpublished materials on gifted and disabled students, including the emotionally disturbed, speech-impaired, learning-disabled, and physically handicapped. Online through BRS, BRS/AfterDark, BRS Colleague. Also available in print, 1966–   , updated quarterly.

Mental Measurements Yearbook. (CD-ROM) The Burros Institute of Mental Measurements of the University of Nebraska-Lincoln, 1993.

Contains descriptive information and critical reviews of more than 1,800 English-language standardized educational, personality, vocational aptitude, and psychological tests. Entries give the amount of time required to administer the tests, plus publisher, price, intended population, and reliability and validity data. Online with BRS, BRS/AfterDark, BRS Colleague, updated monthly. Also available in print as the *Mental Measurements Yearbook*. 11th ed. The Burros Institute of Mental Measurements of the University of Nebraska-Lincoln, 1992.

ProDirect: Education. (CD-ROM) UMI.

This database from Market Data Retrieval lists 3,500 colleges, more than 110,000 schools, fifty state departments of education, and 15,000 public libraries. Includes names of administrators, enrollment and budget data, and special services offered. Also available as *The Educational Directory Online* through Dialog (File 511), with semiannual updates.

PsycLIT. (CD-ROM) SilverPlatter, 1974–   . Quarterly.

Abstracts of articles from more than 1,300 psychology journals representing professional and scientific literature from fifty countries. Compiled by the American Psychological Association. Also available online as *PsycInfo*, 1967–   , with monthly updates. Available on BRS, BRS/AfterDark, BRS Colleague, Data-Star, Dialog (File 11), Knowledge Index (PSYC1), OCLC FirstSearch. Also available in print form as *Psychological Abstracts*, 1927–   , updated monthly.

SOURCES ON CONSUMER SERVICES

On America Online

- College Board Online (lists upcoming test dates and contains the full text of *The College Handbook*).
- Articles from the Association for Supervision and Curriculum Development's journal, *Educational Leadership*.
- ACCESS ERIC, a database with brief consumer articles (e.g., "As Your Child's First Teacher: Helping Children Learn Geography") that are followed by a list of ERIC documents on the topic. There is also a message board where you can communicate with the ERIC staff and find out where you can have an ERIC search done locally. The ERIC Library features reports that can be downloaded, and the Product Catalog lists publications for purchase.

On CompuServe

- OERI Electronic Bulletin Boards: Contains information for education professionals from the U.S. Office of Educational Research and Improvement. This BBS can also be dialed up directly: **202-219-2010/2011.**
- Science Education Forum: Ideas for science experiments, newsletters, software reviews, and software that can be downloaded.

- Educational Research Forum: Sponsored by the American Educational Research Association. Carries news and information on educational research. Users can submit research reports and comments to this BBS.
- Educators Forum: Full-text documents and BBS, stresses the use of computers in education. Contains a directory of members.

On Delphi

- Schole: Information service for education professionals in health and special education. Contains the full text of several journals, news, announcements of upcoming conferences and courses.

On GEnie

- Education RoundTable: Forum to exchange information and ideas. Software libraries to download, real-time conferences.

On NEXIS

- Education Update: Full-text newsletter on policy and trends in U.S. education. Covers education reform, congressional activities. Quarterly.

On NewsNet

- Education Daily: Full-text journal, covering state and federal policies, legislation, and funding. News of court cases, civil rights issues, research and administration.

On the Internet

- News Groups: k12.ed covers art, health/physical education, math, music, science, social studies and special topics. k12.lang covers German-English, Spanish-English, French and Russian.
  Databases on the Internet include:
- ERIC Digests Archive: Short reports of 1,500 words or less with overviews of education topics. Access via **WAIS ERIC-archive.src** and **WAIS eric-digest.src.**
- Educational Leadership: The Association for Supervision and Curriculum Development has put two years' worth of articles from its journal, *Educational Leadership,* online. Access via **WAIS ascd-education.src.**
- Kidsnet: This is a list to foster networking for children and educators. To join, send a message to **kidsnet-request@vms.cis.pitt.edu.** Access via **WAIS kidsnet.src.**

PERIODICALS

Adult Learning. 1989–   . 8/year.
 Published by the American Association for Adult and Continuing Education, this journal reports practical applications of research and innovative instructional strategies.

Change. 1968–   . Bimonthly.
 Broad coverage of issues in higher education.

Chronicle of Higher Education. 1966–   . Weekly.
   Balanced attention to new trends in higher education and the political aspects of the college scene.

Current Contents/Social & Behavioral Sciences. 1961–   . Weekly.
   Reprints the title pages of current issues of more than 1,000 journals. There is a section on education in each issue. Copies of articles can be ordered for a fee.

Education Digest. 1934–   . 9/year.
   Reprints and abridges selected articles from other periodicals, mostly journals covering K-12 education.

Education Week. 1981–   . Weekly.
   This tabloid is subtitled "American education's newspaper of record."

Educational Leadership. 1943–   . 8/year.
   Looks at school issues from an administrator's viewpoint; current articles are on America Online and the Internet.

Instructor. 1891–   . 9/year.
   Features suggested activities for the elementary school classroom and explains approaches that have worked for other teachers.

Phi Delta Kappan. 1915–   . 10/year.
   Short semipopular articles on general education topics. Published by the education honor society.

Young Children. 1944–   . Bimonthly.
   For teachers of children from birth through age eight.

Digest of Education Statistics. 1962–   . National Center for Education Statistics. Annual.
   Provides data from both government and private sources on education from kindergarten through graduate school.

GOVERNMENT PUBLICATIONS

1988–1989 OERI Publications Catalog. U.S. Department of Education. Office of Educational Research and Improvement, 1989.
   This list of materials, many of which are free, is arranged under the headings: Elementary and Secondary Education, Postsecondary Education, General Education Statistics, Libraries, and Miscellaneous.

United States Department of Education Publications. U.S. Department of Education, 1990.

Lists publications on a wide range of topics, including civil rights, computer education, Native American education, special education, and women's equity.

What Works: Research About Teaching and Learning. 2d ed. U.S. Department of Education, 1987.

Lists fifty-nine research findings about what works in education. Topics covered include memorization, cultural literacy, rigorous courses, acceleration, and work experience.

See the following *Subject Bibliographies* from the Government Printing Office for lists of recent government publications on education:

#196—*Elementary and Secondary Education*
#110—*Vocational and Career Education*
#217—*Higher Education*
#085—*Financial Aid to Students*
#137—*Teachers and Teaching Methods*
#214—*Adult Education*
#83—*Educational Statistics*
#88—*Environmental Education*

GOVERNMENT AGENCIES

ACCESS ERIC
1600 Research Blvd.
Rockville, MD 20850
(800) USE-ERIC (800/873-3742)

Office of Educational Research and Improvement
Department of Education
555 New Jersey Ave. NW
Washington, DC 20208-5641
(202) 401-1576

In many states, the state board of education or state department of public instruction produces a school report card and many other publications on education in the state. See *Patterson's American Education* for the addresses of state boards.

ASSOCIATIONS

American Association of University Professors (AAUP)
1012 14th St., Suite 500
Washington, DC 20005
(202) 737-5900

scholars and promote higher education and research.

The College Board (College Entrance Examination Board)
45 Columbus Ave.
New York, NY 10023
(212) 713-8000
A national association of colleges, universities, secondary schools, school systems, and educational associations and institutions. It assists students who wish to attend college through guidance, admissions, placement, financial aid, credit by examination, and other related services. See College Board files on America Online.

Educational Research Service
2000 Clarendon Blvd.
Arlington, VA 22201
(703) 243-2100
ERS serves as both a national source and a clearinghouse for school research and information. By compiling, analyzing, and sharing information that is essential to effective decision making, ERS assists local school districts in both day-to-day operations and long-range planning.

Educational Testing Service (ETS)
Rosedale Rd.
Princeton, NJ 08541
(609) 921-9000
This service provides a number of testing programs (e.g., SAT, GRE, GMAT) and services for admissions, selection, placement, and guidance for educational objectives as well as occupational licensing and certification.

EPIE Institute (Educational Products Information Exchange)
P. O. Box 839
Water Mill, NY 11976
(516) 728-9100
Affiliated with Consumers Union, EPIE analyzes and collects data on instructional materials, educational software, and curriculum development. Publishes *TESS, The Educational Software Selector*, 1987–   .

International Reading Association
800 Barksdale Rd.
P. O. Box 8139
Newark, DE 19714
(302) 731-1600

IRA seeks to improve the quality of reading instruction at all education levels.

National Education Association (NEA)
1201 16th St. NW
Washington, DC 20036
(202) 833-4000
A national organization of teachers, administrators, and other professionals in education. The wide variety of services includes professional publications, research on professional problems and issues, and assistance to members with curriculum and instructional problems. NEA's services are available on America Online: Subscribers can read current articles from its journal, communicate with staff, and download material from its library.

National Society for the Study of Education
5835 Kimbark Ave.
Chicago, IL 60637
(312) 702-1582
A professional society of teachers and officers in school systems and universities that promotes investigation and discussion of educational problems. Publishes a yearbook and a series on contemporary educational issues.

Phi Delta Kappa
Eighth and Union
Box 789
Bloomington, IN 47402
(812) 339-1156
Professional honorary fraternity in education. Publishes books, monographs, papers, proceedings of symposia, the monthly *Phi Delta Kappan*, and an ongoing series of more than 300 short pamphlets in the Fastbacks series, each treating a current topic in education.

LIBRARIES   Any university that grants graduate degrees in education will have a good collection of materials on contemporary education in the United States. The libraries listed below have strong collections of historical materials on education or materials on one aspect of education.

Bank Street College of Education Library
610 W. 112th St.
New York, NY 10025
(212) 663-7200
Specializes in elementary education.

Gutman Library
Harvard University Graduate School of Education
6 Appian Way
Cambridge, MA 02138
(617) 495-4225

Cubberly Education Library
Stanford University
Stanford, CA 94305-6004
(415) 723-2121

Milbank Memorial Library
Teachers College
Columbia University
525 W. 120th St.
New York, NY 10027
(212) 678-3494
The largest special collection on education. Has many historical collections of eighteenth- and nineteenth-century materials.

Education Library
University of Illinois
100 Main Library
Urbana, IL 61801
(217) 333-2305

Education Library
George Peabody College for Teachers
Vanderbilt University
Box 325
Nashville, TN 37203
(615) 322-8095

Reavis Reading Centers

There are almost 3,500 centers, most of them in academic and public libraries, that contain the Phi Delta Kappa Fastbacks collection and other monographs. For locations, contact: Phi Delta Kappa Educational Foundation, 8th and Union, P. O. Box 789, Bloomington, IN 47402; (812) 339-1156.

MICROFICHE COLLECTIONS

ERIC Microfiche. See above under Other Electronic Sources.

Kraus Curriculum Development Library. Contains over 4,900 curriculum guides in every subject area at elementary and secondary levels. Held by some university libraries. Published by Kraus International, Route 100, Millwood, NY 10546; (800) 223-8323.

Tests in Microfiche. A collection of unpublished educational and psychological tests on microfiche available in many university libraries. Published by Educational Testing Service (ETS), Rosedale Rd., Princeton, NJ 08541; (609) 921-9000.

William S. Gray Reading Research Collection. Microfiche copies of the collection of articles and scholarly papers collected by Professor Gray at the University of Chicago and later updated by the Burrows Institute. Available to the public at a few major universities. You can get more information from William S. Gray Reading Research Collection, Alvina Treut Burrows Institute, P. O. Box 49, Manhasset, NY 11030; (516) 869-8457.

LC SUBJECT HEADINGS

To find books in library catalogs, here are some suggested subject headings:

Day care centers

Early childhood education

Education—Costs

Education—Curricula

Education—History

Education, Elementary—Parent participation

Education, Higher

Education, Preschool

Education, Secondary

Group Work in Education (use instead of Cooperative Learning)

Physical education and training

Reading

Schools

Student aid (use instead of Financial aid)

Students

Teaching

Universities and colleges

Education is also a subheading under the names of special populations. For example, Blind—Education and Children of migrant laborers—Education.

And Don't Forget

- Public or private universities offering graduate education programs (master's or doctorate).
- Local school district board of education or school superintendent. These may be sources of local data to integrate into research studies.

24

THE
ENVIRONMENT

See also: *General Reference Sources, Science and Technology*

With the increased awareness of environmental hazards has come an explosion in the amount of information available on this issue. The field known as environmental studies draws on research from many different disciplines, including political science, economics, biology, and geology. Information from these disciplines falls into two broad categories: *Public policy* includes government initiatives as well as actions taken by citizens to intervene in environmental issues. *Ecology* studies the relationships between organisms and their environment; it can also draw on scientific information from other disciplines dealing with physical processes.

Research on environmental topics can be approached from either a public policy or an ecological perspective; sometimes it includes both. Many books on the subject have been published in the last two decades, and numerous magazines cover environmental topics. If an environmental issue is especially important in a particular city or region of the country, then local newspapers will be an important information source.

Local and national organizations such as the Sierra Club can provide information on a host of environmental topics. Many states have Public Interest Research Groups that monitor environmental issues, as do community groups concerned with local environmental issues.

Encyclopedia of Environmental Information Sources. Edited by S. Balachandran. Gale, 1993.

GENERAL REFERENCE SOURCES

This guide to more than 800 environmental topics lists indexes, yearbooks, encyclopedias, online databases, periodicals, research centers, statistical sources, and associations. Some of the topics covered include acid rain, carcinogens, endangered species, global warming, microwave energy, and recycling.

Environmental Hazards: Marine Pollution. By Martha Gorman. ABC-Clio, 1993.

This handbook discusses research resources on legislation, detection, and abatement of marine pollution. Other titles in this series include *Environmental Hazards: Toxic Waste and Hazardous Materials* (1991), *Environmental Hazards: Radioactive Materials and Wastes* (1990), and *Environmental Hazards: Air Pollution* (1989), all by E. Willard Miller and Ruby M. Miller.

The Green Encyclopedia. By Irene Franck and David Brownstone. Prentice-Hall, 1992.

Information on technical terms, endangered species, pesticides, environmental disasters, laws, and parks and wildlife preserves. Also lists organizations and government agencies useful for the environmental activist. "Information and Action Guides" follow major issues. Appendixes list other sources of information.

Gale Environmental Sourcebook: A Guide to Organizations, Agencies, and Publications. Edited by Karen Hill and Annette Piccirelli. Gale, 1992.

Lists contacts at federal and state agencies, books and videos, library collections, corporate environmental contacts, environmental products, and other sources of information.

A paperback similar in scope that will be useful for home libraries is *The Environmental Sourcebook* by Edith Carol Stein (Lyons & Burford, 1992). It lists books and periodicals, organizations, and grant-making foundations.

The Nature Directory: A Guide to Environmental Organizations. By Susan D. Lanier-Graham. Walker, 1991.
Your Resource Guide to Environmental Organizations. Edited by John Seredich. Smiling Dolphins Press, 1991.

These paperback directories will be useful for environmental researchers or activists who need a "portable" list of organizations.

World Directory of Environmental Organizations. 4th ed. California Institute of Public Affairs, 1992.

Comprehensive list of organizations in the United States and foreign countries.

Statistical Record of the Environment. Edited by Arsen J. Darnay. Gale, 1992.

Provides more than 800 charts, tables, and graphs with data on the environment from federal government sources and from environmental organizations.

Atlas of the Environment. Edited by Geoffrey Lean. Prentice-Hall, 1990.
Atlas of United States Environmental Issues. By Robert J. Mason and Mark T. Mattson. Macmillan, 1991.
Gaia: An Atlas of Planet Management. Edited by Norman Myers. Anchor Press, 1984.

Sponsored by the World Wildlife Fund, *Atlas of the Environment* packs an amazing amount of information into colorful and informative maps. It focuses on the impact of human populations on natural environments and addresses everything from education statistics to freshwater pollution. *Atlas of United States Environmental Issues* is a handsome oversized book that shows environmental statistics on maps, charts, tables, and diagrams. *Gaia: An Atlas of Planet Management,* aimed at a more popular audience, uses artwork and charts to convey basic information about the environment and humankind's impact on it.

State of the World: A Worldwatch Institute Report on Progress Toward a Sustainable Society. Norton. Annual.

A yearly report summarizing recent developments in global environmental issues.

ELECTRONIC
SOURCES

Applied Science & Technology Index. (CD-ROM) H. W. Wilson, 1983–   . Monthly.

Indexes 391 journals in such fields as environmental engineering, waste management, and petroleum and gas. Available on CD-ROM with abstracts as *Wilson Applied Science & Technology Abstracts.* Also online with Wilsonline, 1983–   ; in print, 1958–   , updated monthly.

Biological & Agricultural Index. (CD-ROM) H. W. Wilson, 1983–   . Monthly.

Indexes 225 key journals in agriculture and the life sciences covering such disciplines as ecology, environmental science, and forestry. Also available online with OCLC FirstSearch and Wilsonline, 1983–   ; in print, 1964–   , updated monthly.

General Science Index. (CD-ROM) H. W. Wilson, 1984–   . Updated monthly.

Indexes 140 science periodicals geared to students and nonspecialists. Subjects covered include the environment and conservation and oceanography. CD-ROM versions of these indexes can dial up Wilsonline for the most recent citations. *Wilson General Science Abstracts* is a CD-ROM version with abstracts. Also available online through Wilsonline, 1984–   , and OCLC FirstSearch, and in print since 1978, updated monthly.

Environmental Periodicals Bibliography. (CD-ROM) Environmental Studies Institute, 1972–   . Semiannual.

This bibliography reproduces the tables of contents of over 300 periodicals on environmental topics. It covers social, political, and scientific aspects of environmental science. This source is available online through Dialog as *EPB Online* and in print, 1972–   .

ENVIRO/ENERGYLINE Abstracts Plus. (CD-ROM) Bowker, 1971–   . Quarterly.

In addition to abstracts of articles and government documents, this compact disc includes conference proceedings, patents, and unpublished literature. Many of the items are too technical for laypeople. This source is available online in *Enviroline* through Dialog (File 40) and ORBIT; and *Energyline* from Dialog (File 69) and ORBIT, both updated monthly. All indexed documents can be ordered from Bowker. Based on the print products *Environment Abstracts*, 1971–   , *Energy Abstracts*, 1971–   , and *Acid Rain Abstracts*, 1986–   .

Online Sources   The amount of information available over computer networks is staggering. Researchers on the environment are fortunate to have an excellent guide to electronic sources: *Ecolinking: Everyone's Guide to Online Environmental Information* by Don Rittner (Peachpit Press, 1992). In his book, Rittner describes global networks like the Internet, electronic bulletin boards, and commercial services such as America Online and The WELL. He also discusses online databases and CD-ROMs. High-priority reading for the environmental researcher with a computer and modem, this guide will also be useful to researchers in allied disciplines.

EPA National Online Library System

This library catalog lists thousands of EPA documents and can be searched by title, author, and keyword. It is available through the Internet. **Telnet 134.67.180.1.**

EcoGopher at University of Virginia

Dedicated to the collection and dissemination of environmental information, this database includes book and periodical bibliographies, lists of environmental organizations, electronic newsletters, and conference reports. To access this server through the Internet, **telnet ecosys.drdr. virginia.edu.** Log in **gopher.**

Other Internet groups include:

- BIOSPH-L—Anything related to the biosphere, pollution, ecology, habitats, climate, etc. To subscribe, send a message to **listserv%ubvms. bitnet@vml.nodak.edu.**

- ENVBEH-L—Environmental behavior, including environmental stress, human response to artificial and natural settings. Subscribe to **listserv%polygraf.bitnet@mitvma.mit.edu.**

EcoNet: The Ecology Network
A network devoted to environmental concerns. It offers electronic mail services, access to environmental databases, and discussion groups. It is available on the Internet for $3 per hour **(telnet igc.org),** or one can subscribe for $10 per month and dial up directly. Over 200 environmental groups, such as Greenpeace and the Sierra Club, maintain online discussion groups. There are also conferences on such topics as acid rain, population issues, and wind energy. For more information, contact: EcoNet, Institute for Global Communications, 18 De Boom Street, San Francisco, CA 94107; (415) 546-1794.

- America Online: The Environmental Forum
- CompuServe: The Network Earth Forum, The Good Earth Forum

Some examples of bulletin boards:
- EPA Clean-Up Information Bulletin Board: For hazardous waste cleanup professionals. **(301) 566-4699.**
- Eco Systems BBS: Files on recycling and composting, job listings, and public domain MS-DOS software. **(412) 244-0675.**

RACHEL (Remote Access Chemical Hazards Electronic Library): Abstracts from newspapers and magazines, information on corporate waste handlers, and fact sheets on chemicals. Call the Helpline at (202) 328-1119 for a user's guide and free account number.

Buzzworm. 1988–   . Bimonthly.

PERIODICALS

Provides an independent perspective on environmental topics. "Econews" feature in each issue lists environmental publications; "Connections" lists volunteer opportunities and environmental jobs. Each issue has a special directory (e.g., outfitters, environmental organizations).

Environment. 1958–   . 10 times/year.
Published by a nonprofit foundation, *Environment* covers a broad range of environmental issues from a scientific and a public policy perspective.

Topics include conservation, legislation, and scientific advancements. One of the clearest, most up-to-date sources of information on a broad range of environmental issues.

EPA Journal. 1975–   . Bimonthly.
Covers areas in which the Environmental Protection Agency is working, dealing with both government and private efforts to solve environmental problems. Stresses the regulators' point of view. If you want to know what the government says it intends to do about a problem, this is the place to look.

Garbage: The Practical Journal for the Environment. 1989–   . Bimonthly.
Practical information for the "green" home. Articles on composting, water-saving toilets, energy-efficient cars. Reviews environmentally sound products and services.

National Wildlife. 1962–   . Bimonthly.
Published by the National Wildlife Federation. Covers U.S. wildlife and a broad range of environmental issues.

Sierra. 1893–   . Bimonthly.
Published by the Sierra Club. Includes articles on public lands, pollution, wildlife, some fiction. Lists Sierra Club-sponsored trips. Beautiful photography.

Audubon. 1899–   . Bimonthly.
Published by the National Audubon Society, one of the largest and oldest conservation organizations in the United States. Has articles on a range of environmental and conservation issues. Strong coverage of wildlife, especially birds.

Worldwatch. 1988–   . Bimonthly.
The Worldwatch Institute is a nonprofit institute that advocates global solutions to environmental problems. Its magazine contains articles on current environmental trends around the world, including deforestation, soil loss, species extinction, and climate change. Links between economics and environmental policies are emphasized. This magazine is one of the best sources on current environmental issues.

GOVERNMENT AGENCIES

Environmental Protection Agency
401 M St. SW
Washington, DC 20460
(202) 382-2096

Charged with controlling and abating pollution in air, water, solid waste, pesticides, radiation, and toxic substances. Sponsors research, issues many publications. See *EPA Journal* (above), EPA National Online Library System (above), and *Access EPA* (below).

Forest Service
Department of Agriculture
P. O. Box 96090
Washington, DC 20090-6090
(202) 447-3760

Responsible for providing a sustained flow of renewable resources: wood, water, wilderness, wildlife, fisheries. Administers National Forests, conducts forest research.

National Oceanographic and Atmospheric Administration
Department of Commerce
Washington, DC 20230
(202) 377-2985

Responsible for management, research, and services related to the protection and use of living marine resources and their habitats, the atmosphere, and space environment. Conducts satellite observations of the environment. Makes ocean research grants.

U.S. Fish and Wildlife Service
Department of the Interior
1848 C St. NW
Washington, DC 20240
(202) 208-3171

Responsible for migrating birds, endangered species, wildlife law enforcement, surveillance of pesticides, and the environmental impact assessment of dams and other structures.

Access EPA. Environmental Protection Agency. Annual.

 This handy guide contains descriptions of EPA documents, online databases, and the more than two dozen EPA libraries. A number of EPA bulletin boards and clearinghouses may be accessed by modem, and this directory gives information you will need on the procedures for obtaining access.

EPA Publications Bibliography. 1970–76, 1977–83, and 1984–90. NTIS.

 Contains abstracts and indexes for all documents published by the EPA and related organizations. All entries are indexed by keyword, author, and title. Current installments of the bibliography are published four times a

**GOVERNMENT
PUBLICATIONS**

year as the *EPA Publications Bibliography: Quarterly Abstracts Bulletin,
1977–   .* Any report listed in any volume of this bibliography may be
ordered directly from the National Technical Information Service (NTIS).
While many EPA publications are technical, there are also pamphlets
aimed at the consumer: *Recycling Used Oil* (1991), *Citizen's Guide to Pesticides* (1989), *Homebuyer's Guide to Environmental Hazards* (1990).

Other relevant government publications include:

Environmental Trends. Council on Environmental Quality. 1990.
Provides an overview of changes in land use in the United States and the
effect on environmental issues.

Recognition and Management of Pesticide Poisonings. Environmental Protection Agency. 1989.
For health professionals.

Water Quality Indicators Guide: Surface Waters. Department of Agriculture
Soil and Conservation Service. 1990.

See also the following *Subject Bibliographies* from the Government Printing Office:
#46—Air Pollution
#238—Conservation
#306—Energy Conservation and Research Technology
#305—Energy Policy, Issues, and Programs
#88—Environmental Education and Protection
#63—Noise Abatement
#9—Solar Energy
#86—Trees, Forest Products and Forest Management
#50—Water Pollution and Water Resources
#116—Wildlife Management

ASSOCIATIONS   There are close to 100 environmental organizations in the United States.
The following addresses are for the national headquarters of each organization; they may have state or local chapters as well. For additional associations, see one of the directories of organizations listed above under General
Reference Sources.

American Rivers
801 Pennsylvania Ave. SE
Washington, DC 20003
(202) 547-6900
Its goal is the preservation of the remaining free-flowing rivers in the
United States.

Clean Water Action
1320 Eighteenth St. NW
Washington, DC 20036
(202) 457-1286
Advocacy and education on water pollution.

Environmental Defense Fund
257 Park Ave. South
New York, NY 10010
(212) 505-2100
Public education, litigation, and legislation advocacy on a wide range of issues.

Greenpeace U.S.A.
1436 U St. NW
Washington, DC 20009
(202) 462-1177
This group undertakes nonviolent protest to aid endangered species. Monitors conditions of environmental concern, including toxic waste dumping. Online with EcoNet (see above).

National Audubon Society
950 Third Ave.
New York, NY 10022
(212) 832-3200
Interested in ecology, energy, and conservation of natural resources. Conducts research programs to aid endangered species. Sponsors ecology camps and workshops for adults and children.

Nature Conservancy
1815 N. Lynn St.
Arlington, VA 22209
(703) 841-5300
Preserves biological diversity by protecting natural lands.

Sierra Club
730 Polk St.
San Francisco, CA 94109
(415) 776-2211
Concerned with nature and its interrelationships to man. Promotes protection and conservation of natural resources and attempts to influence public policy. Maintains a library. Local chapters sponsor outings, films, and conferences. Online with EcoNet (see above).

Worldwatch Institute
1776 Massachusetts Ave. NW
Washington, DC 20036
(202) 452-1999
Involved in global problem solving, including issues of the environment, renewable energy, family planning. Sponsors research on global warming.

LIBRARIES   Because environmental topics are so popular, it should be possible to find a good deal of information at most public and university libraries. However, some research may require the use of a specialized library collection. Anyone with Internet access can connect to the EPA National Online Library. All the documents in this library can be ordered through the National Technical Information Service (NTIS), 5285 Port Royal Rd., Springfield, VA 22161; (703) 487-4650. Other specialized libraries include:

Solar Energy Collection
Daniel E. Noble Science and Engineering Library
Arizona State University
Tempe, AZ 85287
(602) 965-7210
Also maintains collections in the areas of wind energy and ocean thermal energy conversion.

Minneapolis Public Library
Science and Technology Division
300 Nicollet Mall
Minneapolis, MN 55401
(612) 372-6500
Its Environmental Conservation Library has a strong collection on solar energy.

Forestry Library
260 Mulford Hall
University of California, Berkeley
Berkeley, CA 94720
(415) 642-2936

Forestry Library
Yale University
205 Prospect St.
New Haven, CT 06511
(203) 432-5132

One of the oldest and largest forestry libraries. Forestry is now construed broadly to include environmental studies and natural resources management.

F. Franklin Moon Library
State University of New York College of Environmental Science and Forestry
Syracuse, NY 13210
(315) 470-6715

Use these headings in library catalogs:

Air—Pollution	Environmental protection
Air quality management	Environmental policy
Conservation of natural resources	Green marketing
Deforestation	Hazardous wastes
Ecology	Human ecology
Environmental biotechnology	Pollution
Environmental health	Population biology
Environmental law	Water—Pollution

The subheading Environmental aspects can appear under industries, machines, chemicals, etc. For example:

Automobiles—Environmental aspects
Copper—Environmental aspects

Transcripts: With the growing awareness of environmental problems has come an increase in television coverage. Many television broadcasts—including national news, public television documentaries, and Cable News Network shows—are available in transcript form. You can order them directly, using the address the television program indicates, or you can get them from online sources, including CARL, DataTimes, and NEXIS, which are among the databases that list transcripts of television programming.

25

FILM

See also: *General Reference Sources, Television*

Film may be studied from a business perspective, as a technology, and for its aesthetic, sociological, and political content, among many other approaches, but it is impossible to ignore the role of motion pictures in American culture. Studies of the work of a director or performer or type of film are among the most popular on campuses. Faculty seek information on motion pictures for teaching purposes. Individual film buffs pursue information ranging from the most arcane production credits to the question of which movie to see this weekend. For all these research interests, the menu of resources is a rich one.

GENERAL SOURCES OF INFORMATION

On the Screen: A Film, Television, and Video Research Guide. By Kim N. Fisher. Libraries Unlimited, 1986.

This critically annotated bibliography of important English-language reference works serves as a guide to the literature of motion pictures and television. While the emphasis is on books published after 1960, it does include important works published since the 1920s. Includes chapters on core periodicals, research centers and archives, and societies and associations. Also lists catalogs of scripts and screenplays. Excellent starting place for researchers unfamiliar with the range of film reference literature.

Popular Entertainment Research: How to Do It and How to Use It. By Barbara J. Pruett. Scarecrow Press, 1992.

Lists print and electronic sources and organizations useful for the study of film and other forms of entertainment.

Celebrity Sources: Guide to Biographical Information About Famous People in Showbusiness and Sports Today. By Ronald Ziegler. Garland, 1990.

Annotated bibliography of reference books, collective biographies, periodicals, computerized databases, commercial services, and fan clubs that have information about contemporary stars, plus lists of individual biographies of about 450 show business and sports celebrities.

The Film Encyclopedia. 2d ed. By Ephraim Katz. HarperCollins, 1994.

Over 7,000 entries on individuals and topics (e.g., color cinematography, sound, wide-screen processes). Includes biographical information on directors, producers, screenwriters, composers, cinematographers, art directors, editors, stars, and featured players.

The Encyclopedia of Film. James Monaco and the Editors of Baseline. Perigee Books, 1991.

Biographical entries on 3,000 filmmakers, with emphasis on contemporary artists. International in scope. "All the filmographical and biographical data have been distilled from BASELINE'S databases" (see below).

International Dictionary of Films and Filmmakers. 2d ed. 5 vols. Edited by Christopher Lyon and Susan Doll. St. James Press, 1990–93.

Volume 1, *Films,* is a comprehensive guide to approximately 500 of the "most widely-studied films." Entries include production and cast credits, production and release dates, major awards, and a brief critical essay. Bibliographies for each film provide citations to scripts, books, critical articles, and reviews. *Directors/Filmmakers, Actors and Actresses,* and *Writers and Production Artists* (Volumes 2–4) present a wide spectrum of creative artists from the international film community. Each entry includes biographical data, film credits, bibliography, and critical essay. Volume 5 is the *Title Index.* Excellent starting place for biographical or individual film research.

Sourcebook for the Performing Arts: A Directory of Collections, Resources, Scholars, and Critics in Theatre, Film and Television. By Anthony Slide and others. Greenwood Press, 1988.

Lists libraries with important collections about film.

International Directory of Film and TV Documentation Centres. Edited by Frances Thorpe. St. James Press, 1988.

Directory of 104 archives (not collections of film) belonging to the Fédération Internationale des Archives du Film (FIAF), a worldwide organization dedicated to preserving our motion picture heritage.

Film Review Index. Volume 1: 1882–1949; Volume 2: 1950–1985. By Patricia King Hanson and Stephen L. Hanson. Oryx Press, 1986–87.

Indexes reviews of approximately 8,000 features selected as "films which have, over the years, established themselves as being of the highest interest to researchers and students." Includes citations to reviews in scholarly journals, trade publications, popular magazines, and book chapters.

The New York Times Film Reviews, 1913–1968. Arno Press, 1970.
Supplement, 1969–1970–   . Times Books, 1970–   .
Compilation of reviews arranged by date of publication as they appeared in *The New York Times.* Updated biennially.

Variety's Film Reviews, 1907–   . Bowker, 1982–   .
Compilation of reviews as they appeared in *Variety.* Updated biennially.

The American Film Institute Catalog of Motion Pictures Produced in the United States: Feature Films, 1911–1920. 2 vols. Edited by Patricia King Hanson. University of California Press, 1988.
The American Film Institute Catalog of Motion Pictures Produced in the United States: Feature Films, 1921–1930. 2 vols. Edited by Kenneth W. Munden. Bowker, 1979.
The American Film Institute Catalog of Motion Pictures, 1961–1970. 2 vols. Edited by Richard P. Krafsur. Bowker, 1976.

The first three parts of a set that is to cover all American films. Feature films are defined as films of four reels or more. Entries include title, credits, date of release, physical description, literary source (when known), and detailed plot synopsis. Credits (personal and corporate names), subject, and literary source indexes. The volumes covering 1931 to 1940 are to be published next. The most authoritative work of its kind.

The Motion Picture Guide, 1927–1984. 12 vols. By Jay Robert Nash and Stanley Ralph Ross. Cinebooks, 1985–87. Annual updates, *The Motion Picture Annual,* 1985–   .

Covers 50,000 English-language and notable foreign feature films released theatrically and on videocassette between 1927 and 1984. Volume 10 is devoted to silent films (1910–36). Each entry provides filmographic data (e.g., credits, release date, running time), genre classification, evaluative rating, synopsis, and critical comments. The length of entries varies, ranging from two sentences to several pages. Some correlation exists between the evaluative rating and length of an entry, but it is not consistent. Opinionated and flawed, but useful.

The Holt Foreign Film Guide. By Ronald Bergan and Robin Karney. Henry Holt, 1989.

Selective guide to 2,000 foreign films chosen by the authors as classics, box-office successes, or films that are "representative of trends, fashions, styles, and development." Entries provide credits, running time, brief plot summary, and critical assessment. Originally published in England as the *Bloomsbury Foreign Film Guide,* so arrangement is alphabetical by the British release title. Includes cross-references from the original foreign-language title and U.S. release title.

Film Literature Index. Film and Television Documentation Center, 1973–   . Quarterly, with annual cumulations. **PERIODICAL INDEXES**

Author and subject index to over 300 international periodicals, including serious film journals and "non-film publications presenting film material with some frequency." Designed for the specialist and general reader interested in topics related to film, television, and video.

Some of the following titles also index film periodicals: **ELECTRONIC SOURCES**

Art Index. (CD-ROM) Wilson, 1984–   .

Indexes about a dozen film journals by author and subject. *Wilson Art Abstracts,* an annotated version on CD-ROM, is due to be released in 1995. Also available online as *Art Index* through Wilsonline and OCLC's First-Search and in print, *Art Index,* 1929–   .

A-V Online. (CD-ROM) SilverPlatter, 1964–   . Semiannual.

Database of the National Information Center for Educational Media (NICEM) established in 1964. Bibliographic guide to commercially produced educational audiovisual materials, including 16mm films and videotapes. Also available online through Dialog (File 46), Knowledge Index (EDUC4), and Human Resources Information Network, updated quarterly (1964–   ). Print version *NICEM Film & Video Finder,* 1964–   .

BASELINE. Baseline, Inc. Updated daily.

This online service for the entertainment industry has e-mail capability, bulletin boards, and dozens of data files. For example, its *Titles* file lists 35,000 movies made in the United States from 1970 to the present with distributors, sources of financing, rights information, and ratings. The *In Production* file contains current production information on more than 1,400 films and television series. *Grosses* has data on weekly box office receipts for films released since 1985. There are also files of articles from the *Hollywood Reporter* since 1988, biographical and contact information on industry personnel, and lists of Academy Award nominees since 1927. Baseline will answer questions for nonsubscribers on a pay-per-question basis. (212)254-8235.

Cinemania for Windows. (CD-ROM) Microsoft.

This interactive guide provides reviews, biographies, and famous scenes from hundreds of movies.

Footage '91: North American Film and Video Sources. (CD-ROM) Prelinger Associates, 1992.

Comprehensive directory describing 1,600 collections that supply film and taped images, including stock footage libraries, nonprofit film and television archives, and television news libraries. Entries include address, telephone number, services, description of collection, licensing, restrictions, availability of catalogs, and viewing facilities. Invaluable tool for any researcher attempting to find moving-image footage. CD-ROM version available only for the Macintosh at this writing. Also available in print as *Footage '89: North American Film and Video Sources* and *Footage '91,* edited by Richard Prelinger (Prelinger Associates, 1989–91). Detailed subject index for topics, issues, personalities, and locations.

Magill's Survey of Cinema. (CD-ROM) EBSCO.

Reviews and story line summaries of more than 3,500 films. Also available online on Dialog, Knowledge Index, CompuServe, Prodigy, updated every two weeks, with 30,000 films from 1902 to the present. Can search by title, genre, star, director, or year. For 3,300 films, it includes credits, a lengthy review, and citations to reviews in magazines. There are abbreviated entries for 30,000 additional films. Also available in print as *Magill's Survey of Cinema:* Covers silent films, English-language films, foreign-language films (Salem, 1982–85).

NewsBank Review of the Arts: Film and Television. (CD-ROM) NewsBank. 1986–   . Monthly.

Indexes interviews, reviews, and news stories concerning film from more than 450 U.S. city newspapers. The actual articles are reproduced on microfiche and issued at the same time as the *Review.*

PC Videolog. (Floppy disk) Trade Service Publications, 10996 Torreyana Rd., San Diego, CA 92121. Monthly.

Reports new video releases as they are announced by the manufacturers and film studios. Emphasizes feature films but includes some educational and general-interest titles. Intended for use by retail video stores that rent or sell videocassettes. A loose-leaf version, *Videolog,* updated weekly, is also available.

Social Sciences Index. (CD-ROM) Wilson, 1984–   . Monthly.

Journal articles on the sociological and psychological aspects of film.

Wilson Social Sciences Abstracts is a CD-ROM version with annotations. Also available online with Wilsonline, 1984–   , and in print as *Social Sciences Index*, 1974–   (formerly *Social Sciences and Humanities Index*, 1965–74, and *International Index*, 1907–65).

Variety Video Directory Plus. (CD-ROM) Bowker. Quarterly.

Covers approximately 28,000 entertainment and performance videotapes including feature films, music videotapes, cartoons, television programs, and plays and more than 34,000 documentaries, sports, educational, and other special-interest programs. Can be searched by a number of access points including keyword, subject, performer/director, award, and language. Full-text reviews from *Variety* are available for some of the feature films listed. Available in print as *Bowker's Complete Video Directory* (Bowker, 1990–   ). Annual with midyear supplement. Includes genre, subject, credits, and closed-captioned indexes.

The Video Source Book. (Floppy disk) Gale Research. Annual.

Guide to 125,000 programs currently available on videotape or videodisc from more than 1,300 distributors. Lists feature films, shorts, documentaries, educational and training videotapes available for purchase or rental. Subject and credits indexes. Some overlap with *Variety Video Directory Plus,* but each source lists unique titles. Also available in print.

Visual Materials. RLIN.

An online file of more than 180,000 audiovisual items held by research libraries. Indicates which libraries own individual items.

WorldCat. FirstSearch (OCLC).

This online database available in many libraries provides subject access to over 423,000 records of films, videotapes, and other audiovisual media in OCLC's online union catalog and shows which libraries own individual items.

Roger Ebert's Home Movie Companion. (Data Discman) Quanta.

Thousands of home videos reviewed and rated on a disc for the Data Discman, Sony's portable compact disc player. (See Chapter 9, CD-ROM.)

Commercial Online Services

- Hollywood Hotline. On America Online, CompuServe, Delphi, GEnie, NewsNet. Daily.
  News of entertainment industry.
- Hollywood Hotline's Movie Reviews. On CompuServe. Weekly.
  Provides plot summaries, credits, and ratings.
- Home Video Update. On America Online, EasyLink, GEnie. Weekly.

Such information on recent releases as stars, studio, price.
- Movie Reviews Data Base. On America Online, Dow Jones News/Retrieval, EasyLink, GEnie, Delphi, Prodigy, BASELINE. Weekly. Summaries, credits, and ratings are provided for 5,000 movies from 1920s to present. Reviews of current films by syndicated newspaper columnist Jay A. Brown.
- Prodigy: Critic Leonard Maltin comments on current films and the movie industry.
- GEnie: Show Biz RoundTable, a bulletin board for the discussion of film and the other performing arts.

PERIODICALS *American Film: Film, Video and Television Arts.* 1975–   . Monthly.
Published by the American Film Institute, the focus is Hollywood. Articles chronicle the relationship between art and popular culture.

Film Comment. 1962–   . Bimonthly.
Published by the Film Society of Lincoln Center, it contains articles on recent feature films, interviews with filmmakers, reports on film festivals, retrospective film studies, and television. Emphasis on American films, but foreign films receive good coverage. A serious but not scholarly magazine.

Film Quarterly. 1945–   . Quarterly.
With international coverage, this journal is scholarly but accessible. Has detailed film reviews.

Sight and Sound. 1932–   . Monthly.
Published by the British Film Institute. In 1991, *Sight and Sound* merged with *Monthly Film Bulletin* to make a new magazine, combining critical, in-depth articles on motion pictures with reviews for every feature film released in London as well as new video releases. Includes book reviews, film festival coverage, and news from the international film scene.

Variety. 1905–   . Weekly.
Trade paper covering industry and financial news in motion pictures, television, and theater. Coverage is global, but with an emphasis on the United States. Includes reviews, statistics, special issues, and obituaries, all in *Variety*'s distinctive writing style. The best of its genre.

For a comprehensive list of periodical literature, see Katherine Loughney's *Film, Television and Video Periodicals: A Comprehensive Annotated List* (Garland, 1991).

Motion Pictures, 1894–1912: Identified from the Records of the United States Copyright Office. Copyright Office, Library of Congress, 1953.

Motion Pictures, 1912–1939: Catalog of Copyright Entries Cumulative Series. 1951.

Motion Pictures, 1940–1949: Catalog of Copyright Entries Cumulative Series. 1953.

Motion Pictures, 1950–1959: Catalog of Copyright Entries Cumulative Series. 1960.

Motion Pictures, 1960–1969: Catalog of Copyright Entries Cumulative Series. 1971.

Catalog of Copyright Entries: Motion Pictures and Filmstrips, 1970–   . (Issued on microfiche since 1979.)

This series comprises "an unbroken record of the copyright registrations of motion pictures and also an extensive, although not complete, record of motion picture production in the United States." Entries include titles, name of claimant, copyright data, registration number, physical description, author and title of the work on which the film is based. Covers feature films, television programs, shorts, serials, newsreels, documentaries, and educational films.

Wonderful Inventions: Motion Pictures, Broadcasting, and Recorded Sound at the Library of Congress. Library of Congress, 1984.

Essays by scholars on silent films, golden voices of the silver screen, film restoration, and much more. Two records featuring film music are also included.

See also the Government Printing Office's *Subject Bibliography #73— Motion Pictures, Films and Audiovisual Information.*

National Endowment for the Arts
Media Arts Program: Film/Radio/Television
1100 Pennsylvania Ave. NW
Washington, DC 20506
(202) 682-5452
Awards grants to individuals and nonprofit organizations for film and videotape productions.

National Endowment for the Humanities
Humanities Projects in Media
1100 Pennsylvania Ave. NW
Washington, DC 20506
(202) 786-0278

Independent agency that awards grants to nonprofit media projects in the humanities.

Department of Commerce
International Trade Administration
Office of Service Industries
Information Industries Division
14th and Constitution Avenues
Washington, DC 20230
(202) 377-4781

Coordinates issues concerning import administration, international economic policy, and trade development. Gathers and publishes reports on trade statistics in various industries, including motion pictures.

ASSOCIATIONS

American Film Institute
John F. Kennedy Center for the Performing Arts
Washington, DC 20566
(202) 828-4000

and

2021 N. Western Avenue
P. O. Box 27999
Los Angeles, CA 90027
(213) 856-7600

Participates in film preservation, cataloging, and exhibition. Student filmmakers study at AFI's Center for Advanced Film Studies. Publishes *American Film* (monthly).

Association of Independent Video & Filmmakers
625 Broadway
New York, NY 10012
(212) 473-3400

National trade association of independent producers and individuals involved in independent videotape and film. Provides a wide range of services for members and the general public. Sponsors seminars and workshops. Publishes *The Independent* (monthly).

Society for Cinema Studies
c/o David Desser
2111 FLB/707 S. Mathews
Urbana, IL 61801
(217) 333-3356

Membership organization encouraging scholarship in the fields of film history, theory, and criticism. Publishes *Cinema Journal* (quarterly).

Academy of Motion Picture Arts and Sciences
Margaret Herrick Library
Center for Motion Picture Studies
333 S. La Cienega Blvd.
Beverly Hills, CA 90211
(310) 247-3020
Devoted to the history, sociology, science, and art of filmmaking. The library collection includes more than 18,000 books, pamphlets, and periodicals, 5 million still photographs, 5,000 scripts, and clipping files on 82,000 films and 73,000 film personalities. The Academy Film Archive houses 12,000 films. Use of special collections requires an appointment.

International Museum of Photography at George Eastman House
Film Department
900 East Ave.
Rochester, NY 14607
(716) 271-3361
Research library of film books and motion picture stills. A collection of silent and sound films from the United States, as well as foreign silent films. To view films, apply in writing.

Library of Congress
Motion Picture, Broadcasting and Recorded Sound Division
Room 336, Madison Bldg.
Washington, DC 20540
(202) 707-1000
Research collection of film and television books, clipping files, stills, and copyright descriptions. Extensive moving image collection including feature films, television programs, documentaries, shorts, and newsreels. Viewing restricted to individuals doing research of a specific nature leading to a publicly available work.

Museum of Modern Art
Department of Film
11 W. 53d St.
New York, NY 10019
(212) 708-9400
Reference collection of books, scripts, clipping files, posters, and press books. Large collection of features, documentaries, and shorts. Open to serious researchers only.

National Archives and Records Administration
Motion Picture, Sound and Video Branch
7th and Pennsylvania Avenue NW, Room 2W
Washington, DC 20408
(202) 501-5449

Extensive collection of films created for and produced by the United States government, as well as gift materials from private sources. Includes newsreels, military films, C-Span coverage, Ford Motor Company Collection, and NASA stock footage.

University of California, Los Angeles (UCLA)
Film and Television Archive
1438 Melnitz Hall
Los Angeles, CA 90024
(213) 206-8013

Extensive collection of feature films, animation, and television. Includes *Hearst Metrotone News* collection of releases and outtakes (1914–67) and *Telenews* (1950s–63).

Wisconsin Center for Film and Theater Research
Film and Photo Archive
State Historical Society of Wisconsin
816 State Street
Madison, WI 53706
(608) 262-0585

Features, shorts, and documentaries (1890s–1980s), including Warner Brothers features and shorts (1931–49), RKO features (1930s–1940s), postwar Soviet features and documentaries (1950s–1970s), television documentaries, and Ziv television series (1948–62).

For additional information on film libraries and other resources, see books by Slide and Thorpe under General Sources of Information above.

LC SUBJECT HEADINGS It was only in the late 1980s that the Library of Congress replaced the heading Moving pictures with Motion pictures. Many libraries will not have changed all their records, especially if they still have a card catalog, so be sure to try both headings.

Animated films	Motion picture authorship
Animation (Cinematography)	Motion picture industry
Cinematography	Motion pictures—Production
Documentary films	and direction
Film adaptations	Motion pictures—Social aspects
Motion picture actors and	Social problems in motion
actresses	pictures

There are headings for special populations in film:
   Afro-Americans in motion pictures
   Deaf in motion pictures
   Women in motion pictures
And headings for film genres:

Comedy films	Science fiction films
Detective and mystery films	War films
Musical films	Western films

Two of the most useful and affordable film reference books for a home library are Ephraim Katz's *The Film Encyclopedia* (described above) and *Leonard Maltin's TV Movies and Video Guide* (New American Library). Maltin covers more than 19,000 theatrical and television films. Each entry includes title, date, country of origin, director, cast, running time, critical rating, and capsule review. A symbol indicates the films that are available on home video. Maltin also provides a brief directory of mail-order sources for hard-to-find videotapes. Valuable sources for both the movie buff and the serious researcher.

26

GARDENING

See also: *General Reference Sources, Agriculture, The Home*

Gardening research seems as popular as gardening itself, especially during the nongrowing seasons and, in colder climes, as spring approaches. Whether the goal is food for the family table or plants and flowers to beautify the home, the gardener must know what to plant and when and where to plant it.

Public libraries try to respond to the heavy demand for gardening information with reference materials as well as with circulating items to guide you step by step. Further information may be available from local schools or institutions, such as botanical gardens with programs in agriculture, botany, horticulture, or landscape architecture.

The following resources offer several levels of help, from classic plant identification books to up-to-the-minute data available electronically.

GENERAL REFERENCE SOURCES

The Gardener's Reading Guide: The Best Books for Gardeners. By Jan Dean. Facts On File, 1993.

An annotated list of 2,300 books on a wide variety of popular gardening topics, including biographies of famous gardeners, how-to books, and those on special types of gardens and gardening methods.

Gardening: A Guide to the Literature. By Richard T. Isaacson. Garland, 1985.

An annotated bibliography that lists books on many specialized gardening topics, as well as organizations, periodicals, and book dealers catering to gardeners.

Hortus Third: A Concise Dictionary of Plants Cultivated in the United States and Canada. 3d ed. Compiled by Liberty Hyde Bailey and Ethel Z. Bailey. Macmillan, 1976.

A somewhat technical but authoritive and comprehensive encyclopedia of over 20,000 plant species. Arranged alphabetically by genus.

The New Royal Horticultural Society Dictionary of Gardening. 4 vols. Edited by Antony Huxley and others. Stockton, 1992.

Describes 50,000 plants, with information on cultivation and propagation. Essays discuss environmental issues, plant science, and garden design. Biographical information on horticulturists and landscape architects is also included.

The New York Botanical Garden Illustrated Encyclopedia of Horticulture. 10 vols. Edited by Thomas H. Everett. Garland, 1981–82.

With 7,000 entries written for the amateur gardener, this massive work has become a standard.

Tropica: Color Cyclopedia of Exotic Plants and Trees for Warm-Region Horticulture. 3d ed. By Alfred B. Graf. Roehrs, 1986.

Exotica Series 4 International: Pictorial Cyclopedia of Exotic Plants from Tropical and Near Tropical Regions. 11th ed. By Alfred B. Graf. Roehrs, 1982.

Hortica: Color Encyclopedia of Garden Flora. By Alfred B. Graf. Roehrs/Macmillan, 1993.

These books can be found in many library collections. Brief entries and copious illustrations help readers identify and cultivate tropical, subtropical, and temperate-zone plants. Thousands of color photographs in each volume.

The American Horticultural Society Encyclopedia of Gardening. Edited by Christopher Bricknell. Dorling Kindersley, 1993.

For the Home Reference Shelf

Covers everything from tools and equipment to building walls and decks to houseplants. Beautiful color photos and excellent how-to illustrations for grafting, pruning, dividing plants.

Gardening: The Complete Guide to Growing America's Favorite Fruits & Vegetables. By the National Gardening Association. Addison-Wesley, 1986.

The best single book for the beginning vegetable gardener. A wealth of practical information on what to plant and how and where to plant it.

Complete Handbook of Garden Plants. By Michael Wright. Facts On File, 1984.

An excellent one-volume field guide to over 9,000 varieties of trees, shrubs, annuals, perennials, etc., including concise but useful information on cultivation.

The Garden Sourcebook: A Practical Guide to Planning and Planting. By Caroline Boisset and Fayal Greene. Crown, 1993.

How to plan, plant, and maintain a garden. A plant selector arranges plants by characteristics—autumn color, shade tolerance, etc. Lavishly illustrated.

Random House Book of Perennials. 2 vols. By Roger Phillips and Martyn Rix. Random House, 1991.

Volume 1 covers early (spring) perennials; Volume 2, late (summer) ones. See also the *Random House Book of Vegetables* (1993), the *Random House Book of Bulbs* (1989), the *Random House Book of Roses* (1988).

Taylor's Guides to Gardening. Houghton Mifflin, 1986–87.

This helpful series of field guides is based on the 1961 edition of the classic *Taylor's Encyclopedia of Gardening.* Each volume includes lifelike color photographs, descriptions, and cultivation information. Individual volumes include: Annuals, Perennials, House Plants, Shrubs, Vegetables and Herbs, Bulbs, Roses, and Ground Cover, Vines and Grasses.

The Gardener's Book of Sources. By William B. Logan. Penguin, 1988.

Lists all types of information sources with helpful annotations.

The Encyclopedia of Organic Gardening. Rodale Press, 1978.

The ultimate source for the ecological gardener.

The House Plant Expert. By D. G. Hessayon. Charles Scribner's and Sons, 1981.

This indispensable book, with over 6,000,000 copies in print, will become your houseplant bible.

Wildflowers   A resurgence of interest in and concern for nature has prompted many gardeners to try growing wildflowers. Commercial catalogs have responded to the increased demand with an expanding selection of wildflower seeds, and several reference books are particularly helpful.

Garden of Wildflowers: 101 Native Species and How to Grow Them. By Henry W. A. Art. Storey Communications, 1986.

Charts in the cultivation section summarize hardiness, moisture, light and pH demands, height, color, and flowering dates. One-page descriptions of the 101 recommended species are accompanied by full-page sketches with range maps.

Gardening with Wildflowers. By Francis Tenenbaum. Ballantine, 1973.

Arranged by habitat type, each chapter includes a brief description of suitable species and how to grow them. Includes a list of selected seed suppliers and a brief bibliography.

National Wildflower Research Center's Wildflower Handbook. Texas Monthly Press, 1989.

Describes cultivation techniques and includes an extensive directory of seed, plant, and information sources. Includes a bibliography of books arranged by place.

The last decade has seen a renaissance of the ancient art of herb gardening. Herbs are easy to grow and often thrive in poor soils. Many are hardy perennials. Look under Herbs and Health Food in the phone book Yellow Pages for local nurseries. The Herb Society of America (see Associations below) sells an inexpensive list of herbal suppliers. The following list of titles is only a sample of the literature available in libraries and bookstores:

Herbs

A Modern Herbal. By M. Grieve. Dover, 1971.

A classic, originally published in 1931 and since reprinted many times. A great source for the intriguing histories and traditional household and medicinal uses of herbs.

The Rodale Herb Book. By William H. Hylton. Rodale, 1974.

The first half of this useful compendium covers medicinal, culinary, and aesthetic uses of herbs and their cultivation. The second half describes the history, use, and cultivation of fifty selected herbs.

Magic and Medicine of Plants. Reader's Digest, 1986.

This is a wonderful source of herbal information, beautifully illustrated and lovingly assembled.

Herbal Bounty: The Gentle Art of Herb Culture. By Steven Foster. Peregrine Smith Books, 1984.

A good guide to the cultivation of 124 varieties of herbs, along with suggestions for their use. Includes a bibliography and a directory of suppliers.

Garden Literature: An Index to Periodical Articles and Book Reviews.
1992–   . Quarterly.

Indexes more than 100 magazines, including gardening and horticultural journals as well as titles devoted to environmental issues and alternative farming. Gardening articles from general-interest magazines are also included.

PERIODICAL INDEXES

Magazines for the amateur gardener are also indexed in the general periodical indexes listed in Chapter 18, General Reference Sources.

ELECTRONIC SOURCES

AGRICOLA. (CD-ROM) SilverPlatter, 1972–   . Updated monthly. Also OCLC, 1979–92.

This database from the National Agricultural Library offers comprehensive coverage of worldwide literature on agriculture, fertilizers, hydroponics, soils, and more. Available online with BRS and BRS/AfterDark (CAIN), Dialog (File 10), Knowledge Index (AGRI1), and OCLC First-Search, 1970–   . Corresponds in part to the print product *Bibliography of Agriculture,* 1942–   .

Biological & Agricultural Index. (CD-ROM) H. W. Wilson, 1983–   . Monthly.

Indexes 255 key periodicals dealing with the life sciences and agriculture. Covers such topics as agricultural chemicals, horticulture, plant pathology, ecology, and botany. Also online from OCLC FirstSearch and Wilsonline, 1983–   , and in print, 1964–   . Published from 1919 to 1964 under the title *Agricultural Index.*

HORTCD. (CD-ROM) SilverPlatter, 1973–   . Annual.

A subset of *CAB Abstracts,* also available online (see Chapter 19, Agriculture), this index includes references to horticultural journal articles from all countries of the world, with summaries of their contents.

Bulletin Boards

- CompuServe: Good Earth Forum
- Prodigy: The Victory Garden, sponsored by TV station WGBH, posts articles with hints on gardening. There is also a gardener's bulletin board.
- The Internet has a Gardens and Gardening list for the exchange of information about home gardening. Access via **LISTSERV@UKCC. EDU.**

PERIODICALS

American Horticulturist. 1922–   . Monthly.

Published by the American Horticultural Society for experienced amateur gardeners as well as professionals. Includes plant source list.

Fine Gardening. 1988– . Bimonthly.
Combines high-quality photographs with hands-on articles written by readers.

Horticulture: The Magazine of American Gardening. 1904– . Monthly.
Featuring a broad range of gardening topics, it regularly lists gardens open to the public, arboretums, and museums. Also discusses sources of plants.

National Gardening: The Gardener's Newsmagazine. 1977– . Monthly.
Published by the National Gardening Association, it covers gardening techniques for both novices and experienced gardeners.

Plants and Gardens. 1945– . Quarterly.
From the well-known Brooklyn Botanic Garden, each issue of this magazine addresses a specific topic.

Organic Gardening. 1942– . Monthly.
Formerly *Rodale's Organic Gardening.* Practical information for the gardener who doesn't want to use chemical fertilizers or pesticides.

Wildflower: Journal of the National Wildflower Research Center. 1985– .
Quarterly.
Covers all North American ecosystems—deserts, prairies, forests.

There are dozens of other magazines devoted to general and specific gardening topics and to specific plants. Articles on gardening also appear in general periodicals and newspapers. The publications of local horticultural societies, botanical gardens, arboretums, and garden clubs are especially useful for information appropriate to local growing conditions.

GOVERNMENT PUBLICATIONS

The U.S. Department of Agriculture publishes a Home and Garden Bulletin series with helpful pamphlets for the amateur gardener. USDA's Agricultural Information Bulletin series is also a good source of information. The Quick Bibliography series from the National Agricultural Library includes a series of printed bibliographies extracted from the AGRICOLA database.

Home and Garden Bulletins

Indoor Gardening, no. 220.
Selecting and Growing House Plants, no. 82.
Growing Flowering Perennials, no. 114.
Growing Flowering Annuals, no. 91.

Spring Flowering Bulbs, no. 136.
Spring Flowering Bulbs, no. 151.

USDA Agricultural Information Bulletins

Growing Fruits and Nuts, no. 408.
Growing Your Own Vegetables, no. 409.
Insects and Diseases of Vegetables in the Home Garden, no. 380.

Also see the Government Printing Office's *Subject Bibliography* #41—The Home.

GOVERNMENT AGENCIES

The Cooperative Extension System is a joint effort of the U.S. Department of Agriculture, Extension personnel at the land-grant universities, and Extension agents in nearly all of the 3,150 counties in the United States. In addition to advice on specific gardening problems, county Extension offices provide educational programs for groups and free publications with valuable information on selecting and nurturing plants. In counties where there is sufficient demand, the Extension office may offer a formal training program, resulting in certification as a Master Gardener in return for a specified number of hours of community service. Look for the Extension Service telephone number under the county government listings in your local phone directory.

ASSOCIATIONS

American Horticultural Society
7931 E. Boulevard Drive
Alexandria, VA 22308
(703) 768-5700
Membership organization for amateur and professional gardeners. Operates a seed exchange and gardeners' information service.

National Gardening Association
180 Flynn Avenue
Burlington, VT 05401
(820) 863-1308
A clearinghouse for home and community gardening information. Publishes *National Gardening* (a monthly journal) and *Directory of Seed and Nursery Catalogs*. Offers a Seed Search Service for members seeking particular varieties.

Garden Club of America
598 Madison Avenue
New York, NY 10022
(212) 753-8287
Publishes a bimonthly *Bulletin*. One of its local chapters may be located in your community.

American Herb Association
P. O. Box 353
Rescue, CA 95672
(916) 626-5046

Publishes a quarterly newsletter and helpful annual directories *(Herb Publications and Associations, Sources of Herb Products and Plants)* and offers online searching for herbal information.

Herb Society of America
9019 Kirtland Chardon Road
Mentor, OH 44060
(216) 256-0514

Research-oriented group. Publishes the annual *Herbalist,* a quarterly newsletter, and several booklets.

National Wildflower Research Center
2600 F.M. 973 North
Austin, TX 78725
(512) 929-3600

A clearinghouse for wildflower information, offering online searching for seed and plant sources in local areas. Publishes a journal and a useful handbook (see Periodicals and Wildflowers sections for more information).

For more information, see:

North American Horticulture: A Reference Guide. 2d ed. Edited by Thomas M. Barrett. Macmillan, 1992.

This directory of more than 4,000 horticultural organizations and programs in the United States and Canada covers everything from native plant societies to community gardens. Lists botanical libraries, notable public gardens, university-sponsored horticultural programs.

LIBRARIES

Most of the organizations mentioned above maintain library collections in their areas of interest. Universities and horticultural societies have major collections of importance to both hobbyists and researchers. Following are some examples:

New York Botanical Garden Library
Bronx, NY 10458
(212) 220-6504
One of the largest collections of books on botany in the world.

Hunt Botanic Library
Hunt Institute for Botanical Documentation
Carnegie-Mellon University
Pittsburgh, PA 15213
(412) 268-2436
An important historical collection.

Massachusetts Horticultural Society Library
Horticultural Hall
300 Massachusetts Avenue
Boston, MA 02115
(617) 536-9280
An extensive collection of periodicals and seed and nursery catalogs dating to the eighteenth century. The library has material on botanical art, flower arranging, landscape design, and plant cultivation and identification, including the most influential books from the fifteenth century to the present.

Sterling Morton Library
Morton Arboretum
Route 53
Lisle, IL 60532
(708) 719-2427
Especially good collections on trees and shrubs, but also has considerable material on wild and cultivated plants.

If your city has a botanical garden or arboretum, a library may be located there. Local gardening clubs often have informal libraries.

LC SUBJECT HEADINGS There are scores of gardening titles published every year. When consulting a library catalog, broad subject headings to try include:

Annuals (plants)   Perennials
Flowers   Plants, Ornamental
Herbs   Vegetables
Gardening

Books written about gardening in your specific geographic area can be particularly helpful. Look for geographic subdivisions to locate this material. For example:

Gardening—Southern states
Flowers—Georgia

Specific plant names are also subject headings. The Library of Congress prefers to use the English rather than the Latin names of plants.

Azaleas
Ferns, Ornamental
Miniature orchids

Sweet peppers
Red clover
Roses

Other headings include:
Bonsai
Container gardening
Desert gardening
Gardening in the shade
Herb Gardening
Herbs
Medicinal plants

Native plant gardening
Organic gardening
Plant diseases
Rock gardens
Water gardens
Wildlife Attracting

SOURCES OF EXPERT ADVICE

Most communities have a county Extension agent who is familiar with local growing conditions. See Government Agencies above for more information on this service.

Local nurseries are also good sources of information. Look under Nurseries—Plants, Greenhouses, and Garden Centers in the Yellow Pages. An experienced horticulturalist stocks the varieties that survive best under local conditions.

Other useful sources include 4-H clubs and gardening clubs. Ask a librarian or check the events calendar in your local newspaper for local meetings.

SPECIAL SOURCES: SEED CATALOGS

Sources of seed and stock are as numerous as petals on a dandelion. Catalogs allow you to try things in your garden that local nurseries may not stock.

Many catalogs include a short guide to growing plants from seed, either free with your order or for a nominal fee. Many of the books listed in this chapter include a directory of seed companies.

27

GENEALOGY

See also: *History, Hobbies, Multiculturalism*

We are a nation of immigrants, whether our ancestors came over on the Mayflower, or, like Will Rogers's, "met the boat," or came relatively recently. More and more Americans are discovering the rewards of genealogy, the study of family history. Biographers enlarge the portrait of their subjects through genealogical research. Mormons research their family histories so they can have ancestors baptized and be reunited with them after death. Some citizens find "roots" in the search for their ethnic heritage. Other Americans may be looking for a titled ancestor. For most of us, researching our family history can be a path to self-knowledge, as well as an intriguing treasure hunt. The following sources may be helpful:

GENERAL SOURCES OF INFORMATION

American and British Genealogy and Heraldry: A Selected List of Books. 3d ed. By P. William Filby. New England Historic Genealogical Society, 1983.

Lists more than 9,000 guides, indexes, biographies, and other books arranged by place. The title notwithstanding, it does include some sources for continental Europe.

Ancestry's Red Book: American State, County and Town Records. Edited by Alice Eichholz. Ancestry, 1989.

Lists records available from states and counties and from New England towns.

Ethnic Genealogy: A Research Guide. Edited by Jessie Carney Smith. Greenwood, 1983.

Contains bibliographies, lists of periodicals, and directories of societies for Native American, Asian-American, African-American, and Hispanic-American genealogy.

Guide to Genealogy Software. By Donna Przecha and Joan Lowrey. Genealogical Publishing, 1993.

Software for the home computer has made genealogical research much easier. This book reviews and evaluates more than 100 software packages for the genealogist.

International Vital Records Handbook. By Thomas J. Kemp. Genealogical Publishing, 1990.

Provides addresses, costs, and special instructions for ordering birth, death, and marriage records from U.S. states and sixty-seven foreign countries, along with application forms that can be photocopied to order state records.

Researcher's Guide to American Genealogy. 2d ed. By Val D. Greenwood. Genealogical Publishing, 1990.

Long considered the definitive genealogy text, this book provides lists of sources and sample records. American census returns, legal documents, and military, church, and cemetery records are discussed. There are chapters on genealogical evidence and on computer software.

Searching for Your Ancestors: The How and Why of Genealogy. 6th ed. By Gilbert Harry Doane and James B. Bell. University of Minnesota Press, 1992.

An excellent guide for beginners, this book discusses records and methods in both the United States and foreign countries.

The Source: A Guidebook of American Genealogy. Edited by Arlene Eakle and Johni Cerny. Ancestry, 1984.

A comprehensive guide to U.S. genealogical records. Part I identifies sources such as cemetery, census, church, and legal records. Part II identifies published sources such as newspapers and biographies. Part III emphasizes ethnic sources and includes a chapter on computer databases.

Researchers descended from relatively recent immigrants will quickly exhaust records in this country, but numerous sources are available for researching family history in other nations; for example, *In Search of Your British and Irish Roots* and *In Search of Your European Roots: A Complete Guide to Tracing Your Ancestors in Every Country in Europe,* both by Angus Baxter (Genealogical Publishing). In library catalogs, use the subject heading (name of country)—Genealogy to find a book on records in the country of your forebears. Some countries have free brochures available from an embassy, consulate, or other government office explaining local records. A sampling:

- Britain: "Tracing Your Ancestors." Send a SASE to British Travel Authority, 625 N. Michigan Ave., Chicago, IL 60611.
- Denmark: "Tracing Your Danish Ancestors and Relatives." Telephone (212) 949-2333.
- Ireland: "Tracing Your Ancestors." Telephone (800) 223-6470.
- Norway: "How to Trace Your Ancestors in Norway." Telephone (212) 421-7333.
- Sweden: "Tracing Your Swedish Ancestry." Write Embassy of Sweden, 600 New Hampshire Ave. NW, Washington, DC 20037.

PERIODICAL INDEXES

PERiodical Source Index, 1847–1985. Allen County Public Library Foundation, 1988– .

Also known as PERSI, this periodical index is a major tool covering more than 2,000 periodicals. It will eventually be complete in 16 volumes but at this writing, 12 volumes are available. In the first part of the set, articles are indexed by state and county and then by type of record. The U.S. section is followed by sections for Canada and other foreign countries. In the second part of the set, articles about families are indexed by surname. Annual update volumes have been published covering 1986 to the present.

Genealogical Periodical Annual Index: Key to the Genealogical Literature. Heritage Books, 1962– . Annual.

Indexes fewer magazines than PERSI and covers a much narrower time span, but may be found in more libraries because of its modest price.

PERIODICALS

The American Genealogist, 1932– . Quarterly.

For professional genealogists and experienced amateurs. Publishes family records, ancestral tables, and answers queries.

The Genealogical Helper, 1947– . Bimonthly.

Widely read by amateur genealogists doing their own research. Special issues that contain directories of genealogists, societies, libraries, and family associations are especially helpful.

National Genealogical Society Quarterly, 1912– . Quarterly.

Good source of information on early settlers in America.

New England Historical and Genealogical Register, 1847– . Quarterly.

Oldest continuously published periodical. Good coverage of New England records.

National Archives
Pennsylvania Ave. at Eighth St. NW
Washington, DC 20408
(202) 501-5402

The National Archives is the official depository for records produced by the U.S. government. While it is best known for housing past census records, other important records for the genealogist can be found here, too.

Guide to Genealogical Research in the National Archives. National Archives and Records Service, 1992.

Detailed descriptions of types of records held: census, naturalization, military, land records, claims records, etc. Tells how to order copies of each type.

Genealogical and Biographical Research: A Select Catalog of National Archives Microfilm Publications. National Archives and Records Service, 1983.

Descriptions of records and roll-by-roll lists for each publication.

In addition to its headquarters in Washington, DC, the National Archives has eleven regional branches. *The Archives: A Guide to the National Archives Field Branches,* by Loretto Dennis Szucs and Sandra Hargreaves Leubking (Ancestry, 1988), describes the services and unique holdings of these branches. The regional archives are:

New England Region
380 Trapelo Rd.
Waltham, MA 02154
(617) 647-8100

Southwest Region
501 W. Felix St.
Ft. Worth, TX 76115
(817) 334-5525

Northeast Region
Bldg. 22—MOT Bayonne
Bayonne, NJ 07002-5386
(201) 823-7252

Rocky Mountain Region
Bldg. 48, Denver Federal Ctr.
Denver, CO 80225
(303) 236-0818

Mid Atlantic Region
9th and Market Sts., Rm. 1350
Philadelphia, PA 19107
(215) 597-3000

Pacific Southwest Region
24000 Avila Rd.
Laguna Niguel, CA 92677-6719
(714) 643-4241

Southeast Region
1557 St. Joseph Ave.
East Point, GA 30344
(404) 763-7477

Pacific Sierra Region
1000 Commodore Dr.
San Bruno, CA 94066
(415) 876-9009

Great Lakes Region
7458 S. Pulaski Rd.
Chicago, IL 60629
(312) 581-7816

Pacific Northwest Region
6125 Sand Point Way NE
Seattle, WA 98115
(206) 526-6507

Central Plains Region
2312 E. Bannister Rd.
Kansas City, MO 64131
(816) 926-6272

Federal Censuses, 1790–1920. National Archives.

These census reports list individual names. The federal census is available in print (from several publishers) and on CD-ROM (for the earliest years) and on microfilm. Census records are arranged by place, not alphabetically by name, so you must know the address to find a person. There are, however, name indexes to early censuses. You should be able to find the census for your state on microfilm at a library in the state. Microfilm for other states can be purchased or rented from the National Archives or it can be borrowed from the National Archives through one of its local branches.

State Census Records. By Ann S. Lainhart. Genealogical Publishing, 1992.

This inventory of censuses taken by forty-four states and other state records will help fill in the gaps in the federal census.

ELECTRONIC SOURCES

Biography and Genealogy Master Index CD-ROM. Gale, 1993–   . Updated annually.

Searches 8.25 million references to biographical information in 700 published sources. Also online with Dialog, updated annually. Based on the print product *Biography and Genealogy Master Index.* 2d ed. 8 vols. Gale, 1980. *BGMI 1981–85 Cumulation.* Gale, 1986. *BGMI 1985–90 Cumulation.* 3 vols. Gale, 1991. Annual updates, 1991–   . Also available on microfiche as *Bio-Base.*

Genealogical material available on CD-ROM includes early censuses, state marriage records, social security death benefit records, and others. Some of these discs cost less than $100; for example, the 1820 census for the Northeastern states is about $90. The CD-ROM indexes to the collections of the Family History Library in Salt Lake City described below are also sold to other libraries. Available from GeneSys, 175 N. Freedom Blvd., Salt Lake City, UT 84601.

Bulletin boards: A list of genealogical bulletin boards is maintained by Richard Pence and can be downloaded **(703) 528-2612.**

Genealogical bulletin boards can be found on all the major utilities:
Prodigy, CompuServe, GEnie. Through them researchers in other parts of
the country may be willing to search records for you that aren't available
locally. For instance, if your family comes from Kansas but you are currently
living in Atlanta, you will have access to the Georgia census on microfilm
locally but probably not the Kansas census. On a bulletin board, you can
volunteer to search Georgia records for out-of-staters and request that
someone check the Kansas files for you.

- The CompuServe Genealogy Forum contains a surname exchange and
  shareware.
- GEnie's Genealogy RoundTable has the Genealogy Knowledge Base,
  which tells where to write for further information on a particular topic.

Meyer's Directory of Genealogical Societies in the U.S.A. and Canada. 8th ed. By **ASSOCIATIONS**
Mary Keysor Meyer. Libra Publications, 1990.

Provides addresses for 1,800 genealogical societies. Also lists 250 genealogical periodicals. Some of the important societies listed in this book
include:

Federation of Genealogical Societies
P. O. Box 3385
Salt Lake City, UT 84110-3385
(801) 240-5598
Membership consists of genealogical societies, libraries, historical societies, and family associations. Its objective is to stimulate the activities of
state and local organizations and avoid duplication of effort.

National Genealogical Society
4527 17th St. N
Arlington, VA 22207-2399
(703) 525-0050
Promotes genealogical research by providing a service through which
members can list the families on which they are working and exchange data
with others. Maintains a library and offers a correspondence course in
American genealogy.

New England Historic Genealogical Society
99-101 Newbury St.
Boston, MA 02116
(617) 536-5740
The oldest and largest genealogical society in the United States. Collects
and preserves materials relating to family history and has a large circulating
library. Conducts seminars on genealogy.

Also see the *Encyclopedia of Associations* for the names of more than 150 family name societies, such as the Agnew Association of America or Peck Pioneers.

LIBRARIES

Family History Library
50 E. North Temple
Salt Lake City, UT 84150
(801) 240-2331

This library is a department of the Church of Jesus Christ of the Latter-Day Saints (Mormons). It promotes local and family history and microfilms records in forty countries. The library has more than 8 million family group records and 1.6 million reels of microfilm.

The Library: A Guide to the LDS Family History Library, edited by Johni Cerny and Wendy Elliott (Ancestry, 1988), describes the collections and services of the library in Salt Lake City and its 1,000 U.S. branch libraries. Look in your local phone book under Church of Jesus Christ of the Latter-Day Saints for the nearest branch. Branches have indexes, both on CD-ROM and on microform, to the holdings of the main library in Salt Lake City. Once you identify records that you want to see, your branch LDS library can borrow microfiche or microfilm copies of them for you for a small fee. These indexes are:

International Genealogical Index [IGI]. Index of more than 147 million names extracted from various records from many countries and time periods.
Ancestral File. A computerized file of genealogies, consisting of more than 13 million names.
Library Catalog. A catalog of the 2 million titles in the main library in Salt Lake City.

Library of Congress
Independence Ave. at First St. SE
Washington, DC 20540
(202) 707-5000

Our national library is an important resource for genealogy. *The Library of Congress: A Guide to Genealogical and Historical Research,* by James C. Neagles and Mark C. Neagles (Ancestry, 1990), gives detailed descriptions of records by region and state. For lists of genealogies held by the Library of Congress, see:

Genealogies in the Library of Congress: A Bibliography. By Marion J. Kaminkow. Magna Carta, 1972.

A Complement to Genealogies in the Library of Congress: A Bibliography. By Marion J. Kaminkow. Magna Carter, 1981.
Genealogies Cataloged by the Library of Congress Since 1986. Library of Congress, 1991.

Newberry Library
60 W. Walton
Chicago, IL 60610
(312) 943-9090
Guide to Local and Family History at the Newberry Library, by Peggy Tuck Sink (Ancestry, 1987), describes records in this important regional collection.

LC SUBJECT HEADINGS

Use these headings in library catalogs:
   Genealogists
   Genealogy
   Genealogy—Societies
   Newspapers in genealogy
   A family name can serve as a subject heading if a genealogy of that family has been published as a book; e.g.,
   Gordon family
   Lincoln family
   Genealogy can be a subheading for ethnic groups:
   Afro-Americans—Genealogy
   Jews—Genealogy
   Or for places:
   Ireland—Genealogy
   Ohio—Genealogy
   U.S.—Genealogy

TIPS

Obtain a good genealogical research manual. Gather information from older family members and set about checking its validity.

Gather vital records (birth, marriage, death), usually from local, county, and state authorities.

Much genealogical research can be done by mail, but do not write letters unless you know specifically what it is you need. Be sure you're addressing the right agency and individual to deal with the request. Libraries, archives, and state and local agencies are swamped with letters requesting genealogical information.

As you work with your manual, you'll develop the necessary skills of abstracting, documenting, and analyzing evidence. In preparing group sheets, ancestor charts, and narrative compilations, apply critical standards to your acceptance of information. Ideally, every single genealogical statement will be supported by citations to evidence.

Place each ancestor in historical context with respect to family, neighbors, community, and times. Some of the most difficult genealogical problems can only be solved by extending research beyond the family to associates and neighbors.

Much of genealogical publishing is done by a few specialized publishing companies, among them Genealogical Publishing Co., 1001 N. Calvert St., Baltimore, MD 21202, (301) 837-8271; Ancestry, Inc., Box 476, Salt Lake City, UT 84110, (801) 531-1790; and Genealogical Institute, Box 22045, Salt Lake City, UT 84122, (801) 257-6174. Request copies of their catalogs.

One option is to pay someone to do your research for you. A list of certified genealogists is available from the Board for Certification of Genealogists, Box 19165, Washington, DC 20036.

28

HEALTH
AND
MEDICINE

See also: General Reference Sources, Parenting, Retirement/Aging, Self-Help/Psychology

Today the layperson has access to vastly more health information than ever before; yet the quest for accurate information is daunting. Each day the headlines bring new health crises, new "findings," new confusion.

The following health and medical information sources will guide you to answers to individual problems as well as to general medical information. In addition:

• Your doctors and nurses may be able to give you information customized to your needs; however, you will want to supplement what they tell you in order to become an informed medical consumer.

• Although the search may have to be broadened at times, try to refine your search to the most specific terms. Look under multiple sclerosis, for example, rather than under neurology.

• Public libraries offer a broad selection of general health information for laypeople, referrals to more specialized information, and, often, access to electronic databases. Librarians will not give medical advice, but will help identify sources for it.

• Local medical school and hospital libraries specialize in health materials and house more electronic sources. Reference visits can often be arranged through a call to the library's administrative office or by referral from a public library; circulation of materials usually will be restricted.

• Doctors, hospitals, pharmacies, and other sources listed below provide pamphlets on health topics.

• Check local telephone directories or ask your librarian to help locate a Tel-Med or other telephone service that provides brief taped information on selected health topics.

- Large bookstores stock virtual libraries of medical advice, with many items suitable for the home reference shelves. But here, as with any source, be sure you are comfortable with the authority, any obvious biases, and the currency of the information.

GENERAL SOURCES OF INFORMATION

General Guides

Mayo Clinic Family Healthbook. Edited by David E. Larson. Morrow, 1990.

Describes human development, first aid, and health practices. There are also chapters on safety in the environment, keeping fit, and using modern medical services. Diseases and conditions are covered by organ system and there is a color anatomy atlas and color plates on skin disorders. Also available on CD-ROM (Sony Electronic Publishing), with 500 illustrations (forty-five of them animated) and ninety minutes of sound.

American Medical Association Encyclopedia of Medicine. Random House, 1989.

The A-Z section has more than 5,000 entries and 2,200 clear illustrations on symptoms, procedures, treatments, tests, and drugs. An introductory overview discusses "Medicine Today," and back-of-the-book sections include a glossary of 2,500 drugs and a list of self-help organizations.

Columbia University College of Physicians and Surgeons Complete Home Medical Guide. Rev. ed. Crown, 1989.

Organized by broad subject areas; diseases are discussed in chapters on the various organ systems. Includes sections on first aid and diagnostic tests and a directory of organizations. Also available on CD-ROM as part of the *Health Reference Center* (see below).

The University of California, Berkeley, Wellness Encyclopedia. Houghton Mifflin, 1991.

A guidebook for a healthy lifestyle. Covers diet, exercise, safety at home and at work, self-care, and preventing disease.

Guides on Specific Topics

Many health centers are now lending their names and expertise to popular health guides on specific topics. Here are some examples:

The Johns Hopkins Medical Handbook: The 100 Major Medical Disorders of People over the Age of 50. Random House, 1992.

The Mount Sinai School of Medicine Complete Book of Nutrition. St. Martin's Press, 1990.

The Mount Sinai Medical Center Family Guide to Dental Health. Macmillan, 1991.

The Yale University School of Medicine Heart Book. Hearst, 1992.

Physicians Desk Reference (PDR). Medical Economics. Annual.

In this widely used guide to drugs, the extensive technical information about products is submitted by their manufacturers. The book contains color photos of capsules and tablets. Available on CD-ROM along with *The Merck Manual* (Medical Economics). Since *PDR* is compiled for physicians, the terminology may sometimes be too technical for laypeople. There is now a consumer version crafted explicitly for the general reader: *The PDR Family Guide to Prescription Drugs.* Medical Economics, 1993.

The Complete Drug Reference: United States Pharmacopeia Dispensing Information for the Consumer. Consumers Union. Annual.

This reference work, written in lay language, has information on drugs, their effects, and their interactions with other drugs and foods. It also contains color photos of capsules and tablets.

Essential Guide to Prescription Drugs. By James W. Long and James J. Rybacki. HarperCollins, 1993.

Profiles for the layperson of more than 200 drugs, with brand names, dosages, precautions, and possible interactions.

Essential Guide to Nonprescription Drugs. By David R. Zimmerman. HarperCollins, 1993.

Complementing the book above, describes drugs sold over the counter.

Essential Guide to Psychiatric Drugs. By Jack M. Gorman. St. Martin's Press, 1990.

Provides clear information on drugs used in combating mental illness, their effects and side effects. Written by a psychiatrist, it describes mental illnesses as well.

Complete Guide to Symptoms, Illness & Surgery: Where Does It Hurt? What Does It Mean? 2d ed. By H. Winter Griffith. The Body Press, 1989.

This book contains useful one-page summaries of more than 700 symptoms, 500 illnesses, and 100 surgeries. The diseases section gives information on the condition, what to expect during its course, how to treat it, and when to call a doctor. Griffith also is the author of *Complete Guide to Symptoms, Illness & Surgery for People Over 50* (1992).

Medical Tests and Diagnostic Procedures: A Patient's Guide to Just What the Doctor Ordered. By Philip Shtasel. HarperCollins, 1991.

Describes many diagnostic tests and medical procedures carried out by a wide range of medical and surgical specialists.

Complete Guide to Medical Tests. By H. Winter Griffith. Fisher Books, 1988.
Gives complete coverage of laboratory tests and their purposes.

Directories   *Guide to the Health Care Field.* American Hospital Association. Annual.
Lists all hospitals in the United States by state and then city. Number of beds, total expenses, and all specialized services are noted. A wide range of health care organizations and programs are listed in the last sections.

American Medical Directory. American Medical Association. Biennial.
Lists most physicians in the United States, even those who are not AMA members. Other directories (for example, *The Directory of Medical Specialists*) lists board-certified physicians only.

Alternative Health Care Resources: A Directory and Guide. By Brett Jason Sinclair. Prentice-Hall, 1992.
Directory of organizations, publications, and self-help groups providing assistance and information on alternative medical treatments such as homeopathy, acupuncture, and Oriental healing.

Consumer Health Information Source Book. 3d ed. By Alan M. Rees and Catherine Hoffman. Oryx, 1990.
This useful book is intended primarily for librarians and health education professionals, but any researcher can use it with profit to identify books or magazines on health topics and to obtain addresses of health-related clearinghouses, catalogs, and other resources. Also available on CD-ROM as part of the *Health Reference Center* (see below).

ELECTRONIC SOURCES   Health information is well suited to the currency and searching power of CD-ROM and online databases. Some titles target a specific disease, such as cancer or viral hepatitis, or a medical specialty, such as obstetrics and gynecology or pediatrics. This is a selection of the more general titles. For more complete information, see the *Gale Directory of Databases*.

AIDS Compact Library. (CD-ROM) Macmillan New Media. Quarterly.
Every major AIDS article, conference presentation, and clinical trial from the past ten years. Contains the full text of 10,000 articles from twelve major journals and newsletters, plus abstracts of more than 100,000 additional articles.

Consumer Health and Nutrition Index. (CD-ROM) National Information Services Corp., 1984–   . Quarterly.

Indexes articles from more than sixty newspapers and magazines found in most public libraries, including *Prevention, Harvard Medical School Letter, New England Journal of Medicine,* and *The New York Times.* Also available in print from Oryx Press, 1984– .

Family Doctor. 3d ed. Dr. Allen H. Bruckheim. (CD-ROM) Creative Multimedia Corp., 1993.

This relatively inexpensive compact disc provides brief explanations of and recommendations for treating common ailments. It also includes easy-to-read drug information, color anatomy charts, audio, and video. The author writes the syndicated "Family Doctor" newspaper column. Also available as *The Portable Family Doctor* on Sony Data Discman.

Health Index. (CD-ROM) Information Access. Monthly.

Provides the most current three years of indexing and abstracting of over 160 core journals, consumer magazines, and newsletters. Also online with CompuServe as Health Database Plus.

Health Reference Center. (CD-ROM) Information Access. Monthly.

An expanded version of *Health Index,* this disc contains citations with abstracts of articles appearing in more than 160 health publications from the past three years, plus the full text of approximately 100 consumer magazines and newsletters. In addition, it provides the complete text of more than 500 pamphlets from such organizations as the American Lupus Society and the Parkinson's Disease Foundation. Five books are also offered, including the *Columbia University College of Physicians and Surgeons Complete Home Medical Guide* and the *Consumer Health Information Source Book.*

Health Source. (CD-ROM) EBSCO, 1984– . Bimonthly.

Indexing and abstracting for more than 100 journals in the fields of diet and nutrition, exercise, drugs and alcohol, and medical self-care. The full text is provided for fifteen of the publications, including *Harvard Health Letter, The New England Journal of Medicine,* and *Prevention.*

Mayo Clinic Family Healthbook. (CD-ROM) See General Sources of Information (above).

MAXX. (CD-ROM) Little, Brown. 1989– . 3 times/year.

Contains information on more than 500 diseases plus the full text of fifteen medical reference works published by Little, Brown, such as the *Manual of Allergy and Immunology* and the *Manual of Rheumatology and Outpatient Orthopedics,* as well as the full text of *The Complete Drug Reference: United States Pharmacopeia Dispensing Information for the Consumer.*

MDX Health Digest. (CD-ROM) SilverPlatter, 1988–　　. Quarterly.

More than 12,000 citations with abstracts of consumer health articles. Also available online on Human Relations Information Network, updated monthly.

MEDLINE. (CD-ROM) Available from Dialog OnDisc, Cambridge Scientific Abstracts, EBSCO, SilverPlatter, and CD Plus. Monthly.

The premier medical database, MEDLINE gives references to more than 4,000 professional and scholarly journals, *not* popular or lay magazines. Compiled by the National Library of Medicine, it is the electronic version of the print *Index Medicus,* the *Index to Dental Literature,* and the *International Nursing Index.* The database dates back to 1966, and the complete file fills ten CD-ROMs, but vendors provide versions with selected coverage. Also available online, updated weekly or twice a month, with BRS, BRS/ AfterDark, Dialog (File 155), Knowledge Index, OCLC FirstSearch, and MEDLARS (a service of the National Library of Medicine). The National Library of Medicine offers software called Grateful Med that makes searching MEDLINE easier. A menu-driven version of MEDLINE, PaperChase, is available online with CompuServe, WESTLAW, and other services. Some university libraries make the MEDLINE file available on their online public access catalogs.

Mortality and Morbidity. (CD-ROM) Macmillan New Media. Annual.

The most recent five years of the text and tables of the *Morbidity and Mortality Weekly Report* with statistics from the Centers for Disease Control on illnesses and causes of death.

Nursing & Allied Health. (CD-ROM) Cambridge Scientific Abstracts. 1983–　　. Monthly. Also available as *CD Plus/CINAHL* from CD Plus and *CINAHL-CD* from SilverPlatter.

Citations to articles from 500 nursing and allied health journals, with abstracts. The electronic version of the printed *Cumulative Index to Nursing and Allied Health Literature.* Available online as *Nursing and Allied Health* through BRS, BRS/AfterDark, Dialog (File 218), and Knowledge Index, updated monthly.

Nursing Indisc. Knowledge Access International. 1963–　　. Quarterly.

A subset of MEDLINE corresponding to the *International Nursing Index.*

PDQ (Physician Data Query). (CD-ROM) Cambridge Scientific Abstracts. Quarterly.

Compiled by the National Cancer Institute, it provides information for both laypersons and physicians. Lay information includes description and treatment of and prognosis for common forms of cancer. The physician information section includes names and addresses of physicians who specialize in specific types of cancer. Also available online through BRS, CompuServe, MEDIS, and MEDLARS. If your library does not have access to PDQ online or on CD-ROM, you can obtain information by calling the National Cancer Institute at (800) 4-CANCER.

Physician's Desk Reference. (CD-ROM) See General Sources of Information (above).

Vital Signs: The Good Health Resource. (CD-ROM) Texas Caviar.
   Illustrated library of articles from health organizations such as the American Heart Association, the National Cancer Institute, the National Health Information Center. Materials available in both Spanish and English.

More than 100 medical databases are available online. Here is just a sampling:

Online Services

Comprehensive Core Medical Library. Weekly.
   Available on BRS. Full text of more than seventy medical textbooks and journals. Coverage varies; dates mostly from the late 1980s.

DIRLINE.
   A useful ancillary MEDLINE database. A full-text directory of numerous national and regional health-related organizations, agencies, and libraries. It contains a brief description of each, with address and telephone number. When relevant, the scope of the library collection is given. Available through MEDLARS from the National Library of Medicine.

Health News Daily.
   Newsletter for the industry. Available on BRS and NewsNet.

Health Periodicals Database. 1976–   . Weekly.
   Citations to and, more recently, full text of consumer health periodicals, medical journals, newspapers, and pamphlets from medical associations. Available via CompuServe, Dialog (File 149), BRS, and BRS/AfterDark.

MEDIS. Mead Data Central. Weekly.
   Full text of sixty-six publications in biomedicine, pharmacy, and health care administration. Dates back to mid-1980s.

NORD Rare Disease Database.
   Available via CompuServe, contains information on out-of-the-way medical topics; descriptions for laypersons of diseases that are difficult to find

elsewhere—for example, the "Jumping Frenchmen of Maine" disease. Paper reprints of the descriptions are available for $3.25 each from CompuServe, 5000 Arlington Centre Blvd., Columbus OH 43220.

GEnie offers *Personal Health Abstracts,* which lists 20,000 articles for the consumer, updated monthly. GEnie also has a Medical RoundTable.

Prodigy offers *Consumer Reports* articles on nutrition, exercise, and health; brief reports on health topics such as aromatherapy and foods that heal; daily health news; and a health bulletin board.

America Online, in its Health and Medical Forum, has a *Home Medical Guide,* with articles on diseases, symptoms, tests, and surgeries; reports on patient's rights and alternative medicine; and software files to download. Among these files is "Control Diabetes for Windows," software that enables the diabetic to calculate the sugar, fat, etc., in the daily diet.

CompuServe has forums on cancer, diabetes, disabilities, and health and fitness. In addition to PaperChase and Health Database Plus (Chapter 1), CompuServe also offers HealthNet, with a reference library, a newsletter, and a sports medicine section.

The Internet, with numerous files for medical educators and researchers, also hosts some lists of interest to laypeople: MEDNEWS distributes the Health Info-Com Network Newsletter with weekly AIDS statistics, FDA bulletins, medical news from the United Nations, and the latest *Morbidity and Mortality Weekly Report* from the Centers for Disease Control. Access via: **MEDNEWS%ASUACAD.BITNET2CUNYVM.CUNY.EDU.**

Handicap News BBS Archive is a collection of information and sources for and about the disabled. Access via: **ftp handicap.shel.isc-br.com;** log in **anonymous.**

Bulletin Boards   NAPWA-LINK: Bulletin board for people with AIDS. Voice phone (202) 898-0414.

Handicap News BBS. A list of BBS with handicapped focus. **(203) 337-1607.**

PERIODICALS   *American Health: Fitness of Body and Mind.* 1982–   . 10 times/year.
    Each issue contains health and fitness articles plus twenty departments covering such topics as sports and fitness, mental health, nutrition, health and beauty.

Health. 1967–   . 10 times/year.
    Aimed at women, *Health* contains short articles on many aspects of health and beauty. The oldest existing medical magazine for the layperson.

In Health (formerly *Hippocrates*). 1987–   . Bimonthly.

Contains long and detailed articles on varied medical topics; illustrated with color photos. Each issue also contains some fifteen departmental features, such as an AIDS file with recent discoveries, a list of places to write for health information, and statistics. A high-quality magazine for the layperson.

Prevention. 1950–   . Monthly.
    Covers all aspects of the healthy lifestyle, with an emphasis on the prevention of illness. Articles stress nutrition and vitamins, but also treat exercise, mental health, and other issues.

FDA Consumer. 10 times/year.
    This magazine, issued by the Food and Drug Administration, contains informative articles on food, drugs, and other health-related concerns.

Consumer Reports Health Letter. 1989–   . Monthly.
    Practical information on current topics—carpal tunnel syndrome, dietary supplements, tooth whiteners, and others.

The last decade has seen a flood of health newsletters for the layperson. Some examples:
    Harvard Health Letter
    Health Letter (published by Public Citizen)
    Mayo Clinic Health Letter
    University of California, Berkeley, Wellness Letter

Hundreds of professional journals serve medical researchers and practitioners. The two best-known are:

New England Journal of Medicine. 1812–   . Weekly.
    The most authoritative and widely quoted journal, referred to in newspapers and broadcasts almost every week. In addition to refereed articles, it contains opinion papers, letters, and book reviews. The journal can be found in most libraries. Also available full text on CD-ROM from Macmillan New Media.

JAMA: Journal of the American Medical Association. 1848–   . Weekly.
    The weekly flagship journal of the AMA contains medical articles, medical news, letters, opinion papers, and book reviews. Also available full text on CD-ROM from Macmillan New Media.

The federal government is an excellent source for current health-related information.

GOVERNMENT PUBLICATIONS

Health Information Resources in the Federal Government. 5th ed. 1990.
    A directory of federally sponsored health information resources.

Facing Forward: A Guide for Cancer Survivors. National Institutes of Health, 1990.

Health Hotlines. National Institutes of Health, 1990.

Medicare and Your Physician's Bill. Health Care Financing Administration, 1992.

More Than Snuffles: Childhood Asthma. Food and Drug Administration, 1991.

No Safe Tan. Food and Drug Administration, 1992.

Safe and Sure Self-Care with Over-the-Counter Medicine. Food and Drug Administration, 1992.

Ulcers: Screaming or Silent, Watch Them with Care. Food and Drug Administration, 1991.

When Do You Need an Antacid? Food and Drug Administration, 1992.

Who Donates Blood for You Better Than You? Food and Drug Administration, 1991.

Why Do You Smoke? National Institutes of Health, 1992.

See also the following *Subject Bibliographies* from the Government Printing Office:
#291—Food, Diet, and Nutrition
#122—Public Health
#121—Vital and Health Statistics
#154—Medicine and Medical Science

GOVERNMENT AGENCIES

On topics from pollution and food safety to tobacco use and health education, a wealth of information is available from federal agencies, including the Department of Health and Human Services:

Public Health Service
5600 Fishers Lane
Rockville, MD 20857
(301) 443-2404

Charged with promoting the protection and advancement of the nation's physical and mental health. It has several subagencies:

Centers for Disease Control
1600 Clifton Road NE
Atlanta, GA 30333
(404) 639-3311

Provides information about prevention, epidemiology, and the treatment of disease. Publishes *MMWR (Morbidity and Mortality Weekly Report)*, which is available in most health-oriented libraries. Its information center, (404) 639-3396, contains books, pamphlets, and microforms on a wide range of diseases.

Food and Drug Administration
5600 Fishers Lane
Rockville, MD 20857
(301) 443-1544

Responsible for ensuring the safety of the country's food supply; tests and approves drugs before distribution.

National Center for Health Statistics
1600 Clifton Road NE
Atlanta, GA 30333
(404) 639-3311

This is *the* place to turn to for data on health topics. The Center publishes *Vital & Health Statistics,* which covers everything related to health. The staff is helpful to callers.

National Institutes of Health
9000 Rockville Pike
Bethesda, MD 20892
(301) 496-4000

More than a dozen institutes do research on health and medical conditions. Among them are institutes on cancer, heart disease, diabetes, allergies, dental research, neurological disorders, child health, environmental health, eyes, arthritis, nursing research, and human genome research.

State and Local Government Agencies

City, county, and state agencies may also be helpful. For example, the state Health Services Department is likely to have a Food and Drug section, an Infectious Diseases section, a Licensing and Certification division, and others. A quick look in the Government section of your telephone directory will yield addresses and phone numbers. Similarly, the telephone book can be used to find the names, addresses, and telephone numbers, for example, of the Environmental Health and Mental Health departments of your county or city.

ASSOCIATIONS

There are a large number of disease-specific associations, most of which coordinate support groups and publish informative pamphlets or newsletters. Most have local chapters in large cities. Examples range from famous organizations associated with well-known diseases, such as the American Heart Association, American Lung Association, and American Diabetes Association, to such lesser-known groups as the American Tinnitus Association and National Foundation for Ileitis and Colitis. Three of the more general-interest associations are:

The American Medical Association
515 N. State Street
Chicago, IL 60610
(312) 464-4818
AMA issues a catalog of its publications, some of which can be obtained by the public. AMA has ties to state and local medical associations and it publishes several medical journals in addition to *JAMA* (see above).

American Hospital Association
840 N. Lake Shore Drive
Chicago, IL 60611
(312) 280-600
Publishes hospital statistics, provides continuing education for hospital personnel, administers a library.

American Association of Retired Persons (AARP)
601 E St. NW
Washington, DC 20049
(202) 434-2277
A source of all types of health-related information. Though materials are written for those over 50, they are often relevant to adults of any age. They publish thousands of books and pamphlets and have hundreds of titles on health. Request a free catalog.

For information on additional associations, consult: *Medical and Health Information Directory.* 6th ed. 3 vols. Gale, 1992.
An excellent comprehensive directory of all kinds of institutions, agencies, government departments, publications, libraries, and health services, including clinics, treatment centers, and counseling/diagnostic services.

LIBRARIES

National Library of Medicine
8600 Rockville Pike
Bethesda, MD
(301) 496-6308

The NLM has more than 4 million volumes in its collection. The MED-LINE database (see above) is compiled at the National Library and it supports the MEDLARS online service through which MEDLINE and other databases can be searched. It has an extensive collection in the history of medicine. Also serves as the resource library for the National Institutes of Health, on whose campus it is located.

Francis A. Countway Library of Medicine
Boston Medical Library/Harvard Medical Library
10 Shattuck Street
Boston, MA 02115
(617) 432-2142
The second largest medical library in the United States, after the National Library of Medicine.

New York Academy of Medicine Library
2 E. 103rd St.
New York, NY 10029
(212) 876-8200

Louise Darling Biomedical Library
University of California, Los Angeles
12-077 Center for the Health Sciences
Los Angeles, CA 90024
(310) 825-5781

William H. Welch Medical Library
Johns Hopkins University
1900 E. Monument St.
Baltimore, MD 21205
(410) 955-3411

Use these headings in library catalogs:

LC SUBJECT HEADINGS

Drugs, Nonprescription
Environmental health
Health attitudes
Health behavior (use for Health habits)
Health counseling
Health education
Health facilities
Herbalists
Holistic medicine

Medical care (use for Health care)
Medical care, Cost of
Medical economics (use for the economic aspects of Health care)
Medical personnel
Medical technology
Natural foods (use for Health foods)
Naturopaths

Nutrition
Preventive health services
Public health

Self-care, Health
Voluntary health agencies
Women's health services

Care and hygiene is a subheading under parts of the body, e.g., Foot—Care and hygiene.

The following subheadings can also be used for parts of the body:

Heart—Abnormalities
Heart—Anatomy
Heart—Diseases—Diagnosis
Heart Diseases—Mortality
Heart Diseases—Nutritional aspects

Diseases can also be subdivided:
Diabetes—Diagnosis

COMMERCIAL VENDORS

Commercial vendors publish quality pamphlets, videos, and audiocassettes on a wide range of health topics. Some good sources are listed below:

Channing Bete Company
200 State Road
South Deerfield, MA 01373
(413) 665-7611

Hazelden Educational Materials
15251 Pleasant Valley Road
P. O. Box 176
Center City, MN 55012-0176
(800) 328-9000

Health Edco
P. O. Box 21207
Waco, TX 76702
(800) 433-2677

Johnson Institute
7151 Metro Boulevard
Minneapolis, MN 54439-2122
(800) 231-5165

Krames Communications
1100 Grandy Lane
San Bruno, CA 94066-3030
(800) 333-3032

29

HISTORY

See also: *General Reference Sources, Multiculturalism, Women's Studies*

The study of history is not limited to political and military events, but also includes many aspects of everyday life. Some historians consider history to be part of the humanities; others use techniques from the social sciences. Therefore, when selecting reference materials, you may need to look at sources from both areas. The first historical indexes appeared in the 1950s and have been dramatically improved since then. The introduction of the first CD-ROM indexes after 1985 made searching periodical literature a less cumbersome chore than it used to be. Historical dictionaries and encyclopedias have also proliferated so that there is a specialized historical reference work on virtually every topic from the ancient Greeks to the Gulf War.

Use historical dictionaries and encyclopedias to find out the "basics" of a topic. Then identify the guides to the literature and indexes that cover the subject and the types of material they include. Do they cover books? Periodicals? Primary source materials such as manuscripts, government documents, or newspapers? Is an online database search an option? Finally, evaluate the information you have found. Use book reviews to determine the authority and quality of books. Check the bibliographies of sources you have in hand. Are any of the articles you have found cited? What are the credentials of the author?

The following pages outline basic sources for historical research that will help you answer some of these questions.

Reference Sources in History: An Introductory Guide. By Ronald H. Fritze, Brian E. Coutts, and Louis A. Vyhnanek. ABC-Clio, 1990.

Designed to serve as a basic introduction to the major reference works for all periods of history in all parts of the world, with emphasis on materials published in English. Entries describe several thousand sources, arranged according to type, ranging from historical atlases, to dictionaries and handbooks, to microform collections. Each entry includes an explanatory annotation and tips on how to use the source.

Handbook for Research in American History: A Guide to Bibliographies and Other Reference Works. 2d ed. By Francis Paul Prucha. University of Nebraska Press, 1994.

This helpful guide describes important reference works in American history. The first section covers bibliographies, indexes to periodical literature, maps and atlases, and government publications. Section Two includes chapters on reference sources for broad subject areas such as political history as well as chapters on more specialized topics such as military, diplomatic, ethnic, religious, and women's history. Almost all chapters are prefaced with lengthy introductory notes.

The American Historical Association's *Guide to Historical Literature* (Macmillan, 1961) is an important guide to the literature of history for all nations and time periods but is now very outdated. Oxford University Press will publish a new edition in early 1995.

The Times Atlas of World History. 4th ed. Edited by Norman Stone. Hammond, 1994.

This important atlas includes more than 600 historical maps, a glossary of 100,000 entries, and a 300,000-word text. Sections highlight early man, the first civilizations, the Middle Ages, the emerging West, the age of European dominance, and the age of global civilization. A distinguishing feature is the skewing of maps to reflect different perspectives, a technique now incorporated into many newer atlases. The fourth edition incorporates recent history.

The Atlas of North American Exploration: From the Norse Voyages to the Race to the Poles. By William H. Goetzmann and Glyndwr Williams. Prentice-Hall, 1992.

This colorful atlas illustrates the routes traveled by virtually every explorer in North America from the best known to the most obscure. Four-color maps describe journeys and key settlements and point out where significant events occurred. Coverage includes early settlements, expansion of the frontier, continental explorations, and the quest for the Northwest

Passage and the North Pole. Facsimiles of maps used by the explorers are included.

There are literally hundreds of specialized historical reference works, including the following recent comprehensive works:

Encyclopedia of the North American Colonies. 3 vols. Edited by Jacob Ernest Cooke. Scribner's, 1993.

Designed for nonspecialists, this three-volume set includes articles by historians, anthropologists, geographers, linguists, sociologists, and folklorists. The Spanish Borderlands, New Netherlands, New France, the Acadians, and Russian settlements in Alaska, as well as the thirteen British colonies are covered. Sections describe government and law, economic life, labor systems, racial interaction, folkways, family life, and education.

Encyclopedia of American Social History. 3 vols. Edited by Mary Kupiec Clayton, Elliott J. Gorn, and Peter W. Williams. Scribner's, 1993.

The editors of this encyclopedia describe social history as history "from the bottom up," studying the lives of ordinary people. Essays examine the forces that shape day-to-day existence, such as family structure, work, and popular culture and entertainment. Research aids include annotated bibliographies, maps, and charts and tables. Other reference sets published in the Scribner's American Civilization Series include: *Encyclopedia of the American Religious Experience* (1988); *Encyclopedia of the American Judicial System* (1987); *Encyclopedia of American Political History* (1984); *Encyclopedia of American Economic History* (1980); and *Encyclopedia of American Foreign Policy* (1978).

The Encyclopedia of Southern History. Edited by David C. Roller and Robert W. Twyman. Louisiana State University Press, 1979.

This is the best example of a regional historical encyclopedia. The editors define the South as the sixteen slaveholding states of 1860 plus the District of Columbia. Subjects covered include biography, linguistics, social structure, humor, art, medicine, industry, transportation, and politics. Numerous maps, charts, and tables enhance the volume.

Encyclopedia of Southern Culture. Edited by Charles Reagan Wilson and William Ferris. University of North Carolina Press, 1989.

Defines the South as wherever Southern culture is found. In addition to history, the work also covers the arts and social sciences with articles on such topics as film, country music, agriculture, black life, and media.

The Negro Almanac: A Reference Work on the African American. 6th ed. Compiled by Harry A. Ploski and James Williams. Gale, 1993.

Providing accurate, comprehensive, and well-documented information on African-American culture, this volume uses tables, graphs, illustrations, and vivid text to describe more than 500 years of history. The topical chapters are complemented by a 100-page chronology of black history current through 1993.

Also useful in documenting the black experience in America are the *Dictionary of Afro-American Slavery* (Greenwood Press, 1988) and the *Encyclopedia of African-American Civil Rights: From Emancipation to the Present* (Greenwood Press, 1992).

World

Civilization of the Ancient Mediterranean: Greece and Rome. 3 vols. Edited by Michael Grant and Rachel Kitzinger. Scribner's, 1988.

These volumes contain essays on topics ranging from farming and cooking to taxes, warfare, and divinities in Greece and Rome. The essays cover the period from pre-history to the fall of Rome in A.D. 476. Each essay provides a synthesis of current knowledge and concludes with a bibliography of primary and secondary materials.

Dictionary of the Middle Ages. 13 vols. Edited by Joseph R. Strayer. Scribner's, 1982–90.

This massive set is the standard reference source for medieval studies. Coverage extends from A.D. 500 to A.D. 1500 in the Latin West, the Slavic world, Asia Minor, the lands of the Caliphate in the East, and the Muslim and Christian areas of North Africa.

Encyclopedia of Asian History. 4 vols. Edited by Ainslie T. Embree. Scribner's, 1988.

Prepared by the Asia Society to make available the highest level of contemporary scholarship on Asia to a nonspecialist audience, the encyclopedia covers all aspects of Asian civilization from early history to the present. Geographical coverage includes all of Asia from Iran to Japan, including the Philippines and Indonesia. Articles describe persons, places, geographic features, peoples, periods, the arts, languages, and a host of other topics.

Cambridge Encyclopedia of Latin America and the Caribbean. 2d ed. Edited by Simon Collier, Thomas E. Skidmore, and Harold Blakemore. Cambridge University Press, 1992.

This is one of an ongoing series of encyclopedias that describe the geography, economy, people, and politics of various regions of the world. In the Latin America volume, however, the longest sections focus on the region's history and culture. Other one-volume encyclopedias from Cambridge University Press include: *The Cambridge Encyclopedia of China* (2d ed.,

1991), *The Cambridge Encyclopedia of India, Pakistan, Bangladesh, Sri Lanka, Nepal, Bhutan and the Maldives* (1989), and *The Cambridge Encyclopedia of the Middle East and North Africa* (1988).

Women's Studies Encyclopedia. 3 vols. Edited by Helen Tierney. Greenwood, 1989–91.

Volume III of this set includes a wide range of articles that focus on the history of women's roles, activities, and status. (Volumes I and II cover the sciences and the humanities.) Other Greenwood historical dictionaries include: *Medieval Knighthood and Chivalry* (1986 and 1988), *Tudor England* (1991), *European Imperialism* (1991), *History of France since 1789* (1985–92), *Revolutionary China* (1992), *Russian Revolution* (1989), *Modern Italian History* (1985), *Scandinavian History* (1986), *Modern Spain* (1990), and the *Spanish Empire* (1991). Virtually all include historical chronologies and selected bibliographies.

There are approximately 10,000 periodicals published worldwide with a principal focus on history. The most complete guide is:

PERIODICALS AND INDEXES

Historical Periodicals Directory. 5 vols. Edited by Eric H. Boehm, Barbara H. Pope, and Marie S. Ensign. ABC-Clio, 1981–86.

Among the most popular historical periodicals found in American libraries are:

American Heritage. 1947–   . 8/year.

Sponsored by the American Association for State and Local History and the Society of American Historians, this popular periodical focuses on the history of the United States from prehistoric times through the twentieth century. Profusely illustrated, a recent issue included articles on drugs, the musical *Oklahoma,* Theodore Dreiser, the Deerfield Massacre, and black slaveowners.

American History Illustrated. 1965–   . Bimonthly.

This popular periodical covers all aspects of U.S. history from its prehistory to the Korean War. A recent issue included excerpts from John Faragher's biography of Daniel Boone and articles on nurses in World War II, Wendell Willkie, campaign memorabilia at the University of Hartford, and the movie *Casablanca.*

American Historical Review. 1895–   . 5/year.

This scholarly journal is published by the American Historical Association. Despite its title, its scope includes the history of all nations from their prehistory through the twentieth century. Each issue contains two or three lengthy articles by noted scholars, several review articles, and approximately 200 book reviews.

English Historical Review. 1886–   . Quarterly.

This is the oldest English-language periodical devoted solely to history. Very scholarly in tone, it covers all aspects of world history from the Middle Ages to the present, although articles on British and European topics are most frequent. A typical issue includes articles, a section on notes and documents, and lengthy as well as shorter book reviews.

The Historian. 1938–   . Quarterly.

Sponsored by Phi Alpha Theta, the international honor society in history. Typical issues contain interviews with noted historians, articles by historians and graduate students, and book reviews.

Journal of American History. 1914–   . Quarterly.

Sponsored by the Organization of American Historians, this is the leading scholarly journal devoted solely to the history of the United States. Issues include articles, exhibition reviews, book reviews, and, unique to this journal, reviews of recent movies, both popular and documentary. Occasionally special topical issues are published.

C.R.I.S.: Combined Retrospective Index to Journals in History, 1838–1974. 11 vols. Carrollton Press, 1977–78.

This index provides subject and author access to more than 100,000 articles in 243 journals of history. Volumes 1–9 are subject category indexes and volumes 10 and 11 are author indexes.

See Electronic Sources below for other indexes to history periodicals.

ELECTRONIC SOURCES   *America: History and Life on Disc.* (CD-ROM) ABC-Clio, 1982–   . Updated 3 times/year.

The most comprehensive index of North American history, it includes abstracts of periodical articles on the history and culture of the United States and Canada. Articles are abstracted from 2,100 serial publications in forty languages. Of these, 900 are published in North America. Beginning in 1989, citations for film and video reviews as well as reviews of microforms have been included. Also available online with Dialog (File 38) and Knowledge Index (File HIST 1), 1964–   , updated quarterly. Available in print, ABC-CLIO, 1964–   , updated 5 times a year. Issues 1–3 include indexes. Issue 4 includes abstracts and citations only. Issue 5 is the annual index.

Historical Abstracts. (CD-ROM) ABC-Clio, 1982–   . Updated 3 times/
year.

This index covers all branches of world history except for the United States and Canada, from 1450 to the present, with abstracts and shorter annotations of articles from approximately 2,100 journals published in eighty countries in almost forty languages. In addition, recently published books are selected from book reviews in thirteen major historical and bibliographical journals. Available online with Dialog (File 39) and Knowledge Index (File HIST 2), 1973–   , updated 6 times a year. *Historical Abstracts* is available in print in two parts: Part A: Modern History Abstracts, 4 issues/year; Part B: Twentieth Century Abstracts, 4 issues/year. ABC-Clio, 1955–   . No. 4 of each volume is a cumulative annual index.

History Source. (CD-ROM) EBSCO, 1990–   . Updated bimonthly or 3 times/year.

This history database is available only on CD-ROM. It provides abstract and index coverage of the fifty leading historical journals and full-text coverage of *American Heritage, History Today,* and *Smithsonian.* Coverage begins in July 1990 for most journals.

Humanities Index. (CD-ROM) H. W. Wilson, 1984–   . Quarterly.

An index to approximately 350 periodicals in the humanities, including history and history-related titles. There is a separate listing of citations to book reviews following the main body of the index. *Wilson Humanities Abstracts* is an annotated version on CD-ROM. Also available online with Wilsonline, 1984–   , and OCLC FirstSearch, updated twice a week, and in print, updated quarterly, as *Humanities Index,* 1974–   (formerly *Social Sciences and Humanities Index,* 1965–74; *International Index,* 1907–65).

Social Sciences Index. (CD-ROM) H. W. Wilson, 1984–   . Monthly.

A companion to the *Humanities Index,* this source indexes journals in anthropology, geography, political science, and other disciplines that may be useful to the student of history. Also available on CD-ROM as *Wilson Social Sciences Abstracts.* Available online with Wilsonline and OCLC First-Search and in print.

Constitution Papers. (CD-ROM) Bureau of Electronic Publishing, 1988. **Other Electronic**

Provides the texts of the constitutions of the first thirteen states and other **Sources**
documents of importance to the founding of our nation, such as the Mayflower Compact, Thomas Paine's *Common Sense,* and the complete *Federalist Papers.*

History of the World on CD-ROM. Bureau of Electronic Publishing, 1994.
U.S. History on CD-ROM. Bureau of Electronic Publishing, 1990.
Each of these discs contains the full text of many history books, plus 1,000 maps, photographs, and tables.

U.S. War Series. (CD-ROM) Quanta Press, 1990–91.
Four different discs contain chronologies, biographies, and campaigns of the Civil War, World War II, Korean War, and Vietnam War. *USA Wars: Civil War* is also available for Data Discman.

The National Register of Historic Places Index. Buckmaster Publishing, 1989.
More than 50,000 place names of historical importance from the Department of the Interior.

European Monarchs on CD-ROM. Quanta Press, 1992.
Early kings and queens as well as current royal families.

Internet/Bitnet : Conferences exist for various subfields in history: Russian history, military history, and the history of the American West, for example.
To subscribe to the military list, send an e-mail message to **Listserv @ukanvm.Bitnet.** In the body of the message, type **subscribe Milhst-L your name.** For Russian history, subscribe by sending a message to **Listserv @uscvm.Bitnet** and in the body of the message type **subscribe Rushist your name.** For the Western history list, send a message to **Listserv @uscvm.Bitnet** and in the body of the message type **subscribe Amwest-H your name.**

Project Gutenberg includes the full text of important documents and speeches, such as surrender documents and Martin Luther King's "I have a dream" speech. Access via **University of Minnesota Gopher/Libraries/ Electronic Books/By Title/Historical Documents.**

Mississippi State History Archives has a lot of material on the Internet not relating to Mississippi history, for example, materials on the Vietnam War, medieval studies, French socialism, and Andrew Jackson. FTP via **msstate.edu.** and log in **anonymous. cd docs/history.**

GOVERNMENT PUBLICATIONS   U.S. government documents are an important source of information for students of American history. The government publishes many books on historical topics, and government documents are themselves primary source materials for historical study. All documents listed here are published by the U.S. Government Printing Office unless otherwise noted. Before the late 1800s, government documents were published by private companies, but librarians in government documents collections will be able to help you find them.

Monthly Catalog of United States Government Publications. Government Printing Office. 1885–   .

The most comprehensive index to materials issued by the federal government and thus a major finding tool for primary source material. The cumulative subject index is most helpful. Coverage of publications issued since 1976 is available on CD-ROM from several publishers:

Government Documents Catalog Service. AutoGraphics.
Government Publications Index. Information Access.
GPO CAT/PAC. MARCIVE.
GPO Monthly Catalog. OCLC.
GPO on SilverPlatter. SilverPlatter.

Online access to the *Monthly Catalog* from 1976 is available through Dialog (File 66), BRS and BRS/AfterDark (GPOM), and OCLC's First-Search service.

Historical Statistics of the United States, Colonial Times to 1970. 2 vols. 1976.

Thousands of tables of social, economic, and natural resources data can be accessed by subject and time period. Updated annually by *Statistical Abstract of the United States,* 1878–   . Tables in this publication outline recent social, political, and economic trends in the United States; many of them also contain historical data. The *Statistical Abstract* has two supplements, the *County and City Data Book* (1949–   ) and the *State and Metropolitan Area Data Book* (1979–   ), published at five-year intervals.

Weekly Compilation of Presidential Documents, 1965–   .

The Presidency

Provides speeches, vetoes, executive orders, and other papers of the highest elected official in the United States. This information is retrievable by subject, name, and action (veto, order, proclamation, etc.).

Public Papers of the Presidents, 1957–   .

Initially provided an edited version of what is now included in the *Weekly Compilation of Presidential Documents (WCPD).* Since 1977, everything in the *WCPD* has also been included in the *Public Papers.* Retrospective coverage of the Hoover and Truman administrations as well as the first four years of the Eisenhower administration is included. The papers of Franklin Delano Roosevelt and earlier presidents are available from commercial publishers.

The Presidents of the United States of America. 9th ed. 1982.
The First Ladies. 3d ed. 1981.

Biographies of all the presidents and their wives.

Congressional Masterfile 1. (CD-ROM) Congressional Information Service.

Indexes congressional committee hearings, prints, journals, and other congressional publications from 1789 to 1969. The print equivalent is six publications from the Congressional Information Service: *CIS Unpublished U.S. Senate Committee Hearings Index; CIS U.S. Congressional Committee Hearings Index; CIS U.S. Congressional Committee Prints Index; CIS U.S. Serials Set Index; CIS Unpublished U.S. Senate Committee Hearings Index;* and *CIS Index to U.S. Senate Executive Documents and Reports.* These have been updated by:

Congressional Masterfile 2. Congressional Information Service, 1970–   .
Quarterly.

Indexes publications produced by committees and subcommittees of Congress from 1970 to date. Also online with Dialog (File 101), updated monthly. Print equivalent is *CIS/ Index to Publications of the U.S. Congress.* Congressional Information Service, 1970–   .

Congressional Record, 1874–   . (Preceded by *Congressional Globe, Register of Debates,* and the *Annals of Congress.*)

Transcripts of the debates of Congress. The *Congressional Record* has been online in full text with NEXIS and abstracted with Dialog since 1981.

Biographical Directory of the United States Congress, 1774–1989. 1989.

Brief biographical data on everyone who has ever served in Congress as well as listings of senators and representatives by state and by chamber.

Black Americans in Congress, 1870–1989. 1990.

Women in Congress, 1917–1990. 1991.

Other titles of interest from Congress include:

Presidential Vetoes, 1789–1988. 1992.
Historical Almanac of the United States Senate. 1989.
To Make All Laws: The Congress of the United States, 1789–1989. 1989.
The Senate, 1789–1989: Addresses on the History of the United States Senate. 2 vols. 1988.

Judges of the United States. 2d ed. 1983.

The Supreme Court of the United States: Its Beginnings and Its Justices, 1790–1991. 1991.

Other government publications of historical interest include:

War of the Rebellion: A Compilation of the Official Records of the Union and Confederate Armies. 1880–1901.

U.S. Army in World War II series. 80 vols. 1945–1992.

See also the following lists from the Government Printing Office:

Subject Bibliography #144: American Revolution
Subject Bibliography #192: Civil War
Subject Bibliography #98: Military History
Subject Bibliography #236: Naval History
Subject Bibliography #140: Public Buildings, Landmarks and Historic Sites of the United States

**GOVERNMENT
AGENCIES**

National Archives
Pennsylvania Ave. at Eighth St. NW
Washington, DC 20408
(202) 501-5402

The National Archives is the official depository for records produced by the U.S. government. It produces publications, teaching aids, audiovisual materials, and courses. *Guide to the National Archives of the United States* (1974) gives detailed descriptions of its historical records. Special guides, such as *Black History: A Guide to Civilian Records in the National Archives* (1984) and *Guide to Federal Archives Relating to the Civil War* (1962), are also available. The National Archives has eleven regional branches. See Chapter 27, Genealogy, for a list of addresses and telephone numbers.

The National Archives also administers the following presidential libraries:

Herbert Hoover Library
West Branch, IA 52358
(319) 643-5301

Franklin D. Roosevelt Library
Hyde Park, NY 12538
(914) 229-8114

Harry S. Truman Library
Independence, MO 64050
(816) 833-1400

Dwight D. Eisenhower Library
Abilene, KS 67410
(913) 263-4751

John F. Kennedy Library
Boston, MA 02125
(617) 929-4500

Lyndon B. Johnson Library
Austin, TX 78705
(512) 482-5137

Richard M. Nixon Library
Yorba Linda, CA 92686
(714) 993-3393

Gerald R. Ford Library
Ann Arbor, MI 48109
(313) 668-2218

Jimmy Carter Library
Atlanta, GA 30307
(404) 331-3942

National Endowment for the Humanities
1100 Pennsylvania Avenue NW
Washington, DC 20506
(202) 786-0438
Provides support for fellowships and seminars, grants for the preparation
of publication of texts and reference materials, and grants for programming at the state and local levels.

National Park Service
U.S. Department of the Interior
P. O. Box 37127
Washington, DC 20013-7127
(202) 208-6843
Administers National Register of Historic Places.

Smithsonian Institution
1000 Jefferson Dr. SW
Washington, DC 20560
(202) 357-1300

Supports research, publishes *Smithsonian Magazine,* maintains several
libraries, and manages more than a dozen museums, among them the
National Museum of American History in Washington.

Directory of Historical Organizations in the United States and Canada. 14th ed.
Edited by Mary Bray Wheeler. American Association for State and Local
History Press, 1990.

More than 13,000 organizations listed alphabetically by state with detailed information about their purpose and collections. Particularly helpful
is Part V, which organizes agencies by major program.

Many state historical societies or preservation agencies produce directories of organizations of local interest that may be considered too small for
inclusion in the directory listed above. The address and telephone number
for your state's agency or historical society can be found in the Council of
State Governments' biennial publication, *State Administrative Officials Classified by Function.*

American Association for State and Local History
530 Church St., Suite 600
Nashville, TN 37219
(615) 255-2971
Concerned with research on and teaching of local history, this society
publishes *History News,* technical leaflets, and a bulletin series.

American Historical Association
400 A St. SE
Washington, DC 20003
(202) 544-2422
Members are professional historians who study the history of all parts of
the world, educators, and those interested in history. Maintains a speakers'
bureau, gives awards, provides publications.

National Trust for Historic Preservation
1785 Massachusetts Ave. NW
Washington, DC 20036
(202) 673-4000
Maintains historic properties, gives grants and loans for preservation,
sponsors seminars and workshops, and monitors legislation. Publishes *Historic Preservation,* other periodicals and books.

Newcomen Society of the United States
412 Newcomen Rd.
Exton, PA 19341
(215) 363-6600
Has published more than 1,300 studies on the history of industry, transportation, communication, agriculture, mining, law, education, and related fields.

Organization of American Historians
112 N. Bryan St.
Bloomington, IN 47808
(812) 855-7311
Promotes research and study of American history. Has a speakers' bureau, provides educational programs and publications.

Consult the *Encyclopedia of Associations* for organizations that specialize in a period of history or regional history, e.g., Civil War Historical Association, Western History Association.

LC SUBJECT HEADINGS

History is a Library of Congress subject heading; however, the items categorized under this heading will include materials dealing with the study and teaching of history, the philosophy of history, history research, and other items of a very broad nature. To find material on a particular period of time, consult headings such as:

History, Ancient
History, Modern
Middle Ages

The subheading History may be used under specific topics, classes of persons, or geographic entities. For example:

Automobiles—History	Jews—History
Education—History	Kentucky—History
France—History	Philadelphia—History

History used as a subheading under geographic areas may be further subdivided by time period. For example:

Great Britain—History—Henry VIII, 1509–1547
United States—History—Civil War, 1861–1865
Mozambique—History—1698–1891

Headings that begin with the word historic or historical may also be consulted. For example:

Historic farms
Historical reenactments

In historical research, proper names may be used as subjects as well. These must be searched by last name first. For example:

American Antiquarian Society
185 Salisbury St.
Worcester, MA 01609-1634
(508) 755-5221
Research library with more than 7 million items on American history, including pamphlets, prints, maps, and a strong newspaper collection. Specializes in history through 1876.

William L. Clements Library
University of Michigan
909 S. University Ave.
Ann Arbor, MI 48109
(313) 764-2347
Collections of Americana, discovery through the nineteenth century.

Huntington Library
1151 Oxford Rd.
San Marino, CA 91108
(818) 405-2100
Important collections in history, especially of the West.

John Carter Brown Library
Brown University
Providence, RI 02912
(401) 863-2725
Strong collections on the Americas during the colonial period.

Massachusetts Historical Society Library
1154 Boylston St.
Boston, MA 02215
(617) 536-1608
Important manuscript collections. See *Catalog of Manuscripts of the Massachusetts Historical Society.* 7 vols. G. K. Hall, 1969. Supplement, 1980.

Newberry Library
60 W. Walton
Chicago, IL 60610
(312) 943-9090
A center for the study of Renaissance history.

State Historical Society of Wisconsin
816 State St.
Madison, WI 53706
(608) 264-6534

Large collections of books, manuscripts, newspapers, and nineteenth-century federal and state documents. Scope of collections not limited to Wisconsin or even the Midwest.

Most college and many large public libraries hold large historical collections. For a guide to these collections, see:

Subject Collections. 7th ed. 2 vols. Edited by Lee Ash and William G. Miller. Bowker, 1993.

This edition describes more than 18,000 collections on all topics in over 11,000 academic, public, and special libraries and museums in the United States and Canada.

30

HOBBIES

See also: *General Reference Sources, Automobiles, Film, Gardening, Genealogy, Music, Sports*

A recent survey by Hobby Industries of America found that 70 percent of American households have at least one family member who has a hobby. Research on hobbies may focus on history or technique or collections or supplies. Sources of information range from general directories to specialized electronic bulletin boards.

GENERAL SOURCES OF INFORMATION

Hobbyist Sourcebook. Edited by Denise M. Allard. Gale, 1990.

For each of the forty-three hobbies listed below, this book lists clubs, publications, catalogs and sources of supplies, basic guides, magazines, meetings and conventions, and museums.

Amateur Radio	Dolls
Antique Collecting	Ephemera
Art Collecting	Fish/Aquariums
Astronomy	Games
Autograph Collecting	Gardening
Automotive Hobbies	Genealogy
Beer/Wine Making	Glass
Bird Watching	Humor
Board/Card Games	Insects
Book Collecting	Magic
Caving	Military History
Ceramics	Modelmaking
Collecting	Movies
Crafts	Music Appreciation

Music Performance
Numismatics
Painting
Personal Computing
Pets
Philately
Photography
Printmaking
Railroadiana
Rocks, Minerals, Gems
Shell Collecting
Sports Card Collecting
Treasure Hunting
Weather Forecasting
Woodworking

America's Favorite Pastimes: A Directory of Hobbies. By Robert S. Munson. American Library Association, 1994.

More than 120 high-interest hobbies and avocations are described. A bibliography and a list of associations and museums is included for each.

Aircraft enthusiast
Aircraft, model building
All-terrain vehicles
Antique cars
Archaeology and anthropology
Archery
Art
Astronomy
Backpacking
Badminton
Baseball
Basketball
Basketry
Billiards, pool
Birds, caged
Bird-watching
Board games
Boating
Boats, model building
Bowling
Boxing
Brewing beer
Calligraphy
Camping
Candle making
Card games
Carpentry
Cars, model building
Cats
Ceramics
Coin collecting
Collecting and collectibles
Computer/electronic games
Computer, personal
Cooking
Crochet
Custom/hot rod cars
Cycling
Dance
Dogs
Education, adult
Embroidery
Fencing
Fish, aquarium
Fishing
Football
Frisbee
Gambling
Gardening
Genealogy
Golf
Guns
Gymnastics
Handball
Hiking
History
Hockey, ice
Homes—plans, etc.
Horses
Hunting

Interior decorating
Inventing, patents, copyright
Knitting
Lace making
Lapidary
Leathercraft
Macramé
Martial arts
Mental games
Motion picture/video rental
Motorcycles
Mountaineering
Music
Origami
Parachuting
Photography
Physical fitness
Picture framing
Pigeons
Pottery
Quilting
Racing cars
Racquetball
Radio, amateur
Radio, citizen's band
Radio, shortwave
Railroad enthusiast
Railroad, model building
Recreational vehicles

Refinishing
Rock, fossil, gem collecting
Running
Sewing
Silkscreen
Skating, ice
Skiing
Snowmobile
Soccer
Sports cars
Stained glass
Stamp collecting
Stenciling
Surfing
Swimming
Table tennis
Tennis
Theater
Track and field
Travel
Underwater sports
Volleyball
Voluntarism
Waterskiing
Weather forecasting
Weaving
Woodworking
Wrestling
Writing

The Independent Learners' Sourcebook: Resources and Materials for Selected Topics. By Robert M. Smith and Phyllis M. Cunningham. American Library Association, 1987.

Covers "Thirty-four Popular Subjects for Inquiry," including astronomy, birds and bird-watching, cooking and nutrition, parapsychology, peace/arms reduction, photography, and political action.

What if your favorite pastime is not included in one of these books? Do what the authors of the books did and compile the information yourself. The *Encyclopedia of Associations* lists, by subject, appropriate associations and their meetings. A periodicals directory such as *Ulrich's* or *The Serials Directory* leads to relevant magazines. *Subject Guide to Books in Print* will reveal books about the hobby; the *Catalog of Catalogs*, suppliers of materials. Try a source such as *Guide to Popular U.S. Government Publications* for inexpensive materials published by the government. The *International Museum Directory* and *Subject Collections* will locate museum and library collections. (See Chapter 18, General Reference Sources, for further information about most of these titles.)

PERIODICAL INDEXES

Index to How to Do It Information: A Periodical Index. 1963–   . Annual. Norman Lathrop Enterprises, 2342 Star Dr., Box 198, Wooster, OH 44691.

Indexes sixty-two craft, hobby, and how-to magazines. Publication tends to be delayed; the volume covering 1989 wasn't published until 1991.

Hobby magazines with large circulations are indexed in the general periodical indexes described in Chapter 18. For example, the *Readers' Guide to Periodical Literature* indexes such titles as *Antiques and Collecting Hobbies, Organic Gardening, Popular Photography,* and *Sky and Telescope.*

Many hobby magazines are so specialized that libraries don't subscribe to them. Since periodical indexes are usually compiled for libraries, these magazines aren't indexed anywhere. So seekers of an index to *Error Trends Coin Magazine,* the *Jayne Mansfield Collector's Guide,* or *Scout Memorabilia* are out of luck.

ELECTRONIC SOURCES

Electronic bulletin boards (BBS), especially those catering to very specialized interests, are one of the best sources for the hobbyist.

- ANARC BBS: World Radio/TV Handbook—Short Wave Frequency Lists and Schedules (Association of North American Radio Clubs); **(913) 345-1978**
- Bird Info Network: Breeding, Raising, Taming Exotic Birds; **(303) 423-9775**
- NACD BBS: Cave Scuba Diving (National Association of Cave Divers); **(912) 246-3280**

BBS List Keepers

Some people maintain BBS that list other bulletin boards on a specific topic. Check issues of *Boardwatch Magazine* for monthly updates. Some examples are:

- Starbase III: Astronomy/Space BBS; **(209) 432-2487**
- 3WINKS BBS: Ham/Amateur Radio BBS; **(301) 590-9629**

Commercial Online Services

- America Online calls its BBS "clubs." There are clubs on astronomy, ham radio, photography, radio-controlled models, and many more. Bikenet, the bicycle club, for example, has schedules for League of American Wheelmen rides and workshops, newsletters from local bike clubs, and full-text articles from magazines such as *Bicycle USA.*
- A hobbies section on Prodigy contains more than a dozen specialized

BBS, as of this writing. For example, on the Bird-watching BBS, birders trade lists of birds seen and hints on keeping squirrels away from backyard feeders. Check out the Coins and Stamps, Model Making, Quilting, and Trains BBS, too. Some columns in Prodigy will be helpful for the hobbyist; for instance, Petline on pet care or the Chess file.

- GEnie hosts the Hobby RoundTable, where members share information about dozens of hobbies.
- CompuServe has forums on photography, cooking, wine, aquaria, scuba diving, stamps/coins, pets, and other hobbies.

The Internet

Some examples of news groups (i.e., bulletin boards) that users of the Internet (see Chapter 12) can subscribe to include the following:

rec.crafts.brewing	**rec.models.railroad**
rec.antiques	**rec.pets.birds**
rec.aquaria	**rec.pets.cats**
rec.crafts.textiles	**rec.pets.dogs**
rec.guns	**rec.roller-coaster**
rec.radio.amateur.misc.	**rec.woodworking**

In addition, the Internet has databases that are of interest to hobbyists. Two recent examples, with their Internet addresses, are:

Juggling FTP Archives—Jugglers World Newsletter, lists of vendors, festivals, clubs. **ftp piggy.cogsci.indiana.edu;** log in **anonymous; cd pub/ juggling.**

Homebrew Digest—Software, recipe books, and the Homebrew mailing list. **ftp mthvax.cs.miami.edu;** log in **anonymous; cd Homebrew Digest.**

GOVERNMENT PUBLICATIONS

The federal government publishes lots of popular titles on topics of interest to hobbyists, among them:

Beekeeping for Beginners. Department of Agriculture, 1984.

Stars in Your Eyes: A Guide to the Northern Skies. Army Corps of Engineers, 1981.

For the Fun of It: A Helpful Guide for New Stamp Collectors. Postal Service, 1978.

The Government Printing Office publishes a series of free *Subject Bibliographies* listing current government publications on more than 200 topics and also by issuing agency (Smithsonian Institution Popular Publications). For example:

#177—Birds
#198—Coins and Medals
#72—Photography
#17—Recreational and Outdoor Activities
#11—United States Postage Stamps
#234—Weather

Ask your public library or the nearest depository library (usually an academic library) for the *Subject Bibliography Index*. If you find documents on a *Subject Bibliography* that aren't owned by your local library, you can order them from the Government Printing Office by mail (Superintendent of Documents, Government Printing Office, Washington, DC 20402), by phone ((202)783-3238), or by fax ((202)512-2250) and pay with Master-Card or Visa. (See Chapter 16, Government Publications.)

ASSOCIATIONS

Hobby Industry Association of America
319 E. 54th Street
Elmwood Park, NJ 07407
(201) 794-1133
This is a trade association for suppliers of hobby and craft products.

LC SUBJECT HEADINGS

General subject headings in library catalogs and some indexes include:
Hobbies
Collectors and Collecting
Handicraft
Recreation
Leisure
Play

To find the appropriate terms for specific hobbies, ask a librarian to show you *Library of Congress Subject Headings (LCSH)*. This book will tell you if the term you are using is a recognized subject heading and will list related terms. For example, a check of *LCSH* tells us that Crocheting is a subject heading. We also learn that a broader heading is Fancy work and that narrower terms are Afghans, Beadwork, Doilies, Hairpin Lace, Lace and lace making, and Sweaters.

The subject headings for some hobbies have helpful subheadings: for instance, Autographs—Collectors and collecting or Insects—Collection and preservation.

TIPS

The "Leisure" section of the local newspaper is a good source for information on clubs for hobbyists in your community. Ask if the public library maintains a community referral directory listing clubs. Adult education classes, through the high school, senior center, or recreation department, are an excellent way to learn or improve hobby skills.

31

THE HOME

See also: *General Reference Sources, Consumer Information, Gardening*

Here we treat research on the home mainly as the quest for practical rather than scholarly information. Sources for the scholarly study of housing can be found in this book in such chapters as General Reference Sources, History, and Environment. In these sources, the heading or subheading *Housing* usually pertains to social and economic aspects; the heading *Dwellings,* to the history and description of human shelters.

The first section below suggests key sources for research on buying or building a home. It is followed by a section on home decorating.

There are books on repairs, remodeling, and maintenance of the home. Libraries collect these sources, but unfortunately, the most popular circulating items are usually charged out. Some libraries manage to keep up-to-date titles on the reference shelves; be sure to check there. What can't be found at the library is usually at the local bookstore, and it may pay to buy some basic titles.

PURCHASING/ BUILDING A HOME

Barron's Real Estate Handbook. 2d ed. Barron's, 1988.
Defines real estate terms and contains loan tables, sample real estate documents, and an extensive bibliography.

How to Buy Your Home and Do It Right. By Susan E. Beck. Dearborn Financial Publishing, 1993.
A thorough and detailed guide to the real estate transactions involved in buying a home. Discusses whether to buy, when to buy, where to buy. Also covers financing and moving.

Your New House: The Alert Consumer's Guide to Buying and Building a Quality Home. By Alan and Denise Fields. Windsor Peak Press, 1993.

Provides help in making the decision to buy or build. Information about getting a mortgage, finding an architect or using a real estate agent, and understanding contracts. For the family that chooses to build, the authors give key inspection points for all parts of the house. They list discount catalogs, home centers and warehouse clubs, and sources for discount lighting, carpeting, etc. In an appendix, windows and plumbing fixtures are rated.

Time Saver Standards for Architectural Design Data. 6th ed. By J. Callendar. McGraw-Hill, 1982.
Time Saver Standards for Interior Design and Space Planning. By Joseph De-Chiara. McGraw-Hill, 1991.

These and several related titles are bibles for architects, builders, designers, and interior decorators. They provide thousands of design standards useful in the fields of commercial and residential design.

DECORATING A HOME

In addition to general books, like the titles below, there are books on decorating specific rooms (bedrooms, children's rooms, etc.) and on specific styles, such as Southwest, country, and colonial.

The Complete Book of Home Design. Rev. ed. By Mary Gilliatt. Little, Brown, 1989.

Like the many other works by this author, provides sound advice on home decoration. Arranged by areas: living rooms/halls; kitchens/dining rooms; bedrooms/baths. Guidance on style, function, color, and design.

Decorating with Mary Gilliatt. By Mary Gilliatt. Little, Brown, 1992.

Based on her PBS series, offers checklists of what to buy, advice on caring for the home.

Decorating with Southern Living. By Louis Joyner. Oxmoor House, 1990.

Each section contains information related to a specific area of the home. An especially interesting discussion of first impressions focuses on the atmosphere created at the entrance to the home.

Materials and Components of Interior Design. 3d ed. By J. Rosemary Riggs. Prentice-Hall, 1992.

Provides descriptions of materials used in commercial and residential applications of interior design.

Do-It-Yourself Decorating. Edited by John McGowan and Roger DuBern. Reader's Digest, 1991.

Instructions on painting, wallpapering, sanding floors, making curtains and other sewing projects.

There is a wide range of magazines covering home architecture and furnishings. Some of them target special tastes, such as for log homes or for Victorian, traditional, colonial, or country homes. Other magazines, such as *Southern Living*, treat regional styles.

HomeStyles House Plans. 1986– . Quarterly.
Drawings and floor plans of houses. Blueprints can be ordered from the publisher.

Better Homes and Gardens. 1922– . Monthly.
Filled with useful and affordable projects. Back issues can yield historical reflections of American life.

House Beautiful. 1896– . Monthly.
A bit more upscale than *BH&G* (above); primarily features residential interiors/exteriors. Monthly columns on antiques, wine, food, and gardens.

Architectural Digest. 1925– . Monthly.
Photographic tours of lavish homes. Elegant rooms, gardens, antiques, art, and decorative objects.

Metropolitan Home. 1969– . Monthly.
Casual elegance in contemporary settings.

Elle Decor (American Edition). 1989– . Bimonthly.
International coverage, including homes in Seattle, Chicago, and Paris. Also has feature articles on art, antiques, and food.

Interior Design. 1932– . 16 times/year.
For design professionals; covers design of offices and other public spaces as well as homes. Includes annual Buyer's Guide to products and services.

The New York Times Complete Home Maintenance Almanac: A Season by Season Guide. Random House, 1992.
Information on preventive maintenance and repairs by season; weather-stripping in the fall, painting in the summer, and some tasks for all seasons, such as unclogging drains.

Ortho's Home Improvement Encyclopedia: Problem Solving from A to Z. Edited by Karin Shakery. Ortho, 1985.

From attics to zoning, some 120 topics are discussed, with some how-to information; not as detailed as the other books listed here.

Reader's Digest Complete Do-It-Yourself Manual. Reader's Digest, 1991.
  Gives solutions to common problems relating to household repairs and decoration. Arranged by system: masonry, plumbing, electricity, etc. Provides instructions for laying bricks, fixing sink and tub stoppers, and other common tasks.

Reader's Digest Home Improvement Manual. Reader's Digest, 1982.
  Arranged by project: adding a wing or dormer, increasing electrical capacity. In addition to the usual home improvement projects, this book has chapters on energy-saving improvements, such as solar panels, and on buying a vacation kit home.

The Stanley Complete Step-by-Step Book of Home Repair and Improvement. By James Hufnagel. Simon & Schuster, 1993.
  Gives instructions on installing safety and security systems, along with the typical interior and exterior projects found in home-improvement books.

Time-Life Books Complete Fix-It-Yourself Manual. Prentice-Hall, 1989.
  This covers the basics: kitchen and bathroom plumbing, lighting and electrical repairs, heating and cooling systems. It also deals with the repair of major and small appliances and home electronics.

Time-Life Books Complete Home Improvement and Renovation Manual. Prentice-Hall, 1991.
  From minor renovation projects to putting on an addition. Provides a helpful section on tool selection.

Time-Life Books, Ortho Books, and Sunset all publish series of inexpensive paperbacks on specific skills or projects. For example:
  Time-Life's Home Repair and Improvement Series includes:
Advanced Masonry
Basement and Foundation
Outdoor Structures
  The Ortho Books selection includes:
Basic Carpentry Techniques
How to Design and Remodel Bathrooms
How to Design and Build Decks and Patios
  In the Sunset series are:
Roofing and Siding
Windows and Skylights
Basic Home Repairs Illustrated

Home Improvement Costs for Exterior Projects. Edited by Howard Chandler and others. Means, 1991.

Home Improvement Costs for Interior Projects. Edited by Howard Chandler and others. Means, 1991.

These two books help the homeowner to estimate costs for 128 typical projects, such as sink replacement or patio doors. Each project includes a list of materials and prices, estimated work hours, professional labor costs, and a guide to the difficulty of the project.

Do-it-yourselfers with some experience can consult the sources used by professional tradesmen:

American Electrician's Handbook. 11th ed. Edited by Terrell Croft and Wilford I. Summers. McGraw-Hill, 1987.

Detailed information about circuitry, switches, outlets, conduits, lights, air conditioning, heating, and other electrical matters. Though written for the professional electrician, the instructions require only a basic knowledge of electrical work.

Sweet's Catalog of Products for Homebuilding and Remodeling. McGraw-Hill. Annual.

Sweet's Catalog of Products for General Building and Renovation. McGraw-Hill. Annual.

Two titles from a series of eighteen volumes that reproduce catalogs from hundreds of companies selling products for building and construction. Indispensable for contractors, architects, and interior decorators. A CD-ROM index to manufacturers and product specifications called *SweetSearch* accompanies the series.

The Family Handyman: The Do-It-Yourself Home Improvement Magazine. **PERIODICALS** 1951–   . 10 times/year.

Articles on planning and carrying out structural remodeling and repairs, electrical work, plumbing, interior decorative projects.

Home Mechanix: Managing Your Home in the '90s. 1928–   . 10 times/year.
Formerly *Mechanix Illustrated.* How-to projects for home and auto.

HomeOwner. 1976–   . 10 times/year.
Mostly illustrations of finished projects rather than step-by-step instructions.

Workbench: The Do-It-Yourself Magazine. 1946–   . Bimonthly.
How-to projects for the home.

The Old-House Journal. 1973–   . Bimonthly.

Repair and remodeling of nineteenth- and early twentieth-century houses. Also the source of *The Old-House Journal Catalog,* a buyer's guide to products.

AGRICOLA. (CD-ROM) SilverPlatter, 1972–   . Updated monthly. Also OCLC, 1979–92.

This database from the National Agricultural Library covers many consumer issues, including home purchase, maintenance, and decorating. Available online with BRS and BRS/AfterDark (CAIN), Dialog (File 10), Knowledge Index (AGRI1), and OCLC FirstSearch, 1970–   . Corresponds in part to the print product *Bibliography of Agriculture,* 1942–   .

Applied Science & Technology Index. (CD-ROM) H. W. Wilson, 1983–   . Monthly.

Indexes journals in construction and related fields. Also online with Wilsonline, 1983–   ; in print, 1958–   , updated monthly.

Avery Index to Architectural Periodicals. (Online) RLIN, updated daily, and Dialog, updated semiannually.

Compiled at the Avery Architectural Library at Columbia University, this database includes articles on architecture, interior decoration, furniture, landscape architecture, and housing. Also available in print as *Avery Architectural Index,* 2d ed. (G. K. Hall, 1973) plus supplements.

Consumer Reports. (CD-ROM) Dialog. Quarterly.

Full text of all articles, including those on products for the home, from 1982 to the present, plus *Consumer Reports Health Letter* and *Consumer Reports Travel Letter* (1989–   ). Also available online on Dialog (File 646) and Knowledge Index (REFR6). Available on NEXIS, Prodigy, America Online, and CompuServe, 1988–   .

HUD USER Online. (Online) BRS and BRS/AfterDark. 1967–   . Quarterly.

Abstracts of reports on urban development and housing produced by HUD's Office of Policy Development and Research, as well as by other HUD, federal, and state agencies and commercial publishers. Covers such areas as building technology, housing finance, energy conservation, and elderly/disabled housing.
- America Online: Has a Real Estate Online section with real estate ads; supplies weekly updates of average mortgage rates.
- Prodigy: In the Homelife section are "This Old House" columns on home repair from WGBH and columns on real estate.

- GEnie: Real Estate RoundTable carries real estate ads.
- CompuServe: Offers a monthly mortgage payment calculator. Neighborhood Report offers demographic profiles of communities by ZIP code.
- Homeline BBS: For homeowners and fixer-uppers. Run by a couple who write a newspaper column on home repair. Discuss projects with others who have already undertaken them; download columns on topics such as "How to sand a hardwood floor." **(401) 745-2037.**

Real estate multiple listing services are now maintained electronically, but you must go through a real estate broker to get access to them.

GOVERNMENT
PUBLICATIONS

A Consumer's Guide to Mortgage Refinancing. Federal Reserve Board, 1988.

Home Mortgages: Understanding the Process and Your Right to Fair Lending. Federal Reserve Board, 1990.

A Home of Your Own. Department of Housing and Urban Development, 1990.
 Advice on choosing and buying a home.

Home Buyer's Guide to Environmental Hazards. Department of Environmental Protection, 1990.
 Warns of the dangers of chemical substances (radon, formaldehyde), hazardous substances (asbestos), hazardous waste, contaminated groundwater that can be present in a house.

The Homeowner's Glossary of Building Terms. Department of Housing and Urban Development, 1980.

How to Buy a Manufactured (Mobile) Home. Federal Trade Commission, 1992.

Mortgage Servicing. Federal Trade Commission, 1992.
 Your rights when your lender sells your mortgage to another company.

New Life for Old Dwellings. Department of Agriculture, 1979.

Simple Home Repairs—Inside and *Simple Home Repairs—Outside.* Department of Agriculture, 1986.

Wise Home Buying. Housing and Urban Development, 1987.

See also the following Subject Bibliographies from the Government Printing Office:
#215—Architecture
#41—The Home

GOVERNMENT AGENCIES

Department of Housing and Urban Development
451 Seventh St. SW
Washington, DC 20410
(202) 708-1422
The principal federal agency responsible for programs concerned with the nation's housing needs, fair housing opportunities, and improvement and development of the nation's communities. Provides information on financial assistance for purchase and/or rehabilitation of houses (including Federal Home Administration mortgages), community agencies that administer federal funds, and options available to the homeowner and home buyer. Subsidizes housing for low-income families, operates a lead-based paint abatement program.

Department of Agriculture
14th Street and Independence Avenue SW
Washington, DC 20250
(202) 447-2791
USDA's activities affect housing through rural development and through the Cooperative Extension Department's services to home dwellers. Your county Extension agent can help solve many house and garden problems.

A valuable local government resource is the city or county Building Inspector, who is listed in the Government section of your telephone directory. The inspector enforces building codes and standards and is a good person to consult before beginning any major project.

ASSOCIATIONS

American Society of Interior Designers (ASID)
600 Massachusetts Ave. NE
Washington, DC 20002
(202) 546-3480
Members from professional interior design and related fields. Maintains an educational foundation, awards scholarships, grants, and design awards.

Council of American Homeowners
7927 Jones Branch Dr.
McLean, VA 22102
(703) 761-4648
An advocate for issues affecting homeowners: preserving the home mortgage interest deduction on income taxes, legislation to regulate the home

improvement industry, enforce home builder warranties. Publishes bulletins on second mortgages, insurance, recycling.

Home Furnishings Council
National Home Furnishings Association
P. O. Box 2396
High Point, NC 27261
(800) 521-HOME
This trade association of furniture manufacturers publishes brochures on interior decorating.

National Association of Home Builders of the U.S.
Fifteenth and M Sts. NW
Washington, DC 20005
(202) 822-0200
With members from throughout the building industry, it collects and disseminates research data on home building; lobbies on behalf of the housing industry; and maintains a speakers' bureau and an extensive library on housing.

National Association of Realtors (NAR)
430 N. Michigan Ave.
Chicago, IL 60611-4087
(312) 329-8200
Provides education, standards, professional development via continuing education for realtors. Conducts research and community service projects.

National Association of the Remodeling Industry
4301 N. Fairfax Dr.
Arlington, VA 22203
(703) 276-7600
Trade association for the remodeling industry. Provides books and tapes on the industry; makes referrals.

LIBRARIES

Local historical society libraries can be a gold mine of information if you are interested in the preservation and restoration of an older house. The state historical society library may also be helpful.

Many trade associations maintain libraries, some of which are open to the public. Most universities with a school of architecture will have a good library of books on home design, and you may be able to consult these in certain schools.

Condé Nast Publications Library
350 Madison Ave.
New York, NY 10017
(212) 880-8343
Condé Nast publishes several fashion and home magazines. Subject areas in its library include houses, gardens, home furnishings, interior design, health, personalities. Open by appointment only.

National Association of Home Builders
National Housing Center Library
15th and M Sts. NW
Washington, DC 20005
(202) 822-0200
Subject areas include technical, social, and financial aspects of home building. Publishes *Homes and Homebuilding*, a subject index to periodicals received by the library. Open by appointment only.

SOURCES OF EXPERT ADVICE

Architecture and Planning Research Laboratory
College of Architecture and Urban Planning
University of Michigan
Ann Arbor, MI 48109
(313) 764-1340
Research activities include building-technology development (especially energy conservation and lighting), new ideas in building and community planning, environmental effects, use of simulation in design processes. Special resources: a full-scale simulation laboratory.

Interior Design Institute
Purdue University
West Lafayette, IN 47907
(317) 494-9762
A unit of the Department of Consumer Services and Retailing in the School of Consumer and Family Services. Research fields: space planning, custom design projects, facilities management, including design research and management.

National Institute of Building Sciences
1201 L St. NW
Washington, DC 20005
(202) 289-7800
Nonprofit public/private partnership created by Congress. Seeks to improve construction processes and encourages safe building technology. Includes research on asbestos, homeless rehabilitation, lead-based paints, modular and factory-built housing, etc.

Headings in library catalogs:
    Apartments—Construction and
        restoration
    Apartments—Remodeling
    Apartments—Renovation
    Do-it-yourself work
    Dwellings—Maintenance and re-
        pair
    Dwellings—Remodeling
    Historic buildings—Conserva-
        tion and restoration—
        Amateur's manuals
    Home economics

Home furnishing
Home ownership
House buying
House construction
House painting—Amateur's
    manuals
Interior design

Headings for specific rooms:
    Bathrooms
    Bedrooms
    Dining rooms

Headings for parts of houses:
    Basements
    Roofs

Headings for styles of houses:
    Brick houses
    Bungalows

Headings for equipment:
    Air conditioning
    Electrical equipment
    Heating and ventilating
    Lighting

TIPS

Ask manufacturers and distributors for leaflets and brochures on their products. The staff at your local building supply store or hardware store can give invaluable advice, as can plumbers, electricians, and utilities repair people.

Call your city hall or county government offices and ask which departments might be helpful. Some communities, for example, make loans for home repair to low-income families.

How-to-do-it videotapes may be available from your public library or local building supply store.

When hiring a contractor, check to see if there are any complaints registered against him with the local Better Business Bureau.

32

JOBS AND
CAREERS

See also: General Reference Sources, Business and Finance, Education

Rapid changes in the American economy are causing people of all ages and backgrounds to seek job and career information. Research materials are available to help high school and college graduates seeking their first job, experienced workers looking for new opportunities, and those who are exploring careers at any stage of life.

GENERAL SOURCES OF INFORMATION

Where to Start Career Planning: An Essential Resource Guide for Career Planning & Job Hunting. 8th ed. By Pamela L. Feodoroff and Carolyn L. Lindquist. Peterson's Guides, 1991.

This bibliography, based on Cornell University's career planning library, is arranged by broad categories. It covers books on career fields (*Careers in Journalism,* etc.), overseas employment, second careers, careers for women and minorities, directories of jobs in specific cities, résumés and interviewing, and career planning. This inexpensive paperback will help you find books in the library or in bookstores.

Job Hunter's Sourcebook: Where to Find Employment Leads and Other Job Search Resources. Edited by Michelle LeCompte. Gale, 1991.

Identifies valuable sources for 155 professions and vocations, from accountancy to writing. Lists sources of help wanted ads, placement services, employer directories, employment agencies, job telephone hotlines, computerized résumé services, and electronic bulletin boards. Additional chapters cover interviews, résumés, international and government opportunities, and working at home. This is the first volume in a useful series; the two volumes listed below contain additional information on specific occupations.

Professional Careers Sourcebook. 2d ed. Edited by Kathleen M. Savage and Annette Novallo. Gale, 1992.

Leads to information on more than 110 professional positions. Arranged by occupation, it lists occupational career guides, professional associations, test guides, educational directories and scholarships, periodicals, and professional meetings.

Vocational Careers Sourcebook. Edited by Kathleen M. Savage and Karen Hill. Gale, 1992.

Companion to *Professional Careers Sourcebook,* this book covers 135 occupations that do not require a college degree, such as insurance and real estate sales, the armed forces, production work, and the trades.

Professional's Job Finder. By Daniel Lauber. Planning/Communications, 1992.

This work, like Lauber's *Government Job Finder* and *Non-Profits' Job Finder,* is a directory of job services, salary surveys, journals in which to find job advertisements, and directories for a broad group of career fields. It can serve as a useful supplement to the *Job Hunter's Sourcebook.*

Researching Your Way to a Good Job: How to Find and Use Information on Industries, Companies, Jobs, Careers. By Karmen N. T. Crowther. Wiley, 1993.

Knowledge about a company gives a job applicant an advantage in tailoring a résumé and interview responses to suit the employer. This guide to reference tools and techniques helps job searchers examine potential employers and jobs to find the position and company that is right for them.

American Salaries and Wages Survey: Statistical Data Derived from More Than 300 Government, Business & News Sources. By Arsen J. Darnay. Gale, 1991.

The bulk of salary information in this work is from Area Wage Surveys by the Bureau of Labor Statistics, but many other sources, such as state wage surveys and seventy-three surveys by trade and professional associations, provided data. The list of sources is useful in tracking down even more current salary surveys.

JOB CONTACT INFORMATION

This section does not cover many of the standard business directories, often the most appropriate sources for job seekers (e.g., corporate directories, lists of Fortune 500 and other companies). They are listed in Chapter 21, Business and Finance.

The Career Guide 1993: Dun's Employment Opportunities Directory. Dun & Bradstreet, 1992.

Over 5,000 companies and public institutions, each with at least 1,000 employees, are included in this guide. Company overview, opportunities, benefits, and contact names are given. Geographic and industrial indexes, as well as indexes by discipline and by employers offering work/study or internship programs.

College Placement Annual: A Guide to Employment Opportunities for College Graduates. 4 vols. College Placement Council. Annual.

In this set over 1,000 large employers describe themselves and the kind of employees they are seeking. Occupational, geographical, and special indexes (e.g., M.B.A. Degrees, International Employment) are helpful.

Internships 1992: On-the-Job Training Opportunities for Students and Adults. 12th ed. Peterson's Guides, 1992.

Solid information on hundreds of internship opportunities includes pay, contacts, eligibility, and brief descriptions by former interns.

Peterson's Job Opportunities for Engineering, Science, and Computer Graduates 1993. 4th ed. Peterson's Guides, 1992.

Like the other guides in this series (. . . *Opportunities for Business and Liberal Arts Graduates)*, this volume includes a good section on "Resources for the Job Hunter." Employer profiles form the bulk of each book.

Help! My Job Interview Is Tomorrow!: How to Use the Library to Research an Employer. By Mary Ellen Templeton. Neal-Schuman, 1991.

To help you prepare for an interview and ask intelligent questions, this book offers easy-to-use worksheets to speed information gathering.

CAREER EXPLORATION

Career Information Center. 13 vols. 4th ed. Macmillan, 1990.

In volumes covering occupational fields such as "Transportation" and "Administration, Business and Office," information is provided for jobs requiring (1) no specialized training, (2) some specialized training or experience, and (3) advanced training/experience. Extensive further reading and resource lists note titles for each career.

Chronicle Guidance Briefs (Chronicle Occupational Briefs). Microfiche. Chronicle Guidance Publications. Monthly except June–September.

Each occupational brief includes a picture, a description of the work, the education and training required, employment outlook, and sources of further research. If a career is not in *Occupational Outlook Handbook* (listed under Government Publications), it just might be here.

The Encyclopedia of Careers and Vocational Guidance. 4 vols. 9th ed. Edited by William Hopke. Ferguson, 1993.

This work is similar to but more expansive than the *Occupational Outlook Handbook*. Volume 1 profiles various industries, Volume 2 gives overviews of professional careers, Volume 3 covers general and special careers, and Volume 4, technicians' careers.

The Harvard Guide to Careers. New ed. By Martha P. Leape and Susan M. Vacca. Harvard University Press, 1991.

Excellent, annotated lists of sources for exploring a somewhat narrow range of careers.

Some of these sources may not be found in libraries but rather in college and high school counseling and placement offices.

ELECTRONIC SOURCES

Beacon. (CD-ROM) Macmillan New Media, 1992.

This interactive program includes information on careers as well as on colleges and graduate schools.

Discover for Colleges and Adults: A Computer-Based Career Planning and Information System That Supports Mature Decision-Making. (Diskette) American College Testing Program, 1992.

This CD-ROM product is exemplary of the good sources available in community college and other career centers. It allows users to create lists of occupations or colleges, based on their skills and interests. Local information is also available. Maryland, for instance, has added apprenticeship programs and their sponsors, financial aid programs, and career education/technology programs.

COIN (Coordinated Occupational Information Network). (Diskette) Educational Products, Annual.

Information on a wide range of occupational and educational opportunities, educational and training requirements, job markets, salaries, working conditions, financial aid programs, apprenticeships, and projected employment outlook.

GIS (Guidance Information System). (Diskette) Houghton Mifflin, Semiannual.

Career areas, schools, and financial aid programs.

SIGI (System of Interactive Guidance and Information) PLUS. (Diskette) Educational Testing Service, Annual.

A widely used product in the career decision-making field, this interactive program helps adults and students assess their interests and values and learn about occupations. For each occupation, required skills and preparation are listed.

Most states have specific career information software, usually developed by the State Occupational Information Coordinating Committee. Such software includes information on particular careers as well as on retraining and education. If your public library does not have such material, contact the local high school or community college.

Business Dateline Ondisc. (CD-ROM) UMI/Data Courier. Monthly.
    The full text of articles from the regional business press. Such magazines as *Alabama Business Review, Business First-Buffalo,* and *Tompkins' Central Illinois* are fruitful sources for job seekers.

General BusinessFile. (CD-ROM) Information Access, 1989–   . Monthly.
    Includes business directories as well as references to articles in the regional business press.

Federal Occupational and Career Information System. (Diskette) Office of Personnel Management; distributed by NTIS, 1991.
    This computer-based product helps users match their interests with occupations and positions throughout the federal government.

VGM's Careers Encyclopedia. Sony Data Discman. Sony, 1991.
    Full-text information on thirty careers. A clear and to-the-point narrative of the job, places of employment, potential, and advancement possibilities. Also available in print, 3d ed., VGM Career Horizons, 1991.

The Perfect Resume. (Diskette) By Tom Jackson. Permanx, 1991.
    This software, based on Jackson's popular book, is very helpful. Resumes can also be built on other systems, such as *Discover* and *SIGI Plus.*

Many online systems aid job seekers by listing job openings and/or posting your résumé—for a fee—so it can be seen by employers. Some databases target a specific industry or area of the country; others list jobs and résumés for all fields nationwide. "Job Hunting Online" by Barbara Palladino in the magazine *Online Access* (Winter 1992) is a clear guide to job listings, résumé listings, and in-house company and association listings. This article provides database phone number, cost, parameters, and baud rate for the databases noted below, as well as for Online Career Fair and others. Some states also offer free online listings of job vacancies though the local state employment office, community colleges, and high schools.
1. *Prodigy* offers E-SPAN, a file that typically contains more than 1,000 job openings around the United States. If you are looking for a job in a

particular location, however, you will find these listings skimpy. E-SPAN also has a service where, for $39.50, you can post your résumé for six months.

2. *America Online* contains three job listing services: E-SPAN, Help Wanted USA, and its Classified Bulletin Board, where AOL members can post jobs. Its Chicago Online section posts the help wanted ads from the *Chicago Tribune.* AOL also has a Career Center with many tools for job seekers, including résumé templates and a collection of cover letters than can be downloaded. There are monthly articles on career guidance, an occupational profiles database with 700 occupations, and a Federal Employment Service that describes agencies and types of jobs with the government. The Employment Agencies database lists 2,000 agencies; the Employer Contacts file lists 5,000 companies. There is also online real-time career counseling from two professionals at no extra charge.

3. *CompuServe* has many industry-specific bulletin boards that often contain listings of job openings, and the College Recruitment Database with résumés of recent college grads.

4. If you are looking for a job in a distant city, check and see if you can access its newspaper online through *Dialog* or *DataTimes.*

5. *Human Resources Information Network* has many files of interest to job seekers, including:
   - College Recruitment Database
   - Corporate Jobs Outlook (rating corporations from the employee's perspective)
   - Job Ads USA Database (ads from 100 regional and national newspapers)
   - Minority Graduate Database
   - Military in Transition Database (armed services personnel seeking civilian employment)
   - Personal Employee Profiling (checks references, criminal record, verifies education, etc.)
   - *Recruitment Today* magazine
   - Résumés on Computer

6. *Dialog* has a Career Placement Registry on which, for a fee, job seekers can post their résumés. Potential employers then search the database for likely candidates.

7. *People's Electronic Exchange* contains both job openings and résumés in a classified ad format. Freestanding BBS; call directly **(908) 685-0948.**

8. *The Internet:* Specific academic institutions may post regular job announcements on the Internet.

Federal Career Opportunities. 1974–   . Biweekly.

Listings, by agency, of federal jobs across the country. An electronic version (ACCESS . . . FCO On-Line) is updated weekly. Call (703) 281-0200 for further information.

Federal Jobs Digest. 1976–   . Biweekly.

Lists openings by agency as well as geographically. Includes feature articles on special government programs, such as Administrative Careers with America. Also lists dates for exams for government jobs.

National Ad Search. 1970–   . Weekly.

Reprints 2,000 professional help wanted advertisements from seventy-five metropolitan newspapers across the country.

National Business Employment Weekly. Weekly.

Compiles ads for jobs for the experienced professional in the United States and overseas from the four regional editions of *The Wall Street Journal.* It also includes topical articles on résumés and interviewing, a calendar of career events, and book reviews.

Occupational Outlook Quarterly. 1957–   . Quarterly.

Published by the U.S. Department of Labor Bureau of Labor Statistics, this magazine provides broad discussions of the world of work, making it valuable to career guidance professionals as well as to job seekers. The Summer 1992 issue, for example, focused on college graduates in the labor force. "Job Outlook in Brief," a biennial feature, lists some 200 jobs with a rundown on openings and employment prospects. Used to update the *Occupational Outlook Handbook* (below).

Where the Jobs Are: A Comprehensive Directory of 1200 Journals Listing Career Opportunities. By S. Norman Feingold and Glenda Ann Hansard-Winkler. Garrett Park Press, 1989.

Look up an occupation in this directory and find the periodicals that carry job advertisements for that field. Its "Index Linking Specific Occupations to Appropriate Periodicals" is very helpful.

Occupational Outlook Handbook. Department of Labor. Biennial.

This is the first source for career exploration. It's the bible of the field, with information about education and training requirements, employment outlook, places of employment, and earnings and working conditions for about 225 occupations. *The Job Outlook in Brief* (Department of Labor, 1990) projects job prospects for nearly 250 occupations to the year 2005.

Dictionary of Occupational Titles. 2 vols. 4th ed., revised. Department of Labor, 1991.

DOT provides cogent job descriptions of thousands of occupations. Occupational code numbers are used to organize other personnel reference works. Available online with the Human Resources Information Network (see above).

Careers in Space. National Aeronautics and Space Administration.

Jobs for the Future. Department of Labor, 1988.
Aimed at female high school graduates.

Resumes, Application Forms, Cover Letters and Interviews. Department of Labor, 1987.

Tips for Finding the Right Job. Department of Labor, 1991.

Tomorrow's Jobs. Department of Labor, 1992.

Women on the Job: Careers in the Electronic Media. Department of Labor, 1990.

Many government agencies publish pamphlets describing their employment opportunities, for example, *The G-Women* (Department of the Treasury), *Exceptional Careers* (Customs Service), and *Consider Commerce . . . Career Opportunities for Women in the U.S. Department of Commerce.*

See also the following Subject Bibliographies from the Government Printing Office:

#44—Employment and Occupations
#270—Occupational Outlook Handbook
#300—Office of Personnel Management Publications
#202—Personnel Management, Guidance and Counseling
#110—Vocational and Career Education

GOVERNMENT AGENCIES

Department of Labor
200 Constitution Ave. NW
Washington, DC 20210
(202) 523-8165

Administers laws on worker safety and collects statistics. The Department sponsors many job training and retraining programs administered through state employment services; the Dislocated Worker Program, the Work Incentive Program, and the Veteran's Employment and Training Service are examples.

Equal Employment Opportunity Commission
1801 L St. NW
Washington, DC 20507
(800) USA-EEOC
Works to eliminate discrimination in employment.

National Labor Relations Board
1717 Pennsylvania Ave. NW
Washington, DC 20570
(202) 254-8064
Prevents and remedies unfair labor practices and safeguards employees'
right to organize.

ASSOCIATIONS   American Counseling Association
5999 Stevenson Ave.
Alexandria, VA 22304
(703) 823-9800
Human development and counseling professionals in schools, colleges,
government, and industry. The association maintains a library and publishes many journals.

College Placement Council
62 Highland Ave.
Bethlehem, PA 18017
(215) 868-1421
Members are college career placement counselors. They issue many publications for the recent college graduate: salary surveys, guides to career
planning, directories of employment opportunities.

Forty Plus Clubs   Scattered local chapters of a once-national organization to help workers
over 40 find employment. Check the telephone directory's white pages.

LIBRARIES   Many public libraries have special centralized services to help job seekers.
Community college libraries and high schools may make their career information sources available to the general public.

LC SUBJECT
HEADINGS

Applications for positions	Job descriptions
Career changes	Job hunting
Career development	Job postings
Employee selection	Job satisfaction
Employment agencies	Job sharing
Employment interviewing	Job vacancies
Employment tests	Occupational training

Occupations
Promotions
Professions

Recruiting of employees
Résumés (Employment)
Vocational training

Vocational guidance is a subheading for occupations, e.g., Nursing—Vocational guidance and Television—Vocational guidance. This type of subject heading is used for career information guides, that is, books on nursing or television as a career.

TIPS

Every state has a job training bureau. In many states these offices administer funds for the retraining of dislocated workers.

If you are a college graduate, contact your alma mater's career office. Increasingly, colleges and universities are extending placement services to alumni.

33

LAW

See also: *General Reference Sources, Patents*

This chapter has been designed to help you become a more knowledgeable researcher and consumer of legal issues and services. The law functions at the federal, state, and local levels through legislation (statutory law), regulations (administrative law), and court decisions (case law). Though you may have to consult a lawyer on specific legal matters, it can still be helpful to do your own research. Librarians, of course, can guide you to resources of information, but cannot give legal advice.

The first part of this chapter describes popular legal sources you are likely to find in public and academic libraries and bookstores. The chapter concludes with information on three areas of law likely to be of interest to laypeople: Family Law, Bankruptcy, and Copyright and Literary Property.

GENERAL REFERENCE SOURCES

The Guide to American Law: Everyone's Legal Encyclopedia. 14 vols. West, 1983–85. Annual supplements.

Entries explain legal principles and concepts, landmark laws and trials, and legal documents in language intelligible to laypeople. Volume 11 contains legal forms.

Legal Question and Answer Book. Reader's Digest, 1988.

Uses a question-and-answer format to cover legal issues of greatest interest to the layperson.

You and the Law. By Consumer Guide Editors and the American Bar Association. Signet, 1991.

In a question-and-answer format, this book is similar to the previous entry.

Using a Lawyer . . . And What to Do If Things Go Wrong. By Kay Ostberg.
Random House, 1990.
   Information on legal services plans, fees, terms of employment, and how
to fire a lawyer.

The American Civil Liberties Union Handbook series outlines legal rights
in terms that laypeople can understand. Published by Southern Illinois
University Press.
   Rights of Aliens and Refugees. 2d ed. 1990.
   Rights of Authors and Artists. 2d ed. 1992.
   Rights of Crime Victims. 1985.
   Rights of Indians and Tribes. 1992.
   Rights of Lesbians and Gay Men. 3d ed. 1992.
   Rights of Older Persons. 1988.
   Rights of Patients. 2d ed. 1992.
   Rights of Prisoners. 4th ed. 1988.
   Rights of Single People. 1985.
   Rights of Students. 1988.
   Rights of Teachers. 2d ed. 1984.
   Rights of Women. 2d ed. 1983.
   Rights of Young People. 2d ed. 1985.
   Your Right to Government Information. 2d ed. 1985.
   Your Right to Privacy. 2d ed. 1990.
West Publishing's Nutshell Series includes about 100 paperbacks that
provide an overview of the law in specific areas, such as malpractice, envi-
ronmental, and landlord/tenant law. While written for lawyers and law
students, they are generally accessible to the layperson. Some examples:
   AIDS Law in a Nutshell.
   Art Law in a Nutshell.
   Civil Rights Law in a Nutshell.
   Consumer Law in a Nutshell.
   Energy and Natural Resources Law in a Nutshell.
   Medical Malpractice Law in a Nutshell.
   Mass Communications Law in a Nutshell.
   Military Law in a Nutshell.
   Sex Discrimination Law in a Nutshell.
   Sports Law in a Nutshell.
   Unfair Trade Practices Law in a Nutshell.
   Wills & Trusts in a Nutshell.

Simple Contracts for Personal Use. 2d ed. By Stephen Elias. Nolo Press, 1991.
   Provides thirty-five forms for promissory notes, bills of sale, personal
property leases, deposit and home repair contracts, and releases, with explanations of their use and instructions for filling them out.

Complete Legal Kit. Running Press, 1988.

Approximately 150 forms, covering real estate, employment, credit and collections, loans and debts, sale of personal property, and others. No accompanying explanation is provided.

Do-It-Yourself Guides: A Selection

(See also Family Law and Bankruptcy, below.) Many popular resources on topics such as divorce, making a will, or real estate are found in bookstores or libraries. A sampling:

Divorce Yourself: The No-Fault No-Lawyer Divorce Handbook. 2d ed. By Daniel Sitarz. Nova Publishing, 1991.

Prepare Your Own Will: The National Will Kit. 2d ed. By Daniel Sitarz. Nova Publishing, 1991.

Probate: Settling an Estate: A Step-by-Step Guide. By Kay Ostberg. Random House, 1990.

The Power of Attorney Book. 3d ed. By Denis Clifford. Nolo Press, 1990.

Everyday Contracts: Protecting Your Rights: A Step-by-Step Guide. By George Milko and others. Random House, 1991.

Landlording. 5th ed. By Leigh Robinson. Nolo Press, 1988.

Real Estate: The Legal Side to Buying a House, Condo, or Co-op: A Step-by-Step Guide. By George Milko. Random House, 1990.

Everybody's Guide to Small Claims Court. 4th ed. By Ralph Warner. Nolo Press, 1990.

Guides to Research for Beginners

Finding the Law: A Workbook on Legal Research for Laypersons. By Al Coco. William S. Hein, 1986.

Written for government employees who are involved in legal matters but who have no legal background. Useful for any layperson.

Find the Law in the Library: A Guide to Legal Research. By John Corbin. American Library Association, 1989.

A reference book for librarians and laypersons.

Legal Research: How to Find and Understand the Law. 2d ed. By Stephen Elias. Nolo Press, 1990.

A hands-on guide for paralegals, law students, consumer activists, legal secretaries, businesspersons, and the media.

Legal Research Made Easy: A Roadmap through the Law Library Maze. Nolo
Press/Legal Star Communications.
   A two-hour videotape for law students, paralegals, librarians, and the
public, featuring a Berkeley law professor. Includes a 40-page manual.

Finding the Law. By Morris L. Cohen. West, 1989.
   An abridged edition of *How to Find the Law.* 9th ed. By Morris L. Cohen,
Robert C. Berring, and Kent C. Olsen.

Guides for More Advanced Legal Researchers

Fundamentals of Legal Research. 5th ed. By J. Myron Jacobstein and Roy M.
Mersky. Foundation Press, 1990.

The Legal Research Manual: A Game Plan for Legal Research and Analysis. 2d
ed. By Christopher G. Wren and Jill Robinson Wren. Adams & Ambrose,
1986.

Index to Legal Periodicals. (CD-ROM) H. W. Wilson, 1981–　　. Monthly.
   Indexes about 600 legal periodicals, including law reviews, state publications such as the *Illinois Bar Journal* and *California Lawyer,* and periodicals
from Australia, Canada, and Great Britain. Also available online with Wilsonline, BRS, OCLC FirstSearch, LEXIS, and WESTLAW, 1981–　　, and
in print, 1908–　　.

ELECTRONIC SOURCES

LegalTrac. (CD-ROM) Information Access, 1980–　　. Monthly.
   Indexes about 700 law periodicals. Also online as Legal Resource Index
with BRS, BRS/AfterDark, Dialog (File 150), Knowledge Index, LEXIS,
and WESTLAW. Available in print as *Current Law Index,* Information Access, 1980–　　, updated monthly.

West CD-ROM Libraries. (CD-ROM) West Publishing Company, Annual.
   Full-text packages on subjects such as Bankruptcy; Federal Securities;
Federal Taxation; Government Contracts; Federal Civil Practice; and BNA
Tax Management Portfolios. The libraries typically include collections of
treatise material, case law, digests, statutes, and regulations. West has also
issued Reporters for California, Massachusetts, and New York on CD-ROM.

Search Master. (CD-ROM) Matthew Bender & Company, Quarterly.
   Legal libraries available on *Search Master* include Bankruptcy; Business
Practice; Personal Injury; Intellectual Property; Federal Practice; Tax Li-
brary; and California Practice. These series include the complete texts of
many popular sets, such as *Rabkin's & Johnson's Current Legal Forms with
Tax Analysis, Collier on Bankruptcy,* and *Nimmer on Copyright.*

CaseBase. (CD-ROM) Law Office Information Systems, Quarterly.
Complete texts of Supreme Court and Court of Appeals decisions for eight states. Separate discs for Arkansas, Connecticut, Florida, Kansas, Massachusetts, Mississippi, North Carolina, and Rhode Island.

Many other state legal publications are available on CD-ROM from a variety of publishers. For example:
LawDesk (New York Official Reports)
LawDisc (California civil case decisions)
Florida State Statutes
Georgia Law on Disc
See the *Gale Directory of Databases* for a complete list.

Online   There are several thousand legal databases online. The two most inclusive online services are WESTLAW (West Publishing) and LEXIS (Mead Data Central).

1. WESTLAW has the most extensive collection of legal databases, over 4,000 in all. They include federal statutes and cases, state statutes and cases, Attorney General opinions, and specialized databases on particular legal topics. *Black's Law Dictionary,* legal newspapers, *Shepard's Citations,* access to selected Dialog databases and databases from other publishers, such as the American Bar Association, Bureau of National Affairs, and Commerce Clearing House, are also available. West's *Legal Directory* contains biographical information on lawyers and firms. West has introduced a new system, WIN (Westlaw is Natural), that allows searching using plain English, or what computer scientists call natural language, rather than traditional Boolean connectors.

2. LEXIS gives access to many databases, including codes and statutes, federal and state legislative material, and auxiliary material such as *American Law Reports,* over seventy law reviews, and reports from the Bureau of National Affairs and the American Bar Association. *Shepard's Citations* and the *Martindale-Hubbell Law Directory,* with biographical information on 800,000 lawyers and 50,000 firms, are also available.

Consumer Services   • *America Online,* in its Legal Special Interest Group, has bulletin boards for lawyers to discuss the use of computer technology in law practice and computer law. There are also boards for paralegals and legal secretaries. Software for downloading includes a legal file manager and templates for filing bankruptcy under Chapters 7 and 13.
• *CompuServe* hosts a law forum.
• The Internet has specialized lists on education law and computer law and a forum for law students that can be accessed via: **LAWSCHL %AUVM.BITNET@VM1.NODAK.EDU.**

Project Hermes posts recent Supreme Court decisions on the Internet. Access via: **WAIS supreme-court.src.**

The *Columbia Index to Hispanic Legislation* contains data from the Library of Congress on Hispanic-oriented legislation. Access via: **WAIS columbia-spanish-law-catalog.src.**

Using Internet, you can also access the *Library of Congress's Legislative Information File* (1973–   ) and the *Copyright History Monographs File* (1978–   ). **Telnet locis.loc.gov.**

PERIODICALS

National Law Journal: The Weekly Newspaper for the Profession. 1978–   . Weekly.

The best source for news on fast-breaking legal developments. Special supplements on What Lawyers Earn, Largest Law Firms, etc. Online in full text with NEXIS and WESTLAW.

Nolo News. 1974–   , Quarterly.

A tabloid format catalog published by Nolo Press, the pioneer publisher of self-help legal books and software. Consumer-oriented, it lists primarily its own legal self-help books.

The Practical Lawyer. 1955–   . 8 times/year.

Published by the American Bar Association, this magazine provides nuts-and-bolts information on legal topics as continuing education for lawyers.

GOVERNMENT PUBLICATIONS

Many of the primary sources for law are published by the Government Printing Office. For example:

Code of Federal Regulations.

United States Code. (Note: The *United States Code Annotated* is published by West.)

The federal government also issues popular publications explaining various aspects of the law, among them:

What You Should Know About the Pension Law. Department of Labor, 1988.

The Americans with Disabilities Act: Questions and Answers. Department of Justice, 1991.

The Animal Welfare Act: How It Protects Your Dog and Cat. Department of Agriculture. Animal and Plant Health Inspection Service, 1986.

Handbook on Child Support Enforcement. Department of Health and Human Services, 1989.

United States Immigration Laws, General Information. Department of Justice, 1989.

State Laws and Published Ordinances—Firearms. Department of the Treasury. Bureau of Alcohol, Tobacco, and Firearms, 1989.
　A collection of statutes from the fifty states.

Copyright & Home Copying: Technology Challenges the Law. 1989.
　Focuses on audiotaping.

See also the Government Printing Office's *Subject Bibliography* #126—Copyrights, #185—Digest of U.S. Practice in International Law, and #64—Labor-Management Relations.

GOVERNMENT AGENCIES

Department of Justice
Constitution Avenue and Tenth Street NW
Washington, DC 20530
(202) 514-2000
The Justice Department serves as counsel for U.S. citizens. Plays a key role in protection against criminals, in ensuring healthy business competition, in safeguarding consumers, and in enforcing drug, immigration, and naturalization laws.

Community Relations Service
Department of Justice
5550 Friendship Blvd.
Chevy Chase, MD 20815
(301) 492-5929
Through its ten regional offices, this agency provides on-site resolution by conciliation specialists of any dispute relating to discrimination on the basis of race, color, or national origin.

Legal Services Corporation
400 Virginia Avenue SW
Washington, DC 20024
(202) 863-1820
This quasi-governmental agency makes quality legal assistance available for noncriminal proceedings to those who would otherwise be unable to afford counsel.

Various agencies of the federal government issue numerous publications on legal issues. The agencies often have libraries that are excellent sources of information on legal questions in their specialized areas. For example:

Office of Thrift Supervision
Law Library
1700 G Street NW
Washington, DC 20552
(202) 906-6470
Matters relating to the law of banking and home financing.

United States Department of Commerce
Law Library
14th and E Streets NW
Washington, DC 20230
(202) 377-5517
Legal matters relating to national and international trade.

American Bar Association
750 N. Lake Shore Drive
Chicago, IL 60611
(312) 988-5000
Professional association for attorneys. Affiliated with state bar associations. Sponsors Law Day USA; maintains a library.

ASSOCIATIONS

American Civil Liberties Union
132 W. 43rd St.
New York, NY 10036
(212) 944-9800
Champions rights set forth in the Bill of Rights. Activities include litigation, advocacy, education.

HALT: Americans for Legal Reform
1319 F St. NW
Washington, DC 20004
(202) 347-9600
Aims to make consumers sophisticated shoppers of legal services, to simplify the language and procedures of the law, and to develop alternative means of settling disputes. Publishes citizens' legal manuals on divorce, real estate, small claims court, etc.

Public Citizen
2000 P St. NW
P. O. Box 19404
Washington, DC 20036
(202) 833-3000
Founded by Ralph Nader for citizen empowerment.

To find additional groups, see:

Public Interest Law Groups: Institutional Profiles. By Karen O'Connor and Lee Epstein. Greenwood, 1989.
Provides information on 170 groups that focus on the protection of civil rights, legal aid, consumer interests, capital punishment, etc.

LIBRARIES

Law Library
Library of Congress
101 Independence Avenue
Washington, DC 20540
(202) 707-5079
Comprehensive collections on the law of the United States and of all foreign nations.

State libraries have complete collections of the law for the state and are open to the public. All universities with a law school have law libraries. The degree to which they can be used by the general public varies from institution to institution. In general, the libraries of publicly supported institutions are more accessible to the general public than private ones. Phone before you go.

Most courts have law libraries. Their coverage varies and their use may be limited. Also, in some areas, bar associations have discouraged use of their collections; in others, the public is made welcome. Always check. Ironically, the one place you are almost always likely to have access to a law library is in prison.

LC SUBJECT HEADINGS

A number of headings begin with the word *Law:*
    Law—Codification
    Law—Language
    Law—France
The best approach is to look up the legal topic directly:

Commercial law	Malpractice
Jurisdiction	Natural law
Libel and slander	Violence (Law)

Many direct headings are further subdivided:

Domestic relations—Cases
Domestic relations—Criminal law
Domestic relations (International law)
Many general topics are subdivided by Law and legislation:
Dentistry—Law and legislation

Some local telephone companies or other agencies offer a series of taped **TIPS FOR THE** messages on legal topics of interest to laypeople, such as divorce, immigra- **RESEARCHER** tion and naturalization, and traffic law. Check your phone book for information on these and other legal information services.

The area called family law has evolved over the years to encompass a wide **FAMILY LAW** range of issues involving husbands and wives, people living together but not legally considered to be married, children—their care, well-being, education, etc.—and parents. For this reason, family law is frequently broken down into various components:

Children are no longer considered to be entirely under the control of their **Children** parents until the age of consent, which itself differs from state to state. For various reasons, the courts are increasingly involved in the lives of our nation's children.

Marriage is controlled by the laws of the state in which the couple lives. In **Marriage** general the concept has changed from the old idea that man and wife are one to the notion that the married couple may have separate lives and property rights. An old English legal concept called "dower" was originally established to protect the property rights of females. In many states this cumbersome common law procedure has been replaced by the concept of community property. This means that any property obtained by either of the parties during their marriage is the joint property of both. However, the property each brought to the marriage remains individual.

Again, each state has jurisdiction over the divorce proceedings of its citi- **Divorce** zens. Divorce can involve the division of property, ensuring the education and support of minor children, and visitation rights to those children.

When people are living in retirement they will have to deal with pension **Family Law** plans, health insurance, and plans for the disposition of their property **Questions in** upon their death. At this point, for those with substantial estates, estate **Later Life** planners become involved and devise trusts and wills, with a view to reducing taxes on the estate.

Sources such as the following provide help in drawing up agreements, wills, and divorce papers and in other family matters:

For background reading and the beginner's research:

Nolo's Simple Will Book. 2d national ed. By Denis Clifford. Nolo Press, 1989.

Contains forms and instructions for all states except Louisiana. Covers guardians, minors, updating, trusts, taxes, and power of attorney.

The Transformation of Family Law. By Mary Ann Glendon. University of Chicago Press, 1989.

Traces the historical development of family law.

Legal Rights of Children. By Robert M. Horowitz and Howard A. Davidson. McGraw-Hill/Shepard's, 1984, updated 1990.

Describes the rights of children, their economic interests, public benefit programs, custody, institutional care, education, and handicaps.

The Living Together Kit. 6th national ed. By Toni Ihara and others. Nolo Press, 1990.

Helps unmarried couples to understand the laws affecting them, covering estate planning, agreements, real estate, forms.

Family Law in a Nutshell. 2d ed. By Harry D. Krause. West, 1986.

Background, sources, and applications of family law, including the creation of marriage, regulations, effect of non-compliance with regulations, contracts, support, criminal law, equality, parent-child relationships, legitimacy, adoption, neglect, custody, divorce, economic consequences of divorce, division of property.

Family Law Dictionary. By Robin D. Leonard and Stephen R. Elias. Nolo Press, 1988.

Covers marriage, divorce, living together, related terms; gives examples, charts, and tables.

Readings in Family Law: Divorce and Its Consequences. Edited by Frederica K. Lombard. Foundation Press, 1990.

Emotional and economic effects of divorce; children; mediation. Observations on the legal system.

Divorce, Separation, and the Distribution of Property. By J. Thomas Oldham. Law Journal Seminars-Press, 1987.

Disputes, cohabitation, engagements, requirements for marriage, agreements, distribution of property, including professional education, business, federal benefits.

The Law of Domestic Relations in the United States. 2 vols. 2d ed. By Homer H. Clark. West, 1987.

Family Law Checklist. By Richard E. Crouch. 2 vols. Callaghan & Company, 1990.

Covers 125 topics, including marriage, marital dissolution, alimony, child support, property division, pensions, child custody, tax matters, with appendixes and forms.

Wills, Trusts, and Estates. 4th ed. By Jesse Dukeminier and Stanley M. Johanson. Little, Brown, 1990.

Equitable Distribution of Property. By Lawrence J. Golden. Shepard's/McGraw-Hill, 1983. Updated with pocket parts.

Assists attorneys in drawing up an equitable distribution of property during divorce, including in community property states.

Dissolution of Marriage. By Joyce Hens Green and others. Shepard's/McGraw-Hill, 1986. Updated with pocket parts.

Covers custody, property, taxes, financial planning, accounting, contracts, torts, and mediation.

Domestic Torts: Family Violence, Conflicts, and Sexual Abuse. By Leonard Karp and Cheryl L. Karp. Shepard's/McGraw-Hill, 1989. Updated with pocket parts.

Covers civil legal remedies for spousal abuse, the transmission of sexual diseases, child battering, invasion of privacy, third-party liability, and criminal responsibility.

BANKRUPTCY

Persons or corporations are bankrupt when they have legally been declared unable to pay their debts. Bankruptcy is governed by federal statutes, and the proceedings operate under rules established by the United States Supreme Court. Bankruptcy courts are units of the federal district courts, and the judges are appointed by the United States courts of appeals.

Bankruptcy can be voluntary, in which case the person files for bankruptcy; or involuntary, when the debtor is forced into bankruptcy by creditors. When a bankruptcy petition is filed, a separate bankrupt estate is formed, and a trustee is appointed to represent this estate. The trustee has powers to sue, and may be sued on behalf of the bankrupt estate. The filing of a petition is sufficient to restrain creditors from taking further action to collect their claims.

Most bankruptcy cases are handled by attorneys. Bankruptcy is very complicated, and in all cases except the most simple, following the advice of an attorney is usually the best course. However, informative background research can come from the following sources:

The Bankruptcy Kit. By John Ventura. Dearborn Financial Press, 1991.
Outlines how the process works and what the outcome usually is.

Commercial and Debtor-Creditor Law: Selected Statutes. Compiled by Douglas G. Baird and others. Foundation Press, 1991.

Desk Side Guide to the Rules of Bankruptcy. Rev. ed. By American Bar Association, Young Lawyers Division. American Bar Association, 1988.

How to File for Bankruptcy. 2d ed. By Stephen Elias and others. Nolo Press, 1990.
Helpful aid in deciding whether to file for bankruptcy. Covers instructions for filing, how bankruptcy works, exempt property, and gives forms with instructions.

The Basics of Bankruptcy. By William R. Mapother. Creditors Law Center, 1986.
Introductory text contains terminology, sample forms, walk-through for Chapters 7, 11, and 13, strategies, and glossary.

Creditors' Rights and Bankruptcy. By Steve H. Nickels and David G. Epstein. West, 1989.
Basic principles and issues of bankruptcy.

Personal Bankruptcy and Debt Adjustment. By Kenneth J. Doran. Random House, 1991.
A step-by-step guide to finding a lawyer and then working with the person you have selected to get the best results.

COPYRIGHT AND LITERARY PROPERTY

Copyright gives creators of works (authors, composers, etc.) a statutory right to their work and the opportunity to receive a fair return for its production. In the United States, the copyright laws were extensively revised by the Copyright Act of 1976, as amended by the Computer Software Act of 1980 and the Semiconductor Chip Protection Act of 1984. The acts cover literary, musical, dramatic, graphic, and audiovisual works, computer software, and integrated circuit design.

Under the Copyright Act, a work created after January 1, 1978, is protected for the life of the creator and for fifty years after the creator's death or, if a joint work, for fifty years after the death of the last surviving creator. International copyright is governed by the terms of the Bern Convention, which the United States signed in 1988.

The copyright process is administered by the Register of Copyrights, who serves as the director of the Copyright Office of the Library of Congress. The Copyright Office issues regulations concerning the registration of copyrights, including regulations relative to the reproduction of articles under the control of the office.

There are limitations on copyrights, and by statute certain exceptions exist. The fair use doctrine allows others to use material in a fair manner, balancing the author's right to be paid against the legitimate public interest in the dissemination of ideas. It is a vague area, and courts consider the effect such use will have on the market value of the work, the purpose of the use (commercial or nonprofit educational), the amount of the work used, and the nature of the work copyrighted.

Fair Use

In many cases, the publisher takes care of registering a book for copyright. Though copyrights may be obtained by individuals on their own, consulting an attorney specializing in the area is recommended for important or many-faceted works, if the publisher is not responsible for registration.

Copyright Lawyers

The Writer's Legal Companion. By Brad Bunnin. Addison-Wesley, 1988.
Includes an excellent discussion of copyright law for writers.

Resources for Copyright and Literary Property Law

Copyright Office, Library of Congress, Washington, DC 20559, (202) 479-0700. Ask for Circular One, General Information on Registering a Copyright.

Find the Law in the Library: A Guide to Legal Research. By John Corbin. American Library Association, 1989.
Includes a brief history and overview of copyright laws.

The Beginning Creator's Copyright Manual: A Practical Guide for Authors, Poets, Composers, Programmers, Playwrights, Artists, and Photographers, in Ordinary Language. By H. P. Killough. Harlo Press, 1988. Sold only by the author, P. O. Box 1821, Manhattan, Kansas 66502.

A Writer's Guide to Copyright. 2d ed. Poets & Writers, 72 Spring St., New York, NY 10012, 1987.
A favorite of authors.

How to Copyright Software. 3d ed. By M. J. Sallone. Nolo Press, 1989.
Describes registration, ownership, and protection of software copyrights.

The Copyright Book: A Practical Guide. 3d ed. By William S. Strong. MIT Press, 1990.

Copyright Not Copycat: A Writer's Guide to Copyright. By Sally E. Stuart and Woody Young. Joy Publications, 1987.

Researching Copyright Renewal: A Guide to Information and Procedure. By Iris J. Wildman and Rhonda Carlson. Fred B. Rothman & Co., 1989.

34

LITERATURE

See also: *General Reference Sources, Multiculturalism, Theater and Dance, Women's Studies*

Consisting of works of the imagination, literature can be divided by form: prose (novel, short story), poetry, and drama (plays as they are read, not performed). It can also be organized by language/nationality (French literature, German literature) or by period (Renaissance or modern literature). Some researchers study schools or literary movements such as the Harlem Renaissance or Modernism. The issue of value in literature is an important one and so the critical literature has become part of the body of the discipline and is itself subject to criticism.

Typically, the student or independent researcher is interested in information on one author or even on one work. Writers of literary criticism do not always build on the work of other critics and therefore may not have extensive bibliographies for the researcher to use as a path to additional sources. The immense amount published every year in the discipline of literature makes the use of reference guides especially important. Most of the sources listed here are guides to Western literature, especially British and American literature, but some of the series (e.g., Scribner's, Ungar) do treat Third World literatures and the *MLA International Bibliography* covers literatures in all languages.

Reference Works in British and American Literature. 2 vols. By James K. Bracken. Libraries Unlimited, 1990–91.

GENERAL SOURCES OF INFORMATION

Excellent source for the beginning student. Volume 1 annotates over 500 periodical indexes, bibliographies, biographical sources, core journals, and principal research centers and associations. It has good descriptions of the reference series from Gale, Magill, Chelsea House, Scribner's, and Ungar.

Volume 2 covers reference works (mostly bibliographies and encyclopedias) on 637 specific authors, arranged alphabetically from Louis Adamic to Louis Zukofsky.

Literary Research Guide: A Guide to Reference Sources for the Study of Literatures in English and Related Topics. 2d ed. By James L. Harner. Modern Language Association, 1993.

A comprehensive guide, better for the graduate student and scholar than for the beginning researcher. Covers all literatures in English (including Canadian and Australian) in detail; has cursory coverage of literature in other languages. The Modern Language Association has also published Nancy L. Baker's *Research Guide for Undergraduate Students: English and American Literature* (3d ed., 1989), which has a narrower scope and takes a how-to approach.

A Reference Guide for English Studies. By Michael J. Marcuse. University of California Press, 1990.

This mammoth guide to English and American literature doesn't just list reference books but also includes, for most topics, lists of "frequently recommended works." Marcuse provides fuller descriptions than Harner of most reference sources. Especially good as a guide to libraries and to manuscript collections. For the advanced researcher.

Biography and Criticism

Several publishers have developed series that provide biographical information about authors and summarize critical opinion or reprint criticism on authors from other sources. Among them:

- Beacham: *Research Guide to Biography and Criticism* is a new series on British and American fiction and prose writers and dramatists.
- Chelsea House: *Chelsea House Library of Literary Criticism*, 1985–90. Collection of forty-two volumes on English and American authors from the earliest times to the present.
- Gale: *Contemporary Authors.* 1962–   . Up-to-date source of biographical information on writers from many countries and many fields, not just limited to literary authors. Also available on CD-ROM.

    Dictionary of Literary Biography. 1978–   . Volumes focus on literature by genre and time period (i.e., *American Novelists since World War II* or *British Poets, 1914–1945*). Each volume provides critical essays as well as bibliographies and valuable information on manuscript locations, biographies, collections of letters, diaries, and more. Also *Concise Dictionary of Literary Biography* in 4 volumes.

    Dictionary of Literary Criticism. Gale has seven series that reprint criticism from literature journals, ranging in time from *Classical and Medieval Literary Criticism* to *Contemporary Literary Criticism*, plus sets for poetry and drama. They are useful in libraries that don't own the *MLA International Bibliography* or a large number of the journals it indexes. Also published in smaller sets for high schools; e.g., *Shakespeare for Students.*

A CD-ROM index to all 675 volumes in these and other Gale series is available as *Gale's Literary Index CD-ROM.*

- Salem/Magill: The Masterplots series and the Critical Survey series are basic introductions to authors and their works. Volumes cover fiction, short stories, drama, and poetry in English and foreign languages. Also on CD-ROM.
- St. James: *Contemporary Novelists, Contemporary Dramatists, Contemporary Poets,* and other titles provide biographical information, a list of publications, and a short critical essay on modern American and British authors.
- Charles Scribner's and Son: Multivolume sets combine biography and original criticism. Titles are *British Writers, American Writers, European Writers, Ancient Writers: Greece and Rome, Latin American Writers, African American Writers,* and *Modern American Women Writers.* Also available on CD-ROM.
- Ungar: *A Library of Literary Criticism,* 1966–   . Excerpts of criticism, usually arranged by nationality. Covers non-Western literatures (e.g., Arabic literature) as well as American and European.
- H. W. Wilson: Its authors series now consists of eleven volumes, some of them quite dated. Sample titles are *British Authors before 1800* and *World Authors, 1980–1985.*

Handbooks

Benet's Reader's Encyclopedia. 3d ed. HarperCollins, 1987.

This useful companion to world literature has brief entries on authors, titles, characters, literary allusions, literary movements and terms, and other topics.

A Handbook to Literature. 6th ed. By C. Hugh Holman and William Harmon. Macmillan, 1992.

This dictionary of terms that pertain to literature in English includes poetic terms and terms for periods, theories, and styles. Appendixes include a chronology of literature from *Beowulf* to the death of Graham Greene in 1991 and lists of Nobel and Pulitzer Prize winners for literature.

Oxford Companion to American Literature. 5th ed. By James D. Hart. Oxford University Press, 1983.

Short biographies of authors, plot summaries of novels and plays, entries on literary schools and movements, and more. There are similar volumes for British, Canadian, Australian, French, German, and Spanish literatures.

Reader's Advisor: A Layman's Guide to Literature. 14th ed. Edited by William L. Reese and others. Bowker, 1993–94.

The first two volumes in this six-volume set cover "the best in American and British fiction, poetry, essays, literary biography, bibliography, and reference" and "the best in American and British drama and world literature in English translation." Following a brief description of each author and his/her most important books is a list of books by and about the writer. These lists provide a valuable overview of the most important literature in English and can serve as a guide to reading for the layperson. Volumes 3 through 5 list important books in the social sciences, philosophy and religion, and science and technology; Volume 6 is an index.

See Chapter 18, General Reference Sources, for information on quotation dictionaries.

ELECTRONIC SOURCES

Arts & Humanities Citation Index Compact Disc Edition. Institute for Scientific Information, 1990–   . Updated 3 times/year.

More than 1,100 journals are indexed by author and keyword. In addition, this unique tool enables the searcher to determine who has later cited a particular book or article and which books and articles are influential because they are cited often in leading arts and humanities journals. Also available online as *Arts & Humanities Search,* 1980–   , from Dialog (File 439), BRS, and BRS/AfterDark, updated weekly. Available in print as *Arts and Humanities Citation Index,* Institute for Scientific Information, 1976–   , updated quarterly.

The Columbia Granger's World of Poetry: CD-ROM. Columbia University Press, 1991.
Poetry Finder: On Disk. (CD-ROM) Roth Publishing, 1991.
The English Poetry Full-Text Database. (CD-ROM) Chadwyck-Healey, 1993–94.

The first product is based on a well-known print index to poetry in 550 anthologies. It contains not only first line, author, title, and subject indexes but the full text of 8,500 of the poems (generally older poetry that is no longer covered by copyright). *Poetry Finder* indexes a much larger number of poems and can be searched by first line, author, and title. The third title contains the full text of works by 1,350 poets from 600 to 1900 A.D. on four CD-ROMs. A magnetic tape version is also available for institutions to mount on their own computers. This is a relatively expensive product and will be found only in certain large universities.

Contemporary Authors on CD. Gale, 1993.

Biographical information on almost 100,000 authors, including poets, playwrights, screenwriters, journalists, and other nonfiction writers. Entries include bibliographies of works by and about the author. In addition to name, you can search by nationality of the author, place of birth, college attended, political affiliation, interests, and more.

DiscLit: American Authors and *DiscLit: British Authors.* (CD-ROM) G. K. Hall, 1992.

Full text of the Twayne Authors series volumes, known for their concise critical introductions to the lives and works of major authors. The American Authors series includes 143 authors from Benjamin Franklin to modern writers such as Amiri Baraka and Joan Didion; the British Authors series has 145 authors from the fifteenth century to the present. Each CD-ROM also contains a bibliography of more than 100,000 citations to books by or about the authors from OCLC's online catalog. Every word in the texts and bibliographies can be searched. The advantage of the electronic version of these books is that the researcher can trace a subject or theme across several or all of the authors in the series.

DISCovering Authors: Biographies & Criticism on 300 Most Studied Authors. (CD-ROM) Gale, 1993.

Biographical information plus criticism on 300 of the authors most often studied in high schools and colleges. All time periods and all nationalities are represented: Aristotle to Chinua Achebe and Samuel Pepys to Marcel Proust. In addition to searching by author or title, you can search the disc by theme, time period, characters, or genre. The author biographies can be searched by place and date of birth, religion, media adaptations, and awards. Each entry includes a bibliography listing sources for further reading.

Essay and General Literature Index. (CD-ROM) H. W. Wilson. Annual.

More than 250,000 essays published in 15,000 collections are indexed by author and subject. While not limited to literature, literary criticism is emphasized. Library catalogs do not list the individual essays in collections so this index is an important way to find material that is otherwise lost in libraries. Also available online as part of Wilsonline and OCLC FirstSearch, 1985–   , and in print under the same title, 1900–   .

Humanities Index. (CD-ROM) H. W. Wilson, 1984–   . Quarterly.

Indexes more than 300 general humanities periodicals such as the *American Scholar, Journal of Popular Culture,* and *The Hudson Review.* Available on CD-ROM with abstracts as *Wilson Humanities Abstracts.* Also available online with Wilsonline, 1984–   , and OCLC FirstSearch, updated twice a week, and in print, updated quarterly, as *Humanities Index,* 1974–   (formerly *Social Sciences and Humanities Index,* 1965–74; *International Index,* 1907–65).

MLA International Bibliography. (CD-ROM) H. W. Wilson, 1981–   .
Quarterly.

Covers more than 4,000 periodicals, books, and dissertations on literature in virtually all major languages, with in-depth coverage of English and American literature. Over one million citations are available online through Wilsonline and OCLC FirstSearch, 1981–   , updated monthly. Also available in print, 1921–   , annual. Prior to 1981, the print index had no subject indexing. Citations were arranged by language and then alphabetically by the author being discussed.

Masterplots II on CD-ROM. EBSCO, 1992.

Complete text of volumes in the Masterplots II series covering 2,500 works of literature with plot synopses and brief critical comments. Based on the print *Masterplots II,* Salem Press, 1986–   .

Monarch Notes. (CD-ROM) Bureau of Electronic Publishing.

The entire collection of Simon & Schuster's *Monarch Notes* on more than 200 authors from Austen to Zola can be searched on CD-ROM. Features plot synopses, character analyses, criticism, author biographies, and bibliographies of further reading.

Scribner Writers Series on CD-ROM. Scribner's, 1993.

Full text of essays on 510 writers drawn from nine different Scribner's sets, ranging from *Ancient Writers: Greece and Rome* to *Latin American Writers.* Each essay has a bibliography of scholarly sources for further research. The disc can be searched by genre (poetry, drama, etc.), language, period, race or nationality, or any combinations of these.

RLG Research-in-Progress Database. RLIN. Updated daily.

This online database contains more than 4,000 records of unpublished scholarly work, including articles that have been accepted for publication by fifty literature journals.

Library of the Future. World Library for Data Discman.

Three small discs for Sony's Data Discman ($39.95 each) contain the full text of hundreds of books. Volume 1 has the text of 150 works, including works by Homer, Shakespeare, Swift, and Whitman. Volume 2 has 150 titles, including works by Chaucer, Voltaire, and Dickens. Among the 125 works in Volume 3 are titles from Euripides, Aristophanes, and Virgil. The texts of the 425 works are also available on one CD-ROM as the *Electronic Home Library* (World Library).

- America Online: *Barron's Book Notes,* brief information on the author, plot, and characters of twenty novels, from *Anna Karenina* to *Wuthering Heights.*
- The Internet: Project Gutenberg is an ambitious volunteer effort to get literature into machine-readable form. Among the books available on-line are the complete works of Shakespeare, *Moby Dick, Paradise Lost,* and *O Pioneers!* A newsletter and an index are available via **mrcnext.cso. uiuc.edu.** The texts can be accessed via **ftp mrcnext.cso.uiuc.edu,** log in **anonymous; cd etext** or **ftp quake.think.com,** log in **anonymous;cd pub/etext.**

Online Services

The Dante Project on the Internet contains articles on the *Divine Comedy.* Access via **telnet library.Dartmouth.edu;** then type **connect Dante.**

At least two files contain substantial poetry texts: **U.C. Berkeley Open Computing Facility Gopher/OCF On-Line Library Poetry** and **WAIS poetry.src.**

PERIODICALS

Among the thousands of magazines treating aspects of literature are literary reviews and literature journals. Literary reviews are aimed at the general reader and contain fiction, poetry, drama, and interviews; they may also include literary criticism and social and arts commentary. Literature journals, on the other hand, contain only criticism and are aimed at the specialist.

Literary Reviews: A Sampling

Georgia Review. 1947–   . Quarterly.
The Hudson Review. 1948–   . Quarterly.
The North American Review. 1815–   . Quarterly.
The Paris Review. 1953–   . Quarterly
Partisan Review. 1934–   . Quarterly.
The Southern Review. 1934–   . Quarterly.

Literature Journals

American Literature: A Journal of Literary History, Criticism, and Bibliography. 1929–   . Quarterly.
Published in cooperation with the Modern Language Association, this is the most prestigious journal for American literature. Extensive section of book reviews in each issue.

Comparative Literature. 1949–   . Quarterly.
Articles on international literary history and theory.

ELH: Journal of Literary History. 1934–   . Quarterly.
Covers both English and American literature.

Journal of Modern Literature. 1970–   . 3 times/year.
Covers all national literatures since 1900. One issue per year is devoted to a bibliographical review of literature in English for the year.

PMLA (Publications of the Modern Language Association). 1884–   .
6 times/year.
Articles on the literatures of all nations. Four general issues a year; the other two are the membership directory and the convention program.

World Literature Today. 1927–   . Quarterly.
Essays on and interviews with contemporary writers from many nations. "World Literature in Review" section is divided by language and reviews books of fiction, poetry, criticism, etc.

In addition, hundreds of journals and newsletters devote themselves to specific authors. Examples are *Studies in Browning and His Circle, Chaucer Review,* and *Ellen Glasgow Newsletter.* To find such publications, see: *Author Newsletters and Journals.* By Margaret C. Patterson. Gale, 1979.
Lists 1,129 publications on 435 writers from Shakespeare to Kafka; for post-1970s publications, see the *MLA Directory* below.

For a comprehensive, current list of literature journals (but not newsletters), see *MLA Directory of Periodicals: A Guide to Journals and Serials in Language and Literature.* Modern Language Association, 1979–   . Biennial.

Several book review journals aimed at the general reader provide lengthy critical essays:
The New York Review of Books. 1963–   . Semimonthly.
The New York Times Book Review. 1896–   . Weekly.
TLS: The Times Literary Supplement. 1902–   . Weekly.
Erudite and entertaining essays on new books. Not limited to literature, they cover history, biography, and other fields as well. *TLS* is published in London, but covers important U.S. books, too.

Publishers Weekly: The International News Magazine of Publishing. 1872–   .
Weekly.
Brief prepublication reviews of trade books.

GOVERNMENT PUBLICATIONS Through such agencies as the Library of Congress and its Manuscript Division, the federal government issues occasional publications useful in literary study. For example:

Four Dubliners: Wilde, Yeats, Joyce, and Beckett. From a lecture by Richard Ellmann. Library of Congress, 1986.

George Orwell & Nineteen Eighty-Four: The Man and the Book. Library of Congress, 1985.

Also see the Government Printing Office's *Subject Bibliography* #142—Poetry and Literature, for a list of recent government publications on this topic.

National Endowment for the Humanities
1100 Pennsylvania Ave. NW
Washington, DC 20506
(202) 786-0438
Provides support for fellowships and seminars, grants for the preparation of publication of texts and reference materials, and grants for humanities programming at the state and local levels.

Modern Language Association
10 Astor Place
New York, NY 10003
(212) 475-9500
An association of college and university teachers of English and foreign-language literatures. It holds conventions, awards prizes, produces important publications such as the *MLA International Bibliography* (see above).

National Council of Teachers of English
1111 Kenyon Rd.
Urbana, IL 61801
(217) 328-3870
Teachers of English at all levels, high school and up. Holds conventions, gives grants, publishes many books and journals, e.g., *College English, Teaching English in the Two-Year College, Language Arts.*

Author associations: The T. S. Eliot Society and the James Joyce Society are among the hundreds of associations focusing on one author. They publish author journals and newsletters, some of them mentioned above. See the *Encyclopedia of Associations* (Gale, annual) under the name of the author for further information.

Library of Congress
101 Independence Ave. SE
Washington, DC 20540
(202) 707-5000
In order to be copyrighted, books must be deposited with the Library of Congress. From these deposits and the literary papers it has acquired, the Library of Congress has built a massive collection for research in American

literature. It also has gathered strong collections of foreign literatures. Users of the library are encouraged to show special need, such as having exhausted the resources of local collections. A helpful starting point is the library's National Reference Service, telephone (202) 707-5522, or fax (202) 707-1389.

Humanities Research Center
University of Texas
P. O. Box 7219, University Station
Austin, TX 78713
(512) 471-9119
An important center for research in English and American literature, with more than 800,000 rare books and 9 million literary manuscripts.

Huntington Library
1151 Oxford Rd.
San Marino, CA 91108
(818) 405-2100
Holds 600,000 books and 2.2 million manuscripts for research in British and American literature.

New York Public Library
5th Ave. and 42d St.
New York, NY 10018
(212) 930-0800
Its Berg Collection of English and American Literature is world-famous; important books and literary manuscripts abound elsewhere in the library, such as at the Schomburg Center for Research in Black Culture.

Lilly Library
Indiana University
Bloomington, IN 47405
(812) 855-2452
Important collections of English and American literature from 1640 to the present.

LC SUBJECT HEADINGS In library catalogs, records will be found for writers as authors and as subjects. Looking up James Joyce as an author will lead you to books by Joyce; looking him up as a subject will lead to books about him. For authors about whom much has been written, subheadings such as the following can be used:
Joyce, James, 1882–1941—Allegory and symbolism
Joyce, James, 1882–1941—Archives

Joyce, James, 1882–1941—Bibliography
Joyce, James, 1882–1941—Biography
Joyce, James, 1882–1941—Characters
Joyce, James, 1882–1941—Criticism and interpretation
Joyce, James, 1882–1941—Concordances
Joyce, James, 1882–1941—Correspondence
Joyce, James, 1882–1941—Handbooks, manuals, etc.
Joyce, James, 1882–1941—Humor
Joyce, James, 1882–1941—Influence
Joyce, James, 1882–1941—Manuscripts
Joyce, James, 1882–1941—Musical settings
Joyce, James, 1882–1941—Periodicals
Joyce, James, 1882–1941—Stage adaptations
Joyce, James, 1882–1941—Style
Books about a specific work will be listed under that work:
Joyce, James, 1882–1941— *Ulysses*
Headings also exist for national literatures (often divided by period), for
forms such as fiction or poetry, and for general periods, irrespective of
nationality:
American Literature—Colonial period
American Literature—Mexican American authors
American Poetry—20th century
English Fiction—Middle English, 1100–1500
English Literature—Explication—Dictionaries
French Poetry—20th century
German Literature—Middle High German, 1050–1500
Literature, Modern—19th century
Literature, Modern—History and criticism

35

MULTICULTURALISM

See also: General Reference Sources, Genealogy, History

In recent years there has been increasing debate over the role of ethnicity in American history and the appropriateness of multicultural studies in education. In this chapter we describe some general sources for the study of ethnicity and more specific sources on African Americans, Asian Americans, Native Americans, and Hispanic Americans. You will also want to read more broadly in American history and the social sciences.

GENERAL SOURCES OF INFORMATION

General Works on Ethnicity

Dictionary of American Immigration History. Edited by Francesco Cordasco. Scarecrow, 1990.

Entries cover a broad range of topics relating to immigration to the United States and Canada. Introduction includes a brief history of immigration law.

The Ethnic Almanac. By Stephanie Bernardo. Doubleday, 1981.

A popular compilation of facts on the "top thirty-six" ethnic groups in the United States. Includes an "Ethnic Who's Who," a list of ethnic organizations, and information on tracing ancestry.

Ethnic Information Sources of the United States. 2 vols. 2d ed. Edited by Paul Wasserman. Gale, 1983.

Provides information sources in twenty-six categories, including organizations, libraries, festivals, and books for more than 100 ethnic groups. African Americans, Native Americans, and Native Alaskans are not covered.

Harvard Encyclopedia of American Ethnic Groups. Edited by Stephan Thernstrom. Harvard University Press, 1980.

A one-volume encyclopedia, with entries on 106 ethnic groups, including American regional groups, and twenty-nine thematic essays. Provides short bibliographies, many maps and tables. Unfortunately, most of the statistical data are drawn from the 1970 census and are far from up to date.

Minority Organizations: A National Directory. 4th ed. Garrett Park Press, 1992.

Gives address, phone number, and brief description for 9,700 multiethnic and black, Hispanic, Native American, and Asian-American organizations.

Refugees in the United States: A Reference Handbook. Edited by David W. Haines. Greenwood, 1985.

Contains three essays on general issues and nine essays covering specific refugee groups: the Chinese, Vietnamese, Hmong, Khmer, and Laotians from Southeast Asia, Salvadorans and Guatemalans, Cubans and Haitians, and Soviet Jews. Each essay is accompanied by a bibliography. The volume concludes with a lengthy annotated bibliography of books, articles, and government publications.

We the People: An Atlas of America's Ethnic Diversity. By James Paul Allen and Eugene J. Turner. Macmillan, 1988.

Maps based on 1980 U.S. census data show population distribution by county for sixty-six ethnic and racial groups. The text offers historical interpretation and comparison with 1920 data. Volume includes statistical tables of county ethnic census data and an extensive bibliography.

Afro-American Reference: An Annotated Bibliography of Selected Sources. Compiled by Nathaniel Davis. Greenwood, 1985.

Reference Books on Specific Groups

Useful guide to the most important reference sources for beginning research on African Americans.

African Americans

Black Americans Information Directory. 2d ed. Edited by Julia C. Furtaw. Gale, 1993.

This well-organized directory gathers together extensive information on "black American life and culture." Lists more than 4,000 organizations, agencies, programs, and publications.

Dictionary of American Negro Biography. By Rayford W. Logan and Michael R. Winston. Norton, 1982.

Comprehensive biographical dictionary of individuals who died before January 1, 1970. Lengthy entries cite additional biographical references and primary-source materials.

Encyclopedia of Black America. By W. Augustus Low and Virgil A. Clift.
McGraw-Hill, 1981.

Illustrated one-volume general encyclopedia on African-American history and culture. Includes some 1,400 biographical articles and 125 major
topical articles, with 299 shorter ones. Provides bibliographies with many
entries.

The Negro Almanac: A Reference Work on the African American. Edited by
Harry A. Ploski and James Williams. 5th ed. Gale, 1990.

Topical chapters provide concise coverage of history, biography, and
current status of blacks in American society. Includes illustrations, graphs,
charts, and listings of black firsts, national black organizations, black
media, etc. Extensive bibliography lists publications since 1982.

Statistical Record of Black America. 2d ed. Edited by Carrell Peterson Horton
and Jessie Carney Smith. Gale, 1992.

Compendium of economic and social data on many aspects of black
American life from government, academic, and business sources. The
source documents are always indicated.

The State of Black America. National Urban League, 1976–   .

Annual publication with up-to-date information on black American life.
Surveys significant trends and events, and topical essays by various scholars
address current issues. Includes references and a chronology of the year's
events.

Who's Who Among Black Americans. Edited by Christa Brelin. 7th ed. Gale,
1992.

Provides biographical information on more than 17,000 black American
professionals from all fields. Includes occupational and geographical indexes. Also available online with NEXIS and on floppy disk.

Asian Americans

Asian American Studies: An Annotated Bibliography and Research Guide. Edited
by Hyung-Chan Kim. Greenwood, 1989.

Extensive bibliography of books and periodical articles covering relevant
literature of the social and behavioral sciences and humanities. Does not
include literary topics. Sections are prefaced by concise literature reviews.

Asian Americans Information Directory. Edited by Karen Backus and Julia C.
Furtaw. Gale, 1991.

Guide to organizations and agencies, both regional and national, of
interest to Asian ethnic groups in the United States. Also covers publications, videotapes, and media. Listings include location, phone number,
contact person, and usually a brief description.

Dictionary of Asian American History. Edited by Hyung-Chan Kim. Greenwood, 1986.

Fifteen essays discuss the major ethnic groups in the United States from Asian countries and the Pacific islands and important themes in the Asian-American experience. The dictionary section deals with organizations, laws, relevant court cases, and significant individuals. Appendix includes a select bibliography, chronology of Asian-American history, and 1980 census data by state for the population of Asians and Pacific islanders.

Statistical Record of Asian Americans. Edited by Susan Gall. Gale, 1993.

Data on nineteen Asian nationality groups.

Hispanic Americans

Bibliography of Mexican American History. By Matt S. Meier. Greenwood, 1984.

Opening chapters are organized chronologically, from colonial times to the present. Additional chapters cite material on labor, politics, and culture. The volume concludes with three chapters listing reference works, archives, libraries, and journals.

Dictionary of Mexican American History. By Matt S. Meier and Feliciano Rivera. Greenwood, 1981.

Brief entries and longer essays comment on Chicano history and the contemporary condition of Chicanos in American society. Includes bibliography, chronology, and tables.

The Hispanic Almanac. 2d ed. Hispanic Policy Development Project, 1990.

Compendium of data and other information about the Hispanic population of the United States. Provides a brief historical narrative, a national socioeconomic profile of Hispanics, detailed analysis of the twenty Standard Metropolitan Statistical Areas with the largest Hispanic populations, and a description of voting patterns.

The Hispanic-American Almanac. Edited by Nicolas Kanellos. Gale, 1993.

Modeled after *The Negro Almanac,* this book provides similar types of information about America's fastest-growing ethnic group. Includes a chronology, significant documents, prominent people, and many other topics. Text is supplemented by 400 photographs, maps and charts, and bibliographies.

Hispanic-American Material Culture: An Annotated Directory of Collections, Sites, Archives and Festivals in the United States. Compiled by Joe S. Graham. Greenwood, 1989.

Describes collections in museums, historical societies, and other agencies; and sites on the National Register of Historic Places. Includes bibliography, primarily on arts and crafts. Part of a series; another title covers East and Southeast Asians in America.

Hispanic Americans Information Directory. 2d ed. Edited by Julia C. Furtaw. Gale, 1992.

Guide to approximately 4,700 organizations, federal agencies, research centers, businesses, publishers, library collections, media, etc. In addition to name, address, and telephone number, a brief description is frequently given. Lists the top Hispanic companies and media organizations.

Sourcebook of Hispanic Culture in the United States. By David William Foster. American Library Association, 1982.

Guide to scholarly literature on Mexican Americans, Puerto Ricans, and Cuban Americans. Introductory essays are supplemented by annotated bibliography of the most important books, periodicals, and reports.

Statistical Handbook on U.S. Hispanics. By Frank L. Schick and Renee Schick. Oryx, 1991.

Statistical tables and charts, primarily from U.S. government sources, provide data on population, immigration, economic and social status. Comparative data for whites, Asians, and blacks are often given. See also Gale's *Statistical Record of Hispanic Americans* (1993).

Who's Who Among Hispanic Americans. 2d ed. Edited by Amy L. Unterberger. Gale, 1992.

Includes basic biographical information on 5,000 leaders. Indexed by city, occupation, and ethnic/cultural heritage. Also available online with NEXIS and on floppy disk.

Native Americans

Atlas of the North American Indian. By Carl Waldman. Facts On File, 1985.

Text and maps cover North American Indian history and culture, ancient and modern. The volume includes a chronology, listings of Indian tribes with their historical and current locations, federal and state reservations, major Indian place names, historical and archaeological sites, and a selective bibliography. See also CD-ROM version below.

Guide to Research on North American Indians. By Arlene B. Hirschfelder and others. American Library Association, 1983.

Annotated bibliography of the best books, periodical articles, and government documents on Native Americans. To update this bibliography, use the following work.

Native Americans: An Annotated Bibliography. By Frederick Hoxie and Harvey Markowitz. Salem, 1991.

Selective annotated bibliography of books and scholarly articles on Native American history and culture, most published in the past thirty years. Lists more than 100 reference works covering more than one region or tribe and additional reference material for each culture area.

Handbook of North American Indians. Smithsonian Institution, 1988–   .

A projected twenty-volume series (nine published at this writing) that will be a comprehensive summary of current knowledge about Native Americans. Essays by leading scholars explore history, national policies, politics, economics, religion, tribal customs, etc. Includes illustrations, maps, and bibliographies.

Native Americans Information Directory. Edited by Julia C. Furtaw. Gale, 1993.

Arranged in three broad sections covering Northern American Indians, Native Alaskans, and Native Hawaiians. Lists more than 4,500 organizations, institutions, programs, and publications concerned with Native American life and culture.

The Newberry Library Center for the History of the American Indian Bibliographical Series. Newberry Library, 1976–83.

Bibliographic essays on individual tribes and more general topics, such as United States Indian policy. Indexes indicate titles suitable for use by secondary school students.

Reference Encyclopedia of the American Indian. 6th ed. Edited by Barry T. Klein. Todd, 1992.

Lists information sources on North American Indians (associations, government agencies, reservations, libraries, etc.) and provides bibliographies of periodicals, government publications, and in-print books. The volume concludes with biographical sketches of prominent living Native Americans and other persons active in Indian affairs. Also available on diskette.

Statistical Record of Native North Americans. Edited by Arsen J. Darnay. Gale, 1993.

Historical and statistical data on approximately 200 Native American tribes.

Indexes

General-circulation magazines and newspapers regularly cover civil rights, immigration, other public policy issues related to ethnicity, and many other topics related to multiculturalism. To locate these, use the widely available indexes described in Chapter 18, General Reference Sources. To expand your search, use the specialized indexes listed below and under Electronic Sources.

Index to Black Periodicals. G. K. Hall, 1984–   .
    Covers black periodicals not indexed elsewhere. Former titles: *Index to Selected Periodicals* (1950–59), *Index to Periodical Articles by and about Negroes* (1960–70), and *Index to Periodical Articles by and about Blacks* (1971–83).

Black Newspaper Index. UMI, 1977–   . Quarterly.
    Indexes eight African-American newspapers.

NOTE: Ethnic topics are covered in many specialized journals. For example, to find articles on teaching methods for multicultural education, you will want to use *Education Index* and *Current Index to Journals in Education.*

**ELECTRONIC
SOURCES**

Ethnic NewsWatch. (CD-ROM) SoftLine Information.
    Contains the full text of more than eighty ethnic periodicals and newspapers, from *Armenian Reporter* to *Yakima Nations Review.* Among the perspectives represented are Jewish, Eastern European, Native American, African American, Asian, Middle Eastern, and Hispanic. Many of the Hispanic publications are in Spanish; the whole database can be searched in either English or Spanish.

Afro-American Insight. (Diskette) AfroLink Software, 1815 Wellington Rd., Los Angeles, CA 90019-5945.
    Lists African-American businesses, national organizations and associations, black mayors, elected state and federal officials, black colleges, and travel information.

The American Indian: A Multimedia Encyclopedia. (CD-ROM) Facts On File, 1993.
    Text of the *Atlas of the North American Indian, Who Was Who in American History,* the *Encyclopedia of Native American Tribes, Voices of the Winds,* reproductions of documents from the National Archives, over 1,000 images (including maps), and sound bites of authentic Indian songs.

Chicano Database on CD-ROM. Chicano Studies Library, University of California, Berkeley, 1967–   .
    Bibliographic citations on the Mexican-American experience. The scope of the database has recently been expanded to include material on other Spanish-speaking groups in the United States. Includes portions of several print indexes: *Chicano Periodical Index* (1967–88), *The Chicano Index* (1989–present), which indexes twenty-three periodicals, *Arte Chicano: An Annotated Bibliography of Chicano Art* (1965–81), and *The Chicano Anthology Index.*

Hispanic-American Periodicals Index. (Online) RLIN, 1970–   . Annual.
Indexes 250 scholarly social science and humanities journals published
in Latin America or treating Latin American or U.S. Hispanic topics.

North American Indians. Quanta Press.
A CD-ROM product with images. Provides information on the history of
Native Americans, derived from U.S. Bureau of Ethnology files.

For a more extended search of your topic, use one of the following
databases:

PAIS International. (CD-ROM) SilverPlatter, 1972–   . Quarterly. Also
available as *PAIS on CD-ROM.* Public Affairs Information Service,
1972–   . Quarterly.
Subject index to books, pamphlets, government publications, and more
than 1,200 periodicals, with an emphasis on economic, social, and political
issues. Also available online on BRS (PAIS), BRS/AfterDark, Dialog (File
49), Knowledge Index (SOCS2), FirstSearch (PAIS Decade), 1976–   ,
and on RLIN's CitaDel, 1980–   . Contains records from the print
sources *PAIS Bulletin,* 1976–90 (formerly called *Public Affairs Information
Service Bulletin,* 1915–76), *PAIS Foreign Language Index,* 1972–90, and
PAIS International in Print, 1991–   . Since 1991, *PAIS International* has
included both English-language materials and the materials in French,
German, Italian, Portuguese, and Spanish formerly indexed in *PAIS Foreign
Language Index.*

Social Sciences Index. (CD-ROM) H. W. Wilson, 1983–   . Quarterly.
Indexes by author and subject over 300 leading periodicals in the social
sciences. As with all Wilsondisc products, it is possible to dial up the online
file at no extra charge and find the latest citations. Also available in some
libraries as *Social Sciences Index/Full Text* (1989–   , monthly) with the
full text of the indexed articles on compact disc. Online from Wilson,
1983–   . Print version is *Social Sciences Index,* 1974–   , formerly *Social
Sciences and Humanities Index,* 1965–74; *International Index,* 1907–65.

Social Sciences Citation Index Compact Disc Edition. Institute for Scientific
Information, 1981–   . Quarterly.
Covers more than 1,400 social science journals from around the world
indexed by author and keyword. Searcher can determine who has cited a
particular book or article and which books and articles are influential
because they are cited often. Available also online as *Social SCISEARCH* on
BRS (SSCI) and Dialog (File 7), 1972–   . Corresponds to the print
index *Social Sciences Citation Index,* 1956–   . Because of the extremely

large size of this file, some libraries offering the CD-ROM version of this database may have only the most recent years.

The ability to search by keyword and to combine terms (e.g., "black artists"), a standard feature of online and CD-ROM databases, is particularly useful in the field of ethnic studies. In printed indexes, in many instances it is necessary to scan all entries under a given subject to find the material relating to a particular ethnic group.

Bulletin Boards: Black Issues BBS: list of bulletin boards of interest to African Americans; **(707) 552-3314.**

PERIODICALS

Hundreds of periodicals are published by and about ethnic groups in the United States.

There are popular newsstand titles for the largest ethnic groups, including:

For African Americans

Ebony. 1945–   . Monthly.
American Visions: The Magazine of Afro-American Culture. 1986–   . Bimonthly.

For Hispanic Americans

Hispanic: The Magazine for and about Hispanics. 1988–   . Monthly.

For Asian Americans

A. Magazine: The Asian American Quarterly. 1991–   . Quarterly.

For Native Americans

Akwesasne Notes. 1969–   . Bimonthly.
There are also scholarly journals for these groups:
The Black Scholar. 1969–   . Quarterly.
Journal of Black Studies. 1970–   . Quarterly.

Aztlan: Journal of Chicano Studies. 1970–   . Semiannual.
Latino Studies Journal. 1990–   . 3 times/year.

Amerasia Journal: The National Interdisciplinary Journal of Scholarship, Criticism, and Literature on Asian and Pacific Americans. 1971–   . 3 times/year.

American Indian Culture & Research Journal. 1971–   . Quarterly.
American Indian Quarterly. 1974–   . Quarterly.
Listed below are some of the scholarly ethnic studies journals covering the field as a whole:

Explorations in Ethnic Studies: The Journal for the National Association for Ethnic Studies. 1978–   . Semiannual.
An interdisciplinary journal for professionals concerned with "ethnicity,

ethnic groups, intergroup relations, and the cultural life of ethnic minorities." An annual supplement, *Explorations in Sights and Sounds,* contains reviews of books and nonprint media.

Journal of American Ethnic History. 1982–   . Quarterly.
   Journal of the Immigration History Society. Publishes articles on "immigrant and ethnic history of North American people." Includes review essays and book reviews.

Journal of Ethnic Studies. 1973–   . Quarterly.
   Poetry, fiction, and research notes appear regularly along with scholarly articles on ethnicity and individual ethnic groups in the United States.

For listings of other ethnic periodicals, including those published by various ethnic groups and scholarly journals dealing with specific ethnic groups, consult one of these published bibliographies:

Ethnic Periodicals in Contemporary America: An Annotated Guide. By Sandra L. Jones Ireland. Greenwood, 1990.
   Lists 234 current magazines, newspapers, and newsletters published for 100 ethnic groups, from African to Zionist.

American Indian and Alaskan Native Newspapers and Periodicals. 3 vols. By Daniel F. Littlefield, Jr., and James W. Parins. Greenwood, 1986.

Native American Periodicals and Newspapers, 1828–1982: Bibliography, Publishing Record, and Holdings. Edited by James P. Danky and compiled by Maureen E. Hady. Greenwood, 1984.

At this writing, the library of the State Historical Society of Wisconsin is preparing a bibliography of all African-American periodicals ever published in the United States and where copies are located.

GOVERNMENT PUBLICATIONS

The federal government collects and publishes many statistics by race and ethnic group. Most of these can be found in summary form in the *Statistical Abstract of the United States,* which is published annually. (Chapter 16)
   Following is a representative list of nonstatistical publications on ethnic topics issued by federal agencies:

Community Education and Multiculturalism: Immigrant Refugee Needs and Cultural Awareness. Microfiche. U.S. Conference of Mayors, U.S. Department of Education, 1982.

Guide to Selected Ethnic Heritage Materials, 1974–1980. By Frances Haley. Microfiche. Social Science Education Consortium: ERIC Clearinghouse for Social Studies/Social Sciences Education, 1982.

Public Information Materials for Language Minorities. Prepared by the National Criminal Justice Reference Service. U.S. Department of Justice, National Institute of Justice, 1980.

See also the Government Printing Office's *Subject Bibliography #6*—Minorities.

Lists more than fifty recent government publications on topics relating to minorities.

GOVERNMENT AGENCIES

Civil Rights Division
Department of Justice
10th Street and Pennsylvania Avenue NW
Washington, DC 20530
(202) 514-4224
Responsible for enforcing federal civil rights laws that prohibit discrimination. Coordinates the efforts of federal executive agencies and departments to eliminate discrimination in programs conducted by the federal government or receiving federal assistance.

Equal Employment Opportunity Commission (EEOC)
1801 L Street NW
Washington, DC 20507
(202) 663-4900; (800) USA-EEOC
TDD (800) 800-3302
EEOC directs the federal government's efforts to eliminate discrimination based on color, race, age, religion, sex, or national origin in the employment practices of the private sector and of federal, state, and local government. EEOC publishes data on the employment of minorities and women and maintains fifty offices throughout the United States.

Immigration and Naturalization Service
Department of Justice
425 I Street NW
Washington, DC 20536
(205) 514-4316
Administers and enforces immigration laws. Operates four regional and thirty-three district offices in the United States, three abroad.

U.S. Commission on Civil Rights
1121 Vermont Avenue NW
Washington, DC 20425
(202) 376-8177

Serves as a clearinghouse for civil rights information. Evaluates the effectiveness of federal laws and government equal opportunity programs and presents findings and recommendations to the president and to Congress.

ASSOCIATIONS

Ethnic Cultural Preservation Council
6500 S. Pulaski Road
Chicago, IL 60629
(312) 582-5143

Also known as the *Association of North American Museums, Libraries, Archives, Cultural Centers, and Fraternal Organizations.* A coalition of ethnic and other museums, historical societies, libraries, archives, and cultural centers whose purpose is to facilitate development of arts and humanities programs. Sponsors seminars and exhibits and disseminates information on ethnic activities.

National Center for Urban Ethnic Affairs
P. O. Box 20
Cardinal Station
Washington, DC 20064
(202) 232-3600

Purpose is to develop neighborhood programs and policies that promote appreciation of ethnic cultural diversity. Affiliated with U.S. Catholic Conference.

LIBRARIES

Public libraries located in areas with a significant ethnic population will often have good collections of ethnic material, including archival collections to support the study of local history. Colleges closely associated with a particular ethnic group will also have resources for ethnic studies.

Listed below are a number of specialized collections in this field:

Amistad Research Center
Tulane University
Tilton Hall
New Orleans, LA 70122
(504) 865-5000

Research library with extensive primary source materials on the history of ethnic minorities and race relations in the United States, with an emphasis on African Americans, Native Americans, Chicanos, Asian Americans, and Puerto Ricans. The collection also includes clippings, pamphlets, periodicals, and microfilm. The Center has the archives of such groups as the American Missionary Association and the Race Relations Department of the Jewish Anti-Defamation League.

Auburn Avenue Research Library on African-American Culture and History
Atlanta-Fulton Public Library
Auburn Ave.
Atlanta, GA 30312
(404) 730-1700
This new branch of the Atlanta Public Library will open in the spring or summer of 1994. A noncirculating public library, it is dedicated to research and the study of African-American culture, particularly as it pertains to the Southeast. The library will have reference collections, rare books and materials, and archives for unpublished papers and documents.

Balch Institute for Ethnic Studies
18 South 7th Street
Philadelphia, PA 19106-2314
(215) 925-8090
Independent nonprofit research and educational museum focusing on immigration and ethnicity. Maintains a database of nineteenth-century immigrants to the United States and a collection of ship manifests. Sponsors educational programs and occasional conferences. Maintains a library of some 60,000 volumes and also collects sheet music, manuscripts, microfilm, audiovisual material, and photographs. Two of its special collections are the Philadelphia Jewish Archives Center and the Scotch Irish Foundation Collection.

Center for Migration Studies Library
209 Flagg Place
Staten Island, NY
(718) 351-8800
Contains a noncirculating library of 20,000 volumes and an extensive collection of newsletters and vertical file material. Collecting interests are refugees, international migration, and ethnic studies.

Immigration History Research Center
University of Minnesota
826 Berry Street
St. Paul, MN 55114
(612) 627-4208
Collecting interests of the Center are East, Central, and South European and Near Eastern immigration and ethnic groups from 1880 on. The

Center has an extensive collection of published and manuscript material. Most of the printed titles were published by ethnic presses in North America. Manuscript holdings include the records of ethnic organizations and personal papers of ethnic leaders.

Library of Congress American Folklife Center
Thomas Jefferson Building-G152
Washington, DC 20540
(202) 707-5000
The Center's interests are folk music, ethnomusicology, folklore, folk life, and oral history. Collection includes extensive holdings of field recordings, dating back to 1890, from the United States and other countries, as well as manuscript material, photographs, field notes, folk-related books, etc. Other divisions in the Library of Congress, e.g., Asian, African and Middle Eastern, European, and Hispanic, are also important resources for ethnic material.

Schomburg Center for Research in Black Culture
New York Public Library
515 Malcolm X Boulevard
New York, NY 10037
(212) 862-4000
The library maintains a reference library of nearly 85,000 volumes by and about black people and related clippings, pamphlets, and cultural materials. Major emphases of the collection are African Americans, Africans, and Caribbeans. The Schomburg Center holds many significant special collections from black organizations and individuals.

State Historical Society of Wisconsin
816 State Street
Madison, WI 53706-1482
Library: (608) 264-6535
Archives: (608) 264-6450
The Historical Society's library has strong holdings in the area of minority and ethnic culture and an extensive collection of ethnic newspapers and periodicals, including approximately 40 percent of all African-American periodicals ever published in the United States. The Society also has a major archival collection of civil rights movement material, including the complete papers of the Congress of Racial Equality.

LC SUBJECT HEADINGS

The usual problems in using a library catalog are compounded with ethnic subject headings. Out-of-date terminology is one stumbling block. The Library of Congress has updated some of its ethnic vocabulary, but in many card catalogs older entries under terms such as *Negroes* have not been revised. The heading *intercultural* is used rather than *multicultural*. *LC Subject Headings* will help you find the ethnic terms that are used by catalogers. These include:

Afro-Americans
Asian Americans
Cherokee Indians
German Americans
Indians of North America

In LC headings, the term *Afro-American* is used for "citizens of the United States of black African descent." *Blacks— United States* is used for "works on blacks who temporarily reside in the United States, such as aliens, students from abroad . . ." In general, *Black* and *Blacks* are more inclusive terms. Under Indians of North America, you will also find, by region, the names of all Indian tribes.

As in other subject areas, terms may have geographic or topical subdivisions or may have a subheading indicating the form of publication:

Indians of North America—New Mexico—Bibliography
German Americans—Ethnic identity
Japanese Americans—Evacuation 1942–1945
Puerto Ricans—New York (City)
Ethnic terms are also used as subheadings:
American Literature—Japanese American authors
United States—Race relations
Broad multigroup terms are also used as subject headings:
Ethnic groups
Minorities
Ethnicity
There are many combined terms:
Actors, Jewish
Afro-Americans in the motion picture industry
Ethnic mass media
Intercultural education
Japanese American families
Minorities as artists

When you are not sure whether a term has been used with a preposition or a conjunction or in an inverted form, if your library has an online catalog that allows you to search by keyword it can speed your search, particularly if it has the ability to link keywords with *and;* for example, Puerto Ricans and Actors.

Balch Institute for Ethnic Studies and Center for Migration Studies Library (see under Libraries, above).

MULTI-
CULTURALISM

313

Center for the Study of Ethnic Publications and Cultural Institutions
School of Library Science
Kent State University
Kent, OH 44242-0001
(216) 672-2782
Fosters research on ethnic publishing and ethnic cultural institutions in the United States. Surveys the ethnic press and libraries, archives, and museums with ethnic holdings. Develops a curriculum to prepare librarians for service to ethnic communities.

Center for Studies of Ethnicity and Race in America
University of Colorado/Boulder
Ketchum 30, CB339
Boulder, CO 80309-0339
(303) 492-8852
Conducts research on comparative race and ethnicity, with a focus on African Americans, American Indians, Asian Americans, and Chicanos. Offers lectures and art exhibits; sponsors conferences and workshops for high school teachers and college professors.

Martin Luther King, Jr., Center for Nonviolent Social Change
449 Auburn Avenue NE
Atlanta, GA 30312
(404) 524-1956
Conducts research on nonviolence and on current economic and social issues. Sponsors continuing education on nonviolence and conflict resolution through seminars, conferences, workshops.

Finally, when writing about other ethnic groups, remember to be sensitive to the nomenclature and terminology preferred by the groups themselves. A helpful source here is *The Dictionary of Bias-Free Usage: A Guide to Nondiscriminatory Language,* edited by Rosalie Maggio (Oryx, 1991).

36

MUSIC

See also: General Reference Sources

Music is omnipresent in modern society, in our history, our economy, and our culture. Because of the popularity and varieties of music research, there are numerous sources of information in print, audiovisual, and electronic forms.

GENERAL REFERENCE SOURCES

The sources listed below are concerned mainly, but not exclusively, with "classical" or "serious" music. A later section treats sources for popular music, jazz, and folk music.

Music Reference and Research Materials: An Annotated Bibliography. 4th ed., rev. By Vincent H. Duckles and Michael A. Keller. Schirmer Books, 1993.

Duckles has long been considered the standard guide to music reference tools, listing numerous scholarly and esoteric titles as well as standard reference works found in almost all music collections.

Music: Guide to Reference Literature. By William S. Brockman. Libraries Unlimited, 1987.

More selective, and perhaps more approachable, than Duckles, emphasizing reference tools in English. It contains annotated lists of periodicals and organizations that are quite useful.

The books listed below are the standard sources in which to begin research:

The New Grove Dictionary of Music and Musicians. 20 vols. Edited by Stanley Sadie. Grove's Dictionaries, 1980.

The standard encyclopedia in English on music. International in scope, it includes biographical as well as topical articles. *The New Grove* has generated a number of revised spin-offs, including *The New Grove Dictionary of Musical Instruments* (3 vols., 1984).

The New Grove Dictionary of American Music. 4 vols. Edited by H. Wiley Hitchcock and Stanley Sadie. Grove's Dictionaries, 1986.
This encyclopedic reference work covers all aspects of music making in America and includes entries on both popular and classical music topics.

Baker's Biographical Dictionary of Musicians. 8th ed. Revised by Nicholas Slonimsky. Schirmer Books, 1992.
Baker's should be consulted for brief biographical articles, including those on composers and performers not covered by separate articles in *The New Grove.*

Musical America: International Directory of the Performing Arts. Musical America Publishing. Annual.
Provides listings for North America and the rest of the world for orchestras, opera companies, and other performing groups. Directory information for festivals, music schools, contests, music magazines, publishers, organizations, and other areas of interest to the classical music community. The magazine *Musical America,* of which this used to be a special issue, is no longer published.

The New Harvard Dictionary of Music. Edited by Don Michael Randell. Harvard University Press, 1986.
A useful source for information on music concepts, styles, and terminology.

The New Grove Dictionary of Opera. 4 vols. Edited by Stanley Sadie. Grove's Dictionaries of Music, 1992.
Entries for composers, performers, opera companies, and individual operas.

Opera and Musical Theater

The Definitive Kobbe's Opera Book. By Gustave Kobbe. Edited by the Earl of Harewood. Putnam, 1987.
Covers more than 300 of the more widely known European and American operas. Provides historical background, a list of principal characters, and detailed plot summaries, including numerous interpolations of musical examples.

Songs of the Theater. By Richard Lewine and Alfred Simon. H. W. Wilson, 1984.

The first part of this book lists thousands of song titles included in American musicals from 1891 to 1983, providing information on composer, lyricist, title of show, and date first performed. The second part is a list of shows, with brief background data and a list of song titles from each show.

Guides and Indexes

The music publishing industry issues thousands of pieces of music every year. These series of guides will help you find scores and sheet music:

Music-in-Print Series. Musicdata, 1974–   .
   These guides give bibliographic data (title, composer, publisher, etc.) for music in a particular genre. At this writing, volumes have been issued for sacred and secular choral music, organ music, classical vocal music, orchestral music, string music, and classical guitar music. Master index volumes for composers and titles are issued periodically.

Music Guide Series. Instrumentalist, 1982–   .
   So far, the publisher has issued guides covering the brass and woodwind repertory as well as music for band and other large ensembles.

   As of this writing, pianists and percussionists do not enjoy the advantage of comprehensive and up-to-date tools covering the in-print repertory of their respective instruments. *The Pianist's Resource Guide* (Pallma Music, 1978) and *Solo and Ensemble Literature for Percussion* (3d ed., Percussive Arts Society, 1982) are still useful, though no longer entirely current. If your library offers searches on the OCLC or RLIN databases, this is a good way to look for scores and sheet music. Many music libraries also maintain files of current music publishers' and recording companies' catalogs.

ELECTRONIC SOURCES (CLASSICAL AND POPULAR)

Billboard/Phonolog Music Reference Library. (CD-ROM) Billboard. Quarterly.
   Lists recordings currently available for retail purchase. Includes individual song titles as well as recording titles—one million songs found on 80,000 albums. All genres of music are represented. Also available in print in two parts:
   Phonolog. 1948–   . Weekly.
   Laserlog. 1986–   . Every two weeks. (Compact discs only)
   Both *Laserlog* and *Phonolog* are in loose-leaf format, allowing for frequent updating of individual pages. Most often found in record stores.

Muse (MUsic SEarch): International Bibliography of Writings about Music: RILM Abstracts (Répertoire International de Littérature Musicale). (CD-ROM) National Information Service Corp., 1970–   . Annual.

The most comprehensive source of abstracts of literature about music. International in coverage, it emphasizes musicological and ethnomusicological research. In addition to articles in periodicals, it abstracts books, essays, dissertations, catalogs, and other printed publications about music. It shares with *Music Index* (below) a history of publication delay. For example, coverage as of 1992 extended only through 1987. *Muse* provides a variety of access points, including author, reviewer, title, keyword subject, and journal name. Searches may be modified by the addition of the publication year, publisher, language, or document type. Also available online as *Music Literature International* with DIALOG (File 97), 1972–   , and in print as *RILM Abstracts,* 1966–   , quarterly.

The Music Index on CD-ROM. Chadwyck-Healey, 1981–   . Annual.

Indexes articles on classical and popular music in about 350 music periodicals issued in North America, Europe, and elsewhere. Indexing coverage includes feature articles, news notes, obituaries, and performance notes as well as reviews of books, recordings, and published music. At this writing, the disc covers 1981 to 1989 and may be searched by name, event, musical category, musical instrument, musical group, historical period, and specific subject. Available in print, *Music Index: A Subject-Author Guide to Current Music Periodical Literature,* Harmonie Park Press, 1949–   , monthly. The index has a history of publication delay.

SilverPlatter Music Library. (CD-ROM) SilverPlatter Information, 1991–   . Annual.

This catalog is compiled from the OCLC database and lists more than 400,000 sound recordings on LPs, 45 and 78 rpm records, tape cassettes and reels, compact discs, and cylinders. All types of music are represented, including classical, popular, and music traditions from all over the world.

For Home Use

Multimedia products about music for home use are available on CD-ROM or CD-I (Compact Disc-Interactive, which is used with a TV set instead of a computer). Here are some examples:

Audio Notes. (CD-ROM) Warner New Media.

This series merges audio recordings with text about and images of the composer and his work. Among the titles available are *The Magic Flute, Beethoven's String Quartet No. 14, A German Requiem,* and *The Orchestra.*

Igor Stravinsky: The Rite of Spring. (CD-ROM) Voyager.
Ludwig van Beethoven's Symphony No. 9. (CD-ROM) Voyager.

These interactive discs contain audio, images, and text, plus reference materials such as glossaries.

Microsoft Musical Instruments on CD-ROM. Microsoft.

Multimedia information on 200 instruments. Includes descriptions, pictures, history, and more than 1,500 sound samples.

The Classical Jukebox. (CD-I) Philips.
Jazz Giants. (CD-I) Philips.
Mozart: A Musical Biography. (CD-I) Philips.
Pavarotti: O Sole Mio. (CD-I) Philips.

Selections of music with text and images on the life of the composer or performer on compact disc-interactive.

Online Services   RockNet. America Online, CompuServe.

News of the rock music industry, interviews, concert schedules, record locator service, fan club newsletters.

Bulletin Boards   Aficionados of just about every type of music get together to talk on line. *Prodigy* hosts Grateful Dead and Irish music bulletin boards, for example, and there are pop music boards on *America Online.*

The Internet has dozens of groups that discuss music. The Early Music group discusses medieval, Renaissance, and baroque music and is headquartered at the University of Linz in Austria. Access via: **EARLYM-L@ AEARN.EDVZ.UNI-LINZ.AC.AT.**

Opera buffs discuss their interests on OPERA-L. Access via: **MAILSERV% BRFAPESP.BITNET.@VM1.NODAK.EDU.**

Pop music bulletin boards wax and wane with the popularity of their subjects. At this writing, there are lists for Indigo Girls, Jane's Addiction, Alice Cooper, Bruce Springsteen, Grateful Dead, Kiss, Sinead O'Connor, Siouxsie & The Banshees, and others on the Internet. Check the most recent edition of *Internet: Mailing Lists* for an up-to-date list.

FINDING SONGS IN COLLECTIONS   Songs, both popular and classical, are often published in collections. Individual song titles are *not* listed in library catalogs; access to them can be gained only through secondary sources that index the contents of collections.

Popular Song Index. By Patricia Pate Havlice. Scarecrow, 1975. Supplements: 1978, 1984, and 1989.

Indexes hundreds of songbooks by title, first line of song, first line of chorus, and by composer and lyricist.

Folk Song Index: A Comprehensive Guide to the Florence E. Brunnings Collection. By Florence E. Brunnings. Garland, 1981.

Lists songs in standard, readily available anthologies of folk music. It also indexes sound recordings.

Folio-Dex II: Choral, Orchestral, Band. Folio-Dex Co., 1980– .

A guide to the contents of anthologies currently in print. Emphasis on popular songs.

Song Index. By Minnie Earl Sears. H. W. Wilson, 1926–34.

Covers 281 collections of solo songs published from the nineteenth century through 1934.

Songs in Collections: An Index. By Desiree De Charms and Paul F. Breed. Information Service, 1966.

Indexes art songs and miscellaneous songs (folk songs, Christmas carols, sacred songs, community songbooks, etc.).

American Record Guide. 1935– . Bimonthly.
Opera News. 1936– . Monthly May-November; every two weeks December-April.

Both *American Record Guide* and *Opera News* survey current performances, provide reviews of classical recordings, and offer feature articles on topics of current interest. Beginning with the July/August 1992 issue, *American Record Guide* has offered a level of live music coverage formerly provided by the magazine *Musical America* (1898–1991).

Fanfare: The Magazine for Serious Record Collectors. 1977– . Bimonthly.

Reviews several hundred classical recordings and selected jazz and popular releases in each issue. It also includes feature articles, book reviews, interviews, and brief reports on equipment.

Stereo Review. 1968– . Monthly.

Emphasizes evaluation of equipment, but also includes reviews of current recordings.

The Musical Times. 1844– . Monthly.

Surveys the British classical concert scene, emphasizing London; reviews books, music, and recordings, and publishes a variety of articles on historical topics of broad general interest.

Scholarly articles and articles of general interest to specific professional audiences may be found in numerous journals issued by societies and organizations:

The Journal of the American Musicological Society. 1948–   . 3 times/year.

Notes: The Quarterly Journal of the Music Library Association. 1934–   . Quarterly.

Music Educators Journal. 1914–   . Monthly.

American Music: A Quarterly Journal Devoted to All Aspects of American Music and Music in America. 1983–   . Quarterly.

Results of musicological research are also reported in a number of journals unaffiliated with professional societies. The article "Periodicals" in the *New Grove* (Volume 14, pp. 407–535) includes a list of current and retrospective periodicals by country of publication, with a title index.

National Endowment for the Humanities
1100 Pennsylvania Avenue NW
Washington, DC 20506
(202) 786-0438

National Endowment for the Arts
1100 Pennsylvania Avenue NW
Washington, DC 20506
(202) 682-5400

These independent agencies of the federal government were created to encourage and assist cultural and scholarly activities and programs, to support creativity, and to improve the quality of the arts and humanities nationally. Each agency welcomes inquiries and provides reference and referral services. NEA makes grants to performing artists and groups; NEH makes grants to musicologists, those who study and write about music history. Library resources, including information on agency programs, gaining grants, cultural history, and governmental support, are available to the public (by appointment).

Each state has at least one council or other agency devoted to promoting the arts, including music, within that state. *Musical America*, listed above, provides an up-to-date list, including addresses, telephone numbers, and chief officers of such agencies, as does the following entry on *Information Resources.*

Information Resources in the Arts: A Directory. Compiled by Lloyd W. Shipley. Library of Congress, 1986.

Selective lists of federal, state, and local government agencies; national and regional arts service organizations; arts education agencies and programs; music organizations; and international arts organizations. Additional information is available in the following book from a nonprofit publisher: *A Guide to National and State Arts Education Services.* Edited by John McLaughlin. ACA Books, 1987.

American Federation of Musicians
Suite 600, Paramount Building
1501 Broadway
New York, NY 10036
(212) 869-1330

Performers who are union members belong to more than 400 local and regional chapters of the American Federation of Musicians. Direct your inquiries to the national office.

New York City is a major focal point for musical performances and trade within the United States. The city houses the headquarters of a number of major licensing and service organizations that handle music copyrights, including:

American Society of Composers, Authors, and Publishers (ASCAP)
1 Lincoln Plaza
New York, NY 10023
(212) 595-3050

Broadcast Music, Inc. (BMI)
320 W. 57th St.
New York, NY 10019
(212) 586-2000

National Music Publishers Association
205 E. 42d St.
New York, NY 10017
(212) 370-5330

American Music Center
30 W. 26th St.
New York, NY 10010
(212) 366-5260

Examples of other music associations include:

American Choral Directors Association
P. O. Box 6310
Lawton, OK 73506
(405) 355-8161

American Guild of Organists
475 Riverside Drive
New York, NY 10115
(212) 870-2310

American Musicological Society
University of Pennsylvania
201 S. 34th St.
Philadelphia, PA 19104
(215) 898-8698

American Symphony Orchestra League
777 14th St. NW
Washington, DC 20005
(202) 628-0099

Association for Recorded Sound Collections
P. O. Box 10162
Silver Spring, MD 20914
(301) 593-6552

Hymn Society of the United States and Canada
Texas Christian University
P. O. Box 30854
Fort Worth, TX 76129
(817) 921-7608

Music Educators National Conference
1902 Association Dr.
Reston, VA 22091
(703) 860-4000

Organizations that serve the needs of independent teachers and non-professional musicians and/or promote music at the student level include the Amateur Chamber Music Players and the National Federation of Music Clubs. Among national fraternal groups that recruit at the college level are Phi Mu Alpha Sinfonia and Sigma Alpha Iota. Over fifty national music organizations belong to the National Music Council, which represents the United States on the International Music Council. For addresses, telephone numbers, and a short synopsis of activities and publications, see:

Music: Guide to Reference Literature. By William S. Brockman. 1987. Chapter 21: "Associations, Research Centers, and Other Organizations" (pp. 186–216).

LIBRARIES

Library of Congress
Music Division
Washington, DC 20540
(202) 707-5507

One of the largest music collections in the world, containing printed materials and audiovisual media pertaining to American and European music of all periods, as well as resources on music in other parts of the world. As the national copyright depository, the Library of Congress has extensive holdings of sheet music published in the United States. There are also impressive holdings of composers' manuscripts.

New York Public Library
Music Division
Performing Arts Research Center
111 Amsterdam Avenue
New York, NY 10023
(212) 870-1657

A comprehensive collection, with emphasis on American music and music in New York City. Numerous specialized indexes can be consulted in the Main Reading Room. The Americana Collection has significant manuscript holdings and over 400,000 pieces of sheet music. The Special Collections unit holds rare materials.

Many other public libraries and college and university libraries include music materials among their holdings. Most libraries are quite willing to respond to inquiries from outside the circle of their immediate clientele.

A number of research centers devoted to the work of individual composers or to other specialized research topics are located on college campuses. These include:

Ira F. Brilliant Center for Beethoven Studies
San Jose State University
San Jose, CA 95192-0002
(408) 924-4590

Arnold Schoenberg Institute
University of Southern California
University Park
Los Angeles, CA 90089
(213) 740-4090

Riemenschneider Bach Institute
Baldwin Wallace College
Berea, OH 44017-2088
(216) 826-2207

Center for Black Music Research
Columbia College
600 S. Michigan Ave.
Chicago, IL 60605
(312) 663-1600, ext. 559

Institute for Studies in American Music
Brooklyn College/CUNY
Brooklyn, NY 11210
(718) 951-5655

The following two sources provide further information on music libraries, their specialized holdings, and services to readers:

Directory of Music Research Libraries. Volume 1: *Canada, United States.* 2d rev. ed. Barenreiter, 1983.
Resources of American Music History. By D. W. Krummel and others. University of Illinois Press, 1981.

USING MUSIC LIBRARY CATALOGS

Some types of materials, including those on music, are more difficult to find than others in library catalogs, even in the electronic age. What follows is a brief survey of the problems you may encounter.

1. *Different media.* Music libraries contain a variety of types of material, including books, journals, printed scores, sound recordings on tape, disc, or compact disc, videotapes and discs, and computer disks and tapes. Some libraries have different catalogs for different media; others interfile them all. Most computer catalogs will allow you to retrieve all materials relating to a person or topic irrespective of media. When you

find a record, it will indicate clearly whether it is for a sound recording, printed text, or other medium.

2. *Musicians with many roles.* Many individuals (for example, Leonard Bernstein, Paul McCartney, and Igor Stravinsky) appear in multiple roles as composer, editor, author, performer, arranger, and "arrangee"; their names may also appear as subject headings. In many card catalogs, headings for books about an individual are filed *after* entries for the same person as composer or author. If an individual is both a composer and an author, card catalog entries for literary works are generally interfiled with the entries for musical compositions.

   For further information on search strategies in card catalogs, see *Library Research Guide to Music.* By John E. Druesdow, Jr. Pierian Press, 1982.

3. *Finding smaller works.* Even in computer catalogs, it is often difficult to locate works such as individual songs or short piano works. If they are included in sets or in anthologies, they are rarely cataloged individually. Use published indexes together with the library catalog to help you in your research. See the section Finding Songs in Collections (above) for fuller information on locating individual songs.

4. *Computer catalogs and prolific composers.* In computer catalogs found in colleges, universities, and many public libraries, it can be confusing to look for specific printed music and sound recordings of works by prolific composers such as Vivaldi, Mozart, or Beethoven. Again, consult a librarian when you're having trouble finding what you need.

5. *Uniform titles.* Uniform titles ensure that all the editions of a work are filed together no matter what title appears on the particular piece. Uniform titles in catalog entries for printed music and sound recordings appear, sometimes in brackets, between the name of the composer and the title of the piece of music. A uniform title typically begins with the name of a musical form; a phrase such as "Piano music" for several works for an individual instrument, or the distinctive title of a particular composition. The following entry is an example of the way a uniform title is used to bring together all versions of a Mozart opera, regardless of the language of the title or the medium:

Mozart, Wolfgang Amadeus, 1756–1791. [Nozze di Figaro] *Benita Valente Sings Mozart.*
Mozart, Wolfgang Amadeus, 1756–1791. [Nozze di Figaro] *Figaros Hochzeit.*
Mozart, Wolfgang Amadeus, 1756–1791. [Nozze di Figaro] *Marriage of Figaro.*
Mozart, Wolfgang Amadeus, 1756–1791. [Nozze di Figaro] *Streichquartett in B.*

As with uniform titles, numerous subject headings are based on the form of composition and medium of performance. For example:

Piano music
Piano music (4 hands)
Sonatas (piano)
Songs (high voice) with piano
Symphonies

Other music subject headings are topical or are based on the name of a person. For example:

Christmas music
Railroads—Songs and music
Sea songs
Wedding music
Lincoln, Abraham, 1809–1865—Songs and music
Shakespeare, William, 1554–1616—Musical settings

Many headings begin with the words *music* or *musical,* as part of a phrase or followed by a subdivision:

Music, Influence of
Music—United States—History and criticism
Music and architecture
Music appreciation
Music festivals
Musical instruments
Musical notation

Information about a musical topic can be distinguished from the music itself because the former is often given in the singular and the latter in the plural.

Opera	books about opera
Operas	music editions or recordings

The addition of a subdivision such as "History and criticism" implies books with information about music, not the music itself.

Flute music	music editions or recordings
Flute music—History and criticism	books about flute music

Here are some examples of other important subdivisions used with music subject headings:

Bibliographic

Bach, Johann Sebastian, 1685–1750—Bibliography
Pavarotti, Luciano—Discography
Beethoven, Ludwig van, 1770–1827—Thematic catalogs

Didactic

Flute—Instruction and study
Violin—Methods

Ballet—Scores
Concertos (piano)—Scores and parts
Operas—Vocal scores with piano

Bands (music)—United States—Bibliography
Music—Germany—19th century
Music—History and criticism—18th century
Operas—20th century—Scores

For further guidance, consult the most recent edition of *Library of Congress Subject Headings* or *Music Subject Headings* by Perry Bratcher and Jennifer Smith (Soldier Creek Press, 1988).

Opus. 1990–   . Schwann. Quarterly.
Catalog of currently available classical music recordings.

Spectrum. 1990–   . Schwann. Quarterly.
Lists currently available popular music and jazz recordings. Many libraries keep back issues of the Schwann publications to serve as retrospective finding aids.

See also *SilverPlatter Music Library* and *Billboard/ Phonolog Music Reference Library* under Electronic Sources, above.

The discography, a bibliography of recordings, is another type of retrospective tool. Discographies may be published either in book form or, more typically, as journal articles or appendixes to biographies. Use the following tools to identify discographies:

Bibliography of Discographies. Bowker, 1977–83.
Volume 1: *Classical Music, 1925–1975;* Volume 2: *Jazz;* Volume 3: *Popular Music.*

Classical Music Discographies, 1976–1988: A Bibliography. By Michael Gray. Greenwood, 1989.

Record reviews, another rich source of information, can be located in:

Index to Record Reviews: Based on Materials Originally Published in Notes, the Quarterly Journal of the Music Library Association between 1949 and 1977. Compiled and edited by Kurtz Myers. G. K. Hall, 1978–80. Two updates: *Index to Record Reviews, 1978–1983* and *Index to Record Reviews, 1984–1987.*

In addition, each issue of *Notes* contains an index to current record reviews.

Format

Geographic and/or by period

SPECIALIZED SOURCES

Sound Recordings

In some respects, researching the complex world of classical or art music is child's play compared to making your way through the ever-changing, elusive scene of popular music. No sooner have researchers nailed down the meanings of heavy metal, house music, or hip-hop than they hear of a record label that is pioneering grunge-rock or a new wave of Cuban-influenced dance music. Country music is, for the moment, divided between "new traditionalists" and "glitter-country." The following resources may help you get a handle on the latest genres:

Popular Entertainment Research: How to Do It and How to Use It. By Barbara J. Pruett. Scarecrow Press, 1992.

Lists print and electronic reference sources on pop music, as well as appropriate organizations.

The New Grove Dictionary of Jazz. 2 vols. Edited by Barry Kernfeld. Grove's Dictionaries, 1988.

Scholarly articles about this historically American, now worldwide, musical form.

The Great Song Thesaurus. 2d ed. By Roger Lax and Frederick Smith. Oxford University Press, 1989.

A valuable source of information on composers, lyricists, year of composition, etc., of popular songs.

The Guinness Encyclopedia of Popular Music. 4 vols. Edited by Colin Larkin. Guinness, 1992.

The majority of the 10,000 entries are biographical, focusing on performers, songwriters, producers, and promoters. The scope is international, and the entire twentieth century is covered, with an emphasis on the rock era. There are also entries for record companies, music festivals, organizations, and instruments.

Rock On: The Illustrated Encyclopedia of Rock 'n' Roll. 3 vols. By Norm D. Nite. Harper & Row, 1982–85.

Each year brings more rock encyclopedias of varying quality. Good or not, they are soon of historical interest only. Periodicals are really the only way to keep current on new trends, styles, and movements.

The most important documents of modern popular music tend to be sound recordings rather than printed texts. Consequently, regularly updated reference tools such as *Spectrum* and *Laserlog* (see above) that list recorded music currently available for purchase are very important. Also useful are guides to building personal collections such as:

Jazz on Compact Disc: A Critical Guide to the Best Recordings. By Steve Harris.
Harmony Books, 1987.

The CD Rock & Roll Library: 30 Years of Rock & Roll on Compact Disc. By Bill Shapiro. Andrews and McMeel, 1988.

Rolling Stone Album Guide: Completely New Reviews, Every Essential Album, Every Essential Artist. Edited by Anthony DeCurtis. Random House, 1992.

PERIODICALS

Billboard. 1984–   . Weekly.
   An industry-oriented perspective on popular music.

Down Beat. 1934–   . Weekly.
   The definitive American jazz journal.

Rolling Stone. 1967–   . Weekly.
   Once the voice of the counterculture, *Rolling Stone* is now a mainstream magazine of American popular music and culture.

There are numerous magazines devoted to specific aspects of popular music, for example:

Electronic Musician. 1985–   . Monthly.

Keyboard. 1981–   . Monthly.

ASSOCIATIONS

International Association for the Study of Popular Music/Forschung-szentrum Populare Musik
Humboldt-Universität-Berlin
Am Kupfergraben 5
1080 Berlin, Germany
Telephone: (37-2) 208-1537
Promotes research and supports publication projects on international contemporary popular music.

International Council for Traditional Music
Center for Ethnomusicology
Columbia University
New York, NY 10027
(212) 678-0332
Documents and promotes ethnomusicological research into the historical development of traditional music and dance styles in all areas of the world.

Society for Ethnomusicology
Morrison Hall 005
Indiana University
Bloomington, IN 47405
(812) 855-6672
Sponsors conferences, issues publications, and facilitates scholarly research in the field.

Country Music Foundation
4 Music Square
Nashville, TN 37203
(615) 256-1639
Promotes research, operates a Hall of Fame and library in Nashville, provides consultation services, and issues publications.

National Academy of Songwriters
6381 Hollywood Boulevard, Suite 780
Hollywood, CA 90028
(213) 463-7178
Provides advice on business and legal matters, maintains a library in Hollywood, provides assistance in matters of publicity, and offers professional services to members.

Society for the Preservation and Encouragement of Barber Shop Quartet Singing in America
6315 Third Avenue
Kenosha, WI 53143-5199
(414) 656-8440
Sponsors conventions and contests in the United States and Canada and maintains a library.

Institute of Jazz Studies
135 Bradley Hall
Rutgers University
Newark, NJ 07102
(201) 648-5595
Maintains an extensive collection of books, recordings periodicals, and other materials relating to the development of jazz; sponsors scholarly conferences, concerts, and symposia; sponsors an oral history project; and issues publications.

For fuller information, consult:

Music: A Guide to the Reference Literature. By William S. Brockman. Libraries Unlimited, 1987. Chapter 21: "Associations, Research Centers, and Other Organizations" (pp. 186–216).

The Archive of Folk Culture
American Folklife Center
Library of Congress
Washington, DC 20504
(202) 707-6590

A repository for materials of all types relating to the study of folk music and folklore, including commercial and field recordings, oral history, books, periodicals, manuscript materials, etc. Though international in scope, the collection emphasizes Native American music and English-language folk music traditions within the United States.

Among other libraries with a major focus on folk, ethnic, or popular music are:

Center for Popular Music
Box 41
Middle Tennessee State University
Murfreesboro, TN 37132
(615) 898-2300

Archives of Traditional Music
Morrison Hall, Room 117
Indiana University
Bloomington, IN 47405-2501
(812) 855-4679

Music Library and Sound Recordings Archive
Bowling Green State University
Bowling Green, OH 43403
(419) 372-9929

Resources can also be found in the libraries of the associations and organizations mentioned above.

Popular music
Popular music—United States—1961–1970 (or Music, popular)
Bluegrass music

Contemporary Christian music
Country music
Heavy metal (music)
Rap (music)
Reggae music
Rock music

Jazz
Jazz—Louisiana—New Orleans
Big band music
Blues (music)
Dance-Orchestra music

Dixieland music
Saxophone music (jazz) [and similar headings for other instruments]

Motion picture music
Musicals

Folk dance music
Folk music—Mexico
Folk songs—Spanish

It is not possible to make a clear distinction between folk music and music in general. Some examples are found under the heading *Music* followed by a subdivision:

Music—Japan
Music, Islamic

The term *Songs* subdivided by language and/or place is widely used for songs of an ethnic or national character:

Songs, French

Other folk and ethnic music will be found under the names of specific styles, topics, places, nationalities, and classes of people:

Cuba—Songs and music
Flamenco music
Gypsies—Music
Lumbermen—Songs and music
United States—History—Civil War, 1861–1865—Songs and music

THE MUSIC BUSINESS

See Chapter 33, Law, for sources of information on copyright.

The Business of Music. Revised and enlarged 6th ed. By Sidney Shemel and M. William Krasilovsky. Billboard Books, 1990.

Contains a wealth of information on recording companies and artists, music publishers and writers, and the music industry in general. It concludes with a number of music industry forms, including standard contracts, licenses, and agreements.

The Songwriter's Market: Where & How to Market Your Songs. Edited by Mark Garvey. Writer's Digest Books. Annual.

Provides complete directory information for music publishers, record companies and producers, advertising agencies, managers, and organizations. Other sections are devoted to submitting songs, copyright, contracts, and home demos.

37

PARENTING

See also: General Reference Sources, Education, Health and Medicine

Though "the rearing of children" has been around for some time, the word *parenting* itself emerged less than fifty years ago in American English. Now, there are thousands of parenting books, magazines, agencies, guidelines, and regulations.

Some people may question whether this material has made for better child rearing, but certainly the parent or care giver has many more resources than ever before for addressing the challenges of raising children. Some of the most useful sources are given below. Several of them take into account the nontraditional patterns of parenthood in America.

GENERAL REFERENCE SOURCES

Sourcebook on Parenting and Child Care. Edited by Kathryn Hammell Carpenter. Oryx Press, 1994.

Chapters on such topics as preparing for parenthood and finding qualified day care list both print and electronic sources and telephone hotlines.

The Parent's Desk Reference: The Ultimate Family Encyclopedia from Conception to College. By Irene Franck and David Brownstone. Prentice-Hall, 1991.

A convenient source of basic information on parenting topics with references to more detailed sources of information. Provides reading lists of recent publications, including resources for or by children. A section of special help offers model school curricula, charts of normal skill development, and lists of organizations and reference works dealing with special children.

What's New for Parents: The Essential Resource to Products and Services, Programs and Information, New for the 90s. By Irene Franck and David Brownstone. Prentice-Hall, 1993.

Franck and Brownstone update *The Parent's Desk Reference* (above) with lots of specific sources.

Caring for Your Baby and Young Child: Birth to Age Five. By the American Academy of Pediatrics; edited by Steven P. Shelove and others. Bantam, 1991.

Authoritative and comprehensive manual on child care. Covers physical and psychological development of infants and toddlers and provides health information and safety tips. The Academy also publishes similar volumes on older children: *Caring for Your School-Age Child: Ages 5–12; Caring for Your Adolescent: Ages 12–21,* which covers the legal and health rights of adolescents in addition to medical and developmental issues.

The following series of ten titles from the Gesell Institute of Child Development (now the Gesell Institute of Human Development) provides helpful and readable material for parents:

Your One-Year-Old: The Fun-Loving, Fussy 12-to-24 Month-Old. By Louise B. Ames. Delacorte, 1982.
Your Two-Year-Old: Terrible or Tender. By Louise B. Ames and Frances L. Ilg. Delacorte, 1976.
Your Three-Year-Old: Friend or Enemy. By Louise B. Ames and Frances L. Ilg. Delacorte, 1976.
Your Four-Year-Old: Wild and Wonderful. Delacorte, 1976.
Your Five-Year-Old: Sunny and Serene. By Louise B. Ames and Frances L. Ilg. Delacorte, 1979.
Your Six-Year-Old: Defiant But Loving. By Louise B. Ames and Frances L. Ilg. Delacorte, 1979.
Your Seven-Year-Old: Life in a Minor Key. By Louise B. Ames and Carol C. Haber. Delacorte, 1985.
Your Eight-Year-Old: Lively and Outgoing. Delacorte, 1989.
Your Nine-Year-Old. By Louise B. Ames. Delacorte, 1990.
Your Ten- to Fourteen-Year-Old. Rev. ed. By Louise B. Ames and others. Delacorte, 1988.

Touchpoints: Your Child's Emotional and Behavioral Development: The Essential Reference. By T. Berry Brazelton. Addison-Wesley, 1992.

Brazelton is a popular and authoritative pediatrician, author, and television personality. This book gives a readable survey of child development during the first three years, followed by a topical section addressing the common emotional and behavioral problems of the first six years. A final section discusses the impact of parents, grandparents, friends, and other care givers on a child.

Your Growing Child: From Babyhood through Adolescence. By Penelope Leach. Knopf, 1986.

An easy-to-use source that covers almost all of a parent's questions, including questions about childhood illnesses and many aspects of social, emotional, and physical development. Topics are organized in a straightforward encyclopedic format so that you can simply turn to the item of current concern.

Dr. Spock's Baby and Childcare. 6th ed. By Benjamin M. Spock and Michael Rothenberg. Dutton, 1992.

This classic work is still considered the bible for new parents and remains a basic and indispensable reference source. For the sixth edition, new chapters were prepared on divorce, stepparenting, AIDS, and other current topics.

The First Three Years of Life. Rev. ed. By Burton L. White. Prentice-Hall, 1990.

Continues to be a first source for information on the social, emotional, and physical development of children during the first three years. The first half of the book concentrates on all aspects of development, in a series of progressive phases. The second half covers issues such as discipline, toys, play, and toilet training. Dr. White has been the center of controversy because of his opinion that substitute care during the first three years is not in the best interests of any child. He has added a chapter on current topics such as the "superbaby phenomenon" to this edition and restated his concern about substitute care.

Guides to Children's Media

The American Library Association Best of the Best for Children. Edited by Denise Perry Donavin. Random House, 1992.

The best recent books, magazines, audios, videotapes, software, toys, and games for children from birth through age 14. Includes suggestions for thematic connections between books and other media. Describes some 1,500 selections, most of them award winners and "kid-tested."

The New York Times Parent's Guide to the Best Books for Children. Rev. ed. By Eden Ross Lipson. Random House, 1991.

Brief annotations on more than 1,000 books in five categories: wordless books, picture books, story books, early reading books, middle reading books, and young adult books. There are subject and age-appropriate indexes.

Research Guide for Studies in Infancy and Childhood. By Enid E. Haag. Greenwood, 1988.

Describes databases, reference works, and subject bibliographies. Includes citations to books, articles, and reports from the social sciences, medicine, and the arts.

Infancy: A Guide to Research and Resources. By Hannah Nuba-Scheffler and others. Garland, 1986.

Addresses child development from the prenatal period to two years.

Resources for Early Childhood: An Annotated Bibliography and Guide for Educators, Librarians, Health Care Professionals, and Parents. By Hannah Scheffler and others. Garland, 1985.

Covers children ages two to six.

Resources for Middle Childhood: A Source Book. By Deborah Lovitky Sheiman and Maureen Slonim. Garland, 1988.

Focuses on the six- to twelve-year-old child.

Designed for use by educators, health care professionals, and parents, each of the three sources just cited includes brief essays on various topics followed by annotated bibliographies of related books.

Childhood Information Resources. By Marda Woodbury. Information Resources Press, 1985.

Youth Information Resources: An Annotated Guide for Parents, Professionals, Students, Researchers, and Concerned Citizens. By Marda Woodbury. Greenwood, 1987.

Comprehensive guides to literature about childhood and adolescence. Detailed annotations describe printed reference works and electronic sources.

Child Development Abstracts and Bibliography. Society for Research on Child Development, 1927– .

Covers all aspects of child development and related areas in both books and periodicals.

Inventory of Marriage and Family Literature. Sage, 1975– .

Provides indexing for the published marriage and family literature from approximately 1,500 journals.

Children's Reference Plus. (CD-ROM) Bowker. Annual.

Searches the full text of many bibliographies of children's books: e.g., *Best Books for Children, Books for Children to Read Alone, Books for the Gifted Child, Fantasy Literature for Children and Young Adults,* plus titles from *Children's Books in Print,* with reviews.

ERIC. (CD-ROM) Available as *DIALOG OnDisc: ERIC.* UMI, 1966–   , and *ERIC on SilverPlatter,* 1966–   . Quarterly.

Many topics covered in this education database are of importance in parenting: child development, gifted children, disabled children, and language development. These files are also online through CompuServe, Dialog (File 1), Knowledge Index (EDUC1), BRS, BRS/AfterDark, and OCLC FirstSearch from 1966–   , updated monthly. Corresponds to two print indexes, *Current Index to Journals in Education* (Oryx, 1969–   ) and *Resources in Education* (U.S. Government Printing Office, 1966–   ), updated monthly.

Family Resources. (Online) National Council on Family Relations, 1970–   . Monthly.

Available online on Dialog (File 291), BRS (NCFR), BRS/AfterDark, and HRIN. A CD-ROM version, *Family Resources on Disc,* is under development at this writing. Indexes over 400 family-related journals and other print literature, as well as audiovisual material. The database also includes information on family-centered programs and services. A portion of the database corresponds to the print index *Inventory of Marriage and Family Literature.*

PsycLIT. (CD-ROM) SilverPlatter, 1974–   . Quarterly.

Abstracts of articles from more than 1,300 psychology journals representing professional and scientific literature from fifty countries. Compiled by the American Psychological Association. Also available online as *PsycInfo,* 1963–   , with monthly updates. Available on BRS, BRS/AfterDark, Dialog (File 11), Knowledge Index (PSYC1), OCLC FirstSearch. Also available in print form as *Psychological Abstracts,* 1927–   , updated monthly.

Social Work Abstracts Plus. (CD-ROM) SilverPlatter. 1977–   . Annual.

This database produced by the National Association of Social Workers contains materials on child and family welfare and children with developmental disabilities. Also available on BRS and BRS/AfterDark, updated quarterly. Corresponds to the print index *Social Work Research and Abstracts.*

SocioFile. (CD-ROM) SilverPlatter, 1974–   . 3 times/year.

Covers the international literature of sociology, including articles, dissertations, conference papers, and books. Provides lengthy abstracts. Also available online on BRS (SOCA, SOCZ), BRS/AfterDark, Dialog (File 37), Knowledge Index (SOCS1), and FirstSearch (SocioAbs), 1963–   . Corresponds to the print *Sociological Abstracts,* 1963–   .

Child Care Database. HRIN. Monthly.

Information on more than 90,000 licensed or certified child care establishments in forty-five states. Data given include care giver training in first aid, type of care available (before and after school, all day, etc.), admission policy for mildly ill children, program activities, size of yard or playground, meals served, fees.

HRIN also has special reports of interest to parents online, for example:
Caring for Children with Special Needs
Training Corporate Managers to Ease Work and Family Conflicts
The Work and Family Manager: Evolution of a New Job
Work and Family Programs for Lower-Income Workers

Online Services

National Adoption Database. CompuServe. Updated periodically.

This file from the National Adoption Center lists more than 1,500 children with special needs available for adoption and the names of families seeking children for adoption.

New Parents Network. Available as a forum on Delphi and as a BBS, NPNet has more than 300 files on such topics as prenatal care and childbirth, product recalls, poison control, home schooling, and health. NPNet is carried on thirty BBS around the country, so you may be able to find it on a local board. If not, it can be reached at its headquarters in Arizona at **(602) 326-9345.**

Prodigy has a parenting guide with 600 articles by experts; *Consumer Reports* articles on such topics as saving for college and student accident insurance; articles on children's health (car sickness, teen sexuality); parenting columns; and bulletin boards on which parents can discuss parenting practices.

America Online, in its Parents' Information Network, stresses educational issues. There are files to download and bulletin boards on home schooling, school choice, child abuse, and giftedness. Another section lists TV and radio programs of educational value for children.

American Baby Magazine. 1938–   . Monthly.

Designed for expectant parents and new parents, *American Baby* covers pregnancy, the care of newborns and toddlers through the age of three, early learning, and related topics. The magazine contains a profusion of advertisements and is sometimes available free for the first six months through pediatricians' offices.

PERIODICALS

Child. 1985–   . 10 times/year.

Targeted at the well-educated, high-income family. Articles are written by well-known contributors. Columns review books, software, and videotapes.

Growing Child (Growing Parent). 1971–   . Monthly.

An ad-free newsletter. The first issue a subscriber receives deals with birth and the newborn. Each subsequent issue discusses concerns about the development of the child as it grows; for example, the eighth issue discusses the baby at seven months, the thirtieth issue the child at two years, five months. The series ends at six years. In addition to child development topics, *Growing Child* explores health issues, play activities, and social skills. *Growing Parent* is a supplement that is included as part of a subscription.

Parenting. 1987–   . 10 times/year.

Similar to *Parents,* this newsstand magazine appeals to the two-income upscale urban family. Emphasis on consumerism and children's fashion, along with topics on child rearing.

Parents' Choice: A Review of Children's Media. 1978–   . Quarterly.

Reviews of books, TV shows, movies and videotapes, computer software, and toys and games.

Parents Magazine. 1926–   . Monthly.

This popular magazine features issues and concerns of interest to parents of children from birth through age 18. With its solid reputation, it is a reliable choice among general magazines on the topic.

Gifted Children Monthly. 1980–   . 9 times/year.

"For the parents of children with great promise." Provides suggestions on enrichment activities for children.

Teaching Exceptional Children. 1968–   . Quarterly.

Practical journal intended for teachers of disabled and gifted children but also useful for parents.

More than thirty U.S. cities have parenting magazines or newspapers, often free tabloids. They are excellent sources of information on local museums, summer camps, and special educational programs.

Professional Journals

Numerous professional publications address family issues and various aspects of child development and child rearing. The following is a sampling of major titles:

Child Development. 1930–   . Bimonthly.

Publishes articles on all aspects of development from the prenatal period through adolescence.

Childhood Education. 1924–   . 5 times/year.
   Articles are aimed at parents as well as at professionals involved in the education of children and adolescents.

Adolescence. 1966–   . Quarterly.
   An interdisciplinary journal devoted to the psychological, sociological, and educational aspects of adolescence.

Exceptional Children. 1934–   . Bimonthly.
   Covers current research. Includes articles on curriculum development and suggestions for the classroom.

Infant Care. By Elaine Brata Arken. Department of Health and Human Services, Bureau of Maternal and Child Health and Resource Development, 1989.
   This updated edition of a popular booklet covers current information about caring for a baby during its first year of life.

GOVERNMENT PUBLICATIONS

Books for Children. Library of Congress. Annual.
   A list of the best picture books and fiction and nonfiction for children, selected by the Children's Literature Center of the Library of Congress.

Dealing with the Angry Child. National Institute of Mental Health, 1992.

Feeding Baby: Nature and Nurture. Food and Drug Administration, 1990.

Seal Out Dental Decay. National Institutes of Health, 1991.

You Can Help Your Young Child Learn Mathematics. Department of Education, 1991.

Choosing a School for Your Child. Department of Education, 1989.

Children Today: An Interdisciplinary Journal for the Professional Serving Children. 1954–   . Bimonthly.
   Contains information on child development and other child-related issues of interest to parents. The periodical will be of primary interest to day care providers, social services workers, and youth leaders. Available online with Dialog.

   See also the Government Printing Office's *Subject Bibliography #35—* Children and Youth.

Several agencies in the U.S. Department of Health and Human Services support programs for children and families:

Administration for Children, Youth, and Families
Mary E. Switzer Building
330 C Street SW
Washington, DC 20201
(202) 245-03471

Responsible for planning, developing, and implementing programs to support family development and for administering related grants to the states. Head Start, services for runaway youth, and programs to prevent or remedy the effects of child abuse and neglect are among the responsibilities of this agency. Also manages the National Clearinghouse on Child Abuse and Neglect.

Maternal and Child Health Bureau
Public Health Service
Parklawn Building
5600 Fishers Lane
Rockville, MD 20857
(301) 443-3376

Directs, coordinates, and monitors policies and programs dealing with the health of mothers and children. The Bureau administers grants and sponsors research, education, and training programs. It is specifically responsible for research on pediatric AIDS, hemophilia in all age groups, and pediatric emergency systems.

Center for Research for Mothers and Children
National Institute of Child Health and Development
6130 Executive Boulevard
Rockville, MD 20857
(301) 496-5133

Conducts and supports biomedical and behavioral research on child and maternal health and problems of human development. The Center provides funding for research and disseminates research results to practitioners and the general public. Some of the Center's areas of concern are learning disabilities, genetic diseases, pediatric and maternal AIDS, and the causes of infant morbidity and mortality.

Many state, county, and city agencies provide services to families and/or facilitate access to federal programs. Check the government pages of your telephone directory or ask for help in identifying appropriate agencies at your local public library.

Hundreds of organizations provide support and training for parents and advocacy on children's issues, for example, Mothers at Home or Compassionate Friends (for parents who have lost a child). The directory below is designed to help parents find such groups:

Who to Call: The Parent's Source Book. By Daniel Starer. Morrow, 1992.

An annotated directory of agencies that provide information to consumers over the phone. Includes associations concerned with fertility, child care, health, safety, education, missing children, and recreation; also lists mail order catalogs.

Action for Children's Television
20 University Road
Cambridge, MA 02138
(617) 876-6620
Membership organization promoting quality television programming for children and elimination of commercialism from children's programming. Conducts symposia, commissions studies, and bestows awards for outstanding children's shows.

Children's Defense Fund
122 C Street NW
Washington, DC 20001
(202) 628-8787
Sponsors research, monitors federal agencies, drafts legislation in the areas of child welfare, child care, child development, and family services. Publishes *CDF Reports,* a monthly newsletter on issues relating to children and youth, and other books and handbooks on issues affecting children.

Council for Exceptional Children
1920 Association Drive
Reston, VA 22091
(703) 620-3660
Concerned with children who are gifted or who are handicapped in any way. Disseminates information to parents and teachers on the education of exceptional children through workshops and publications. Operates the ERIC Clearinghouse on Handicapped and Gifted Children. Publishes *Exceptional Children, Teaching Exceptional Children,* and *Exceptional Child Education Resources.*

Family Service America
11700 West Lake Park Drive
Milwaukee, WI 53224
(414) 359-1040
Assists member agencies in developing and providing family services.
Conducts research, sponsors competitions, and publishes a newsletter and
a journal, *Families in Society.*

National Association for Gifted Children
1155 15th St. NW
Washington, DC 20005
(202) 785-4268
Promotes interest in programs for the gifted. Distributes information on
the development of the gifted and sponsors an institute to provide training
in curriculum planning for and parenting of the gifted. Publishes a newsletter and the *Gifted Child Quarterly.*

National Association of Child Care Resource and Referral Agencies
2116 Campus Dr. SE
Rochester, MN 55904
(507) 287-2220
Community-based child care agencies that promote a high-quality child
care system accessible to all families.

National Committee for Prevention of Child Abuse
332 S. Michigan Ave., Suite 1600
Chicago, IL 60604
(312) 663-3520
An advocacy organization promoting public policies, research, and programs to assist in preventing all forms of child abuse. Publishes a monthly
newsletter, books, and pamphlets.

National Information Center for Children and Youth with Handicaps
P. O. Box 1492
Washington, DC 20013
(703) 893-6061
Provides information to parents and educators on the rights of children
and youth with special needs and on the services available to them. Pub-
lishes a free quarterly newsletter, *News Digest,* and an annual *Disability Fact
Sheet,* as well as booklets and issue papers.

National PTA-National Congress of Parents and Teachers
330 N. Wabash
Chicago, IL 60611
(312) 787-0977
Membership organization for parents, teachers, students, and administrators. Coordinates the efforts of home, school, and community through local groups. Publishes a newsletter, *PTA in Focus,* and disseminates information on many topics relating to parents and children.

LIBRARIES

Check your local public library first for materials on parents and children; public libraries everywhere purchase materials on parenting skills. A nearby college or university with a program in teacher education, home economics, psychology, social work, or sociology will also have material on child development and parent education.

Two particularly large academic collections are listed here, but many of the organizations mentioned in this chapter also maintain specialized collections.

Family Resource Coalition—Clearinghouse on Family Resource Programs
230 N. Michigan Avenue
Chicago, IL 60601
(312) 726-4750
Collects information on programs for teens and their parents, parent education and support. Maintains files on 1,000 family resource and child-rearing programs.

Education Library
Peabody College, Vanderbilt University
P. O. Box 325
Nashville, TN 37203
(615) 322-8095
Especially concerned with child study, education, psychology, and special education.

Milbank Memorial Library
Teachers College, Columbia University
525 W. 120th Street
New York, NY 10027
(212) 678-3494
Extensive collections in education and psychology. The library has an historical collection of children's books and a textbook collection dating from the eighteenth century.

When using your library's catalog to find books on parenting, the broad subject headings to try include:

Parenting

Child rearing

Parent and child

Parents

Families

Many headings beginning with the word *Child* will be of interest:

Child development

Child psychology

Child study

Relevant books can be located under headings for each age level:

Infants

Toddlers

Children

Teenagers

Youth

For books on particular aspects of child rearing or child development, narrow terms can be useful:

Learning disabilities

Play and playthings

Asthma

All of these terms will frequently have topical or geographical subdivisions. Topical headings may have age-level subdivisions:

Abortion—in adolescence

Children—Management

Toddlers—Books and reading

Infants—Care and hygiene

Teenagers—Family relationships

Youth—Mexico

Joint custody of children

Mentally handicapped children

Minority teenagers

Music and teenagers

Psychological child abuse

Single parents

Television and children

To locate more elusive subject headings, consult the *Library of Congress Subject Headings* list or ask a librarian for help.

ACCESS ERIC
1600 Research Boulevard
Rockville, MD 20850
(800) USE-ERIC

Sponsored by the Educational Resources Information Center of the U.S. Office of Educational Research and Improvement. Helps parents and teachers to locate and obtain information on education.

Center for Early Adolescence
University of North Carolina at Chapel Hill
Suite 211, Carr Mill Mall
Carrboro, NC 27510
(919) 966-1148

In addition to its research program, the Center seeks to provide information and training to organizations working with ten- to fifteen-year-olds to prevent adolescent pregnancy, substance abuse, and dropout problems. Maintains a database of young adolescent organizations in the United States.

Center for Parent Education
55 Chapel Street
Newton, MA 02160
(617) 964-2442

Develops parent education materials. Holds professional training institutes and workshops. Provides consultation services for research projects and service programs.

Center for the Study of Families, Children and Elderly
Vanderbilt University
1208 18th Avenue S.
Nashville, TN 37212
(615) 322-8505

In addition to its research programs, the Center offers consultation services to federal, state, and local governments on issues related to at-risk children and social welfare policies.

Gesell Institute of Human Development
Louise Bates Ames Parenting Center
310 Prospect St.
New Haven, CT 06511
(203) 777-3481

In addition to its programs of research and publication, the Gesell Institute sponsors lectures and workshops on early childhood development and provides psychological counseling and consultation services.

La Leche League International
9616 Minneapolis Avenue
P. O. Box 1209
Franklin Park, IL 60131
(708) 455-7730

Membership group promoting breast-feeding as a means of fostering good mothering. The organization has a medical advisory board and offers accredited seminars for physicians. Nearly 3,000 local groups provide training for pregnant women and new mothers and telephone counseling by trained volunteers. Maintains a free hotline, 800-LA LECHE, and distributes information on the medical and psychological benefits of breast-feeding.

Parents Helping Parents
535 Race Street, Suite 220
San Jose, CA 95126
(408) 288-5010

Membership organization of parents, lay counselors, and professionals. Offers support, information, and training for parents of children with special needs.

Local branches of the YMCA, PTA, American Red Cross, and similar organizations, as well as churches, school systems, and hospitals, frequently offer training classes for parents and/or sponsor support groups. The Girl Scouts, Boy Scouts, 4-H clubs, and other youth organizations in your community may offer child-rearing programs or parent-child activities. Family and human development specialists in the U.S. Department of Agriculture's Extension Service provide training through county Extension offices. Watch your local newspaper for listings or check with a librarian to find out what is available in your community. The best leads may come from people in your own community who are active in parent education and organizations for children and youth.

SPECIALIZED SOURCES

Videotapes on parent and child issues are popular. A three-part *Parents Video Magazine* series issued by *Parents Magazine* covers many concerns important to parents:

Baby Comes Home: Parents Video Magazine. Volume 1. Gruner & Jahr USA, 1986. 50 minutes, color.

Recommended for parents of children newly born through eighteen months. Features topics include bonding, breast-/bottle-feeding, crying and the parents' role, and a baby's first teacher.

Meeting the World: Parents Video Magazine. Volume 2. Karl-Lorimar Home Video, 1986. 50 minutes, color.

Recommended for parents of children six months to twenty-four months. Featured topics include stages of development, child-proofing your home, sleep, discipline, and day care.

Learning about the World: Parents Video Magazine. Volume 3. Gruner & Jahr USA, 1986. 50 minutes, color.

For parents of children eighteen months to four years. Featured topics include chores, sharing, bath time, preschool, and games.

To locate other videotapes on child rearing, use the latest edition of *The Video Source Book* or the CD-ROM product *Video Plus.*

38

PATENTS

See also: *Law, Science and Technology*

Patents are granted by the government to give inventors exclusive rights to their inventions and to prevent unauthorized people from making commercial use of them for a specified period of time. In the United States, patent protection is granted for seventeen years and cannot be renewed. The right extends throughout the United States and its territories only; therefore, many inventors apply simultaneously for foreign patents.

A new patent is issued somewhere in the world every ten seconds; more than a million patents and related documents are published each year. While patents are sometimes granted for trivial and even silly inventions, and patent documents are difficult to read because of what has become known as "patentese" (the legal language used by their writers), they represent a rich and varied source of information about new products, processes, plants, microorganisms, and chemical compositions. In some cases, patents surpass the scholarly journal as a source of information.

In the United States and in many other patent-granting countries, the inventor is required in the application for a patent to provide a detailed description of the invention and to set forth the best mode contemplated for carrying it out. Every patent includes a statement of a technical problem, an inventive idea designed to solve that problem, a product or process to be patented, and a record of the previous level of scientific and technical information or knowledge out of which it grew. When appropriate, a drawing is also required. The information recorded in patent specifications becomes an indispensable part of the technical literature for the future researcher, playing a significant role in the development of a nation's technology and its dissemination. Patent information is also critically important in the transfer of foreign technology.

350

For the inventor, a patent search is necessary to determine if an invention or idea has previously been patented. Corporations need to know if a patent has expired. Some types of patent searches are usually undertaken by a patent attorney, but many searches can be done by anyone who is persistent and willing to ask for help.

An Introduction to U.S. Patent Searching: The Process. By Susan B. Ardis. Libraries Unlimited, 1991.

Gives an overview of the history of patents and discusses their importance as a source of social, historical, and technical information. Ardis explains the elements of a patent document and the structure of the U.S. Patent and Trademark Office files. Explanations of the types of searches that can be done are accompanied by sample searches and hints on techniques.

Inventing & Patenting Sourcebook. 2d ed. By Richard C. Levy. Gale, 1992.

Includes reproducible forms for filing patents and copyrights, plus lists of federal laboratories that offer advice, inventors associations, venture capitalists, invention trade shows, journals and newsletters, and registered patent attorneys. Also includes the phone directory for the U.S. Patent and Trademark Office. Also available in a concise paperback edition, *The Inventor's Desktop Companion.*

Introduction to Patents Information. 2d ed. Prepared by the Patents Information Staff, Science Reference and Information Service, British Library. Edited by Stephen van Dulken. British Library, 1992.

Good general introduction to patent documentation. Both British and international patents are covered.

Patent It Yourself. By David Pressman. Nolo Press, 1992.

Instructions on filing a patent application without a lawyer.

Scientific and Technical Literature: An Introduction to Communication Forms. By Richard D. Walker and C. D. Hurt. American Library Association, 1990.

Chapter 4, "Patents," is an excellent guide to bibliographic tools and a general introduction to the characteristics of patents and their literature.

Commission of the European Communities. *Patent Information and Documentation in Western Europe.* 3d ed. Edited by B. M. Rimmer. K. G. Saur, 1988.

Also includes information on Japan, the United States, the former Soviet Union, and international organizations and associations.

The ability to search patent databases electronically relieves some of the tedium of manual searching. But patents often have vague titles and abstracts that give only a general overview of an invention, making keyword searching difficult. A standardized vocabulary may not exist for an invention in a new field. The researcher must be prepared to look through a good deal of irrelevant material when attempting a subject search. On the positive side, some searches, such as those for patent families (U.S. and foreign patents for the same item) and for patent citations, can be done only in electronic sources.

There is a great variety of patent databases, each differing somewhat in search features, as the following sources indicate:

CASSIS (Classification And Search Support Information System). U.S. Patent and Trademark Office, 1790–   .

Free, unlimited access to this service, available on CD-ROM and online, is provided at all patent depository libraries. The file is updated every six months. *CASSIS* can be searched by patent number, classification, and status (on CD-ROM only). Keyword searching is available only for recent years. *OG/PLUS* is the CD-ROM version of the *Official Gazette of the U.S. Patent and Trademark Office* (the publication that announces new patents). *Patent History* is the CD-ROM record of all patents issued during the most recent seventeen years.

All patent databases are derived from information produced by the national patenting agencies. The commercial vendor enhances this information with added features, such as expanded abstracts and titles, citation searching, and patent family searching. Some commercially available databases are:

INPADOC. (Online) 1968–   . Weekly.

Available from Dialog (File 345), ORBIT, and STN, this important source of patent information from the European Patent Office includes about 19 million patent records from fifty-six patenting authorities, or 96 percent of the world's patents. Contains only bibliographic data for records, and shows legal status for ten major patenting offices. *Inpamonitor* is mounted on STN as a separate file, with patent records for the most recent four weeks. *Inpane* on ORBIT maintains a file of the most recent six to ten weeks.

World Patents Index. (Online) Derwent Publications. 1965–   . Weekly or monthly.

Available on Dialog (Files 350, 351), ORBIT, and from the producer. More than 6 million citations for patents from thirty-one countries, some

of these for only a short time. Part of this database, including the special
Derwent classification, is available only from this publisher.

APS Automated Patent Searching. (CD-ROM) MicroPatent, 1975–   .
Monthly.
    Citations to and abstracts of U.S. patents.

FullText. (CD-ROM) MicroPatent, 1975–   . Monthly.
    Full text of all U.S. patents issued since 1975.

PatentImages. (CD-ROM) MicroPatent, 1990–   . Biweekly or weekly.
    Full-text images for U.S. patents.

CLAIMS/Patent CD. (CD-ROM) IFI/Plenum Data.
    Covers U.S. chemical patents from 1950, mechanical and electrical pat-
ents from 1963, and design patents from 1980. Corresponds in part to the
online databases *CLAIMS/Reassignment and Reexamination* and *CLAIMS/
U.S. Patents Abstracts* (below).

CLAIMS (CLass Assignee Index Method Search). (Online) IFI/Plenum
Data.
    A series of products available on Dialog, ORBIT, and STN. The CLAIMS
database is divided into seven different files, the major ones being:
    CLAIMS/U.S. Patent Abstracts. Weekly.
        Available from Dialog (Files 23, 24, 25, 340), ORBIT, and STN. Con-
    tains citations and abstracts for all U.S. chemical patents issued since
    January 1950 and all mechanical and electrical patents issued since
    January 1963.
    CLAIMS/Uniterm. 1950–   . Monthly.
        Available on Dialog (Files 223, 224, 225, 341), ORBIT, and STN.
    Includes citations to all U.S. patents, with in-depth indexing for all
    chemical patents.
    CLAIMS Comprehensive Data Base. 1950–   . Weekly.
        Available on ORBIT and STN. This file is based on *CLAIMS/Uniterm,*
    with additional enhancements to the chemical indexing. The database is
    available only to companies that purchase a subscription to the master
    database for in-house searching. It is not offered by Dialog.

OG/PLUS. (CD-ROM) Research Publications. Weekly.
    Full text of patents issued in the current year plus patent status file and
citations to cases involving patent violations. The latter two files are available online with ORBIT.

Patent History. (CD-ROM) Research Publications. 1973 to previous year. Annual.

> Historical equivalent of *OG/PLUS.*

LEXPAT. (Online) Mead Data Central. 1975–   . Weekly.

> Covers U.S. utility, plant, and design patents as a separate "library" in the LEXIS system of databases. *LEXPAT* contains the complete text of more than one million U.S. patents. All significant words in the text can be searched.

Other Online Sources

Many online databases in science and technology include patents among the literature sources covered, but search features may be more limited than in the specialized patent files. *Chemical Abstracts* and its online equivalent, *CA Search,* provide an excellent source of chemical patents information. Coverage for most of the twenty-five countries and two international bodies begins in 1967 and now constitutes 15 percent of the database.

There are many other patent databases, including those prepared by patent agencies in Europe and Japan. To find out about them, use the latest edition of the *Gale Directory of Databases.*

PERIODICALS

World Patent Information. 1979–   . Quarterly.

> Has a regular column on patent searching.

Every patenting authority that is a member of the Paris Union is required to issue a patent journal or gazette such as the *Official Gazette of the U.S. Patent and Trademark Office* (see below). The *Official Journal (Patents)* is published by the British Patent Office. In Canada, applications and notices of searches are published in the *Official Bulletin (Bulletin Officiel de la Propriété Industrielle).* The World Intellectual Property Organization (WIPO, see below) publishes the *PCT Gazette; Gazette of International Patent Applications* in which bibliographic information, abstracts, and drawings of all PCT applications are printed in English and French.

GOVERNMENT PUBLICATIONS

To conduct a patent search, you will need to use the indexes, guides, and manuals prepared by the U.S. Patent and Trademark Office. They are available in all patent depository libraries, regional government documents depository libraries, and many selective documents depository libraries.

Official Gazette of the U.S. Patent and Trademark Office: Patents. 1872–   . Weekly.

> The official journal of the U.S. Patent and Trademark Office, it lists the patents, design patents, and other patent documents granted the previous week. Contains an index of inventors and a subject index by class and

subclass numbers of the U.S. Patent Classification System. Since 1975, there has been a separate publication for trademarks.

Index of Patents Issued from the United States Patent and Trademark Office. Annual.

Index to the *Official Gazette.* Part 1 lists inventors and assignees granted patents during the year. Part 2 is a list of patents of that year by class and subclass.

Index to the U.S. Patent Classification System. Annual.

One begins a patent subject search here by locating all relevant terms and phrases that might identify a product or process.

Manual of Classification. Annual.

A loose-leaf service containing numbers and descriptive titles for all classes and subclasses used to classify inventions patented by the Patent and Trademark Office. Pages are issued as needed to update the system.

Patent Classification Definitions. Microfiche. Irregular.

Gives changes in classification of patents and definitions of new and revised classes and subclasses.

Other useful government publications include:
General Information Concerning Patents: A Brief Introduction to Patent Matters. Annual.

Provides nontechnical answers to the most commonly asked questions about patents. Includes blank copies of patent application forms.

Directory of Registered Patent Attorneys and Agents Arranged by States and Counties. 1966–   .

Some patent searches are most appropriately conducted by an attorney—for example, to find whether a proposed invention might infringe on another patent or whether an unexpired patent is valid and enforceable. This publication can be used to find a patent lawyer.

Directory of Patent Depository Libraries. 1988.

Lists all patent depository libraries and describes the staff, collections, and services available.

See also the Government Printing Office's *Subject Bibliography #21—Patents and Trademarks.*

Patent and Trademark Office
2011 Crystal Drive
Arlington, VA 22202
(703) 557-3341

An agency of the Department of Commerce, this office administers patent laws, examines applications for patents, grants patents, records and indexes them, and represents the United States in international cooperative efforts on patent and trademark matters. Also publishes and sells copies of patents, operates the patent depository system, and maintains a library for public use.

World Intellectual Property Organization
34, chemin des Colombettes
CH-1211 Geneva 20, Switzerland
22 7309 111

This specialized agency of the United Nations, with 116 members, is concerned with patents, trademarks, and copyrights. It administers treaties and offers technical assistance and training for member nations.

American Association of Inventors
2853 State Street
Saginaw, MI 48602
(517) 791-3444

Assists with the development of ideas, the patent application process, production, and marketing.

Inventors Clubs of America
P. O. Box 450261
Atlanta, GA 30345
(404) 938-5089; (800) 336-0160

Sponsors local clubs. Conducts education programs and competitions. Maintains a library, a biographical archive, and a museum.

National Council of Intellectual Property Law Associations
U.S. Patent and Trademark Office
2001 Jefferson Davis Highway
Arlington, VA 22202
(703) 415-0780

Coalition of state and local patent law associations. Provides for exchange of information on patent, trademark, and copyright law. Sponsors the National Inventors Hall of Fame.

Patent and Trademark Office Society
P. O. Box 2089
Arlington, VA 22202
(703) 557-6038
Membership consists of Patent Office employees and patent and trademark practitioners. Provides continuing professional education for its members and publishes the *Journal of the Patent and Trademark Office Society.*

Public Search Room
U.S. Patent and Trademark Office
2021 Jefferson Davis Highway
Arlington, VA 22202
(703) 557-3158
The most important patent library in the United States. Open to the public, this library contains all U.S. patents and those from fifty-two major patenting countries.

Patents are not routinely acquired by all libraries, even very large ones. The U.S. Patent and Trademark Office distributes all patents and related documentation to sixty-nine patent depository libraries (PDL) in the United States. In order to qualify as a PDL, the university, public, or state library must provide public access, have a technical/scientific collection, and have a patent collection going back at least twenty years. More detail about the scope of each library's collection and the services offered can be found in the list of patent depository libraries on pages 358–59.
Major patent collections are found in the following libraries:

Kurt F. Wendt Engineering Library
University of Wisconsin-Madison
215 N. Randall Avenue
Madison, WI 53706
(608) 262-3493
Complete collection of U.S. patents.

Franklin Research Institute
20th Street and Ben Franklin Parkway
Philadelphia, PA 19103
(215) 448-1239

Sunnyvale Public Library
Patent Information Clearinghouse
1500 Partridge Avenue
Sunnyvale, CA 94088
(408) 730-7290

LIST OF PATENT DEPOSITORY LIBRARIES

Reference Collections of U.S. Patents and Trademarks
Available for Public Use in Patent and Trademark Depository Libraries

The following libraries, designated as Patent and Trademark Depository Libraries (PTDLs), receive patent and trademark information in various formats from the U.S. Patent and Trademark Office. Many PTDLs have on file all full-text patents issued since 1790, trademarks published since 1872, and select collections of foreign patents. All PDTLs have both the patent and trademark sections of the *Official Gazette of the U. S. Patent and Trademark Office.* The full-text utility and design patents are distributed numerically on 16 mm microfilm, and plant patents on color microfiche. Patent and trademark search systems on CD-ROM are available at all PTDLs to increase utilization of and enhance access to the information found in patents and trademarks. It is through the CD-ROM systems that preliminary patent and trademark searches can be conducted through the numerically arranged collections. All information is available for use by the public free of charge.

In addition, each PTDL offers reference publications which outline and provide access to the patent and trademark classification systems, as well as other documents and publications which supplement the basic search tools. PTDLs provide technical staff assistance in using all materials. Facilities for making paper copies of patent and trademark information are generally provided for a fee.

Since there are variations in the scope of patent and trademark collections among the PTDLs, and their hours of service to the public vary, anyone contemplating use of these collections at a particular library is urged to contact that library in advance about its collections, services, and hours in order to avert possible inconvenience.

State	Name of Library	Telephone Contact
Alabama	Auburn University Libraries	(205) 844-1747
	Birmingham Public Library	(205) 226-3680
Alaska	Anchorage: Z. J. Loussac Public Library	(907) 562-7323
Arizona	Tempe: Noble Library, Arizona State University	(602) 965-7010
Arkansas	Little Rock: Arkansas State Library	(501) 682-2053
California	Los Angeles City Library	(213) 612-3273
	Sacramento: California State Library	(916) 654-0069
	San Diego Public Library	(619) 236-5813
	Sunnyvale Patent Clearinghouse	(408) 730-7290
Colorado	Denver Public Library	(303) 640-8847
Connecticut	New Haven: Science Park Library	(203) 786-5447
Delaware	Newark: University of Delaware Library	(302) 831-2965
Dist. of Columbia	Washington: Howard University Libraries	(202) 806-7252
Florida	Fort Lauderdale: Broward County Main Library	(305) 357-7444
	Miami-Dade Public Library	(305) 375-2665
	Orlando: University of Central Florida Libraries	(407) 823-2562
	Tampa: Tampa Campus Library, University of South Florida	(813) 974-2726
Georgia	Atlanta: Price Gilbert Memorial Library, Georgia Institute of Technology	(404) 894-4508
Hawaii	Honolulu: Hawaii State Public Library System	(808) 586-3477
Idaho	Moscow: University of Idaho Library	(208) 885-6235
Illinois	Chicago Public Library	(312) 747-4450
	Springfield: Illinois State Library	(217) 782-5659
Indiana	Indianapolis-Marion County Public Library	(317) 269-1741
	West Lafayette: Siegesmund Engineering Library, Purdue University	(317) 494-2873

Iowa	Des Moines: State Library of Iowa	(515) 281-4118
Kansas	Wichita: Ablah Library, Wichita State University	(316) 689-3155
Kentucky	Louisville Free Public Library	(502) 561-8617
Louisiana	Baton Rouge: Troy H. Middleton Library, Louisiana State University	(504) 388-2570
Maryland	College Park: Engineering and Physical Sciences Library, University of Maryland	(301) 405-9157
Massachusetts	Amherst: Physical Sciences Library, University of Massachusetts	(413) 545-1370
	Boston Public Library	(617) 536-5400 Ext. 265
Michigan	Ann Arbor: Engineering Library, University of Michigan	(313) 764-5298
	Big Rapids: Abigail S. Timme Library, Ferris State University	(616) 592-3602
	Detroit Public Library	(313) 833-1450
Minnesota	Minneapolis Public Library and Information Center	(612) 372-6570
Mississippi	Jackson: Mississippi Library Commission	Not Yet Operational
Missouri	Kansas City: Linda Hall Library	(816) 363-4600
	St. Louis Public Library	(314) 241-2288 Ext. 390
Montana	Butte: Montana College of Mineral Science and Technology Library	(406) 496-4281
Nebraska	Lincoln: Engineering Library, University of Nebraska-Lincoln	(402) 472-3411
Nevada	Reno: University of Nevada, Reno Library	(702) 784-6579
New Hampshire	Durham: University of New Hampshire Library	(603) 862-1777
New Jersey	Newark Public Library	(201) 733-7782
	Piscataway: Library of Science and Medicine, Rutgers University	(908) 932-2895
New Mexico	Albuquerque: University of New Mexico General Library	(505) 277-4412
New York	Albany: New York State Library	(518) 473-4636
	Buffalo and Erie County Public Library	(716) 858-7101
	New York Public Library (The Research Libraries)	(212) 714-8529
North Carolina	Raleigh: D.H. Hill Library, North Carolina State University	(919) 515-3280
North Dakota	Grand Forks: Chester Fritz Library, University of North Dakota	(701) 777-4888
Ohio	Cincinnati and Hamilton County, Public Library of	(513) 369-6936
	Cleveland Public Library	(216) 623-2870
	Columbus: Ohio State University Libraries	(614) 292-6175
	Toledo/Lucas County Public Library	(419) 259-5212
Oklahoma	Stillwater: Oklahoma State University Center for International Trade Development	(405) 744-7086
Oregon	Salem: Oregon State Library	(503) 378-4239
Pennsylvania	Philadelphia, The Free Library of	(215) 686-5331
	Pittsburgh, Carnegie Library of	(412) 622-3138
	University Park: Pattee Library, Pennsylvania State University	(814) 865-4861
Rhode Island	Providence Public Library	(401) 455-8027
South Carolina	Charleston: Medical University of South Carolina Library	(803) 792-2372
	Clemson University Libraries	Not Yet Operational
Tennessee	Memphis & Shelby County Public Library and Information Center	(901) 725-8877
	Nashville: Stevenson Science Library, Vanderbilt University	(615) 322-2775
Texas	Austin: McKinney Engineering Library, University of Texas at Austin	(512) 495-4500
	College Station: Sterling C. Evans Library, Texas A & M University	(409) 845-2551
	Dallas Public Library	(214) 670-1468
	Houston: The Fondren Library, Rice University	(713) 527-8101 Ext. 2587
Utah	Salt Lake City: Marriott Library, University of Utah	(801) 581-8394
Virginia	Richmond: James Branch Cabell Library, Virginia Commonwealth University	(804) 367-1104
Washington	Seattle: Engineering Library, University of Washington	(206) 543-0740
West Virginia	Morgantown: Evansdale Library, West Virginia University	(304) 293-4510
Wisconsin	Madison: Kurt F. Wendt Library, University of Wisconsin Madison	(608) 262-6845
	Milwaukee Public Library	(414) 278-3247

Patents are arranged by subject in this collection of more than 5 million patents. U.S. coverage begins with 1962.

Milwaukee Public Library
814 W. Wisconsin Avenue
Milwaukee, WI 53233
(414) 278-3000
Has British patents back to number 1 for 1617.

New York Public Library, Annex Services
521 W. 43d Street
New York, NY 10036
(212) 714-8520
Complete files of U.S. and British patents; partial coverage for other countries.

LC SUBJECT HEADINGS

Patent laws and legislation
Patent lawyers
Patent literature
Patent searching
Patents

Any of these subject headings may be subdivided by place, topic, or form of publication:
Patents—United States—Handbooks, manuals, etc.
Patents, Government owned—United Kingdom
Patents—Bibliography—Japan

Patents can also be a subdivision of specific products or processes:
Automobiles—Patents
Molecular sieves—Patents

SOURCES OF PATENT DOCUMENTS

Patent documents can be purchased from many patenting authorities, including the U.S. Patent and Trademark Office. If speed is important, you may wish to purchase them from a commercial service. Some of the vendors of patent databases also offer patent delivery services. For a fee, these companies can provide overnight or even same-day delivery. These companies market a variety of patent services:

Research Publications
Rapid Patent Service
1921 Jefferson Davis Highway
Arlington, VA 22202
(800) 336-5010

Offers the most complete patent service available in the United States. It has an "on-demand" paper copy delivery service. Copies are sent by fax or overnight mail upon request. It also provides a weekly confidential alerting service for purposes of monitoring newly issued U.S. patents by competition, technology, or inventor/assignee. Search and translation services are also available for any patent included in any online database from any vendor. Research Publications also sells microfilm copies of all U.S. patents granted, beginning in 1790. Many other countries' patents and applications are also available from this company.

Derwent, Inc.
1313 Dolley Madison Boulevard
Suite 303
McLean, VA 22101
(800) 451-5451; (703) 790-0400

Derwent analyzes, classifies, indexes, abstracts, and codes patent documents from over thirty major patent-granting countries. The company produces a series of electronic, print, and microfilm services that make patents available and usable. Its services are designed to monitor competitive activities and technological trends, offering weekly updates in several fields. Subject searching, company and inventor searching, patent family searching, and statistical analysis are available to Derwent customers.

39

POLITICS
AND
GOVERNMENT

See also: General Reference Sources, Government Agencies, Government Publications, History, Law, Newspapers

This chapter describes research sources on politics and government available to political science students, other researchers, and political activists in search of contacts in government. Though it offers some state resources, it concentrates on those of the federal government.

Political science, the academic discipline, is an interdisciplinary field and a relatively new one. Before the twentieth century, the study of politics was the province of historians and economists. Today political scientists study such fields as public policy and public administration.

One of the special challenges of political study is the constant round of new activity and the coverage it generates in the media. Electronic sources offer an improved, if still daunting, means of keeping up with the daily deluge of materials.

GENERAL SOURCES OF INFORMATION

The Social Sciences: A Cross-Disciplinary Guide to Selected Sources. Edited by Nancy L. Herron. Libraries Unlimited, 1989.

The chapter on political science is useful for the beginning researcher; other chapters discuss tools from related social science disciplines that may be useful for the student of government.

Political Science: A Guide to Reference and Information Sources. By Henry E. York. Libraries Unlimited, 1990.

Another good guide for the beginning researcher, with more detail on political science than *The Social Sciences.* Also lists associations, research institutes, journals.

The Almanac of American Politics: The President, the Senators, the Representatives, the Governors: Their Records and Election Results, Their States and Districts. National Journal. Biennial.

Provides a compact summary and analysis of politics at the national and state levels. Its state-by-state analysis points out the many factors at work in each state and provides an understanding of how those factors influence political actions. Each senator and representative's votes on key issues as well as the ratings given them by selected interest groups are included. *The Almanac* is the first source to try for U.S. political information. Available online with NEXIS.

Congressional Quarterly Almanac. Congressional Quarterly. Annual.

A good annual summary and analysis of U.S. politics that highlights key actions, compiles annual voting records, describes major legislation, and analyzes Supreme Court decisions. Updated by *CQ Weekly Report* (see below).

Congressional Quarterly's Guide to Congress. 3d ed. 1982.
Congressional Quarterly's Guide to the Presidency. 1989.
Congressional Quarterly's Guide to the U.S. Supreme Court. 2d ed. 1990.

In-depth guides to the workings of all three branches of government. Useful appendixes include important documents, glossaries, and biographies.

Congressional Index. Commerce Clearing House, 1937– . Biennial with weekly updates.

A constantly updated index to bills that lists their current status. One section reports all roll call votes for the week. This information is also available electronically (see below).

Washington Information Directory. Congressional Quarterly. Annual.

Describes both governmental and nongovernmental organizations. It is especially useful for locating lobbying groups and special-interest organizations.

Washington Representatives. Columbia Books, 1977– . Annual.

List of lobbyists, foreign agents, and legal counsels in Washington representing special-interest groups.

The Washington Almanac: A Guide to Federal Policy. 2d ed. By Lawrence J. Haas. Henry Holt, 1993.

Essays on every major area of government (civil rights, labor, trade, foreign affairs, etc.) are followed by profiles of major players who shape policy, including government officials, lobbyists, and scholars from Washington think tanks. Addresses and telephone numbers are provided for each of these 350 people.

Who's Who in American Politics. R. R. Bowker, 1967–   . Biennial.
Biographical sketches of nearly 25,000 men and women who are active in national and state politics. Also available on CD-ROM as part of *The Complete Marquis Who's Who Plus* and online with Dialog.

Voting Information

America Votes. Congressional Quarterly. Annual.
An annual compliation of federal and state election returns.

Congressional Roll Call. Congressional Quarterly. Annual.
A detailed and highly organized record of all roll call votes in Congress. The motion or bill associated with each vote is described and the vote information presented in chart form. Extensive analysis of the voting is also provided. Also see Electronic Sources below.

State Legislatures

State Legislative Sourcebook: A Resource Guide to Legislative Information in the 50 States. By Lynn Hellebust. Government Research Service. Annual.
Describes each state legislature and its publications. Provides telephone numbers for checking the status of bills in each state. These phone numbers are also listed in *Lesko's Info-Power* (Information USA, 1990).

ELECTRONIC SOURCES

Almost all current legislative information is available electronically. Services that provide voting records and the status and text of bills, such as LEXIS/NEXIS, CQ's Washington Alert, Commerce Clearing House's Electronic Legislative Search System, and LEGI-SLATE, are available only by subscription. They are used primarily by corporations, law firms, and lobbying groups, but rarely by libraries because of the high cost.

Brief recorded messages on bill status and voting records are available on a daily basis at these numbers:

U.S. House of Representatives Floor Votes
Democratic Cloakroom (202) 225-7500
Republican Cloakroom (202) 225-7430
U.S. Senate Floor votes
Democratic Cloakroom (202) 224-8541
Republican Cloakroom (202) 224-8601

The Library of Congress now makes its bill tracking system available through the Internet. There is a forty-eight-hour time lag in making status reports available. **Telnet locis.loc.gov.**

The Inter-University Consortium for Political and Social Research at the University of Michigan is a consortium of 260 institutions that collect social science data in machine-readable form, usually on magnetic tape. Member institutions can borrow data files from each other. Many files are useful for political scientists. See the ICPSR's annual catalog, *A Guide to Resources and Services,* for a list of the materials available. This guide is also available online with RLIN.

ABC POL SCI on Disc. (CD-ROM) ABC-Clio, 1984–   . Updated 3 times/ year.

Table of contents listing for more than 300 current periodicals covering political science and government. Available in print as *ABC POL SCI: A Bibliography of Current Contents,* 1969–   , updated bimonthly.

Congressional Masterfile 2. (CD-ROM) Congressional Information Service, 1970–   . Quarterly.

Indexes publications produced by committees and subcommittees of Congress from 1970 to date. (An index to congressional reports and hearings from 1789 to 1969 is available as *Masterfile 1.*) Also online with Dialog (File 101), updated monthly. Print equivalent is *CIS/Index to Publications of the U.S. Congress,* Congressional Information Service, 1970–   .

LEXIS/NEXIS. (Online)

More than a dozen databases are available online for the political researcher or activist. For example, BILLTEXT has the full text of all bills introduced during the current session of Congress. Bill Tracking is a service that gives daily status information on bills introduced during the current session. The Capital Source gives biographical information on more than 7,000 persons and organizations operating within the Beltway, including government, the media, corporations, and trade and professional associations. Bill Tracking is also provided for the legislatures of all fifty states. Some academic libraries and virtually all law school libraries subscribe to this service.

PAIS International. (CD-ROM) SilverPlatter, 1972–   . Quarterly. Also available as *PAIS on CD-ROM.* Public Affairs Information Service, 1972–   . Quarterly.

Subject index to books, pamphlets, government publications, and more than 1,200 periodicals, with an emphasis on economic, social, and political issues. Includes articles on both federal and state politics. Also available online on BRS (PAIS), BRS/AfterDark, Dialog (File 49), Knowledge Index (SOCS2), FirstSearch (PAIS Decade), 1976–   , and, from 1980–   , on RLIN's CitaDel. Contains records from the print sources *PAIS Bulletin,* 1976–90 (formerly called *Public Affairs Information Service Bulletin,* 1915–

76), *PAIS Foreign Language Index*, 1972–90, and *PAIS International in Print*, 1991–   .

Social Sciences Index. (CD-ROM) H. W. Wilson, 1984–   . Monthly.

Indexes journals in area studies, geography, international relations, political science, public administration, policy sciences, and other disciplines. *Wilson Social Sciences Abstracts* is an annotated version on CD-ROM. Also available online with Wilsonline, 1984–   , and OCLC FirstSearch, updated twice a week, and in print, updated quarterly, as *Social Sciences Index,* 1974–   (formerly *Social Sciences and Humanities Index,* 1965–74; and *International Index,* 1907–65).

Social Science Source. (CD-ROM) EBSCO, 1984–   . Bimonthly.

Indexing and abstracting for 353 periodicals. Full text is provided for fifteen of them, including *Congressional Quarterly Weekly Report, Foreign Policy, The Nation, National Review,* and *The New Republic.*

Staff Directories on CD-ROM. Staff Directories. Biennial.

Contains all the listings of government employees from the *Congressional Staff Directory, Federal Staff Directory,* and *Judicial Staff Directory.* Includes over 50,000 names with job title, address, and telephone number. See Chapter 17, Government Agencies, for further information.

United States Political Science Documents. (Online) 1975–   .

Indexes scholarly political science journals. Available from Dialog (File 93). Print version compiled by the University of Pittsburgh, University Center for International Studies, 1975–   , updated annually.

Winning Elections. (CD-ROM) Wayzata.

Text of seven books on disc: *Congressional Directory, U.S. Government Manual,* and books on campaign strategy and finance, with texts of political speeches.

Online Services

- *Prodigy,* in its Politics section, has a file of current presidential speeches.
- *America Online* in its White House Forum has daily press releases from the White House and a file of current speeches given by the President.

PERIODICALS

American Political Science Review. 1906–   . Quarterly.

Published by the American Political Science Association, this scholarly journal has an extensive book review section.

CQ Weekly Report. 1946–   . Weekly.

Published by a commercial firm, this news service provides a factual account of congressional activities, highlighting the most newsworthy events of the week. Online with DataTimes and CQ Washington Alert Service. Material is summarized and published at the end of the year as the *Congressional Quarterly Almanac* (see above).

Foreign Affairs. 1922–   . 5 times/year.

Published by the Council on Foreign Relations, this is the best-known journal of world affairs, with nonpartisan articles on international relations.

National Journal. 1969–   . Weekly.

A magazine that provides current reporting on politics, Congress, and federal agency activities, similar to *CQ Weekly Report.* Online with LEXIS/ NEXIS, 1977–   , and LEGI-SLATE, 1985–   .

Political Science Quarterly. 1886–   . Quarterly.

An academic journal that is also accessible to the serious general reader interested in politics and world affairs. Emphasis is on American politics.

Washington Post. 1877–   . Daily.

This Washington newspaper provides extensive coverage of national politics. Available on CD-ROM from UMI and online with Dialog, Knowledge Index, Dow Jones News/Retrieval, NEXIS, CompuServe, and DataTimes.

In addition to these publications, which feature purportedly "objective" coverage of politics and government, many magazines of opinion discuss the political scene from a particular perspective. Among the best known are:

Dissent. 1954–   . Quarterly. Liberal.
Human Events. 1944–   . Weekly. Conservative.
The Nation. 1865–   . 47 times/year. Liberal.
National Review. 1955–   . Biweekly. Conservative.
New Republic. 1914–   . Weekly. Liberal.

Budget System and Concepts of the United States Government. 1991.

GOVERNMENT PUBLICATIONS

Overview of the budget process that explains some of the more important budget concepts.

Congressional Record. U.S. Congress. (Online) 1985–   . Daily with a four-day lag.

Official transcript of action on the House and Senate floors. It also includes a wide range of other information inserted into the record by senators and representatives. Online in full text from NEXIS and LEGISLATE; a weekly abstracted version is available from Dialog. Available in print from the Government Printing Office, 1873–   .

How Our Laws Are Made. U.S. Congress. House. 1990.
Gives a clear description of the complicated legislative process.

Nomination and Election of the President and Vice President of the United States. 1992.
A compilation of constitutional provisions, federal and state laws, and rules of the two major political parties.

United States Government Structure. 2 vols. 1987.
Describes the basis of the U.S. government—the Constitution. Discusses the three branches of government and the importance of each. The different levels of government—federal, state, and local—are explained and compared. Part of the Federal Citizenship Text Series.

See also the following *Subject Bibliographies* from the Government Printing Office:
#204—Budget of the United States and Economic Report of the President
#207—Civil Rights and Equal Opportunity
#141—Federal Government
#75—Foreign Affairs of the United States
#210—Foreign Relations of the United States
#211—Intergovernmental Relations
#191—Treaties and Other International Agreements of the United States
#245—Voting and Elections

GOVERNMENT AGENCIES

Federal Election Commission
999 E St. NW
Washington, DC 20463
(202) 219-3420 or (800) 424-9530
The governmental agency responsible for overseeing federal elections and campaigns. It publishes some reports and collects a wide range of statistics and information regarding elections that can be requested directly.

Congressional Research Service
Library of Congress
101 Independence Ave. SE
Washington, DC 20540

Some 800 highly trained researchers do nonpartisan studies on policy issues for members of Congress. The more than 450 reports compiled each year are available as: *Major Studies and Issue Briefs of the Congressional Research Service* (Research Publications). Coverage in this set dates back to 1916. The printed index to the reports is published quarterly. The reports are on microfiche. Members of Congress can also get copies of these reports for their constituents. See *Lesko's Info-Power* (Information USA, 1990) for a partial list of reports.

American Political Science Association
1527 New Hampshire Ave. NW
Washington, DC 20036
(202) 483-2512

ASSOCIATIONS

Members are university teachers of political science, public officials, and laypersons. Its Congressional Fellowship Program allows political scientists and journalists to spend a year working with members of Congress.

American Conservative Union
38 Ivy St. SE
Washington, DC 20003
(202) 546-6555

Lobbying organization to mobilize responsible conservative thought. Maintains a speakers bureau, conducts research programs, rates members of Congress on their voting records.

Americans for Democratic Action
1511 K St. NW
Washington, DC 20005
(202) 785-5980

This liberal group works for legislation to reduce inequality, curtail defense spending, and prevent encroachment on civil liberties. Rates members of Congress on their voting records.

Democratic National Committee
430 S. Capitol St. SE
Washington, DC 20003
(202) 863-8000

Republican National Committee
310 First St. SE
Washington, DC 20002
(202) 863-8500

The two major political parties can provide a gamut of material from campaign brochures to information regarding their political platforms.

Common Cause
2030 M St. NW
Washington, DC 20036
(202) 833-1200

This citizens' lobby works for more open government and against the influence of Political Action Committees.

Congress Watch
215 Pennsylvania Ave. SE
Washington, DC 20003
(202) 546-4996

A subdivision of Ralph Nader's group, Public Citizen (see Chapter 22). Lobbies Congress on behalf of citizens' interests. Publishes educational materials.

League of Women Voters of the United States
1730 M St. NW
Washington, DC
(202) 429-1965

A nonpartisan organization that promotes education about the political process. The many local branches of the League are a resource for political information.

National Women's Political Caucus
1275 K St. NW
Washington, DC 20005
(202) 898-1100

Seeks to gain an equal place and voice for women in the political process at local, state, and national levels. This multipartisan group supports women candidates and raises women's issues in campaigns.

LIBRARIES More than 1,400 academic and public libraries are designated as federal depository libraries and automatically receive U.S. government publications. (See Chapter 16, Government Publications, for a more detailed discussion of this system.) The public may use these government publications collections, even in libraries with otherwise restricted access. The following publication lists the depositories:

U.S. Congress, Joint Committee on Printing, *A Directory of U.S. Government Depository Libraries.* Annual.

The presidential libraries operated by the National Archives are important sources for research on government in the twentieth century. See Chapter 29, History, for a complete list of these libraries.

Many research institutes in this field have a political approach that you should be aware of when you consult them.

American Enterprise Institute
1150 Seventeenth St. NW
Washington, DC 20036
(202) 862-5800
This moderate conservative research and educational organization issues publications on government regulation, economics, foreign affairs, and politics.

Brookings Institution
1775 Massachusetts Ave. NW
Washington, DC 20036
(202) 797-6000
A left-of-center institute, Brookings sponsors research in economics, social programs, government, and foreign policy.

Heritage Foundation
214 Massachusetts Ave. NE
Washington, DC 20002
(202) 546-4400
Conducts public policy research focusing on domestic and foreign policy issues from a conservative point of view.

Institute for Policy Studies
1601 Connecticut Ave. NW
Washington, DC 20009
(202) 234-9382
This think tank on the left of the political spectrum studies national security, foreign policy, human rights, and domestic reconstruction.

Business and politics	Political action committees	**LC SUBJECT**
Campaign funds	Political activists	**HEADINGS**
Campaign literature	Political conventions	
Electioneering (i.e., political	Political corruption	
campaigns)	Political ethics	
Lobbying	Political parties—Platforms	

Political science
Political scientists
Politicians
Politics, Practical (i.e., methods
used in political party work)

Presidential candidates
Press and politics
Public opinion
Television in politics
Women political activists

The subheading Politics and government can be used with the names of countries, states, cities, and other places, and under ethnic groups, e.g., Illinois—Politics and government. Political activity can be a subheading under classes of persons, types of businesses, corporate bodies, e.g., Catholic Church—Political activity and Trade unions—Political activity. Ethics can be a subheading under the names of legislative bodies, e.g., U.S. Congress—Ethics.

40

RELIGION

See also: General Reference Sources

Religious studies, perhaps more than most fields, can be confusing for two reasons: the tremendous breadth of the field (nearly every event, artifact, or person can be said to have a religious dimension); and the lack of a clear line dividing religion as it is practiced from the academic study of religion. Until the mid-twentieth century, graduate studies in religion were conducted almost exclusively at theological seminaries. The University of Iowa School of Religion, founded in 1946, was the first state university program in religious studies, and the first to begin to evolve an approach that wasn't rooted in Christian theological categories.

Academic professionals currently devoted to studying religion fall into two main groups: those who employ traditional historical, theological, and comparative approaches to religion (epitomized by the American Academy of Religion) and those who employ methods derived from the social sciences to study religion as a societal phenomenon (epitomized by the Society for the Scientific Study of Religion).

Researchers should be aware of their own preconceptions about religion and not expect from or impose upon other religious traditions the same kinds of belief or behavior that are characteristic of Western religion.

The way libraries in the United States are organized reflects a Christian, indeed a Protestant, bias. The Dewey Decimal Classification devotes nearly the entire range of 200s to Christianity. After an initial category called "Natural Religion" (210s), Christianity takes up the 220s through the 280s; all other religious traditions are crammed into the 290s at "Other and Comparative Religions." The Library of Congress classification system reflects the same bias, but has been revised in recent years to minimize the subservient status accorded non-Christian religions.

Religious Information Sources: A Worldwide Guide. By J. Gordon Melton and Michael A. Koszegi. Garland, 1992.

While about half the 2,500 sources in this guide relate to Christianity, all world religions are covered, and there is a section on occult, New Age, and esoteric religions. In addition to listing print, microform, and electronic materials, it also includes lists of associations, research centers, and archival collections.

Guides to the
Literature

Theological and Religious Reference Material: General Resources and Biblical Studies. By G. E. Gorman and Lyn Gorman. Greenwood, 1984.

An extensive guide to sources for research on Christian theology and related fields, listing handbooks, collections, and bibliographies. A companion volume on comparative and non-Christian religions is in preparation.

Research Guide to Religious Studies. By John F. Wilson and Thomas P. Slavens. American Library Association, 1982.

An introduction to religious studies as an academic discipline. Includes a survey of the field and an annotated list of major reference works. Although dated, it is useful for beginning researchers.

Encyclopedias

The Encyclopedia of Religion. 16 vols. Mircea Eliade, editor-in-chief. Macmillan, 1987.

A comprehensive treatment of all aspects of religion, designed for "educated, nonspecialist readers." Scholars describe religious traditions and theological systems, including ancient and non-Western religions; discuss religion in various geographical regions; and analyze the relationships between religion and other aspects of culture. Extensive bibliographies lead to other sources.

The Encyclopedia of American Religions. 4th ed. Edited by J. Gordon Melton. Gale, 1992.

Intended to be a "comprehensive survey of religious and spiritual groups in America," the volume covers 1,600 groups arranged in nineteen major religious families and traditions. Includes directory information (address, current membership, publications, affiliated colleges) and extensive bibliographies.

Encyclopedia of the American Religious Experience: Studies of Traditions and Movements. 3 vols. Edited by Charles H. Lippy and Peter W. Williams. Scribner's, 1988.

Multi-author work presenting the "best of current scholarship on religion in America," designed for a broad general audience. Essays treat approaches to religion in America; Jewish and Christian traditions; religions outside those traditions; American religious thought and literature; liturgy, worship, and the arts; and religion and the political and social order.

Concise Encyclopedia of Islam. By G. Glasse. HarperCollins, 1989.
Brief articles describe Islamic beliefs, religious leaders, rituals, law, and culture. Includes illustrations, maps, a chronology, and a bibliography.

The Encyclopedia of Eastern Philosophy and Religion: Buddhism, Hinduism, Taoism, Zen. By Ingrid Fischer-Schreiber and others. Shambhala, 1989.
Intended for general readers. Includes definitions, biographical sketches, and discussions of historical and cultural traditions. Lengthy bibliography.

Encyclopedia of Judaism. Edited by Geoffrey Wigoder. Macmillan, 1989.
Illustrated encyclopedia reflecting scholarship from Reform, Conservative, and Orthodox Judaism.

Encyclopedia of Unbelief. 2 vols. Edited by Gordon Stein. Prometheus Books, 1985.
Articles on atheism, humanism, rationalism, and other free thought movements. Covers the history of unbelief in various countries and time periods. Also lists meetings, organizations, publishers, and periodicals.

New Age Encyclopedia. Edited by J. Gordon Melton and others. Gale, 1990.
Objective description of New Age groups and philosophies on health and healing, higher consciousness, and spiritual development. Includes biographies of leaders and a chronology.

The Spiritual Seeker's Guide: The Complete Guide for Religions and Spiritual Groups of the World. By Steven S. Sadler. Allwon Publishing, 1992.
Covers thirty-four religions, including traditional Eastern and Western faiths, plus "Spiritual Paths," such as Druidism, wiccan, and Freemasonry, "Metaphysical Teachings," such as Baha'i, Alcoholics Anonymous, and channeling, and "Masters and Movements," including various swamis, babas, maharishis, gurus, and yogis.

World Christian Encyclopedia. Edited by David B. Barrett. Oxford University Press, 1982.
Surveys Christianity, country by country. Includes statistics, maps, biographical information, a bibliography, and a directory.

Yearbook of American and Canadian Churches. Abingdon, 1916–   . Annual.

Compiled by the National Council of Churches, this yearbook provides statistics, profiles, and descriptions of all major religious groups, not just Christian ones, in the United States and Canada. Statistics vary in reliability because editors rely on surveys returned by the organizations described. Also includes lists of regional church agencies, seminaries, church-related colleges, and religious periodicals.

Statistics

The People's Religion: American Faith in the 90's. Edited by George Gallup, Jr. and Jim Castelli. Macmillan, 1989.

Summarizes Gallup polls on religious institutions and beliefs over the past fifty years. Covers such topics as denominational membership, attendance, confidence in clergy, and interest in religion. It also includes profiles of Americans' attitudes towards a wide variety of religious and ethical issues and profiles of major American religious groups. On the basis of these findings, Gallup forecasts the future of American religion in the coming decade.

Other Sources

World Spirituality: An Encyclopedic History of the Religious Quest. Crossroad, 1985–   .

Seeks to present the historical unfolding of the variety of spiritual wisdom. To be complete in twenty-five volumes; each volume is edited by a noted scholar or team of scholars. At the end of 1993, twenty-one volumes in this series had been published:

Christian Spirituality: Origins to the Twelfth Century. Edited by Bernard McGinn and others. 1985.
Christian Spirituality: High Middle Ages and Reformation. Edited by Jill Raitt and others. 1987.
Christian Spirituality: Post-Reformation and Modern. Edited by Louis Dupre and others. 1991.
Classical Mediterranean Spirituality: Egyptian, Greek, Roman. Edited by A. H. Armstrong. 1986.
Hindu Spirituality: Vedas through Vedanta. Edited by Krishna Sivaraman. 1988–   .
Islamic Spirituality. Edited by Seyyed Hossein Nasr. 1991.
Jewish Spirituality: From the Bible through the Middle Ages. Edited by Arthur Green. 1986.
Jewish Spirituality: From the Sixteenth-Century Revival to the Present. Edited by Arthur Green. 1987.
South and Meso-American Native Spirituality. Edited by Gary H. Gossen. 1993.
Modern Esoteric Spirituality. Edited by Antoine Faivre and Jacob Needleman. 1992.

Another series, Asian Philosophies and Religions Resource Guides, edited by David J. Dell and Edward S. Haynes and published by G. K. Hall, introduces each of the great Asian religions. Each volume is entitled "Guide to . . ." Three examples:

Guide to Chinese Religion. By David C. Yu. 1985.
Guide to Islam. Edited by David Ede. 1983.
Guide to Hindu Religion. Edited by David J. Dell. 1981.

Also see indexes under Electronic Sources.

Christian Periodical Index. 1956–   . Quarterly.
    Published by the Association of Christian Librarians. Indexes sixty titles, with emphasis on evangelical magazines.

Catholic Periodical and Literature Index. 1930–   . Bimonthly.
    Published by the Catholic Library Association. Indexes 160 magazines, some in foreign languages.

Index to Jewish Periodicals. 1963–   . Semiannual.
    Indexes fifty English-language periodicals, both popular and scholarly.

Arts & Humanities Citation Index Compact Disc Edition. (CD-ROM) Institute for Scientific Information, 1990–   . Updated 3 times/year.
    More than 1,100 journals are indexed by author and keyword. In addition, this unique tool enables the searcher to determine who has later cited a particular book or article and which books and articles are influential because they are cited often in leading arts and humanities journals. Also available online as *Arts & Humanities Search,* 1980–   , from Dialog (File 439), BRS, and BRS/AfterDark, updated weekly. Available in print as *Arts and Humanities Citation Index,* 1976–   , updated quarterly.

Humanities Index. (CD-ROM) H. W. Wilson, 1984–   . Quarterly.
    Indexes 290 humanities periodicals, including *Biblical Archaeologist, Catholic Biblical Quarterly, Church History, Harvard Theological Review, History of Religions, Muslim World,* and *Religious Studies. Wilson Humanities Abstracts* is an annotated version on CD-ROM. Also available online with Wilsonline, 1984–   , updated twice a week, and in print, updated quarterly, as *Humanities Index,* 1974–   (formerly *Social Sciences and Humanities Index,* 1965–74; *International Index,* 1907–65).

Religion Indexes. (CD-ROM) H. W. Wilson, 1975–   .
    Compiled by the American Theological Library Association, this database contains more than 600,000 records. It provides indexing and ab-

stracts for articles in more than 200 journals plus books and covers all religions and all theological points of view. Corresponds to the following print indexes: *Religion Index One: Periodicals* (1975–   ), *Religion Index Two: Multi-Author Works* (1975–   ), *Research in Ministry* (an index of theses and reports, 1981–   ), and *Index to Book Reviews in Religion* (1986–   ). Available online with BRS, BRS/AfterDark, Dialog (File 190), Knowledge Index, and Wilsonline, updated monthly. Available in print as *Religion Index* (formerly *Index to Religious Periodical Literature,* (1949–   ).

REX (Religious Index). (CD-ROM) FABS International, 1959–   . Quarterly.

More than 60,000 citations, with abstracts, to articles in 200 journals. Nonsectarian, it includes Christian, Jewish, and Muslim publications. Corresponds to *Religious and Theological Abstracts.*

There are several CD-ROMs that contain the complete text of the Bible. For example, *CDWord* contains the text of four editions of the Bible (King James, New American Standard, New International, and Revised Standard), plus the Bible in Greek, and study aids such as dictionaries and *Harper's Bible Commentary. Master Search Bible* (Tri-Star Publishing) is similar. The King James Version of the Bible is available on disc for Sony Data Discman. Franklin Electronic Publishing has three versions of the Bible available for its handheld reader: King James, New International, and Revised Standard.

The King James Version of the Bible is available online in full text with Dialog (File 297) and also through America Online and the Internet (see below).

Online Services

- *NewsNet* has the full text of such services as *Catholic News Service, Church News International, Episcopal News Service, Lutheran News Service,* and *Religious News Service Daily News Reports.*
- *America Online,* in its Ethics and Religion Forum, has the full text of the King James Version of the Bible, searchable by keyword. There are bulletin boards for many religious traditions, from Islam to Scientology, and software files that include Bible quizzes, an online Christian magazine, a sermon outliner, and church budgeting software.
- *Prodigy* has a religion bulletin board with lively conversation about Christianity, Islam, and several other faiths.
- *GEnie* has a Religion and Ethics RoundTable.
- *CompuServe* offers the Religion Forum.
- *The Internet* has many files for the religious researcher. Here is just a sample:

A complete King James Bible, with cross-references and lexicon. Access via: **ftp wuarchive.wustl.edu;** log in **anonymous; cd pub/bible.**

A translation of the Koran. Access via: **ftp quake.think.com;** log in **anonymous; cd pub/etext/koran.**

The Torah, Prophets, and Writings from the Torah in Hebrew is accompanied by other files. Access via: **ftp nic.funet.fi;** log in **anonymous; cd pub/doc/bible/hebrew.**

Buddha-L provides a means for those interested in Buddhist studies to exchange information. Access via: **LISTSERV@ULKYVM.LOUISVILLE .EDU.**

Christian Life is a mailing list for discussions on practical Christian life. Access via: **CHRISTIA%FINHUTC.BITNET@MITVMA.MIT.EDU.**

PERIODICALS

America. 1909–   . Weekly.
   Edited by Roman Catholics; topics are of wide interest.

Christian Century: An Ecumenical Magazine. 1908–   . Weekly.
   A nondenominational magazine, moderate to liberal in viewpoint. Publishes articles on ethical and social issues.

Christianity Today. 1956–   . Biweekly.
   Provides news of the evangelical Christian world and articles on current religious topics.

Commentary. 1945–   . Monthly.
   Published by the American Jewish Committee, presents discussion of Jewish concerns in the United States and abroad. The voice of moderate, rather than liberal, Jewish thought.

Commonweal. 1924–   . Biweekly.
   Reflects a liberal Roman Catholic perspective on contemporary issues.

Judaism: A Quarterly Journal of Jewish Life and Thought. 1952–   . Quarterly.
   For the general reader as well as the scholar.

Sojourners. 1971–   . 11 times/year.
   Combines biblical perspective with an interest in current political and social issues.

Tikkun: A Bimonthly Critique of Politics, Culture, and Society. 1986–   . Bimonthly.

Contains articles, poetry, and fiction. Devotes a portion of each issue to contemporary Jewish concerns.

To find denominational periodicals, consult the *Yearbook of American and Canadian Churches* (above).

Among the journals in religious studies that publish historical and theological scholarship are:

Journal of the American Academy of Religion. 1933–   . Quarterly.
Scholarly articles on a variety of theological topics. Includes a lengthy book review section.

Religious Studies Review. 1975–   . Quarterly.
Published by the Council of Societies for the Study of Religion, this journal includes review articles that discuss a series of recent books or articles on a single topic. Also publishes lengthy book reviews, though most are not of current books.

To identify other scholarly religious studies journals, consult:

Religious Periodicals of the United States: Academic and Scholarly Journals. Edited by Charles H. Lippy. Greenwood, 1986.
Profiles more than 100 periodicals of diverse religious orientations.

GOVERNMENT PUBLICATIONS   Although strict application of the First Amendment precludes government publication in the area of religion, census reports from 1850 through 1936 included a great deal of information about religious affiliation and religious organizations. Some of those figures are given in summary form in: *Historical Statistics of the United States.* 2 vols. Bureau of the Census, 1975.

In the current era, all this information must be gathered independently of government information sources. In lieu of official government statistics, two publications provide vital statistics and information about institutional religion: *Yearbook of American and Canadian Churches* and *The People's Religion* (see above under Statistics).

ASSOCIATIONS   The Council of Societies for the Study of Religion
Mercer University
Macon, GA 31207
(912) 741-2376
The Council is a federation of learned societies in religious studies. It currently includes the American Society of Church History, American Society of Missiology, Association of Professors and Researchers in Religious

Education, Association for the Sociology of Religion, Catholic Biblical Association, Catholic Theological Society of America, College Theology Society, Institute of Religion in an Age of Science, National Association of Baptist Professors of Religion, North American Association for the Study of Religion, and Society of Christian Ethics.

American Academy of Religion
Department of Religion
501 Hall of Languages
Syracuse University
Syracuse, NY 13244
(315) 443-3861
AAR is the professional society of religious studies scholars and teachers; it is affiliated with the American Council of Learned Societies.

Society for the Scientific Study of Religion
Purdue University
Pierce Hall No. 193
West Lafayette, IN 47907
(317) 494-6286

To find other organizations, consult:

Directory of Religious Organizations in the United States. By J. Gordon Melton. Gale, 1992.
Brief descriptions of more than 1,600 religious organizations. Includes statement of purpose, address, founding date, membership, and publications.

New Religious Movements Research Collection
Graduate Theological Union Library
2400 Ridge Road
Berkeley, CA 94709
(510) 649-2500
Movements new to America since 1960 and unorthodox movements resurgent since 1960. Has materials on Asian religions in the United States, the occult, feminist spirituality, etc.

SPECIAL LIBRARIES/
LIBRARY
COLLECTIONS

Union Theological Seminary Library
3041 Broadway
New York, NY 10027
(212) 662-7100
One of the largest theological collections in the United States.

Jewish Division
New York Public Library
5th Avenue and 42d Street
New York, NY 10018
(212) 930-0601
Materials on Judaism in all languages from earliest times to date. Catalog in print as *Dictionary Catalog of the Jewish Collection.* 14 vols. G. K. Hall, 1960. *Supplement.* 8 vols. G. K. Hall, 1975.

Jesuit-Krauss-McCormick Library
1100 E. 55th Street
Chicago, IL 60615
(312) 753-0700
Large collection resulting from the merger of Jesuit, Lutheran, and Presbyterian seminary libraries.

The American Theological Library Association recently began an important project, the North American Theology Inventory, in which all accredited theological libraries are evaluating their holdings, determining the level of their collections in various areas. When completed, it will provide an important research tool for the field of religious studies.

Two sources offer some assistance in locating collections in religion and theology:

Association of Theological Schools in the U.S. and Canada Directory. Annual.
Lists accredited theological institutions and their libraries.

Women Religious History Sources: A Guide to Repositories in the United States. Edited by Evangeline Thomas and others. Bowker, 1983.
This specialized resource describes library collections related to monasticism and religious orders for women.

Many of the most specialized collections of materials in religious studies are located in small, religiously affiliated colleges or in seminaries. Religious studies researchers need to use OCLC and other national databases to locate the resources they need.

LC SUBJECT HEADINGS   Catalogers use two major headings to designate works in religion: Religion and Religious life and customs. These terms are used as subdivisions under geographical locations, historical periods, ethnic groups, types of institution, names of corporate bodies or of individuals. For example:
Appalachian region, Southern—Religious life and customs
Afro-Americans—Religion—Bibliography

Japan—Religious life and customs

Bryan, William Jennings—Religion

For books about individual religions or denominations, use the specific name of the group, for example:

Afro-American Methodists—Periodicals

Christianity—Morocco

Methodists in the U.S.—Hymns

Presbyterians—Illinois—History

Some of the standard subheadings used with specific faiths include Doctrines, Prayer books and devotions, Rituals, and Study and Teaching. For example:

Islam—Doctrines

Buddhism—Prayer books and devotions

Hinduism—Rituals

There are subject headings for sacred books, for example:

Koran

Prior to 1981 it was common to add "moral and religious aspects" to particular subject headings, but three new subheadings have now been added: Religious aspects; Mythology; Moral and ethical aspects. For example:

Euthanasia—Religious aspects

Cinema—Moral and ethical aspects

Corn—Mythology

American Theological Library Association

820 Church Street, Third Floor

Evanston, IL 60201

(708) 869-7788

ATLA publishes a newsletter that gives invaluable information about collection development, preservation and microfilming projects, and personnel changes in theological libraries.

SOURCES OF EXPERT ADVICE

41

RETIREMENT/ AGING

See also: General Reference Sources, Consumer Information, Health and Medicine, Hobbies, Travel

Advancing age may dictate certain changes in lifestyle, but it also brings opportunities not always available to the nonretired worker: a new career, a business, hobbies, travel, study programs, scholarly projects.

Personal research can help direct your choices, as well as provide information on aging itself and its impact on the individual and on society. For the first time in our nation's history, there are as many people over 65 as there are teenagers.

Whether you have special interests in the aging, have just begun your preretirement planning, or have already received your gold watch, the following resources may help to guide your research:

GENERAL SOURCES OF INFORMATION

Aging with Style and Savvy: Books and Films on Challenges Facing Adults of All Ages. By Denise Perry Donavin. American Library Association, 1990.

A list of books and films covering all aspects of aging, from planning to health to poetry and fiction.

A Consumer's Guide to Aging. By David H. Solomon and others. Johns Hopkins University Press, 1992.

Written by a team of physicians and social workers, this book discusses fitness, emotional health, sex and intimacy, and other issues for people over 50. Each chapter concludes with a list of resources for further information.

The Henry Holt Retirement Sourcebook. By Wilbur Cross. Holt, 1993.

This "information guide for planning and managing your affairs" comes with a list of 500 organizations that have useful programs and publications.

Older Americans Sourcebook. Edited by Ronald Manheimer. Gale, 1993.

   Broad subject chapters cover a wide range of topics on aging and list information resources and support groups.

The Only Retirement Guide You'll Ever Need. By Kathryn and Ross Petras. Poseidon Press, 1991.
   Information on finances, estate planning, housing, health, and active retirement, with sources for additional information.

Over Fifty: The Resource Book for the Better Half of Your Life. By Tom and Nancy Biracree. HarperCollins, 1991.
   Advice and sources of further information on finances, health care, recreation, housing, and social life.

The Retirement Sourcebook: Your Complete Guide to Health, Leisure, and Consumer Information. By Edward L. Palder. Woodbine House, 1989.
   Lists hotlines, books, free or inexpensive brochures, and other sources of information on such topics as travel, volunteering, con artists, computers, and condominium living.

Senior Citizens Services: How to Find and Contact 21,000 Providers. 4 vols. Edited by Charles B. Montney. Gale, 1993.
   In four regional volumes, this title lists state and area agencies on aging, plus private sector agencies that provide adult day care, health screening, legal assistance, and more.

Choices and Challenges: An Older Adult Reference Series. ABC-Clio.
   This series explains the options available to today's older person. Part II of each volume lists associations, self-help groups, books, periodicals, government publications, videotapes, and databases appropriate to the topic. Titles available include:

Healthy Aging. By Robin Mockenhaupt and Kathleen Nelson Boyle. 1992.
Housing Options and Services for Older Adults. By Ann E. Gillespie and Katrinka Smith Sloan. 1990.
Legal Issues and Older Adults. By Linda Josephson Millman. 1992.
Making End-of-Life Decisions. By Lee E. Norrgard and Jo DeMars. 1992.
Mental Health Problems and Older Adults. By Gregory A. Hinrichsen. 1990.
Older Workers. By Sara E. Rix. 1990.
Paying for Health Care After 65. By Elizabeth Vierck. 1990.
Travel and Older Adults. By Allison St. Clair. 1991.
Volunteerism and Older Adults. By Mary K. Kouri. 1990.

Fact Book on Aging. By Elizabeth Vierck. ABC-Clio, 1990.
Statistical Handbook on Aging Americans. By Frank L. Schick. Oryx Press, 1986.
Two sources of statistics on older Americans.

ELECTRONIC SOURCES

AgeLine. (Online) 1978–   . Updated monthly.
Maintained by the American Association of Retired Persons, this database lists publications on the social, psychological, and economic aspects of middle age and aging. It covers retirement, employment, housing, leisure, and consumer aspects. Available on Dialog (File 163), Knowledge Index, BRS, and BRS/AfterDark.

SeniorNet.
A nonprofit network for people 55 or older who are interested in learning about computers. It includes bulletin boards on topics ranging from retirement to cooking to grandparenting. The Community Center is SeniorNet's live chat area. The Computer Learning Center is a message board on which questions can be asked about computers. In the Showcase and Exchange area, members share files or projects. The *SeniorNet Sourcebook* is a compilation of creative computer projects developed by members. Seniors who don't own computers can visit one of the fifty-three SeniorNet Learning Centers around the country and use the network there. It can also be accessed through America Online or directly through SeniorNet. Memberships are currently $25, or $35 for couples. For more information or for locations of SeniorNet Learning Centers, contact SeniorNet, 399 Arguello Blvd., San Francisco, CA 94118; (415) 750-5030.

PERIODICALS

Aging. 1951–   . Quarterly.
Published by the U.S. Administration on Aging, this publication is aimed at geriatric practitioners, service providers, and older people themselves. In a newsmagazine format, it provides information on innovative community programs for seniors.

Modern Maturity. 1958–   . Bimonthly.
This feature magazine comes with a membership in the American Association of Retired Persons.

New Choices for the Best Years. 1960–   . 10 times/year.
Formerly *Retirement Living.* Upscale popular magazine on retirement living and planning. Covers travel, finances, health, and lifestyles.

Perspectives on Aging. 1972–   . Bimonthly.
Published by the National Council on the Aging, this newsmagazine for

professionals who work with the elderly will be of interest to older people, too.

Abstracts in Social Gerontology: Current Literature on Aging. Sage Publications, 1990–   . Quarterly.

Supersedes the National Council on the Aging's *Current Literature on Aging.* Indexes periodical articles on medical issues, middle age, economic issues, and work and retirement.

Funerals: A Consumer Guide. Federal Trade Commission, 1992.
Guide to Choosing a Nursing Home. Health Care Financing Administration, 1992.
Guide to Health Insurance for People with Medicare. Health Care Financing Administration, 1992. Free.
Innovative Developments in Aging: Area Agencies on Aging: A Directory. 1982.
Medicare and Advance Directives. Health Care Financing Administration, 1992. Free. Explains how to set up a living will or durable power of attorney.
Reverse Mortgages. Federal Trade Commission, 1991.
Staying Independent: Planning for Financial Independence in Later Life. Department of Agriculture, 1990.
Understanding Social Security. Social Security Administration, 1992.

See also the following Government Printing Office *Subject Bibliographies:*
  #39—Aging
  #285—Retirement
  #165—Social Security

The first three agencies are part of the Department of Health and Human Services.

Social Security Administration
6401 Security Blvd.
Baltimore, MD 21235
(410) 965-1234
Administers national program of contributory social insurance and medical care for retirees (Medicare).

Administration on Aging
330 Independence Ave. SW
Washington, DC 20201
(202) 619-0556
Develops plans and programs to promote the welfare of older persons; makes grants to states for community programs.

National Institute on Aging
National Institutes of Health
9000 Rockville Pike
Bethesda, MD 20892
(301) 496-5345
Conducts and supports research on the aging process.

Senior Community Service Employment Program
Department of Labor
200 Constitution Ave. NW
Washington, DC 20210
(202) 535-0500
Subsidizes part-time job opportunities in community service activities for low-income persons 55 and older. Money is distributed through state programs.

ACTION
1100 Vermont Ave. NW
Washington, DC 20525
(202) 606-4855
ACTION sponsors three programs for older people. Foster Grandparents pays low-income persons 60 and older to serve in schools, hospitals, day care centers, children's homes, and other community institutions. Retired Senior Volunteers provides community service opportunities for people over 60. The Senior Companion Program enables low-income people to provide volunteer services to other elderly.

ASSOCIATIONS

American Association of Retired Persons
601 E St. NW
Washington, DC 20049
(202) 434-2277
With more than 30,000,000 members, this organization is a powerful political force. Members are entitled to publications, discounts, group health insurance, and pharmacy benefits. The AARP's Institute for Lifetime Learning has affiliates nationwide that provide educational opportunities on the topics of aging and retirement.

Elderhostel
80 Boylston St., Suite 400
Boston, MA 02116
(617) 426-7788 or (800) 733-9753
For domestic and foreign travel-study opportunities for seniors.

Gray Panthers
1424 16th St. NW
Washington, DC 20036
(202) 387-3111
Activist group that combats ageism. Publishes *Gray Panther Network*.

National Council of Senior Citizens
1331 F St. NW
Washington, DC 20004
(202) 347-8800
Federation of local autonomous clubs for seniors that carry out educational and action projects.

National Council on the Aging
409 Third St. SW
Washington, DC 20024
(202) 479-6665
This research organization provides a referral and reference service; has a large publications program with inexpensive materials.

Pension Rights Center
918 16th St. NW
Washington, DC 20006
(202) 296-3776
Serves as an information clearinghouse concerned with pension rights.

LIBRARIES

National Gerontology Resource Center
American Association of Retired Persons
601 E St. NW
Washington, DC 20049
(202) 434-2277

Institute of Gerontology Library
University of Michigan
300 N. Ingalls St.
Ann Arbor, MI 48109
(313) 665-1126
Large collection of unpublished research papers, and newsletters from associations for the elderly and centers on aging.

Policy Center on Aging
Brandeis University
Heller Graduate School
Waltham, MA 02254
(617) 736-3874
Issues publications in the area of retirement income adequacy, long-term health care, aging and mental health, and other topics.

Ethel Percy Andrus Gerontology Center
University of Southern California
University Park—MC 0191
Los Angeles, CA 90089-0191
(213) 740-6060
Publications and conferences on the biological, behavioral, social, and environmental aspects of aging.

LC SUBJECT HEADINGS

Afro-American aged
Age discrimination in employment
Aged—Abuse of
Aged—Economic conditions
Aged—Government policy
Aged—Institutional care
Aged—Long-term care
Aged—Political activity
Aged—Recreation
Aged—Respite care
Aged—Travel
Aged as authors
Aged as consumers
Aged automobile drivers
Aged women

Aging (used primarily for biological and physiological aspects; e.g., Aging—Nutritional aspects)
Architecture and the aged
Day care centers for the aged
Early retirement
Frail elderly
Gerontology
Life care communities
Pain in old age
Pensions
Physical fitness for the aged
Retirement, Places of
Retirement communities
Retirement income
Social security

42

SCIENCE
AND
TECHNOLOGY

See also: General Reference Sources, Agriculture, The Environment, Health and Medicine

To do research in science requires learning the highly technical language that makes a great deal of scientific information inaccessible to the layperson. But it is possible to find good, well-written science materials that intelligent laypeople can understand. The emphasis in this chapter is on resources that can be used by nonscientists.

Recent years have seen the publication of several stimulating books that explain science to the general reader. For example, *Chaos: Making a New Science* by James Gleick (Penguin, 1988) is a first-rate, believable introduction to a complex scientific concept. *The Double Helix: A Personal Account of the Discovery of the Structure of DNA* by James D. Watson (Athenaeum, 1968) is a fascinating account that describes the accomplishments and the frustrations of Nobel Prize-level scientists. Another recent popular science book is *A Brief History of Time: From the Big Bang to Black Holes* by Stephen Hawking (Bantam, 1988).

Science is usually a collaborative effort. It is also international. Research crosses national boundaries. The diffuse nature of science means that the literature is diffuse as well. The following sources have been chosen to help the layperson approach the field.

Information Sources in Science and Technology. By C. D. Hurt. Libraries Unlimited, 1993.

The strength of this work is that it is selective and makes critical judgments on specific titles, giving the reader an informed choice on whether to seek further. Covers seventeen major disciplines, such as chemistry, geology, and medicine, as well as general titles.

GENERAL
REFERENCE
SOURCES

Guides to the
Literature

Science and Technology Information Sourcebook. By H. Robert Malinowky. Oryx, 1994.

An annotated bibliography of print and electronic reference tools arranged by major disciplines: science, engineering, medicine, and agriculture. Introductory essays discuss channels of sci-tech communication and new sources of information.

Scientific and Technical Information Sources. 2d ed. By Chen Ching-Chen. MIT Press, 1987.

More inclusive than Hurt but lacks critical annotations; Chen only describes the works listed. Depending on the use the researcher wishes to make of general guides, Chen gives better universal coverage; Hurt gives better selective coverage.

Using Science and Technology Information Sources. By Ellis Mount and Beatrice Kovacs. Oryx Press, 1991.

An instructional guide to the complex array of sci-tech materials.

Dictionaries   One of the difficulties in working with science is the technical language, so a good scientific dictionary is of critical importance.

Van Nostrand's Scientific Encyclopedia. 2 vols. 7th ed. Edited by Douglas M. Considine and Glenn D. Considine. Van Nostrand Reinhold, 1989.

This is the classic in the field. Articles stress the practical when possible and cover a broad spectrum of topics, from math to medicine. Includes numerous illustrations and charts.

McGraw-Hill Dictionary of Scientific and Technical Terms. 4th ed. Edited by Sybil Parker. McGraw-Hill, 1989.

Provides definitions for more than 100,000 terms in all areas of science and technology. Available on CD-ROM (see below).

Academic Press Dictionary of Science and Technology. Edited by Christopher Morris. Academic Press, 1992.

The newest dictionary in this field, it is also the most comprehensive, with more than 130,000 entries. Covers 124 fields, from acoustical engineering to zoology. Includes brief biographies of scientists.

Hammond Barnhart Dictionary of Science. By Robert K. Barnhart with Sol Steinmetz. Hammond, 1986.

For those who may find the previous three titles too technical, this is an excellent science dictionary. It includes far fewer words (15,000), but they are defined in terms laypeople can understand. Also published as the *American Heritage Dictionary of Science* (Houghton Mifflin).

The Facts On File Dictionary of Science. 1986.
The Facts On File Dictionary of Biology. Rev. ed. 1988.
The Facts On File Dictionary of Botany. 1984.
The Facts On File Dictionary of Chemistry. Rev. ed. 1988.
The Facts On File Dictionary of Geology and Geophysics. 1987.
The Facts On File Dictionary of Mathematics. Rev. ed. 1988.
The Facts On File Dictionary of Physics. Rev. ed. 1988.

This series of dictionaries is aimed at the student and layperson. Each contains from 2,000 to 7,000 clear definitions.

McGraw-Hill Encyclopedia of Science and Technology. 20 vols. 7th ed. McGraw-Hill, 1992.

This unique multivolume and general-purpose scientific encyclopedia offers up-to-date, authoritative, and comprehensive coverage of all disciplines in science and technology. More than 13,000 tables, charts, drawings, and photographs help make concepts clear. Some articles require advanced mathematical skills for complete comprehension. Not for the beginner, this set is useful for those with some science background to be released on CD-ROM in 1994. Also available in a one-volume concise version. Several spin-off titles are available, e.g., *McGraw-Hill Encyclopedia of Geological Sciences.*

Encyclopedia of Earth System Science. 4 vols. Edited by William A. Nierenberg. Academic Press, 1991.
Encyclopedia of Human Biology. 8 vols. Edited by Renato Dulbecco. Academic Press, 1991.
Encyclopedia of Microbiology. 4 vols. Edited by Joshua Lederberg. Academic Press, 1992.
Encyclopedia of Physical Science and Technology. 18 vols. 2d ed. Edited by Robert A. Meyers. Academic Press, 1992.

These specialized Academic Press encyclopedias are more detailed and more technical in approach than the McGraw-Hill set. Excellent for college science majors and people with a science background.

Handbooks containing formulas and algorithms are important to scientists and may be helpful to some laypeople who are doing research in science and are fairly knowledgeable. These classic handbooks should be in most libraries:

CRC Handbook of Chemistry and Physics. CRC Press. Annual.

Tables, charts, and formulas make up most of this book, which scientists use regularly. It may be difficult for the nonscientist despite explanatory material and references. Also available in a smaller, student edition.

Encyclopedias

Handbooks

American Institute of Physics Handbook. 3d ed. McGraw-Hill, 1972.

Where the *CRC Handbook* is comprehensive, the *AIP Handbook* is selective and therefore possibly quicker to use. Also a classic in the field, this handbook contains formulas and tables used in general science as well as, specifically, in physics.

Bibliographies

Core List of Books and Journals in Science and Technology. By Russell H. Powell and James R. Powell, Jr. Oryx Press, 1987.

Lists scholarly books and journals in English for nine disciplines, from agriculture to physics. There is a separate chapter on reference materials.

LC Science Tracer Bullets. Library of Congress, 1972–   .

More than 200 of these brief bibliographies on topics of current interest in science and technology, such as the brain, dolphins, earthquakes and earthquake engineering, and Japanese technology, are available free from the Library of Congress. A typical list notes important books and journal articles, dictionaries and encyclopedias, indexes and abstracts, government publications, and subject headings under which books can be found in library catalogs. Order these bibliographies from the Library of Congress Science and Technology Division, Independence Avenue at First Street SE, Washington, DC 20540, or call (202) 707-5664. The most recent Tracer Bullets are available online through America Online and on the Internet: **telnet marvel.loc.gov.** Log in **marvel.**

PERIODICALS

Discover. 1980–   . Monthly.

This attractively illustrated magazine has popular articles on all areas of science, including medicine. For all levels of readership.

Natural History. 1900–   . Monthly.

Published by the American Museum of Natural History, this magazine has articles on biology and natural and earth sciences accompanied by beautiful photographs. The popular science writer Stephen Jay Gould has a column here.

Nature. 1869–   . Weekly.

This is a British publication, but the focus is international. While *Science* (below) has an international focus for its research reports, *Nature* has better coverage of the international science policy scene. Either of these titles will give the casual or new reader in science a sense of where science is moving and the forces that drive it.

Science. 1880–   . Weekly.

Published by the American Association for the Advancement of Science

(AAAS) and used by scientists and nonscientists alike. It is a combination of opinion, letters, news of general science, and research reports. It is especially good for helping the reader to keep up with national trends and issues in science policy. The research reports may be beyond the initial grasp of the casual reader of science materials. Available online with BRS.

Science News. 1921–   . Weekly.
    Aimed at the layperson, this well-illustrated magazine has short articles that are easy to read but always well documented. Also contains reviews of new books.

Scientific American. 1845–   . Monthly.
    An excellent general-purpose science journal with articles that are usually accessible to the general public. There is also a news and comment section that will give the reader some indication of the hot points in general science.

Mammals: A Multimedia Encyclopedia. (CD-ROM) National Geographic.
    Features text, range maps, vital statistics, and 700 color images of mammals.

ELECTRONIC SOURCES

McGraw-Hill Science and Technical Reference Set. (CD-ROM) Release 2.0. McGraw-Hill, 1992.
    Contains the text of the one-volume *McGraw-Hill Concise Encyclopedia of Science and Technology,* 2d ed., and the *McGraw-Hill Dictionary of Scientific and Technical Terms,* 4th ed.

SciTech Reference Plus. (CD-ROM) Bowker. Annual.
    Contains the full text of *American Men and Women of Science* (a biographical directory), *Directory of American Research and Technology, Corporate Technology Directory,* and the science and technology books and periodicals from *Books in Print* and *Ulrich's International Periodicals Directory.*

General Science Index. (CD-ROM) H. W. Wilson, 1984–   . Monthly.
    Designed specifically for students and nonspecialists, this is an index to 140 science periodicals. Unlike *Applied Science and Technology Index* (below), it is less focused on applications of science. Some of the subjects covered include astronomy, chemistry, earth science, mathematics, medicine and health, oceanography, and physics. Also available on CD-ROM with abstracts as *Wilson General Science Abstracts. General Science Index* is available online via Wilsonline, 1984–   , and OCLC FirstSearch, and in print, 1978–   .

Applied Science & Technology Index. (CD-ROM) H. W. Wilson, 1983–   .
Monthly.

Indexes 391 journals in such fields as chemistry, computer technology, civil, electrical, and mechanical engineering, geology, meteorology, plastics, solid state technology, and telecommunications. Available on CD-ROM with abstracts as *Wilson Applied Science & Technology Abstracts.* Also online with Wilsonline, 1983–   ; in print 1958–   , updated monthly.

Biological & Agricultural Index. (CD-ROM) H. W. Wilson, 1983–   .
Monthly.

Indexes 255 key periodicals in the life sciences and agriculture. Covers such topics as biochemistry, biotechnology, botany, entomology, genetics, microbiology, and zoology. Also online from OCLC FirstSearch and Wilsonline, 1983–   , and in print, 1964–   . Preceded by *Agricultural Index,* 1919–64.

Science Citation Index Compact CD-ROM Edition. Institute for Scientific Information, 1980–   . Quarterly.

This is the only index with extensive coverage of the international scholarly literature from 3,200 journals from all branches of science. Its major contribution is that it allows tracking of citations from one scientist to another. For the purposes of general science, it may be most often used to locate material by a particular author or in a specific subject area. Also available on CD-ROM with abstracts. Because of the huge size of this database (one CD-ROM holds only a year's worth of *SCI*), libraries may own only the most recent years. Available online as SCISEARCH from Dialog (File 434) and ORBIT, 1974–   , and in print, 1955–   , semimonthly. The format of the print set is initially intimidating, but time spent learning to use this work is very well spent.

Abstracts and Indexes in Science and Technology: A Descriptive Guide. 2d ed. By Dolores B. Owen. Scarecrow, 1985.

This is a convenient way to determine the coverage and the level of sophistication of the many specialized indexes, such as *Chemical Abstracts* and *Engineering Index,* that are not covered in this chapter.

Other Databases

Hundreds of online databases are available in science, far too many to list here. Some of them are large general files such as Chemical Abstracts or Biosis Previews (biology). Others reflect the narrow specializations of science, for example, from Dialog:

Aluminum Industry Abstracts (File 33)—Aluminum technology.
Analytical Abstracts (File 305)—All aspects of analytical chemistry.

Ceramic Abstracts (File 335)—Scientific and engineering literature on ceramics.

Engineered Materials Abstracts (File 293)—Science of polymers, ceramics, and composite materials.

Kirk-Othmer Online (File 302)—Text of the *Kirk-Othmer Encyclopedia of Chemical Technology.*

Mathsci (File 239)—World's mathematical research literature.

Metadex (File 32)—International literature on metallurgy.

Directory of Periodicals Online: Science and Technology. Globe and Mail, 1990–   .

List of periodicals whose full text is available online.

The backbone of the Internet is the National Science Foundation's NSFNET, which was established to enable scientists to access the regional supercomputers. Numerous databases of interest to scientists are available on the Internet, such as the Bionic Sequence Analysis Bibliography, and GenBank, a catalog of all published nucleic acid sequences. Many of the science files found on the Internet are too esoteric for the layperson, but there are some files for the nonspecialist, including these:

Internet

Periodic Table of Elements. Access via **University of Minnesota Gopher/ Libraries/Reference Works.**

Science and Technology Information Service provides information about programs sponsored by the National Science Foundation. The NSF Bulletin, Guide to Programs, press releases, and a listing of awards are available. Access via: **telnet stis.nsf.gov;** log in **public NSF Gopher.**

Network Sources for Meteorology and Weather describes how this type of data may be found on the Internet. Search here to find sources for weather maps, weather reports, climatological studies. Access via: **ftp bears.ucsb.edu;** log in **anonymous; cd pub/windsurf, get net-weather.**

The first two bulletin boards list other bulletin boards on their respective topics:

Bulletin Boards

Engineering-Related BBS   Computer Plumber   **(319) 337-6723**
Astronomy/Space BBS   Starbase III   **(209) 432-2487**
Geological Survey BBS, Department of the Interior
    (9600 bps). Files on mapping and earth science.   **(703) 648-4168**
NASA Headquarters Information Technology Center
    BBS Current information on computer applica-
    tions.   **(202) 453-9008**

Prodigy, in its Science Center, has articles from NOVA, WGBH's television series, and from *National Geographic.* Other features provide science news and a science bulletin board.

America Online hosts a section from the National Space Society, an organization of laypeople interested in space and space exploration. It contains a bulletin board, files from the NSS magazine, *Ad Astra,* and files to download.

GOVERNMENT AGENCIES

National Aeronautics and Space Administration
600 Independence Ave. SW
Washington, DC 20546
(202) 453-1000
Conducts research for solutions to problems of flight, conducts explorations of space, and arranges for the most effective use of U.S. scientific and engineering resources. Manages such field installations as the Jet Propulsion Lab in Pasadena, California, the Lyndon B. Johnson Space Center in Houston, and the John F. Kennedy Space Center in Florida. Issues many popular publications, including charts and posters.

National Science Foundation
1800 G St. NW
Washington, DC 20550
(202) 357-5000
Promotes science and technology through research and education. Makes grants for research and postdoctoral fellowships. Also awards money for science teaching and curriculum development at the secondary school level.

Smithsonian Institution
1000 Jefferson Dr. SW
Washington, DC 20560
(202) 357-1300
Administers many museums, including the National Air and Space Museum and the National Museum of Natural History in Washington, D.C. Also has libraries to support these museums and their research programs. Other facilities include the Smith Astrophysical Observatory and the Tropical Research Institute.

GOVERNMENT PUBLICATIONS

The U.S. government has a deep and continuing investment in science and technology. Agencies such as the National Science Foundation fund extensive scientific research. Accordingly, the government is a major producer of publications that examine and describe aspects of science and technology.

Government Reports Announcement and Index. National Technical Information Service, 1946– . Biweekly.

This title contains lists of reports available from the science and technology clearinghouse for the federal government, the National Technical Information Service (NTIS). It is one of the primary tools for scientists and engineers. Available on CD-ROM from SilverPlatter, 1983– , and online with Dialog (File 6) and Knowledge Index (GOVE2), 1964– . Some larger libraries are also NTIS depositories, which means that they will have not only the index but also copies of the reports.

NTIS adds an average of 1,200 titles to its collection every week. Researchers who need to stay abreast of what is being published can subscribe to one of eighty-five *NTIS Alerts.* Twice a month, they summarize the latest government-sponsored projects and their findings on topics such as food technology, human factors engineering, and environmental health and safety. Customized *Alerts* are also available. Call (703) 487-4650 and request catalog PR-797.

Beehives of Invention: Edison and His Laboratories. Department of the Interior, 1973.
A biography of the man who harnessed electricity.

Exobiology in Earth Orbit. NASA, 1989.
Explains scientific experiments of exobiology—biological processes occurring in space—to be carried out in earth-orbiting spacecraft.

Handbook of Mathematical Functions with Formulas, Graphs, and Mathematical Tables. National Bureau of Standards, 1981.

Inside the Cell. National Institutes of Health, 1990.

Poisonous Snakes of Europe. Defense Intelligence Agency, 1986.

Questions About the Oceans. Naval Oceanographic Office, 1985.
One hundred questions and answers about marine life, the oceans' uses, and other interesting information.

Sentinels in the Sky: Weather Satellites. NASA, 1988.

SETI: Search for Extraterrestrial Intelligence. NASA, 1990.

See *LC Science Tracer Bullets* above.

See also the following *Subject Bibliographies* from the Government Printing Office:

#115—Astronomy and Astrophysics
#200—Atomic Energy and Nuclear Power
#51—Computers and Data Processing
#160—Earth Sciences
#53—Electricity and Electronics
#308—Engineering
#34—Insects
#70—Mammals and Reptiles
#24—Mathematics
#151—Minerals and Mining
#99—Minerals Yearbooks
#222—NASA Educational Publications
#257—NASA Scientific and Technical Publications
#32—Oceanography
#48—Radiation and Radioactivity
#243—Science Experiments and Projects
#297—Space, Rockets and Satellites
#296—Telecommunications
#234—Weather

ASSOCIATIONS

The American Association for the Advancement of Science
1333 H Street NW
Washington, DC 20005
(202) 326-6400

Founded in 1848, AAAS aims to increase public understanding and appreciation of the importance and promise of science. Represents all areas of science, works on public policy issues and science education. AAAS is the publisher of *Science* (see above) and *Science Books and Films,* a newsletter listing new materials for adults and children.

National Academy of Sciences
2101 Constitution Ave. NW
Washington, DC 20418
(202) 334-2138

Scientists and engineers are elected to membership in this prestigious honorary organization. Its National Research Council has 1,000 study committees that serve as official advisers to the federal government on science and technology.

New York Academy of Sciences
2 E. 63d St.
New York, NY 10021
(212) 838-0230

Educates the public on scientific issues, promotes the role of science in human welfare. Publishes *The Sciences,* a useful journal for the educated layperson.

All science disciplines have their own associations, such as the American Chemical Society and the American Institute of Physics. Membership usually is limited to scientists in the specific field.

One of the best ways to become involved in science is to join a local science club. Institutions of higher education will often sponsor such groups. Local public libraries should be a source of information on these clubs.

Most college and university libraries have good collections in basic science. Major public libraries should also have collections adequate to begin most research. The libraries listed here have unusally large collections:

LIBRARIES

Linda Hall Library
5109 Cherry St.
Kansas City, MO 64110
(816) 363-4600
Privately endowed library with comprehensive collections in science, except clinical medicine.

Science and Technology Division
Library of Congress
Independence Ave. at First St. SE
Washington, DC 20540
(202) 707-5000
One of the world's major collections of technical report literature. Also issues *LC Science Tracer Bullets* (see above).

Natural history	Science—Information Services	**LC SUBJECT**
Science	Science—Nomenclature	**HEADINGS**
Science—Abstracts	Science—Periodicals	
Science—Bibliography	Science—Social Aspects	
Science—Dictionaries	Science—Study and Teaching	
Science—Experiments	Science—Terminology	
Science—History		

These subheadings can also be used with specific science disciplines, e.g., Chemistry—Dictionaries or Physics—Periodicals.

There are subject headings for both broad and narrow disciplines in science. For example:

Life sciences
Biology
Zoology
Microbiology
Bacteriology

Science, Renaissance
Science and civilization
Science and industry
Science and law
Science and state
Science and the humanities
Science news
Scientific apparatus and instruments
Scientific literature

Scientists—Biography
Scientists—Directories
Scientists—United States
Scientists in government
Also for specific disciplines:
Chemists
Geologists
Ornithologists

The ability to search by keywords is often a feature of online catalogs and online databases. Because scientists usually give their books and journal articles literal titles that describe what the content is, this can be an effective way of searching. However, scientists occasionally use terminology from other disciplines. For example, in astronomy a black hole is defined as a collapsed star that had a mass so great that no light could escape. Looking for the term *black hole* in a broad science database might also turn up the use of the term in gastroenterology. A physician, reading an x-ray showing a perforation in the stomach or intestines of a patient, will see a black hole on the x-ray. The same terminology may be used in different areas of science for entirely different concepts. Within a disciplinary database, however, keywords will usually lead to the desired subject.

43

SELF-HELP/
PSYCHOLOGY

See also: *General Reference Sources, Health and Medicine*

The self-help concept is anything but new. "One's own hand is the surest and promptest help," said the seventeenth-century fabulist La Fontaine. Since the founding of Alcoholics Anonymous in 1935, however, self-help groups and activities have proliferated, as have books on various aspects of the subject. Though there is a great deal of information available for people with physical problems, the mental health self-help topics fall mainly within the field of psychology. This chapter, therefore, describes some of the general resources of that discipline and related fields in addition to what are commonly called self-help materials.

Psychology: A Guide to Reference and Information Sources. By Pam M. Baxter. Libraries Unlimited, 1993.

An annotated guide to reference sources in all areas of psychology, including educational and industrial psychology, consumer behavior, even parapsychology.

The Social Sciences: A Cross-Disciplinary Guide to Selected Sources. Edited by Nancy L. Herron. Libraries Unlimited, 1989.

An annotated listing of "best, most used" reference sources in the social sciences, including psychology. Both electronic and print sources are included, along with suggestions for search strategies.

Library Use: A Handbook for Psychology. 2d ed. By Jeffrey G. Reed and Pam M. Baxter. American Psychological Association, 1991.

Intended as an introduction to library research for undergraduates. Reed

**GENERAL
REFERENCE
SOURCES**

Guides

and Baxter present advice on defining a topic and using major print and electronic sources in psychology, including tests and measures and current awareness services.

A Guide to Information Sources for Social Work and the Human Services. By Henry N. Mendelsohn. Oryx, 1987.

Describes reference sources, including government publications, for historical and current information on social work and related disciplines. An annotated list of 1,200 social work and social welfare journals is included. Though Mendelsohn discusses online databases, this work was published before CD-ROM products were widely available.

Encyclopedias   *Encyclopedia of Alcoholism.* 2d ed. By Robert O'Brien and Morris Chafetz. Facts On File, 1991.

More than 600 entries provide information on alcohol and alcoholism and on related legislation, organizations, social and economic issues. The volume includes graphs and tables and references for further reading. Appendixes list periodicals, organizations, and state agencies dealing with alcohol issues.

Encyclopedia of Drug Abuse. 2d ed. By Robert O'Brien and others. Facts On File, 1992.

In dictionary format, this encyclopedia covers drug abuse "from its earliest recorded history to its current state as a major worldwide problem." Entries cover physical and psychological data on drugs and the impact of drug use and abuse on social institutions and customs. The book includes a dictionary of street language and a list of slang synonyms, figures on drug use and drug control laws, and lists of state agencies, international organizations, and major periodicals.

Encyclopedia of Phobias, Fears, and Anxieties. By Ronald M. Doctor and Ada P. Kahn. Facts On File, 1989.

Defines more than 2,000 psychological conditions and describes forms of psychotherapy and medication. Historical notes and information on prominent specialists are also included. Cross-references between technical and popular terms are provided. Many of the entries cite related books and journal articles. Other titles in this Facts On File series include *The Encyclopedia of Depression, The Encyclopedia of Schizophrenia and the Psychotic Disorders,* and *The Encyclopedia of Mental Health.*

Encyclopedia of Psychology. 4 vols. 2d ed. Edited by Raymond J. Corsini. Wiley, 1994.

Articles in this encyclopedia, which covers all major aspects of psychology, were written by prominent scholars and practitioners and directed to a lay audience. Volume 4 contains an extensive bibliography and subject and name indexes. Some libraries may have the abridged version, *Concise Encyclopedia of Psychology.*

The Columbia University College of Physicians and Surgeons Complete Home Guide to Mental Health. Edited by Frederic I. Kass, John M. Oldham, and Herbert Pardes. Holt, 1992.

    Clearly written articles prepared by more than fifty experts in the mental health field. Describes common problems and disorders of children, adolescents, and adults, and discusses treatment options. Also addresses the concerns of special groups, such as the elderly, women, and AIDS patients.

The Psychotherapy Handbook: The A-Z Guide to More than 250 Different Therapies in Use Today. Edited by Richie Herick. New American Library, 1980.

    The originator of each treatment or other authority in the field defines the therapy and discusses its history, technique, and applications. A bibliography accompanies each section.

Handbooks

Addictionary: A Primer of Recovery Terms and Concepts. By Jan R. Wilson and Judith A. Wilson. Simon & Schuster, 1992.

    An overview of twelve-step recovery programs for a broad variety of addictions: alcohol, work, gambling, etc. The entries include psychological concepts, specific substances, various recovery programs, and each of the twelve steps. Addresses and telephone numbers are given for all programs in the book.

The Alcohol/Drug Abuse Dictionary and Encyclopedia. By John J. Fay. Charles C. Thomas, 1988.

    Defines more than 1,400 terms and phrases, including both idioms and technical vocabulary. Appendixes include lists of street jargon, state agencies for alcohol and drug abuse control, drug poison information centers, and resource agencies, and a bibliography. A list matching generic and brand names of commonly abused substances is also included.

Dictionary of Behavioral Science. 2d ed. Compiled by Benjamin B. Wolman. Krieger, 1989.

    An authoritative, up-to-date source for accurate and concise definitions of some 20,000 terms in psychology and related sciences.

The Penguin Dictionary of Psychology. By Arthur S. Reber. Penguin, 1986.

    Covers psychology and related disciplines. Brief entries define both technical vocabulary and informal, colloquial terms.

Dictionaries

Whatever your concern, there is probably a self-help group or organization that deals with the problem. The directories below are listed in order of usefulness:

Directories   *Directory of National Helplines: A Guide to Toll-Free Public Service Numbers.* Pierian Press, 1993.

Information on more than 500 helplines for teenage runaways, battered wives, the disabled, etc. Also health and environmental helplines. Notes whether publications are available from the group. Access by subject as well as organization name.

Self-Help Sourcebook: Finding and Forming Mutual Aid Self-Help Groups. 3d ed. Self-Help Clearinghouse, Saint Clare's-Riverside Medical Center, 1990.

Lists toll-free helplines and clearinghouses around the world, arranged by topic. Also includes a chapter on how to start a self-help group.

Recovery Resourcebook. By Barbara Yoder. Simon & Schuster, 1990.

A comprehensive survey of self-help groups concerned with recovery from addictions, with extensive essays on various aspects of addictions and descriptions of the groups concerned with recovery. The volume also includes a bibliography and a list of professional treatment facilities.

Clearinghouse Directory: A Guide to Information Clearinghouses and Their Resources. Edited by Donna Batten. Gale, 1991.

Lists local self-help clearinghouses that provide reference and referral service to existing programs or assistance in starting a new self-help group. For each organization the directory gives address, telephone number, publications, and services.

Encyclopedia of Associations: National Organizations of the U.S. Gale. Annual.
Encyclopedia of Associations: Regional, State and Local Organizations. Gale. Biennial.

Standard directories owned by most libraries, also available online and on CD-ROM (see below). In the *Regional, State, and Local Organizations* set, each volume covers a geographic region. Local organizations and the local chapters of national organizations are arranged by state and city. Since many local organizations are run by volunteers and do not maintain offices, this source is not as inclusive as the national volumes are.

In locating a treatment center, the following directories will be useful:

The 100 Best Treatment Centers for Alcoholism and Drug Abuse. Avon Books, 1988.

A selective directory of centers recommended by professionals in the field of substance abuse treatment. An introductory chapter offers advice on selecting a treatment center. Entries in the directory include program information; admission policy; and statistics on number of beds, length of stay, number of staff, and cost. There is also a directory of resources and services and the names and addresses of specialists in the treatment of addiction.

Drug, Alcohol, and Other Addictions: A Directory of Treatment Centers and Prevention Programs Nationwide. 2d ed. Oryx, 1993.

A comprehensive directory to nearly 18,000 programs and facilities. Programs for treating behavioral addictions are included. Entries include address, phone number, and the name of a contact person. Occasionally other information is provided, such as treatment method, number of patients served, and principal source of funding.

For additional directories, see also the Government Publications section of this chapter.

Local telephone books can be very useful for those seeking self-help groups, hotline numbers, clearinghouses, etc. Local Yellow Pages include listings under such categories as Clinics, Alcoholism Information and Treatment Centers, Drug Abuse Addiction Information and Treatment, and Psychologists. The white pages, too, sometimes yield information under likely terms: Alcoholics, Overeaters, Depressives, etc.

ELECTRONIC SOURCES

Health Source. (CD-ROM) EBSCO, 1984–   . Bimonthly.

Indexes and abstracts 160 journals in the fields of drugs and alcohol, medical self-care, and other topics.

Social Sciences Index. (CD-ROM) H. W. Wilson, 1984–   . Monthly.

Indexes journals in psychology, psychiatry, social work, and other disciplines. *Wilson Social Sciences Abstracts* is an annotated version on CD-ROM. Also available online with Wilsonline, BRS, and FirstSearch, 1984–   , updated twice a week, and in print, updated quarterly, as *Social Sciences Index,* 1974–   (formerly *Social Sciences and Humanities Index,* 1965–74; *International Index,* 1907–65).

Social Science Source. (CD-ROM) EBSCO, 1984–   . Bimonthly.

Abstracts 353 journals in psychology and other social science disciplines. Also includes the full text of fifteen journals, including *Journal of General Psychology, Journal of Social Psychology,* and *Psychology Today.*

For a more comprehensive search of the scholarly literature, a number of databases are available. Depending on your particular interest, psychology, sociology, and social work databases can all be useful in examining psychological problems, substance abuse issues, and self-help techniques. Medical and education databases are also useful for examining certain aspects of these issues; see the chapters on Health and on Education for suggestions.

Alcohol and Alcohol Problems Science Database. (Online) U.S. National Institute on Alcohol Abuse and Alcoholism, 1972–   . Monthly.

Worldwide literature on alcohol research. Available on BRS and BRS/AfterDark.

Alcohol Information for Clinicians and Educators Database. (Online) Dartmouth Medical School, 1978–   . Quarterly.

Literature on alcohol use and abuse. Available on BRS and BRS/AfterDark.

DRUG INFO. (Online) University of Minnesota College of Pharmacy, 1968–   . Quarterly.

Available online on BRS (DRSC, DRUG) and BRS/AfterDark. Covers educational, sociological, medical, and psychological aspects of substance abuse, including alcohol abuse. Provides citations and abstracts for books, journal articles, instructional guides, conference papers, and other materials.

Encyclopedia of Associations CD-ROM. SilverPlatter. 3 times/year.

Gives access to information on some 87,000 organizations included in Gale's three directories: national; international; and regional, state, and local. Keyword, acronym, and subject searching are available. Also available online on Dialog (File 114) or on diskette.

Mental Health Abstracts. (Online) IFI/Plenum Data, 1969–   . Monthly.

Formerly *NIMH Data Base.* Available online on Dialog (File 86) and Knowledge Index. Covers all aspects of mental health and mental illness. The materials cited come from books, conference proceedings, and more than 1,200 journals. Nonprint materials are also included.

National Directory of Treatment and Prevention Programs. (Online)

Available from Human Relations Information Network. Information on 19,000 programs for addictions.

PsycLIT. (CD-ROM) SilverPlatter, 1974–   . Quarterly.

Abstracts of articles from more than 1,300 psychology journals representing professional and scientific literature from fifty countries. Compiled by the American Psychological Association. Also available online as Psyc-Info, 1967–   , with monthly updates. Available on BRS, BRS/After-Dark, Dialog (File 11), Knowledge Index (PSYC1), OCLC FirstSearch. Also available in print form as *Psychological Abstracts,* 1927–   , updated monthly.

Social Work Abstracts Plus. (CD-ROM) SilverPlatter, 1977–   . Annual.

This database produced by the National Association of Social Workers contains materials on psychiatric social work and counseling. Also available online on BRS and BRS/AfterDark, updated quarterly. Corresponds to the print index *Social Work Research and Abstracts.*

SocioFile. (CD-ROM) SilverPlatter, 1974–   . 3 times/year.

International literature of sociology, including articles, dissertations, conference papers, and books. Provides lengthy abstracts. Also available online on BRS (SOCA, SOCZ), BRS/AfterDark, Dialog (File 37), Knowl-edge Index (SOCS1), and FirstSearch (SocioAbs), 1963–   . Corre-sponds to the print *Sociological Abstracts,* 1963–   .

Other Electronic Sources

- PsyComNet: Available on GEnie, includes a monthly bibliography of the literature on mental health.
- A growing number of subscription electronic services, such as PsychNet and American Psycho/Info Exchange, provide bulletin board, electronic mail, and online conference features to users interested in the field of psychology. For current information on electronic databases and other services, consult the latest edition of the *Gale Directory of Databases.*
- The Internet has several files on psychology. The American Psychologi-cal Association sponsors a refereed journal called *PSYCOLOQUY.* It contains both newsletter-type information and short articles. Access via: **PSYC2PUCC.PRINCETON.EDU.**
- The Psychology Graduate Students Discussion Group enables students to communicate. Access via: **PSYCGRAD2ACADVM1.UOTTAWA.CA.**
- America Online has a section, Issues in Mental Health, with bulletin boards on which members discuss divorce, teen issues, and problems of daily living. Files to be downloaded include "How to Evaluate Self-Help Books."

PERIODICALS

New Age Journal. 1974–   . Bimonthly.

This popular journal publishes many articles on various self-help topics and techniques and also profiles important personalities in the New Age/self-help movement.

Psychology Today. 1967–   . Monthly.

After a brief publication lapse, *Psychology Today* is again available at newsstands. The magazine is written for a general audience and covers topics in all areas of psychology.

Re-Vision: The Journal of Consciousness and Change. 1978–   . Quarterly.

A New Age periodical for individuals interested in personal transformation, with contributors from a variety of disciplines.

Sober Times: The Recovery Magazine. 1987–   . Monthly.

Aims to inform, educate, and entertain people who have addictive and compulsive disorders.

There are a variety of newsletters on self-help issues, but these are not usually available in libraries. For subscription information on such publications as *The Brown University Family Therapy Letter, The Addiction Letter, Alcoholism and Drug Abuse Week,* and the *Harvard Mental Health Letter,* consult the latest edition of *Ulrich's International Periodicals Directory* or the *Oxbridge Directory of Newsletters.*

Journals   Many journals dealing with psychology, mental health, alcoholism, substance abuse, and related issues are intended primarily for professionals in the fields of medicine and/or psychology. The following entries are selected for their potential interest to the lay reader:

American Psychologist. 1946–   . Monthly.

Published by the American Psychological Association, contains articles on policy issues and clinical practice as well as theoretical and research material.

American Journal of Drug & Alcohol Abuse. 1974–   . Quarterly.

Sponsored by the American Academy of Psychiatrists in Alcoholism and Addictions and the American Medical Society on Alcoholism and Other Drug Dependencies. Medically oriented journal for the exchange of ideas among professionals involved in the study and treatment of substance abuse.

Community Mental Health Journal. 1965–   . Bimonthly.

Sponsored by the National Council of Community Mental Health Centers. Covers theory, practice, and research in mental health and social work. Includes articles on such topics as crisis intervention, suicide prevention, etc.

Journal of Counseling Psychology. 1954–   . Quarterly.
    Published by the American Psychological Association, includes articles on techniques, training, and materials and methods applicable to specific population groups and problem areas.

Journal of Drug Issues. 1971–   . Quarterly.
    Readable articles with a focus on policy issues.

Journal of Alcohol and Drug Education. 1955–   . 3 times/year.
    Published by the Alcohol and Drug Problems Association of North America. Provides a "forum for varying educational philosophies and differing points of view in regard to alcohol and drugs." Serves as a reference resource for teaching materials and techniques and programs for the family and community.

Drug Use Among American High School Seniors, College Students, and Young Adults, 1975–1990. 2 vols. By Lloyd D. Johnston, Patrick M. O'Malley, and Jerald G. Bachman. National Institute on Drug Abuse, 1991.
    This is the fourteenth such report on an ongoing program of national research. The document gives statistics on and analyzes trends in the use of illicit drugs, alcohol, and cigarettes by young people in the United States and reports their attitudes on the harmful effects, legality, and exposure to these substances.

GOVERNMENT PUBLICATIONS

Mental Health Directory, 1990. Compiled by A. S. Fell and others. National Institute of Mental Health, 1990.
    Nationwide listing of mental health organizations and related resources, including outpatient, residential inpatient, and supportive care facilities (halfway houses, group homes, etc.).

Mental Health, United States, 1992. Edited by Ronald W. Manderscheid and Mary Anne Sonnenschein. Center for Mental Health Services and National Institute of Mental Health, 1992.
    Data from national surveys on the characteristics of seriously mentally ill patients and trends in availability, volume, staffing, and expenditures of mental health services in the United States.

National Directory of Drug Abuse and Alcoholism Treatment and Prevention Programs. National Institute on Drug Abuse and National Institute on Alcohol Abuse and Alcoholism, 1990.
    Name, address, and phone number for approximately 9,000 federal, state, local, and private agencies. Entries are coded to indicate the function, type of care, and specialized programs of each facility.

Prevention Pipeline. National Clearinghouse for Alcohol and Drug Information, 1987–   . Bimonthly.

Publishes news about government substance abuse programs and current research findings generated by government agencies. The newsletter also identifies resources to assist in planning, implementing, and evaluating substance abuse prevention programs.

A Consumer's Guide to Mental Health Services. National Institute of Mental Health, 1987.

Answers commonly asked questions, helps identify warning signals, discusses various treatments, and lists resources for help and information.

Depression. National Institute of Mental Health, 1989.

An overview of depression's symptoms and causes, how it is diagnosed and treated, and how to help.

Plain Talk About Mutual Help Groups: People Who Know Just How You Feel. National Institute of Mental Health, 1981.

An overview of the many support groups active in the United States.

Obsessive-Compulsive Disorder. National Institute of Mental Health, 1991.
Panic Disorder. National Institute of Mental Health, 1991.

These two books describe symptoms, treatments, and where to get help.

Also see the Government Printing Office's *Subject Bibliography #167—* Mental Health.

GOVERNMENT AGENCIES

The federal government has established seven major clearinghouses that provide a wide range of drug- and alcohol-related information, resource materials, and referrals. These are sponsored variously by the Department of Health and Human Services, the Department of Justice, and the Department of Housing and Urban Development. In 1991 the Office of National Drug Control Policy linked the clearinghouses by setting up the Federal Drug, Alcohol, and Crime Clearinghouse network. By dialing a single number, (800) 788-2800, callers can reach all of the clearinghouses in the network. Callers can also contact an individual clearinghouse directly. Two of the most useful are:

National Clearinghouse for Alcohol and Drug Information
P. O. Box 2345
Rockville, MD 20785
(800) 729-6686
(301) 468-2600

An agency of the U.S. Office for Substance Abuse Prevention. Disseminates a wide range of materials on drug and alcohol prevention and treatment. The agency maintains an extensive library, publishes a newsletter *(Prevention Pipeline)*, and coordinates the Regional Alcohol and Drug Awareness Network (RADAR), which facilitates access to state and local sources of information.

Drug Abuse Information and Treatment Referral Line
(800) 662-HELP
Spanish telephone (800) 66-AYUDA
Hours—Monday through Friday: 9:00 A.M.–3:00 A.M.
Saturday and Sunday: noon–3:00 A.M.
Information about drug use, treatment, support groups, and services. Information counselors can discuss problems and provide referrals to state and local drug treatment facilities and programs.

National Institute of Mental Health
Parklawn Building
5600 Fishers Lane
Rockville, MD 20857
(301) 443-3877
NIMH conducts and supports research and research training in all aspects of mental health, mental illness, and mental health services. The agency and its many subdivisions collect, analyze, and disseminate data on the incidence of mental illness and information on resources for its treatment.

Many state, county, and city agencies provide services and/or facilitate access to federal programs:

Nonfederal Agencies

The National Directory of State Agencies. Cambridge Information Group. Annual.

Covers all states, listing agencies first by state and then by functional areas such as budget, mental health, etc. Agency name, director, address, and telephone number are provided.

For local offices, check the government pages, usually blue, of your telephone directory or ask for help in identifying appropriate agencies at your local public library. Your library or some other organization in your community may operate an information and referral service, a valuable source for local information.

International Network for Mutual Help Centers
St. Clare's-Riverside Medical Center
Pocono Road
Danville, NJ 07834
(201) 625-7101
Seeks to promote and support mutual help by encouraging awareness, utilization, and development of self-help groups. Facilitates communication between clearinghouses.

National Self-Help Clearinghouse (NSHC)
25 W. 43d Street, Room 620
New York, NY 10036
(212) 642-2944
Answers telephone and mail inquiries. Provides referrals and information on self-help programs nationwide and conducts research and training. Publishes *Self-Help Reporter*.

Self-Help Center
1600 Dodge Ave.
Suite S-122
Evanston, IL 60201
(800) 322-MASH
(708) 328-0470
A clearinghouse for the collection and dissemination of information on all types of self-help groups. Organizes workshops and publishes pamphlets, workbooks, and articles on self-help.

Because most colleges and universities offer courses in psychology, academic libraries generally have the major reference sources for psychology as well as the important journals and books in the field. Public libraries are more likely to hold a selection of popular psychology and self-help titles.

Addiction Research Center Library
National Institute on Drug Abuse
P. O. Box 5180
Baltimore, MD 21213
(410) 550-1488
Collects books and periodicals in the area of drug addiction and the related areas of biochemistry, neurology, pharmacology, physiology, psychology, and psychiatry.

Center of Alcohol Studies Library
Rutgers University, Busch Campus
Smithers Hall
Allison Road
Piscataway, NJ 08855
(908) 932-4442
The major research collection for all scientific and scholarly aspects of
alcohol problems. Actively collects current popular self-help/recovery ti-
tles.

Research Library
National Institute on Alcohol Abuse and Alcoholism
1400 I St. NW
Suite 600
Washington, DC 20005
(202) 842-7600
Maintains a specialized collection of books and periodicals.

Self-Help Clearinghouse Library
St. Clare's-Riverside Medical Center
Pocono Road
Danville, NJ 07834
(201) 625-7101
Collects self-help literature, material on how to start and maintain self-
help groups, and related directories.

For further information on libraries that collect materials on substance
abuse, contact:

Substance Abuse Librarians and Information Specialists
c/o Andrea Mitchell
P. O. Box 9513
Berkeley, CA 94709-0513
(510) 642-5208
This is an organization of individuals and institutions interested in the
collection and dissemination of material on substance abuse. Publishes the
SALIS Directory, a list of 170 substance abuse collections.

If you are looking for books on topics in psychology or self-help in your **LC SUBJECT**
library's catalog, broad subject headings to try include: **HEADINGS**

Alcoholism   Psychotherapy
Mental health   Substance abuse
Psychology

More specific subject headings are also available:

Adult children of alcoholics (or narcotic addicts)	Group psychotherapy
	Meditation
Behavior modification	Personality disorders
Co-dependence (psychology)	Relationship addiction
Community mental health services	Self-actualization (psychology)
	Self-help groups
Depression (mental)	Self-help techniques
Drug abuse	Stress (psychology)
Group counseling	Twelve-step programs

Names of groups are also used as subject headings:

Alcoholics Anonymous

Gamblers Anonymous

National Alliance for the Mentally Ill

Overeaters Anonymous

Any of these and other related subject headings will sometimes have topical or geographical subheadings; terms relating to psychology and self-help may also be used as subheadings for other topics.

Adolescent girls—Drug abuse	Mental health facilities—Georgia
Alcoholism—Psychological aspects	Substance abuse—Law and legislation
Hospitals—Substance abuse services	Twelve-step programs—Religious aspects
Indians of North America—Alcohol use	Women—Mental health

It is not always easy to anticipate how a subject heading will be phrased. To locate elusive headings, use the *Library of Congress Subject Headings* list or ask a librarian for help.

SPECIALIZED SOURCES

There are a few specialized publishers in the field of self-help/recovery that issue annotated catalogs of their titles. These firms also produce and distribute audiotape and videotape versions of their books.

CompCare Publishers
2415 Annapolis Lane
Minneapolis, MN 55427-0777
(800) 328-3330

Hazelden Educational Materials
15251 Pleasant Valley Road
P. O. Box 176
Center City, MN 55012-0176
(800) 328-9000

Health Communications, Inc.
U.S. Journal, Inc.
3201 S.W. 15th Street
Deerfield Beach, FL 33442-8190
(800) 851-9100

44

SEXUALITY

See also: General Reference Sources, Health and Medicine, Self-Help/Psychology

For the researcher in this complex and controversial field, the news is good: More is known about sexuality and more information is available than ever before. The advent of AIDS has resulted in funding for new studies of sexual behavior. The topic of human sexuality touches many disciplines. This section concentrates on sources for the lay researcher on sexual health, sexual lifestyles, and sexuality in general.

GENERAL REFERENCE SOURCES

Here are some of the landmark research works in the field of sexuality:

Sexual Behavior in the Human Male. By Alfred C. Kinsey and others. W. B. Saunders, 1948.
Sexual Behavior in the Human Female. By Alfred C. Kinsey. W. B. Saunders, 1953.

To this day the most exhaustive studies on American sexual life and mores. The scholarly work of Alfred Kinsey and his associates made an enormous impact on American sexual perspectives, though many contemporary experts now question the original research techniques or feel that the material is seriously outdated.

The Kinsey Institute New Report on Sex: What You Must Know to Be Sexually Literate. By June M. Reinisch and Ruth Beasley. St. Martin's Press, 1990.

A readable compendium written for a popular audience. Presents straightforward answers to 650 of the most frequently asked questions of the Kinsey syndicated newspaper column. Topics covered include sexual development, male and female anatomy, sexual response, sexual dysfunctions, sexually transmitted diseases, sex and the disabled, and sex and aging.

Human Sexual Response. By William H. Masters and Virginia E. Johnson. Little, Brown and Company, 1966.

Masters and Johnson stand with Kinsey among what *Time* magazine used to call the "sexperts." They were among the first scientists to investigate human sexual response through direct observation and physical measurement in the laboratory. Their book is, however, almost thirty years old and questions have been raised about the original research techniques.

The Janus Report on Sexual Behavior. By Samuel S. Janus and Cynthia Janus. Wiley, 1993.

Thousands of men and women share their beliefs and feelings about sexual practices in the age of AIDS.

"The Sexual Behavior of U.S. Adults," by Barbara C. Leigh, Mark T. Temple, and Karen Trocki. *American Journal of Public Health,* vol. 83, no. 10 (October, 1993): 1400–1408.

This national survey asked 2,058 people questions about number of partners, condom use, and other AIDS-related issues.

AIDS: Sexual Behavior and Intravenous Drug Use. Edited by Charles F. Turner, Heather G. Miller, and Lincoln E. Moses. National Academy Press, 1989.
AIDS: The Second Decade. By Heather G. Miller, Charles F. Turner, and Lincoln E. Moses. National Academy Press, 1990.

These reports, by a committee of the National Research Council, assess the status of research into sexual behavior related to AIDS, discuss prevention strategies, and identify future lines of research.

Constructing the Sexual Crucible: An Integration of Sexual and Marital Therapy. By David Schnarch. Norton, 1991.

Posits a new model for sexual/marital therapy that integrates both the physiological and emotional aspects of intimacy and sexuality.

Studies in Human Sexuality: A Selected Guide. By Suzanne G. Frayser and Thomas J. Whitby. Libraries Unlimited, 1987.

Specialized
Bibliographies

A broad, interdisciplinary overview of important books on human sexuality. Each entry contains a descriptive abstract. The book has three parts: general (reference books and general subjects); a topical guide (behavioral, physiological, developmental, and social/cultural aspects); and bibliographies.

Women and Sexuality in America: A Bibliography. By Nancy A. Sahli. G. K. Hall, 1984.

Provides a historical, cross-disciplinary look at changing views of female sexuality, 1800s–1980s. Includes chapters on special populations and subjects—older women, the disabled, transsexuals, masturbation, sexual dysfunction. Entries for books and pamphlets have annotations.

Lesbianism: An Annotated Bibliography and Guide to the Literature, 1976–1986. By Dolores J. Maggiore. Scarecrow, 1988.

A guide to social and behavioral sciences literature, arranged under five headings: the individual lesbian, minorities, lesbian families, oppression, and health issues. Lists relevant organizations at the end of each section.

Homosexuality: A Research Guide. By Wayne R. Dynes. Garland, 1987.

A comprehensive, annotated research guide arranged under twenty-four topical headings. Highlights neglected themes and diverse viewpoints.

AIDS Information Sourcebook. 3d ed. Edited by H. Robert Malinowsky and Gerald J. Perry. Oryx, 1991.

Aimed at the general public, the third edition has been updated to include more data on intravenous drug users and minorities. Includes a directory of organizations for testing, treatment, advocacy, education, and research; a bibliography including books, articles, posters, pamphlets, curricula, databases, and videotapes; and a glossary of AIDS-related terminology and slang.

Guides, Dictionaries, and Other Reference Materials

Human Sexuality: An Encyclopedia. Edited by Vern L. Bullough and others. Garland, 1994.

A compilation of articles by experts covering all aspects of sexuality.

Encyclopedia of Homosexuality. 2 vols. By Wayne R. Dynes. Garland, 1990.

Information on almost any topic relevant to gays and lesbians.

Language of Sex from A to Z. By Robert M. Goldenson. World Almanac, 1989.

A dictionary of sexology that uses easy-to-understand language. Includes technical terms, colloquial expressions, biographical entries, and descriptions of landmark sex studies.

The Language of Sex: An A to Z Guide. By Michael A. Carrera. Facts On File, 1992.

Contains entries on HIV/AIDS, safer sex, and new drugs; a topical bibliography of core titles; and a list of resource organizations.

Sexuality Education: A Resource Book. Edited by Carol Cassell and Pamela M. Wilson. Garland, 1989.

This is a comprehensive, practical guide to developing sex education programs in churches, schools, the home, and communities, and to identifying resources for the programs.

Materials on human sexuality are to be found in many disciplines. Sources thus range from all-inclusive, cross-disciplinary indexes to more specialized databases. The following is a selective list:

AIDS. (CD-ROM) ABC News InterActive.
Interactive program about AIDS, for school use.

AIDS Knowledge Base. (Online) 1986–   . Monthly.
Available on BRS. Contains the complete text of approximately 200 textbook chapters on AIDS plus citations to other relevant literature.

AIDS Weekly. (Online) 1988–   . Weekly.
Available on NewsNet. Full text of a newsletter on the prevention, detection, and treatment of AIDS.

AIDSLINE. (CD-ROM) SilverPlatter, 1980–   . Quarterly.
Subset of MEDLINE database (see below). Also available online with BRS, Dialog (File 157), and Knowledge Index (MEDI17). Updated weekly or monthly, depending on the vendor.

Combined Health Information Database. (Online) National Institutes of Health. Quarterly.
A good database for locating educational materials on health topics, particularly the sexual aspects of diseases and syndromes. Covers programs, care manuals, brochures, fact sheets, and audiovisual materials. Includes twenty-one separate files, including one on AIDS Education. Available on BRS and BRS/AfterDark.

Family Resources. (Online) National Council on Family Relations, 1970–   . Monthly.
Available online on Dialog (File 291), BRS (NCFR), BRS/AfterDark, and HRIN. A CD-ROM version, *Family Resources on Disc,* is under development at this writing. Indexes over 400 family-related journals, as well as audiovisual material. The database also includes information on family-centered programs and services. Coverage includes marriage, sexual attitudes and behavior, family relationships and counseling, and reproduction.

A portion of the database corresponds to the print index *Inventory of Marriage and Family Literature,* 1973–   .

MEDLINE. (CD-ROM) National Library of Medicine. Available from Dialog on Disc, 1984–   ; Compact Cambridge, 1976–   ; and SilverPlatter, 1966–   . Updated monthly.

Includes indexing of articles on the health care and biomedical aspects of sexuality. Also available online with BRS, BRS/AfterDark, Dialog (File 155), Knowledge Index (MEDI2), STN, and others. Also available as part of MEDIS from Mead Data Central.

PsycLIT. (CD-ROM) SilverPlatter, 1974–   . Quarterly.

Abstracts of articles from more than 1,300 psychology journals representing professional and scientific literature from fifty countries. Provides excellent coverage of literature on sexual behavior, sex variations, gender issues, counseling, and therapy. Compiled by the American Psychological Association. Also available online as PsycInfo, 1967–   , with monthly updates. Available on BRS, BRS/AfterDark, Dialog (File 11), Knowledge Index (PSYC1), OCLC FirstSearch. Also available in print form as *Psychological Abstracts,* 1927–   , updated monthly.

Teenage Sexuality. (CD-ROM) ABC News InterActive, 1992.

For classroom use, this interactive disc contains information on teenage pregnancy, sexually transmitted diseases, and human reproductive systems.

Consumer Online Services

- CompuServe: *Human Sexuality* from the Human Sexuality Medical Information and Advisory Service. The service includes online self-help and discussion groups. The tone in answering questions is friendly and easy to understand. Other databases on CompuServe, such as *Health Database Plus* and *Magazine Database Plus,* are also very useful.
- America Online: Gay and Lesbian Forum
- The Internet: Queer Resources Directory has sections concerned with AIDS, contact information for activist groups, a bibliography of publications, and portions of the GLAAD Newsletter. Access via: **ftp.nifty. andrew.cmu.edu.**

Bulletin Boards

The writer William Burroughs once said that sex is a virus that infects every new medium. As an illustration, the electronic media now contain hundreds of sexually oriented bulletin boards, making it difficult to single out the boards providing serious information.

PERIODICALS

Advocate: The National Gay and Lesbian Newsmagazine. 1967–   . Biweekly.

The leading national magazine on gay and lesbian issues. For other titles,

see *International Directory of Gay and Lesbian Periodicals*. Compiled by H.
Robert Malinowsky. Oryx, 1987.

Family Life Educator. 1982–   . Quarterly.
   Information on family life education, reviews of films and books.

Family Planning Perspectives. 1969–   . Bimonthly.
   Information on family planning from the Alan Guttmacher Institute,
including op ed pieces, special reports, and news digests.

Human Sexuality. Dushkin, 1985–   . Annual
   Reprints articles written for a lay audience that appeared originally in
popular magazines. Covers topics from sexual biology to sexuality through
the life cycle.

Psychology Today. 1967–   . Monthly.
   A popular journal of psychology that often includes articles dealing with
sexuality.

Sex over Forty. 1982–   . Monthly.
   Newsletter on the sexual concerns of the mature adult.

SIECUS Report. 1965–   . Bimonthly.
   A newsletter from the Sex Information and Education Council of the
United States, reporting on current issues relating to human sexuality and
promoting comprehensive sex education and HIV/AIDS education. Includes articles, commentaries and advocacy pieces, special bibliographies,
and a conference/seminar calendar.

Washington Memo. 1968–   . 20 issues/year.
   A newsletter from the Alan Guttmacher Institute covering federal and
state policies on reproductive health issues.

The following is a selective list of major scholarly research journals: **Journals**

Archives of Sexual Behavior. 1971–   . Bimonthly.

Journal of Homosexuality. 1974–   . Quarterly.

Journal of Sex Education & Therapy. 1976–   . Quarterly.
   Contains articles of interest to a broad professional audience. Resources
sections include reviews of audiovisual materials.

The Journal of Sex Research. 1965–   . Quarterly.
Published by the Society for the Scientific Study of Sex (see below).

GOVERNMENT PUBLICATIONS

AIDS and the Education of Our Children: A Guide for Parents and Teachers.
Department of Education, 1988.

Child Sexual Abuse Prevention: Tips to Parents. Clearinghouse on Child
Abuse and Neglect Information, 1986.

Condoms and Sexually Transmitted Diseases. Food and Drug Administration,
1990.

HIV/AIDS Surveillance. Centers for Disease Control, 1989–   . Monthly.

Introduction to Sexually Transmitted Diseases. National Institute of Allergy
and Infectious Diseases, 1987.

The Pill: 30 Years of Safety Concerns. Food and Drug Administration, 1992.

GOVERNMENT AGENCIES

Centers for Disease Control
Public Affairs Office
U.S. Department of Health and Human Services
1600 Clifton Road NE
Atlanta, GA 30333
(404) 329-3524 (publications)
Provides information on sexually transmitted diseases and public health.

Food and Drug Administration
U.S. Department of Health and Human Services
5600 Fishers Lane
Rockville, MD 20857
(301) 443-3170 (consumer affairs)
Evaluates medical devices and new drugs, including contraceptives.

National AIDS Information Clearinghouse
P. O. Box 6003
Rockville, MD 20850
(800) 458-5231

National Health Information Center
Office of Disease Prevention and Health Promotion
U.S. Department of Health and Human Services
P. O. Box 1133
Washington, DC 20013
(800) 336-4797
Provides information and makes referrals.

American Association of Sex Educators, Counselors, and Therapists
435 N. Michigan Avenue, Suite 1717
Chicago, IL 60611
(312) 644-0828

ASSOCIATIONS

American Association for Marriage and Family Therapy
1717 K Street NW, Suite 407
Washington, DC 20006
(202) 429-1825

National Gay and Lesbian Task Force
1517 U Street NW
Washington, DC 20009
(202) 332-6483
Membership organization that lobbies for gay and lesbian civil rights.
Has antiviolence and other projects and a resource center.

Sex Information and Education Council of the U.S. (SIECUS)
130 West 42d Street, Suite 2500
New York, NY 10036
(212) 819-9770
Membership organization that promotes sexual health and sexuality
education among diverse populations. Its services include publications, a
speakers bureau, educational consultants, and a library.

Society for the Scientific Study of Sex
P. O. Box 208
Mount Vernon, IA 52314
(319) 895-8407

Collection on Human Sexuality
Cornell University
John M. Olin Library
Ithaca, NY 14853-5301
(607) 255-4144

**LIBRARIES/LIBRARY
COLLECTIONS**

A strong archival collection of primary resources on human sexuality, particularly of gay and lesbian materials. Open access. Catalog records are available online with RLIN.

Institute for Advanced Study of Human Sexuality
1523 Franklin Street
San Francisco, CA 94109
(415) 928-1133

A professional graduate school granting degrees in human sexuality. Scholars may apply to use the Institute's library.

Kinsey Institute for Research in Sex, Gender, and Reproduction
313 Morrison Hall
Bloomington, IN 47405
(812) 855-7686

A world-renowned, comprehensive collection of human sexuality materials, including print, film/videotape, and photography materials, art and artifacts, and sexual ephemera. Access is restricted to qualified researchers. Reference and referral services are available to the public through the Institute's Information Services Department.

LC SUBJECT HEADINGS

AIDS (Disease)
Birth control
Bisexuality
Climacteric
Conception
Contraception
Gay men
Gay teenagers
Generative organs
Group sex
Gynecology
HIV (Viruses)
Homosexuality
Human reproductive technology
Hygiene, Sexual
Lesbians
Masturbation
Premarital sex
Psychosexual disorders
Puberty

Safe sex in AIDS prevention
Sex
Sex change
Sex counseling
Sex customs (Use instead of Sexual behavior)
Sex in literature
Sex in marriage
Sex instruction (Use instead of Sex education)
Sex oriented businesses
Sex role (Use instead of Gender role)
Sex therapy
Sexual abstinence
Sexual addiction
Sexual attraction
Sexual deviation
Sexual disorders
Sexual ethics

Sexual fantasies
Sexual intercourse
Sexually transmitted diseases
Sterilization (Birth control)

Teenage pregnancy
Transsexuals
Transvestism

See also Sexual behavior as a subheading under Aged, College students, Men, Physically handicapped, etc. For example,
College students—Sexual behavior

Alan Guttmacher Institute
111 5th Avenue
New York, NY 10003
(212) 254-5656
Conducts research and public education on reproductive health, fertility, and population.

American Social Health Association
P. O. Box 13287
Research Triangle Park, NC 27709
(919) 361-8488
Works to expand biomedical research and education programs on sexually transmitted diseases.

Center for Population Options
1025 Vermont Avenue NW
Suite 210
Washington, DC 20005
(202) 347-5700
Provides technical assistance on programs to reduce adolescent pregnancy, STDs, and AIDS. Operates support center for school-based clinics.

Coalition on Sexuality and Disability
122 E. 23d Street, Suite 109
New York, NY 10010
(212) 242-3900
Promotes sexual health care services for people with disabilities. Promotes research in the area of sexuality and disability.

Planned Parenthood Federation of America
810 Seventh Ave.
New York, NY 10019
(212) 541-7800
Undertakes education, research, and medical services.

**SPECIALIZED
SOURCES**

AIDS Hotline: (800) 342-AIDS; (800) 344-7432 (Spanish); (800) 243-
    7889 (TTY, deaf access)
National Gay and Lesbian Hotline: (800) 767-4297
Sex Addiction Hotline: (800) 321-2066
STD Hotline: (800) 227-8922

45

SMALL
BUSINESS

See also: *Business and Finance*

People starting their own businesses or already operating them have many materials and organizational resources available to them. Business proprietors can join trade and professional associations, and also familiarize themselves with government agencies that can provide money, consulting services, and regulatory information. How-to resources in books and the electronic media provide practical advice on everything from personality inventories to tax tips. The resources listed here are focused specifically on the needs of small business.

In addition to the guides listed here, readers are also urged to make use of general guides to the field of business, including *Business Information: How To Find It, How to Use It; Handbook of Business Information;* and *Basic Business Library: Core Resources.*

GENERAL SOURCES OF INFORMATION

Business Information Desk Reference: Where to Find Answers to Business Questions. By Melvyn N. Freed and Virgil P. Diodato. Macmillan, 1991.
The first third of this source takes specific questions that businesspersons might have (e.g., "How can I apply for a Small Business Administration loan?") and then links them to books and other publications in which answers to the questions may be found. Each source is fully described in the second third of the book. The last third of the book lists questions that can be answered through online databases; each suggested database is fully described. The final chapter of the book lists and describes business and trade organizations from which various kinds of help can be obtained.

The Entrepreneur's and Small Business Problem Solver: An Encyclopedic Reference and Guide. 2d ed. By William A. Cohen. Wiley, 1990.

Section I covers the legal and financial aspects of starting a business, Section II treats marketing, and Section III concentrates on management problems such as personnel management, security, and computers. A directory of small business contact sources is in the appendixes.

Franchise Opportunities Handbook. U.S. Department of Commerce. Minority Business Development Agency. GPO, 1972–   . Annual.

Franchise Annual. Info Press, 1969–   . Annual.
Source Book of Franchise Opportunities. Business-One Irwin. Annual.

McDonald's, Holiday Inn, and Ace Hardware are all franchises. These three directories of franchises provide information that the potential owner will need to have to make an informed decision about buying a franchise. Information includes cost of initial investment, descriptions of the franchise's principal business, and the kinds of managerial assistance that are provided by the franchisors. The *Franchise Opportunities Handbook* lists U.S. franchises only; *Franchise Annual* includes U.S., Canadian, and overseas franchises; and the *Source Book of Franchise Opportunities* covers U.S. and Canadian franchises.

How to Form Your Own . . . Corporation. By Anthony Mancuso. Nolo Press.
Volumes for California, Florida, New York, and Texas tell how to incorporate.

How to Set Up Your Own Small Business. 2 vols. By Max Fallek. American Institute of Small Business, 1993.

This extremely readable guide provides an introduction to the nuts and bolts of all aspects of setting up a small business. Among the topics covered are market research, sales forecasting, site selection, financing, advertising, purchasing, bookkeeping, accounting, selling, insurance, use of computers in a small business, writing a business plan, and franchising. Another useful book by this author is *How to Write Your Own Business Plan Project Kit,* 1989.

The Legal Guide for Starting & Running a Small Business. By Fred S. Steingold. Nolo Press, 1992.

Advice on whether to form a sole proprietorship, partnership, or corporation or buy a franchise or existing business. Information on negotiating a lease, hiring employees, working with independent contractors, and resolving business disputes.

RMA Annual Statement Studies. Robert Morris Associates. Annual.

This association of bank loan and credit officers compiles financial data on manufacturing, wholesaling, retailing, service, and contracting businesses. Banks and other creditors use this information to determine the viability of a company wanting to buy on credit or borrow money. The information is also helpful in determining how a business ranks relative to a particular industry. For businesses as varied as health food stores, pest control services, photocopy services, and swimming pool construction companies, this book provides such data as typical debt-to-worth ratio, profit before taxes to total-assets ratio, and gross profits.

The Small Business Information Handbook. By Gustav Berle. Wiley, 1990.

A miscellany of terms, tips, strategies, and contacts of interest to the small business owner. A sampling of entries includes Advertising Media Selection, Bank Loans, Incubators, National Retail Hardware Association, and Waste Disposal.

Small Business Sourcebook. 2 vols. 6th ed. By Carol A. Schwartz. Gale, 1993. Interedition supplement, 1993.

The first place to look for sources of information on small business. Volume 1 lists, for 224 small businesses, relevant associations, print sources, newsletters, consultants, conventions and trade shows, sources of supplies, computer software, educational programs, and audiovisual material. Small businesses covered include retail, service, and manufacturing operations ranging from an accounting/tax preparation service through a pizzeria to a word-processing business. The sources in the second volume are listed under general categories such as accounting, inventory, marketing, minority-owned business, and workplace safety. This volume also lists federal and state resources, including university small business development centers and incubator/research and technology parks for each state.

World Chamber of Commerce Directory. World Chamber of Commerce Directory. Annual.

Addresses and telephone numbers of U.S. Chambers of Commerce, U.S. Convention and Visitors Bureaus, Canadian Chambers of Commerce, American Chambers of Commerce Abroad, Foreign Tourist Information Bureaus, Foreign Chambers of Commerce in the United States, and Foreign Chambers of Commerce. A wealth of local business and demographic information can be obtained from local Chambers of Commerce, often free of charge.

PERIODICALS

Black Enterprise. 1970–   . Monthly.

This magazine focuses on business and jobs and careers in business from a black perspective. Articles profile black entrepreneurs and businesses, as

well as non-black enterprises, give travel tips, and cover issues of importance to African Americans in business.

Business Age: The Magazine for Small Business. 1986–   . Monthly.
How-to tips for owners and managers of businesses with up to 250
employees.

Entrepreneur. 1979–   . Monthly.
This magazine's coverage has a definite "start-up" flavor. Its articles
cover issues of importance to small businesses, provide how-to advice, and
profile specific small businesses and places where small businesses flourish.
There are also many paid advertisements for start-up kits for specific retail
and service businesses.

Inc.: The Magazine for Growing Companies. 1979–   . Monthly.
The articles in this magazine deal with issues of importance to small and
medium-size businesses, provide profiles of successful small businesses and
their owners, and provide how-to advice.

Journal of Small Business Management. 1963–   . Quarterly.
Official publication of the International Council for Small Business with
practical articles for managers and advisers of small businesses.

Nation's Business. 1912–   . U.S. Chamber of Commerce. Monthly.
The newsy articles in this magazine cover trends in business, people and
companies, how-to advice, and national news on small businesses.

NFIB Quarterly Economic Report for Small Business. 1974–   . Quarterly.
The National Federation of Independent Businesses' report on the economic climate for small business. Tables, charts, and text describe sales,
employment, inventories, and more.

Small Business Opportunities. 1988–   . Bimonthly.
How-to information on starting and running a business. Profiles of successful entrepreneurs.

Small Business Reporter. 1958–   . Irregular.
A series of reports for small businesses, published by the Bank of Amer-
ica. Examples are "How to Buy and Sell a Small Business" and "Financial
Records for Small Business."

Also be sure to read the appropriate local business magazines and newspapers, such as *Crain's Chicago Business* or *Business First—Buffalo.*

There is only one periodical index that is specifically for small business. Researchers should also consult the general business periodical indexes listed in Chapter 21.

PERIODICAL INDEXES

Small Business Start-Up Index: A Guide to Practical Information Related to Starting a Small Business. By Michael Madden. Gale, 1990–   . 3 times/ year.

Index to articles in periodicals, chapters in books, audiovisual materials, pamphlets, computer software, and reports that provide how-to information on starting specific businesses, profiles of specific small businesses, and information about entrepreneurs. Over 600 specific types of small businesses appear as subject categories.

ELECTRONIC SOURCES

For electronic indexes to business periodicals, see Chapter 21, Business and Finance.

Bulletin Boards

SBA Online. U.S. Small Business Administration. (800) 697-4636.

This free bulletin board connects people with resources and information that will help them to start, maintain, or expand a small business. Perhaps the most helpful information provided is the full text of SBA publications, which can be downloaded or printed out. The service also plans to provide leads to information available from other agencies and companies. For people who need help accessing the database, a voice information answer desk can be reached at (800) 827-5722.

- GEnie: Home/Office Small Business RoundTable.
- CompuServe: The Entrepreneurship Institute's International Computer Network promotes sharing of information among members of this national organization.

  The Small Business Report contains ideas and guidelines on operating a small business from syndicated columnist Mark Stevens.

  A Guide to Incorporating offers information and order entry procedures for incorporating a business in any state.

  The Working from Home Forum features summaries of articles from relevant periodicals, tutorials, and electronic conferences.
- America Online: The Microsoft Small Business Center has software to download, articles by business columnists, and a bulletin board on which small business owners can share ideas.
- Prodigy: The Entrepreneurs bulletin board has letters posted on franchises, multilevel marketing (Amway, etc.), health insurance, and other topics of interest to the prospective small business owner.

  The Home Office area offers Consumer Reports Home Office, with articles evaluating equipment such as fax machines, a home business column on computing, and reviews of software for the home office.

A Basic Guide to Exporting. Commerce Department, 1986.

Census of Retail Trade. Bureau of the Census, 1991.

GOVERNMENT PUBLICATIONS

Financial Management: How to Make a Go of Your Business. Small Business Administration, 1986.

Guide to Business Credit for Women, Minorities, and Small Businesses. Small Business Administration, 1990.

The Small Business Directory. Small Business Administration, 1992.
  Lists books and videotapes on starting and managing a small business.

Starting and Managing a Business from Your Home. Small Business Administration, 1988.

The State and Small Business: A Directory of Programs and Activities. Small Business Administration, 1989.

See also the Government Printing Office's *Subject Bibliography #307—Small Business.*

GOVERNMENT AGENCIES

Small Business Administration
409 Third St. SW
Washington, DC 20476
(202) 205-6600 or (800) U-ASK-SBA

The SBA has, among its responsibilities, to represent small business interests in Congress; provide information, referral, and educational services directly to small businesses; provide grants and loans to small businesses; help small businesses obtain government contracts to provide goods and services; and assist in the development of small businesses owned by women and minorities. The SBA publishes a Small Business Bibliographies series. For example, #92 is entitled "Effective Business Communication." To obtain information about SBA publications, call (800) 827-5722, or order a free list of publications by writing the Small Business Administration.

The SBA's Office of Small Business Development Centers sponsors over 700 centers. Their goals are to provide information and training for small businesses and to do research to stimulate the growth of local small businesses. To locate the nearest Small Business Development Center, call the Small Business Administration Office or access the information via SBA Online. There are more than 500 Small Business Institutes located at local universities. Other divisions of the SBA include Minority Small Business and Capital Ownership, Veterans Affairs Office, and Women's Business Ownership.

Department of Commerce
14th St. between Constitution Ave. and E St. NW
Washington, DC 20230
(202) 377-2000
Promotes international trade, economic growth, and the technological advancement of American business. Collects economic statistics, grants patents and registers trademarks, and assists in the growth of minority businesses. Its Bureau of Economic Analysis publishes such titles as *The Survey of Current Business* and *Business Statistics,* both available from the Government Printing Office.

ASSOCIATIONS

National Business Association
5025 Arapaho, Suite 515
Dallas, TX 75248
(800) 456-0440
Promotes the growth of small businesses by helping members obtain government loans; offers insurance and software in conjunction with the U.S. Small Business Administration; sponsors seminars and trade shows.

National Small Business Benefits Association
2244 N. Grand Ave. East
Springfield, IL 62702
(217) 753-2558
Offers businesses with fewer than 200 employees discounts on group dental and life insurance, travel programs, fax equipment, office supplies, and cellular phone service. Provides management consulting, accounting services, and owner-to-owner networking.

National Federation of Independent Businesses
150 W. 20th Ave.
San Mateo, CA 94403
(415) 341-7441
The nation's largest organization representing small and independent businesses. Provides a variety of services from lobbying to surveys on economic trends.

Service Corps of Retired Executives (SCORE)
409 3d St. NW, Suite 5900
Washington, DC 20024
(202) 205-6759

The members of SCORE, in 450 local groups, provide free consulting and training for people in small business.

Trade Associations

For almost every type of small business, there exists a specific trade association at both the state and national level. For small businesses, the state associations are especially helpful since they lobby at the state level and can provide information about state regulations and legislation, health care, workman's compensation, group buying services, insurance plans, and pension plans. National and state trade associations often sponsor conferences where owners can meet other people in similar businesses, buy merchandise, or receive training. These organizations also provide consulting services and help maintain networks through which small business operators can contact each other. See the *Small Business Sourcebook* (above) for the appropriate association. If none is listed for your business, try the *Encyclopedia of Associations* or *National Trade and Professional Associations of the United States,* Columbia Books, 1966–   . Annual.

Local Information

This type of information is best obtained via contact with local people, such as lawyers, accountants, bankers, and merchants. Customers are another important resource. They can tell you whether a business's product or service serves local needs as well as provide intelligence about the services and products of competing businesses.

LC SUBJECT HEADINGS

The most relevant heading is Small Business. Other headings that will yield information include:

Cottage industries	Sole proprietorship
Franchises (Retail trade)	Small business—Finance
Home based businesses	Small business—Cash position
New business enterprises	Small business—Purchasing
Sale of business enterprises	Small business—Research

46

SPORTS

See also: *General Reference Sources, Hobbies*

Research on sports may take you to social history, medicine, and psychology, as well as to the actual statistics and details of any individual sport. To appreciate the integration of sports and athletics with mainstream issues, one has only to consider a few sports figures recently in the news: Earvin "Magic" Johnson and Arthur Ashe in relation to the plight of HIV and AIDS victims; Pete Rose and the issue of gambling; Mike Tyson and standards of private behavior; Billie Jean King and freedom of sexual orientation. Sports permeate much of American culture.

Not all of the 120 million people who watched Super Bowl XXVII will engage in academic sports research, but many people do have questions about their own sports interests. General reference works such as almanacs will often answer the casual question; for more ambitious research, many print and electronic sources lead to detailed and specialized information.

GENERAL SOURCES OF INFORMATION

Biographical Dictionary of American Sports. 5 vols. Edited by David L. Porter. Greenwood.

> *Baseball.* 1987.
> *Football.* 1988.
> *Outdoor Sports.* 1988.
> *Basketball and Other Indoor Sports.* 1989.
> *Supplement.* 1992.

With primary emphasis on athletes who are retired or deceased, this book features both professional and college athletes, coaches, sports writers and announcers, and others. Each biography is followed by a list of materials for further reading. An index to all five volumes was published in 1993.

Celebrity Sources: Guide to Biographical Information About Famous People in Showbusiness and Sports Today. By Ronald Ziegler. Garland, 1990.

Annotated bibliography of reference books, collective biographies, periodicals, computerized databases, commercial services, and fan clubs that have information about contemporary luminaries, plus lists of individual biographies of about 450 show business and sports celebrities.

The Encyclopedia of North American Sports History. By Ralph Hickok. Facts On File, 1992.

Historical sketches of sports, topics such as Television in Sports, short entries on important people and sporting events, cities having at least one major league team, important stadiums and arenas, and organizations.

Information Please Sports Almanac. 1990–   . Houghton Mifflin. Annual.

Essays and statistics survey the past year for both professional and college sports. Historical statistics cover the Olympic Games from 1896 to date.

The Leisure Literature: A Guide to Sources in Leisure Studies, Fitness, Sports, and Travel. Edited by Nancy Herron. Libraries Unlimited, 1992.

Aimed at the academic researcher, this book lists the standard reference books, core journals, and statistical sources for sport. Appendixes include lists of important publishers on sports, degree programs in sports, and sports-related associations.

The Olympics Factbook: A Spectator's Guide to the Winter Games. By Martin Connors and others. Visible Ink, 1993.

Statistics on the Winter Olympics from their inception through 1992. A companion volume covers the Summer Olympics. Online with NEXIS and Prodigy.

Oxford Companion to World Sports and Games. Edited by John Arlott. Oxford University Press, 1975.

This handbook of international sports provides a digest of rules and diagrams of fields or courts, accompanied by some history and records. Useful for more obscure sports.

Rules of the Game: The Complete Illustrated Encyclopedia of All the Major Sports of the World. Rev. ed. By The Diagram Group. St. Martin's, 1990.

Provides for each sport a brief history, a description of the playing area and equipment, rules, and a synopsis of players and officials. Over 2,000 illustrations.

Sports: A Reference Guide. By Robert J. Higgs. Greenwood, 1982.

Bibliographic essays describe sources on the history of sport; sports in art and popular culture (e.g., films, cartoons); sports, race, and sex; sports in education; and other topics. Also describes research centers and directories by sport.

Sports Fan's Connection: An All-Sports-in-One Directory to Professional, Collegiate, and Olympic Organizations, Events, and Information Sources. Edited by Bradley J. Morgan and Peg Bessette. Gale, 1992.

For almost fifty sports, this book lists books, magazines, videotapes, radio and TV stations, sports information services, and online services. Chapters also have special material appropriate to the topic; "Baseball," for instance, has a list of fantasy camps. Covers every major participatory sport, including luge, tractor pulling, lacrosse, and rodeo.

USA Today Sports Atlas. Rev. ed. By Will Balliett and f-stop Fitzgerald. Gousha/Simon & Schuster, 1993.

State maps show professional and college sports facilities, and sites for skiing, bowling, horse and greyhound racing, and other sports. In the back of the book, state-by-state lists of spectator venues and outdoor venues provide addresses. Scattered throughout the book are such features as lists of sports bars and *USA Today* graphics.

SPORT Discus. (CD-ROM) SilverPlatter. 1975–   . Updated semiannually.

ELECTRONIC SOURCES

Over 200,000 records covering exercise physiology, coaching, psychology, and sports medicine. Based on more than 2,000 sources from around the world. Also online with BRS and Dialog as *Sport* database. Print version is *SportSearch,* Sport Information Resource Centre, 1974–   .

Sporting News Baseball Guide and Register. (CD-ROM) Quanta, 1992.

Last six years of *Sporting News* on a disc. Smaller version available for Data Discman.

DIALOG OnDisc: ERIC. UMI, 1966–   . Updated quarterly.
ERIC on SilverPlatter, 1966–   . Updated quarterly.

Abstracts of articles from 750 education journals and hundreds of thousands of research reports, including research in physical education. These files are also available online through CompuServe, Dialog, Knowledge Index, BRS/AfterDark, BRS Colleague, and OCLC EPIC and FirstSearch. Updated monthly.

The print versions of *CIJE* (Oryx, 1969–   ) and *RIE* (U.S. Government Printing Office, 1966–   ) are updated monthly. See Chapter 23, Education, for more information.

MEDLINE, 1966–   , available on CD-ROM from Dialog, EBSCO, and SilverPlatter, and online with Dialog (File 155) and Knowledge Index (MEDI1 and MEDI2), updated twice a month, and BRS, updated weekly.

Useful for sports medicine and physiology. Compiled by the National Library of Medicine, it is available in print as *Index Medicus.*

Online Sources

- Human Resources Information Network: Timeout for Sports profiles people in the sports world.
- CompuServe: Provides Sports Forum, Sports Network, scores, statistics, standings, schedules. Computer SportsWorld offers real-time scores, news analysis of college and pro sports. Contains both current and historical data.
- GEnie: Sports Roundtable.
- Delphi, Prodigy: Events Online, schedules.
- Dow Jones News/Retrieval: Offers Sports Report, stories, scores, statistics, standings, and schedules.
- NEXIS: Has complete text of *Sporting News, Sports Illustrated.*
- America Online: Sportslink has many files for downloading (e.g., final 1992 American League statistics), plus USA Today Sports, and bulletin boards.

PERIODICALS

Journal of Sport History. 1974–   . 3 times/year.

Detailed scholarly articles view the sporting world from an academic perspective.

Sport. 1946–   . Monthly.

Comparable to *Sports Illustrated,* with photo essays.

Sporting News. 1886–   . Weekly.

A tabloid, the longest continuously published sports magazine.

Sports Illustrated. 1954–   . Weekly.

General-audience magazine with large circulation highlighting sports news at all levels, from high school through professional sports.

SPECIALIZED PERIODICAL INDEXES

Physical Education Index. BenOak Publishing, 1978–   . Quarterly.

Subject index to 200 periodicals. Comprehensive coverage of dance, physical education, physical therapy, recreation, sports, sports medicine.

Sports Periodicals Index. National Information Systems, 1985– Monthly.

Access by subject and name to 100 sports journals. Includes the most popular magazines in virtually all sports.

See also *SPORT Discus* under Electronic Sources.

Congress occasionally holds hearings on gambling and professional sports, most notably boxing, and those hearings in printed form are sent to depository libraries. These publications can be identified through the *Monthly Catalog of United States Government Publications.*
    Other government agencies publish popular titles on fitness:

GOVERNMENT PUBLICATIONS

Introduction to Running: One Step at a Time. U.S. Department of Health and Human Services. President's Council on Physical Fitness and Sports, 1987.

Walking for Exercise and Pleasure. U.S. Department of Health and Human Services. President's Council on Physical Fitness and Sports, 1984.

Playing for a Living: The Dream Comes True for Very Few. Department of Labor, 1987.
    For high school athletes who want to pursue sports as a career.

    See also *Subject Bibliography* #239—Physical Fitness, from the Government Printing Office.

President's Council on Physical Fitness and Sports
U.S. Public Health Service
200 Independence Ave. SW
Washington, DC 20201
(202) 619-1296

GOVERNMENT AGENCIES

Amateur Athletic Union of the United States
3400 W. 86th St.
Indianapolis, IN 46268
(317) 872-2900
    Composed of regional amateur sports associations. Maintains a library and biographical archives. Has youth sports programs in twenty sports and conducts local, state, regional, and national championships.

ASSOCIATIONS

National Collegiate Athletic Association
6201 College Blvd.
Overland, KS 66211
(913) 339-1906

Administers intercollegiate athletics. Committees oversee forty-two college sports. Operates a statistics service and publishes rule books, handbooks, and special reports on sports programs, finances, and television.

U.S. Olympic Committee
1750 E. Boulder St.
Colorado Springs, CO 80909
(719) 632-5551
A federation of sports governing bodies that represents the United States in the events of the Olympic and Pan-American games. It selects, finances, equips, and transports team members, as well as operating two training centers and maintaining historical archives and a library.

Women's Sports Foundation
342 Madison Ave.
New York, NY 10173
(800) 227-3988
Supports the participation of women in sports by conducting seminars, developing educational guides, providing travel and training grants, and supporting the enforcement of Title IX, which ensures gender equity in school and other sports programs. Sponsors an information and resource clearinghouse on women's sports, maintains biographical archives, and compiles statistics.

LIBRARIES

University of Notre Dame Libraries
Edmund Joyce Collection
Hesburgh Library
Notre Dame, IN 46556
(219) 631-8252
Said to be the largest collection of sporting materials in the world, representing more than 500 sports and games. A major research center for sports.

Sport Information Resource Centre
1600 James Naismith Dr.
Gloucester, Ont.
Canada K1B 5N4
(613) 748-5658
Compiler of *Sport* database. Subscribes to more than 1,400 periodicals.

Amateur Athletic Foundation
2141 W. Adams Blvd.
Los Angeles, CA 90018
(213) 730-9696
Large library and museum on sports and the Olympics.

Applied Life Studies Library
146 Library
University of Illinois
1408 W. Gregory Dr.
Urbana, IL 61801
(217) 333-3615
Good coverage of physical education. Catalog published as *Dictionary Catalog of the Applied Life Studies Library, University of Illinois* (G. K. Hall, 1977) and *Supplement* (1982).

Look also under individual sports, e.g., Baseball, Football, Hockey, and under types of sport facilities, e.g., Bowling alleys, Tennis courts.

LC SUBJECT HEADINGS

Athletic clubs
Athletic shoes
Athletics
Ball games
Coaching (athletics)
College sports
Doping in sports
Games
Mass media and sports
Olympics
Outdoor life
Physical education and training
Professional sports
Sex discrimination in sports
Sporting goods
Sports and state
Sports betting
Sports camps
Sports for the physically handicapped
Sports for women
Sports officiating
Sportscasters
Television broadcasting of sports
Tournaments
Violence in sports

An extremely wide range of materials is available on specific sports. The following sources on sailing provide only one example.

GENERAL SOURCES

The Annapolis Book of Seamanship. Rev. ed. By John Rousmaniere. Simon & Schuster, 1989.
A heavily illustrated guide to every aspect of sailing. Covers navigation, weather, safety, and sailing skills.

The Sailing Dictionary. 2d ed. By Joachim Schult. Revised by Jeremy Howard-Williams. Sheridan House, 1992.

Many of the 4,000 terms here are accompanied by line drawings that illustrate the definitions.

SEA-D series. (CD-ROM) Laser Plot. Semiannual.

Optically scanned government nautical charts displayed in full color for use with electronic positioning systems such as Loran. Separate files available for Chesapeake Bay, Florida West Coast, the Great Lakes, and many other U.S. and foreign locations.

• CompuServe: Sailing Forum has data libraries on types of boats, outfitting, etc., and regular online conferences.

Cruising World. 1974–   . Monthly.

One of the most popular sailing magazines, with descriptions of cruising worldwide. Referral service links readers who own specific boats with others who have experience with those boats.

Practical Sailor. 1970–   . Semimonthly.

The *Consumer Reports* of boating. Field-tests and evaluates sailboats and equipment.

Sail. 1970–   . Monthly.

For sailors at various levels, from novices to experts, with an emphasis on racing.

Sailing World. 1962–   . Monthly.

Covers sailboat design, sailing technique and equipment, seamanship, racing events.

Yachting. 1907–   . Monthly.

The oldest boating magazine, covers both sail and motor yachts. Articles on cruising and racing and the lifestyle aspects of yachting.

National Ocean Survey
National Oceanic and Atmospheric Administration
U.S. Department of Commerce
1825 Connecticut Ave. NW
Washington, DC 20235
(202) 673-5122

Charged with exploring, mapping, and charting the global ocean, this agency publishes nautical charts used by sailors. The four large charts (maps) listed below serve as indexes to the hundreds of charts available. They also list authorized dealers of the charts.

U.S. Atlantic and Gulf Coasts, 1988
U.S. Pacific Coast, 1988

Alaska, 1988
Great Lakes, 1988

The National Weather Service, another department of the National Oceanic and Atmospheric Administration, broadcasts marine forecasts.

U.S. Coast Guard
Department of Transportation
2100 Second St. SW
Washington, DC 20593
(202) 267-2229

Maintains aids to navigation, provides boating safety program, search and rescue service, and marine environmental response. Has district offices.

American Sailing Association
13922 Marquesas Way
Marina Del Rey, CA 90292
(213) 822-7171

ASSOCIATIONS

Promotes sailing safety and standards for sailing education by accrediting sailing schools and instructors. Operates library on sailing and the handicapped.

U.S. Yacht Racing Union
P. O. Box 209
Newport, RI 02840
(401) 849-5200

The coordinating and governing body of sailboat racing. Sponsors sailing championships.

America's Cup Races (and the names of other specific races)
Multihull sailboats
Navigation
Ocean travel
Sailboat living
Sailboat racing
Sailboats—Auxiliary engines
Sailboats—Chartering
Sailing
Sailing, Single-handed
Seamanship
Windsurfers (Sailboats)
Yacht building
Yacht designers
Yacht racing
Yachts and yachting

LC SUBJECT HEADINGS

47

STANDARDS AND SPECIFICATIONS

Standards and specifications are basic to the development of products and services. They exist within every industry, from weapons manufacture to, say, book publishing, where certain technical measures of uniformity and quality have been adopted, including the standard for "Permanence of Paper for Printed Library Materials." Students in technical fields and researchers in many areas of commerce will need access to the sources that record and describe these measures and to the agencies involved in their development.

The terms *standard* and *specification* are often used interchangeably, although *standard* is the broader term and *specification* the narrower one. Both identify acceptable levels of quality and performance. The American National Standards Institute (ANSI) defines a standard as "a specification accepted by recognized authority as the most practical and appropriate current solution of a recurring problem." ANSI defines a specification as "a concise statement of the requirement for a material, process, method, procedure or service, including, whenever possible, the exact procedure by which it can be determined that the conditions are met within the tolerances specified in the statement."

Because new products, methods, and materials are constantly being created, refined, and otherwise modified, there is need frequently to revise standards. Nearly seventy countries have organizations at a national level that prepare, approve, and publish standards and specifications. These organizations consist of representatives of industry, professional societies, trade associations, consumer groups, and government agencies. Through ongoing publication programs the organizations announce new, revised, and amended standards. Most standards are intended to be observed voluntarily, to serve both the producers of materials, products, and services and the consumers of them.

There has been a need for international standardization for as long as there has been international exchange of materials and the import and export of products and services. The International Organization for Standardization (ISO) was formed in 1946 to achieve "international agreement on industrial and commercial standards and thus facilitate international trade." With members from over sixty nations (including ANSI as the U.S. representative), ISO accomplishes much useful standardization.

The development of standards and specifications is an activity shared by government agencies and organizations in the private sector. The guides, indexes, and other literature on standards are, therefore, a mix of government, association, and trade publications.

GENERAL REFERENCE SOURCES

A Sourcebook on Standards Information: Education, Access, and Development. Edited by Stephen M. Spivak and Keith A. Winsell. G. K. Hall, 1992.

This anthology of articles on issues pertaining to standards concludes with a list of sources for accessing standards, a list of standards information centers, and a bibliography.

Standards: A Resource and Guide for Identification, Selection, and Acquisition. By Patricia Ricci and Linda Perry. Stirtz, Bernards, 10 World Trade Center, St. Paul, MN 55101, 1990.

A directory of government and industry associations that develop standards. Also includes information on libraries, standards vendors, newsletters, and other publications on standards.

Standards and Specifications Information Sources: A Guide to Literature and to Public and Private Agencies Concerned with Technological Uniformities. By Erasmus J. Struglia. Gale, 1973.

Guide to standards agencies, primarily in the United States. Also covers indexes to periodical literature, and catalogs and indexes of standards.

Access to Standards Information; How to Enquire or Be Informed about Standards and Technical Regulations Available Worldwide. ISO, 1986.

How to find out about standards in other countries.

ELECTRONIC SOURCES

Worldwide Standards Service on CD-ROM. Information Handling Services. Updated every two months.

Indexes 90 percent of the world's standards. Permits comprehensive searching of U.S., Japanese, German, British, French, Canadian, Australian, and Saudi Arabian national standards. Also available online as *IHS Industry and International Standards and Specifications* with Dialog (File 92), updated weekly, and in part in print as *Index and Directory of Industry Standards*, 7 vols., Information Handling Services, 1991. The company also supplies the standards themselves on microfilm and reports that documents from over sixty U.S., six international, and nineteen foreign national societies are available.

Other CD-ROM products are available from Information Handling Services. The first such product was ASME *Boiler and Pressure Vessel Code,* with fully searchable text of the entire code with all graphs, illustrations, drawings, and schematics.

SPECMASTER. (CD-ROM) National Standards Association. Monthly.
Includes U.S. voluntary standards from over 400 organizations. Also available online as *Standards and Specifications Database* with Dialog (File 113) and ESA-IRS (File 44).

Standards Search. (CD-ROM) Society of Automotive Engineers and the American Society for Testing Materials. Annual.

PRINTED INDEXES TO STANDARDS

See also the electronic indexes to standards listed above.

Book of ASTM Standards. American Society for Testing Materials, 1939–   . Annual.

Catalog of American Standards. American National Standards Institute, 1964–   . Annual.
Sales catalog for ANSI-approved standards.

Index of Federal Specifications, Standards and Commercial Item Descriptions. U.S. General Services Administration, Federal Supply and Services Office, 1952–   . Annual with five supplements.

Index of Specifications and Standards. U.S. Department of Defense. Annual.

KWIC Index of U.S. Voluntary Engineering Standards. National Center for Standards and Certification Information, National Institute of Standards and Technology. Annual.
Issued annually on microfiche; available from the National Technical Information Service (see below). Also available as a computer printout from the National Center for Standards and Certification Information, A629 Administration Building, National Institute of Standards and Technology, Gaithersburg, MD 20899; (301) 975-9040.

ISO Catalogue. ISO. Annual.

KWIC Index of International Standards. 3d ed. ISO, 1987.

Journal of Testing and Evaluation. 1966–   . Bimonthly.

Published by the American Society for Testing and Materials, provides technical information on the performance of materials, products, systems, and services.

Journal of Research of the National Institute of Standards and Technology (formerly *Journal of Research of the National Bureau of Standards*). 1928–   . Monthly.

Data and specifications on all types of standards.

ANSI Reporter. 1967–   . Monthly.

Newsletter highlighting activities of the American National Standards Institute (see under Associations, below) and of related groups.

National Institute of Standards and Technology (NIST)
Gaithersburg, MD 20899
(301) 975-2000
Research Information Center: (301) 975-3052

Formed in 1901 as the National Bureau of Standards to ensure the compatibility of measurement standards used in the United States. There are nine technical units within NIST:

1. Computer Systems Laboratory
2. Technology Services
3. Electronics and Electrical Engineering Laboratory
4. Manufacturing Engineering Laboratory
5. Chemical Science and Technology Laboratory
6. Physics Laboratory
7. Materials Science and Engineering Laboratory
8. Building and Fire Research Laboratory
9. Computing and Applied Mathematics Laboratory

The Research Information Center is the central repository for information to assist in the work of these units. The National Center for Standards and Certification Information was established in 1965 as the repository for copies of U.S. and foreign standards.

National Technical Information Service (NTIS)
5285 Port Royal Road
Springfield, VA 22161
(703) 487-4604

Source of U.S. regulations and ANSI and other standards adopted by government agencies.

U.S. Government Printing Office
Washington, DC 10402
(202) 783-3238.
Miscellaneous nonmilitary government standards from U.S. agencies and departments.

Naval Publishing and Printing Service
700 Robbins Ave.
Philadelphia, PA 19111
(215) 697-2667
Naval standards.

General Services Administration
Specification and Consumer Information Distribution Section
Washington Navy Yard, Bldg. 197
Washington, DC 20407
(202) 472-2205
Federal standards and other materials included in the *Index of Federal Specifications, Standards and Commercial Item Descriptions* (see above, under Printed Indexes).

International Organization for Standardization (ISO)
Case Postale 56 CH-1211
Geneva 20, Switzerland
Telephone: 41/22/34-1240.
New standards, revisions, and amendments are announced monthly in *ISO Bulletin.*

ASSOCIATIONS

American National Standards Institute (ANSI)
1430 Broadway
New York, NY 10018
(212) 642-4900
Serves as a clearinghouse for nationally agreed-on voluntary standards and represents the United States in international standardization discussions. Sells approved U.S. industry standards and foreign standards and catalogs. Membership is open to nonprofit educational institutions.

American Society for Testing and Materials (ASTM)
1916 Race Street
Philadelphia, PA 19103
(215) 299-5400
Indexes formally approved ASTM standards, practices, specifications, guides, test methods, terminology, and related materials.

National Standards Association
1200 Quince Orchard Blvd.
Gaithersburg, MD 20878
(301) 590-2300; (800) 638-8094
Sales of U.S. standards.

Engineering libraries at major universities and technology departments at large public libraries will frequently have excellent collections of standards and specifications. Some examples are:

LIBRARY COLLECTIONS

Science and Technology Department
Cleveland Public Library
325 Superior Ave.
Cleveland, OH 44114
(216) 623-2932

Science and Business Department
Milwaukee Public Library
8914 W. Wisconsin Ave.
Milwaukee, WI 53233
(414) 278-3000

Linda Hall Library
5109 Cherry St.
Kansas City, MO 64110
(816) 363-4600
A privately endowed library of science and technology.

Science and Technology Department
Carnegie Library of Pittsburgh
4400 Forbes Ave.
Pittsburgh, PA 15213
(412) 622-3100

Science and Technology Department
Los Angeles Public Library
630 W. Fifth St.
Los Angeles, CA 90071
(213) 612-3200

In library catalogs, Standardization is used for books on the "establishment of standards of quality for commodities and services." Specifications is used for works on "particular qualities prescribed for a product to meet specific

LC SUBJECT HEADINGS

requirements." Geographical subheadings or subheadings indicating form of publication may be used with these terms.

Specifications—Bibliography—Catalog

Standardization—Periodicals

Standardization—Public policy—Europe

Standardization and Specifications may also be used as subheadings under headings for industries, products, or types of engineering.

Construction—Specifications

Drugs—Standardization

Heat engineering—Specifications

Standards is not used alone as a subject heading but will appear with a modifying term or as a subheading.

Standards, Engineering

Standards, Military

Electric engineering—Standards

Materials—Standards

48

TELEVISION

See also: General Reference Sources, Film

Television is one of the most potent social, financial, political, and cultural forces in modern society and there is obviously a high level of interest in gathering facts about it. This section gives guidance to the researcher seeking information about television—its history, technology, finances, performers, and place in society.

Les Brown's Encyclopedia of Television. 3d ed. Gale, 1992.
    Almost 3,000 entries on people, programs, and companies, as well as on legal and technological issues in the industry. Covers such topics as family viewing time, violence, children's advertising. Individual programs are not covered in as much detail as in some of the sources that follow.

Television: A Guide to the Literature. By Mary Cassata and Thomas Skill. Oryx, 1985.
    Topics covered include the communication/mass communication process, the history of television, reference sources, children and television, television news, television and politics, literature of the industry, criticism.

Popular Entertainment Research: How to Do It and How to Use It. By Barbara J. Pruett. Scarecrow Press, 1992.
    Lists print and electronic reference sources for research on radio and TV.

Television sources are also listed in more comprehensive works on broadcasting or the mass media as a whole. The best of these are:

Mass Media Bibliography: An Annotated Guide to Books and Journals for Research and Reference. 3d ed. By Eleanor Blum and Frances Goins Wilhoit. University of Illinois Press, 1990.

Lists almost 2,000 sources. Do not look for specialized materials here; one of the criteria for entry in the bibliography is that works "deal with the subject in broad general terms." The entries deal with mass communications and their theory, economics, structure, function, and content. Books and journals are listed in categories, including broadcasting media, directories and handbooks, journals, and indexes to mass communications literature.

On the Screen: A Film, Television, and Video Research Guide. By Kim N. Fisher. Libraries Unlimited, 1986.

An excellent starting place for someone unfamiliar with television sources. A critically annotated bibliography of important English-language reference books on motion pictures and television. The emphasis is on books published after 1960, but it does include some references to earlier works. Includes chapters on core periodicals, research centers and archives, societies and associations.

Radio and Television: A Selected, Annotated Bibliography. Compiled by William E. McCavitt. Scarecrow, 1978.
Supplement One, 1977–1981. 1982.
Supplement Two, 1982–1986. Compiled by Peter K. Pringle and Helen H. Clinton. 1989.

Annotated bibliographies of books, pamphlets, and reports on all aspects of broadcasting. Coverage begins with 1920.

Reviews   *Variety Television Reviews, 1923–1988.* 15 vols. Garland, 1989.

Though *Variety* has shed some of its idiosyncratic language ("THESP INKS TERMER WITH MGM") over the years, it has lost none of its authority. What the reviewers in *Variety* and *Daily Variety* thought of television shows as they appeared is found here in chronological order, with a title index.

Programming Guides   Programming guides list and/or evaluate TV programs. They are an excellent source not only of information on the programs themselves but also on personalities, producers, and production companies.

The Complete Directory to Prime Time Network TV Shows, 1946–Present. 5th ed. By Tim Brooks and Earle Marsh. Ballantine, 1992.

Covers regular series carried on the commercial networks in the evening. Note: Only the most well-known syndicated shows are included. There is an essay on the history of network television, and appendixes on prime-time schedules, Emmy winners, series that also aired on radio, hit theme songs.

Harry and Wally's Favorite TV Shows. By Harry Castleman and Walter J. Podrazik. Prentice-Hall, 1989.

Harry and Wally give their views on 2,100 series or miniseries that originally aired or currently play in the evening hours. They award zero (awful) to four (a gem) stars. An appendix lists shows that are available on home video.

Total Television: A Comprehensive Guide to Programming from 1948 to the Present. 3d ed. By Alex McNeil. Penguin Books, 1991.

The most current and detailed guide to TV programming. Contains descriptions of more than 4,700 daytime and prime-time TV series. It covers shows not only on ABC, CBS, and NBC, but also on Fox, Dumont, and PBS. In addition, entries describe syndicated programs, selective cable series, and specials. Also contains a chronological list of special programs, charts of fall schedules, Emmy and Peabody Award winners.

Syndicated Television: The First Forty Years, 1947–1987. By Hal Erikson. McFarland, 1989.

Coverage of syndicated shows that appeared originally "off-network." This listing is highly selective for religious, sports, and informational (news/documentary) shows.

Television Drama Series Programming: A Comprehensive Chronicle, 1947–1959. By Larry James Gianakos. Scarecrow, 1980. With supplements.
    1959–1967.   1978
    1975–1980.   1981
    1980–1982.   1983
    1982–1984.   1987
    1984–1986.   1992

The most comprehensive guide to television drama. These volumes outline individual episodes of TV drama series. Each entry includes episode title, broadcast date, actors. Later volumes include (when the information is available) directors and writers. Appendixes list TV adaptations of literary works such as Pulitzer Prize winners, Nobel Prize winners, classical Greek drama, Shakespeare, nineteenth- and twentieth-century writers.

Encyclopedia of Television: Series, Pilots, and Specials, 1937–1984. 3 vols. By Vincent Terrace. New York Zoetrope, 1986.

Describes more than 8,000 series, pilots, special programs, and experimental programs aired through 1984. The index includes every name listed in each entry, including actors, directors, producers, writers, musicians. It is a product of Baseline (see below).

Television is a great promoter and consumer of people—and "Whatever happened to . . . ?" must be the most frequently asked television question. Here are some sources that will answer queries about TV personalities:

The Complete Actors' Television Credits, 1948–1988. 2d ed. By James Robert Parrish and Vincent Terrace. Scarecrow, 1989–90.
The television work of more than 3,000 actors.

Contemporary Theatre, Film, and Television. Gale. Annual.
Concentrates on persons currently active in the media in the United States and the United Kingdom, but also includes those who have made significant contributions in the past. The entries give personal and professional data and, usually, a business address. Covers performers, directors, writers, producers, designers, managers, technicians, composers, critics.

Variety Obituaries, 1905–1990. 13 vols. Garland, 1991. With semiannual updates.
More than 90,000 obituaries and news stories from *Variety* covering show business personalities.

Celebrity Sources: Guide to Biographical Information about Famous People in Show Business and Sports Today. By Ronald Ziegler. Garland, 1990.
This annotated bibliography lists collective and individual biographies, reference books, periodicals, computer databases, commercial services, and fan clubs.

Broadcasting & Cable Market Place. Bowker. Annual.
This directory of radio, television, and cable systems also features special sections on Federal Communications Commission (FCC) regulations and executives, satellites, programming, advertising, technology, professional services. Formerly *Broadcasting Yearbook.*

Television and Cable Factbook. Warren Publishing. Annual.
Provides more detailed information about television stations than the previous entry, including Arbitron ratings and technical facilities.

Film Literature Index. Film and Television Documentation Center, 1973–   . Quarterly.
The title notwithstanding, this index covers television and videotape as well as motion pictures. Since 1986, articles on TV have been listed in a

separate section of each issue. Covers more than 300 periodicals, including scholarly and nonspecialist journals.

Footage '91: North American Film and Video Sources. (CD-ROM) Prelinger Associates, 1992.

Comprehensive directory describing 1,600 collections that supply film and taped images, including nonprofit television archives and television news libraries. Entries include address, telephone number, services, description of collection, licensing, restrictions, availability of catalogs, and viewing facilities. Invaluable tool for any researcher attempting to find moving-image footage. CD-ROM version available only for the Macintosh at this writing. Also available in print as *Footage '89: North American Film and Video Sources* and *Footage '91,* edited by Richard Prelinger (Prelinger Associates, 1989–91). Detailed subject index for topics, issues, personalities, and locations.

Humanities Index. (CD-ROM) H. W. Wilson, 1984–   . Quarterly.

Indexes 290 humanities periodicals, including *Journal of Broadcasting & Electronic Media* and *Journal of Popular Film and Television. Wilson Humanities Abstracts* is an annotated version on CD-ROM. Also available online with Wilsonline and OCLC FirstSearch, 1984–   , updated twice a week, and in print, updated quarterly, as *Humanities Index,* 1974–   (formerly *Social Sciences and Humanities Index,* 1965–74; *International Index,* 1907–65).

PAIS International. (CD-ROM) SilverPlatter, 1972–   . Quarterly. Also available as *PAIS on CD-ROM.* Public Affairs Information Service, 1972–   . Quarterly.

Subject index to books, pamphlets, government publications, and more than 1,200 periodicals, with an emphasis on economic, social, and political issues. Indexes *Television Quarterly* and other relevant titles. Also available online on BRS (PAIS), BRS/AfterDark, Dialog (File 49), Knowledge Index (SOCS2), FirstSearch (PAIS Decade), 1976–   . Contains records from the print sources *PAIS Bulletin,* 1976–90 (formerly called *Public Affairs Information Service Bulletin,* 1915–76), *PAIS Foreign Language Index,* 1972–90, and *PAIS International in Print,* 1991–   .

NewsBank Review of the Arts: Film and Television. (CD-ROM) NewsBank. 1975–   . Monthly.

Indexes interviews, reviews, and news stories about television from more than 450 U.S. city newspapers. Note: The actual articles are reproduced on microfiche and issued at the same time as the *Review.*

Social Sciences Index. (CD-ROM) H. W. Wilson, 1984–   . Monthly.

Indexes such journals as *Journal of Communication* and *Communication Research. Wilson Social Sciences Abstracts* is an annotated version on CD-ROM. Also available online with Wilsonline and OCLC FirstSearch, 1984–   , updated twice a week, and in print, updated quarterly, as *Social Sciences Index,* 1974–   (formerly *Social Sciences and Humanities Index,* 1965–74; *International Index,* 1907–65).

Variety Video Directory Plus. (CD-ROM) Bowker. Quarterly.

A comprehensive listing of entertainment and performance video-tapes—including music videotapes, television programs, and cartoons—and special-interest videotapes—including documentaries, sporting events, and educational programs. This is the CD-ROM equivalent of Bowker's *Complete Video Directory* (1990–   ). It allows searching by subjects, performers, directors, awards, languages, and keywords in titles.

Online Databases   *Gale Database of Publications and Broadcast Media.* Dialog. Semiannual.

This is the electronic form of the *Gale Directory of Publications and Broadcast Media.* It lists radio, TV, and cable companies in the United States and Canada. Also available on diskette (annual).

NewsNet. This vendor makes available the full text of several newsletters for the television industry. Most of them are updated weekly. For example:
FCC Report. Full text of *FCC Week* with information on federal communications policy.
Public Broadcasting Report. Newsletter covering public radio and TV.
Television Digest.

Soap Opera Summaries. CompuServe. 1984–   . Daily.
Plot summaries and cast news.

TRANSCRIPT. CompuServe. 5 times/week.
Catalog of transcripts of shows available from Journal Graphics. You can place orders online.

Baseline. Baseline. Daily.
Provides access to current information on credits for television personnel, current television productions, and company information. Baseline will answer questions of nonsubscribers on a pay-per-question basis and can be reached at:

Baseline, Inc.
838 Broadway
New York, NY 10003
(212) 254-8235

Burrelle's Broadcast Database. Burrelle's Information Service. 1989–   .
Daily.

Contains the full text of more than 150,000 transcripts of news and public affairs programs. To use, you must subscribe directly from:

Burrelle Information Service
75 E. Northfield Rd.
Livingston, NJ 07039-9873
(800) 631-5122

Also available in print as *Burrelle's Index of Television Transcripts,* 1992–   .

- Prodigy has a television bulletin board that collects and sends messages to popular TV personalities.
- America Online has a list of radio and TV programs with educational value for children from KidsNet.
- The Internet has several TV sources.

   Television Shows Archive has guides to many TV series, mostly sitcoms. It includes cast and episode summaries. Access via: **ftp pitmanager@mit.edu;** log in **anonymous cd pub/TV.**

   Monty Python—a large collection of sketches. Access via: **U.S. Berkeley Open Computing Facility/OCF On-Line Library/Python.**

   The Simpsons Archive—summaries of episodes, casts, etc. Access via: **ftp.cs.widener.edu;** log in **anonymous; cd pub/simpsons** or **WAIS simpsons.src.**

PERIODICALS

Film, Television, and Video Periodicals: A Comprehensive Annotated List. By Katharine Loughney. Garland, 1991.

A comprehensive guide to magazines and journals containing current information on the dynamic world of television.

Broadcasting: The Fifth Estate. 1931–   . Weekly.

This is the trade journal for the broadcasting industry and covers radio, TV, cable, and home videotape. News of new technology, legislation, FCC regulations.

TV Guide. 1953–   . Weekly.

This programming guide is published in regional editions and contains, in addition to network and cable listings, articles on performers, series, and specials. All of *TV Guide* from its beginning and all of its regional editions are available on microfilm.

Variety. 1905–   . Weekly.
A trade journal that covers, among other things, the television industry and financial news. Coverage is worldwide but centers on the U.S. It includes reviews, statistics, special issues and themes, and obituaries.

Scholarly Journals Two journals aimed primarily at the scholar can be of use to independent researchers:

Journal of Broadcasting & Electronic Media. 1956–   . Quarterly.
Includes articles on broadcast journalism, regulation, and international communications. Analyzes content of news and entertainment programming.

Television Quarterly. 1962–   . Quarterly.
This publication of the National Academy of Television Arts and Sciences contains articles by scholars, critics, and television professionals. It concentrates on television's role in society, new technologies and their impact, and influential individuals in television, some of whom are interviewed.

GOVERNMENT PUBLICATIONS As a consequence of its oversight and scrutiny of television, the government publishes laws and regulations; relevant committees and subcommittees of Congress publish hearings; and government agencies, particularly the Federal Communications Commission and its subdivisions, publish reports and studies on television.

The Arts on Television. National Endowment for the Arts, 1990.
Provides a synopsis, credits, and air dates for arts programming on the Public Broadcasting System. Includes theater, opera, and dance. Gives names of distributors from which some of the programs may be rented or purchased.

The Impact on Children's Education: Television's Influence on Cognitive Development. Office of Educational Research and Improvement, Department of Education, 1988.

TV with Books Completes the Picture. Library of Congress, 1991.
Activities for children to enhance learning.

Three Decades of Television: A Catalog of Television Programs Acquired by the Library of Congress, 1949–1979. By Sarah Rouse and Katharine Loughney. Library of Congress, 1989.

The Library of Congress has a major collection of television programs. This catalog lists more than 14,000 programs, including "series, serials, telefeatures, specials, and documentaries; daytime and prime-time programs; local, network, DuMont, and syndicated broadcasts; and educational materials from NET and PBS." It has a content descriptor (adventure, public affairs, variety, etc.) index.

See also the Government Printing Office's *Subject Bibliography #296—Telecommunications*.

Federal Communications Commission
1919 M Street NW
Washington, DC 20554
(202) 632-7000
The FCC has a considerable degree of power over all the broadcast media, and, in the television industry, it controls local stations, the networks, cable systems, and satellite communications. FCC units also issue reports, do studies, and hold hearings and conferences. The Commission's library, with holdings on all aspects of the communications industry, is open to the public; telephone (202) 632-7100. Among the library's publications is *Telecommunications Legal Research Manual*.

National Endowment for the Arts
Media Arts Program: Film/Radio/Television
1100 Pennsylvania Avenue NW
Washington, DC 20506
(202) 682-5452
Awards grants to individuals and to nonprofit organizations for film and video productions. NEA's library, (202) 682-5485, contains materials on, among other things, public policy and the arts, and cultural policy.

National Endowment for the Humanities
Humanities Projects in Media
1100 Pennsylvania Avenue NW
Washington, DC 20506
(202) 786-0438
Awards grants to nonprofit organizations for projects connected with the mass media and the humanities. NEH's library, (202) 786-0224, is open to the public *by appointment only* and contains materials on a wide range of humanities and public and private philanthropy matters.

Motion Picture, Broadcasting and Recorded Sound Division
Library of Congress
Room 336, Madison Building
Washington, DC 20540
(202) 707-1000
This major research library contains an extensive collection of books on television, clipping files, and copyright descriptions. The extensive moving image collection includes many television programs. Note: Viewing the moving image collection is limited to individuals doing research of a specific nature leading to a publicly available work.

UCLA Film and Television Archive
University of California, Los Angeles
46 Powell Library
405 Hilgard Avenue
Los Angeles, CA 90024-1517
(310) 206-5388
After the Library of Congress, the second-largest collection of television programs. This archive is available to researchers only.

The Museum of Broadcast Communications
78 E. Washington
Chicago, IL 60607
(312) 987-1510
Contains numerous television shows and commercials. The collection is national in scope but has a special emphasis on the Midwest, especially Chicago. It is open to the public.

The Museum of Television and Radio (formerly Museum of Broadcasting)
25 W. 52d Street
New York, NY 10022
(212) 752-4690
Its extensive collection of television programs (1939–   ) and radio broadcasts (1929–   ) is available to the general public. The museum also has a small library of books, journals, and radio scripts.

Television News Archive
Vanderbilt University
Jean & Alexander Heard Library
419 21st Avenue South
Nashville, TN 37240
(615) 322-2927

This archive is the largest collection of television newscasts in the United States, with network evening newscasts on videotape from 1968 and a collection of special network newscasts. It is open to the public for research, and tapes are available on loan. Programs are indexed in *Television News Index and Abstracts: A Guide to the Videotape Collection of News Programs in the Vanderbilt News Archive.* 1968–   . Monthly.

Descriptive abstracts are arranged by network, date, and time and indexed by names, places, and subjects. Introductory material explains the fee structure for ordering copies of videotapes.

For additional information on special libraries and collections in television see:

Sourcebook for the Performing Arts: A Directory of Collections, Resources, Scholars, and Critics in Theatre, Film, and Television. By Anthony Slide, Patricia King Hanson, and Steven L. Hanson. Greenwood, 1988.

Afro-Americans in television
Broadcasting
Cable television
Closed caption television
Color television
Crime in television
High definition television
Mass media
Minorities in television
Physicians in television
Sex in television
Soap operas
Television—Law and legislation
Television—Production and direction
Television actors and actresses
Television advertising
Television and children
Television and politics
Television authorship
Television broadcasting
Television broadcasting—Social aspects
Television broadcasting of news
Television comedies
Television film
Television frequency allocation
Television in education
Television in politics
Television programs
Television programs for children
Violence in television

BIB Television Programming Source Books. Edited by Heidi Holland. North American Publishing Company, 1993.

Although intended for television programmers, the source books are useful to anyone researching production and distribution information on television films and series. Volumes 1 and 2, *Films/Alphabetical,* list more than 30,000 films that were recently produced or have already been shown on television. Volume 3 lists *Film Packages,* and Volume 4, *Series,* lists 20,000 television series in syndication and their distributors. Distributors to the home videotape market are not listed.

International Directory of Film and TV Documentation Centers. Edited by Frances Thorpe. St. James Press, 1988.

Lists 104 archives belonging to the FIAF (Fédération internationale des archives du film), a worldwide organization dedicated to preserving the world's film and videotape heritage.

49

THEATER
AND DANCE

See also: *General Reference Sources, Film, Literature*

Because theatrical works have both literary and performing arts aspects, research sources are found in a library's literature section as well as in its arts collections. Literature collections will yield material on plays, playwrights, and the history of drama. Performing arts sources, which are emphasized in this chapter, provide information on such topics as theatrical production and its technical aspects, management, players, directors, design and designers. Often these sources cross over into film and television.

Theater also has its own body of reference works, including those offering historical and biographical information, and others providing access to the plays themselves.

Dance has been included in this chapter. General humanities and arts sources provide some coverage of the topic, but, like theater, dance has specialized reference compilations of considerable detail and range.

American Theater and Drama Research. By Irene Shaland. McFarland, 1991.
  A guide to the literature of theater since 1945. Lists databases, organizations, and research centers, as well as books. Treats musical theater and ethnic theater along with drama.

American Theatre History. By Thomas J. Taylor. Salem Press, 1992.
  An annotated list of books on theater in America from its beginnings to the present. Sections on regional, experimental, ethnic, community, academic, and children's theater. Also contains a list of theater periodicals.

REFERENCE SOURCES

Theater

465

Best Plays of [year]. Edited by Otis Guernsey, Jr., and Jeffrey Sweet. Applause Books. Annual.

Best Plays is the continuation of a comprehensive survey that began more than seventy years ago as *Best Plays of 1919–20 and the Year Book of the American Drama,* edited by Burns Mantle. In addition to short review articles on each season's productions, it provides excerpts of the editor's choice of the year's ten best plays, along with photographs, a directory of new productions, and an index of performers. Coverage includes Broadway, Off-Broadway, and regional theater. This is a standard reference source that reflects the historical panorama of twentieth-century American theater. Drawings by Hirschfield enliven the text.

The Cambridge Guide to American Theatre. By Don B. Wilmeth and Tice L. Miller. Cambridge University Press, 1993.

Provides coverage of American theater from its earliest time to the present, including not only legitimate New York theater but also alternative theater and popular forms such as vaudeville, the circus, and burlesque. There are articles on a wide range of topics, including theater in major U.S. cities, Shakespeare on the American stage, theater architecture, principal theaters, lighting, and costume, as well as entries for individual plays. A biographical index provides life dates and major occupations for more than 3,000 names mentioned in the entries.

The Cambridge Guide to World Theatre. 2d ed. Edited by Martin Banham. Cambridge University Press, 1994.

This heavily illustrated guide is especially useful for the information it provides on theater outside Europe and the United States. As an example, while *The Oxford Companion to the Theatre* (see below) offers five pages on theater in India, *The Cambridge Guide to World Theatre* provides ten, along with numerous cross-references to entries on various uniquely Indian theater forms, both secular and religious. There are also detailed articles on national theaters that are absent from the Oxford guide, such as theater in Indonesia and Nigeria.

Catalog of the Theatre and Drama Collections. 51 vols. By New York Public Library Research Libraries. G. K. Hall, 1967–76.

The collections of the New York Public Library are an extremely important source for information in all areas of the performing arts. This mammoth set lists titles in the NYPL's collections, including more than 120,000 plays, as well as works relating to all aspects of the theater, such as stage history, biography, criticism, acting, and stage management. The catalog also reproduces cards for several hundred thousand nonbook items, such as reviews, press clippings, and photographs. *Bibliographic Guide to Theatre*

(G. K. Hall, 1976–   ) is an annual publication that lists materials cataloged since 1976.

Contemporary Theatre, Film, and Television. Gale, 1984–   .
   This series is intended as a supplement to *Who's Who in the Theatre,* which
ceased publication in 1981. It is broader in coverage, since it includes
information on film and television as well as theater. You will find here
biographical information on performers, directors, writers, producers, designers, managers, choreographers, technicians, composers, executives,
dancers, and critics in the United States and Great Britain.

The New York Times Theater Reviews, 1870–1990. 26 vols. Garland, 1992.
   Reprints, in chronological sequence, reviews of theater productions as
they appeared in *The New York Times.* Included are appendixes of awards
and prizes and of productions and runs by season. The same reviews can be
retrieved by using *The New York Times Index* and the microfilm of the
newspaper.

McGraw-Hill Encyclopedia of World Drama: An International Reference Work. 5
vols. 2d ed. Edited by Stanley Hochman. McGraw-Hill, 1984.
   A set that provides information about both the literary and the performance aspects of theater. Most of the entries are on dramatists, but there are
also articles on national and ethnic theaters, theater companies, and per-
formance-related topics. The information for each major dramatist includes a biographical sketch, criticism of the work, summaries of selected
plays, and bibliographies of primary and secondary sources. Briefer overviews are provided for less well-known dramatists. Other material includes
a glossary of terms, an index of play titles, and a general index.

Notable Names in the American Theatre. James T. White & Co., 1976.
   Provides detailed entries on living persons, as of 1976, including actors,
designers, directors, and dramatists, active in American theater. There are
shorter entries on 8,000 others from all periods of American theater. Other
information includes facts about Broadway and Off-Broadway productions,
awards, and histories of important theater companies and theater buildings.

*Ottemiller's Index to Plays in Collections: An Author and Title Index to Plays
Appearing in Collections Published Between 1900 and 1985.* 7th ed. By Billie M.
Connor and Helene G. Mochedlover. Scarecrow, 1988.
   A standard work for locating plays in collections, *Ottemiller's* indexes over
3,000 plays in more than 1,300 collections. It covers full-length plays from
all periods and literatures, as well as those plays excerpted in the *Best Plays*
series.

The Oxford Companion to American Theatre. 2d ed. By Gerald Bordman. Oxford University Press, 1992.

Like other titles in the Oxford Companion series, this is a useful and accessible source on all aspects of American theater. The more than 3,000 entries cover American playwrights, producers and directors, individual plays, lyricists and composers, performers, companies, organizations, and theaters. Emphasis is on Broadway and the New York stage, though there is some coverage of regional theater as well as of ephemeral figures and productions. A briefer version, *The Concise Oxford Companion to the American Theater,* was published in 1987. For a source that provides more information on theater outside New York, see *The Cambridge Guide to American Theatre* (above).

The Oxford Companion to the Theatre. 4th ed. By Phyllis Hartnoll. Oxford University Press, 1983.

A basic source that provides definitions of theater terms, biographical sketches of personalities, articles on important theater companies and buildings, and historical surveys of theater in specific countries and cities. This edition reflects the spread of alternative and experimental theater. Focus is on legitimate theater, with only limited coverage of popular genres, such as music hall, vaudeville, and musical comedy. *The Concise Oxford Companion to the Theatre* (2d ed., Oxford University Press, 1992) omits some of the illustrations and longer articles.

Play Index. 8 vols. H. W. Wilson, 1953–93.

This is an index to more than 30,000 plays that were published between 1949 and 1992, ranging from puppet plays to classical drama. It provides author, title, subject, and dramatic style entries for each play, as well as a brief synopsis, and information about size of the cast and number of sets. Not only full-length stage plays are included, but also radio, television, and one-act plays, and plays for children and young adults. This book is very useful for amateur stage groups.

Samuel French's Basic Catalogue of Plays. Samuel French, 7623 Sunset Blvd., Hollywood, CA 90046. Biennial.

French's Catalogue provides annotated listings of all plays published or controlled by Samuel French, either in manuscript or published form. Among the headings under which plays are listed are: full-length royalty plays, full-length nonroyalty plays, one-act plays, musicals and operettas, monologues, holiday plays, children's plays, skits, and stunts. A similar catalog is available from Dramatists Play Service (440 Park Avenue South, New York, NY 10016). Both Samuel French and Dramatists Play Service are major sources for scripts and major rights organizations for copyright and royalties. Their catalogs are available free of charge.

Theatre World. Theatre World, 1944–   . Annual.

This annual survey gives brief summaries and cast lists for Broadway productions, but also covers Off-Broadway and regional theater. Contains awards, biographies, obituaries, and lots of photographs.

Who's Who in the Theatre: A Biographical Record of the Contemporary Stage. 1st–17th eds. Pitman, 1912–81.

Biographies of persons connected with all aspects of theater, including actors, composers, dramatists, critics, designers, and historians. The emphasis in earlier volumes is on London stage personalities, but later volumes also cover New York. Stratford-upon-Avon and the Stratford Festival in Ontario are included as well. Besides biographies, there are playbills for the productions in the period covered. Supplemented by *Who Was Who in the Theatre, 1912–1976* (4 vols., Gale, 1978), which reproduces the latest biographical sketch of those dropped from *Who's Who in the Theatre* because of death or inactivity.

No index devotes itself specifically to theater. Two indexes include considerable theater material:

**ELECTRONIC
SOURCES**

Humanities Index. (CD-ROM) H. W. Wilson, 1984–   . Quarterly.

Indexes 290 humanities periodicals, including such theater titles as *Theatre Journal, Theatre Research International,* and *Theatre Survey,* as well as more general titles such as *Performing Arts Journal. Wilson Humanities Abstracts* is an annotated version on CD-ROM. Also available online with Wilsonline and OCLC FirstSearch, 1984–   , updated twice a week, and in print, updated quarterly, as *Humanities Index,* 1974–   (formerly *Social Sciences and Humanities Index,* 1965–74; *International Index,* 1907–65).

MLA International Bibliography. (CD-ROM) H. W. Wilson, 1981–   . Quarterly.

Covers more than 4,000 periodicals, books, and dissertations on literature, including both drama and theater, in virtually all major languages, with in-depth coverage of English and American literature. Over one million citations are available online through Wilsonline and OCLC FirstSearch, 1981–   , updated monthly. Also available in print, 1921–   , annual. Prior to 1981, the print index had no subject indexing. Citations were arranged by language and then alphabetically by the author/playwright being discussed.

American Theatre. 1984–   . Monthly.

PERIODICALS

Though fairly recent in origin, this is one of the most important theater magazines in the United States. It covers primarily nonprofit professional theater. Included are profiles of actors in current productions, coverage of legal and political issues that affect theater, articles on theater companies and play scripts, and a monthly calendar of productions around the country. *Drama,* published in Great Britain, is a quarterly that provides similar coverage of British and European theater.

Theatre Crafts. 1967–   . 10 times/year.

Subtitled "The Magazine for Professionals in Theatre, Film, Video, and the Performing Arts," this periodical is aimed at those concerned with lighting, costume, stage design, advertising, and other technical aspects of theatrical production.

Plays: The Drama Magazine for Young People. 1941–   . 7 times/year.

Intended for students through the high school level, *Plays* offers a supply of royalty-free dramatic material for schools, young people's clubs, and libraries. Each issue includes eight to ten plays.

Theatre Journal. 1941–   . Quarterly.

Published in cooperation with the Association of Theatre in Higher Education, *Theatre Journal* is more scholarly than the other periodicals listed here. In addition to articles dealing with various aspects of theater throughout the world, it provides book reviews, and reviews of professional, international, and university/college productions.

Variety. 1905–   . Weekly.

This newspaper of show business contains reviews of Broadway and Off-Broadway plays and shows abroad, information on casting and money grossed each week by Broadway and road shows. Covers regional as well as New York theater.

GOVERNMENT PUBLICATIONS

Children + Parents + Arts. National Endowment for the Arts, 1992.

Five pamphlets with creative ideas to help children develop skills in theater, dance, music, writing, and the visual arts.

GOVERNMENT AGENCIES

National Endowment for the Arts
Theater Program
1100 Pennsylvania Ave. NW
Washington, DC 20506
(202) 682-5425

Awards grants to professional theater companies, to individuals for professional theater training, and to playwrights. There is also a Dance Program that offers assistance to choreographers and dance companies. Telephone (202) 682-5435.

National Endowment for the Humanities
1100 Pennsylvania Ave. NW
Washington, DC 20506
(202) 786-0278

American Society for Theatre Research
Theatre Arts Program
University of Pennsylvania
Philadelphia, PA 19104
(215) 898-5271
An organization for scholars of the theater. Sponsors research projects, publishes a newsletter and *Theatre Survey* (semiannual) as well as books on the stage and the theater.

Dramatists Guild, Inc.
234 W. 44th Street, 11th Floor
New York, NY 10036
(212) 398-9366
Founded in 1920 to protect the rights of dramatists, this organization now has more than 8,000 members, including playwrights, lyricists, and composers. It offers symposia, seminars, and workshops, maintains a library of theater reference material, and publishes *Dramatists Guild Newsletter*.

Theatre Guild
226 W. 47th Street
New York, NY 10036
(212) 869-5470
Begun in 1917 as a theatrical producing organization, the Theatre Guild aims to encourage and promote attendance at dramatic, musical, and theatrical performances. It pioneered the subscription plan to guarantee audiences in New York and elsewhere and currently sponsors the American Theatre Society, a national subscription service for major Broadway attractions touring the United States.

New York Public Library for the Performing Arts
111 Amsterdam Avenue
New York, NY 10023
(212) 870-1639
The collection contains more than one million books, scripts, scrapbooks, playbills, promptbooks, posters, letters, photographs and photographic negatives, manuscripts, documents, scenery plans, and costume designs. Maintains files on all active theater groups in the New York area. Special collections related to theater include archives and memorabilia of

theater groups and important individuals, such as Richard Rodgers and Hal Prince. Some other important collections are the William Seymour Theatre Collection at Princeton University; the Humanities Research Center Theatre Arts Collection at the University of Texas, Austin; and the School of Drama Library at Yale.

LC SUBJECT HEADINGS

Material dealing with drama as acted on the stage is listed under Theater:
Theater—Production and direction
It may be subdivided geographically, e.g., Theater—United States.

(Note that although the British spelling *theatre* is used in the titles of many American publications and may be found, therefore, in the title files of library catalogs, the subject heading is always spelled *theater*.)

Acting	Dramatic criticism
Actors	Passion plays
Amateur theater	Stage lighting
Children's plays	Vaudeville
Costume	

Material dealing with theater buildings, architecture, decoration, etc., is listed under Theaters.

Materials dealing with the literary aspects of theater are listed under Drama; American drama; English drama; etc.

REFERENCE SOURCES

Dance

Dance is not as well documented as are other performing arts and, until recently, was notoriously underindexed. Nevertheless, several ambitious reference works will keep the researcher on the move.

Balanchine's Complete Stories of the Great Ballets. By George Balanchine and Francis Mason. Doubleday, 1977.

The great choreographer Balanchine provides information on over 400 ballets, both classical and modern, that are important in terms of their music, choreography, design, or performance. The entries include information on first productions and important revivals, often accompanied by Balanchine's own commentary. Detailed, scene-by-scene descriptions are given for the more important ballets. Additional sections include how to appreciate ballet, children's ballets, choreography, dancers, and careers in ballet, a brief history of ballet, and a chronology of significant events in ballet history, as well as an illustrated glossary of ballet terms.

Biographical Dictionary of Dance. By Barbara Naomi Cohen-Stratyner. Macmillan, 1982.

Brief sketches of nearly 3,000 figures from four centuries of American and European dance history. Genres covered include circus, burlesque,

Hollywood movies, Broadway musicals, and television variety shows. Also treated are composers, impresarios, teachers, designers, and others associated with dance, as well as performers and choreographers.

The Dance Encyclopedia. By Anatole Chujoy and P. W. Manchester. Simon & Schuster, 1967.

Provides lengthy, encyclopedic articles on various forms of dance, including ballet, tap, modern, ballroom, and folk. Briefer articles focus on personalities, stage design, instruction, terms, and techniques.

Complete Guide to Modern Dance. By Don McDonagh. Doubleday, 1976.

By profiling 100 significant twentieth-century choreographers, this title provides a survey of modern dance up to about 1975. Coverage ranges from forerunners of modern dance, such as Isadora Duncan and Ted Shawn, to contemporary figures like Twyla Tharp. In addition to biographical information, there are detailed descriptions of at least one representative work. For each choreographer, a "choreochronicle" lists titles and dates of all known works. The guide, though one of the best sources on modern dance, is nearly twenty years old and lacks information on today's choreographers.

The Concise Oxford Dictionary of Ballet. 2d ed. By Horst Koegler. Oxford University Press, 1982.

Covering 400 years of ballet history, this guide provides brief entries on all aspects of ballet, including personalities, works, companies, places of performance, ballet schools, and technical terms. It is translated and adapted from a work published in German in 1972, with much material added on American and British ballet. As with all titles in the Oxford Companion series, this is an excellent one-volume source for those who need to research a few facts, but do not need in-depth information. Note also that the book will not include more contemporary dancers and works, since it was published in 1982.

Dance Handbook. By Allen Robertson and Donald Hutera. G. K. Hall, 1990.

This accessible guide offers more than 200 entries grouped under eight broadly chronological categories, such as "Romantic Ballet," "Ballets Russes," and "Birth of Modern Dance." Each category offers both factual and critical information on ballets, choreographers, and composers. A "databank" provides brief, directory-type information on magazines, companies, organizations, festivals, and sources for research, arranged by country.

A Dictionary of Ballet Terms. By Leo Kersley and Janet Sinclair. Da Capo, 1979.

The language of ballet is quite technical, and this is the place to look for definitions. The entries, some of which are quite long, are accompanied by line drawings. A similar title is Gail Grant's *Technical Manual and Dictionary of Classical Ballet* (Dover, 1982), which, though newer, is no longer in print. Grant's definitions tend to be shorter than those found in *A Dictionary of Ballet Terms*.

International Dictionary of Ballet. 2 vols. St. James, 1993.

Over 700 entries on dance companies and ballets, noting first and/or significant performances. Biographical entries list roles for dancers and works for choreographers, with critical essays.

ELECTRONIC SOURCES

Dance on Disc. (CD-ROM) G. K. Hall. Annual.

As in other areas of the performing arts, the collections of the New York Public Library are an essential resource. From ballet to break dancing, this compact disc lists around 96,000 items cataloged for the collection, including choreographic diagrams, films, and dance notebooks. Includes material on costumes, set designs, and the cultural aspects of dance. Also available in print as *Dictionary Catalog of the Dance Collection: A List of Authors, Titles, and Subjects of Multi-Media Materials in the Dance Collection of the Performing Arts Research Center of the New York Public Library*, 10 vols., G. K. Hall, 1974. Covers materials cataloged prior to October 1, 1973. It is supplemented by *Bibliographic Guide to Dance* (G. K. Hall), which has been published annually since 1975.

PERIODICALS

Dance Magazine. 1926–   . Monthly.

The oldest continuously published dance periodical in the country and the single most important periodical on dance. It covers ballet, modern, and Broadway styles of dance across the country, combining attractive photographs with articles by noted dance scholars. Each issue also includes a monthly performance calendar.

Dance and Dancers, published in Great Britain, provides similar coverage of both modern dance and ballet from an international perspective. More technical than *Dance Magazine*, it will be of particular interest to professionals and serious students of dance history and criticism.

PERIODICAL INDEXES

Index to Dance Periodicals. By the New York Public Library Research staff. G. K. Hall, 1991–   . Annual.

This new annual index fills a serious gap. It provides references to current periodical literature on dance and dance-related topics from fifty-one titles in the dance collection of the Performing Arts Research Center of the New York Public Library, including *Dance Magazine, Dance and Dancers*,

Dance Research Journal, New York Magazine, and the *New Yorker.* Twenty-seven of the indexed titles are American. The rest, twelve of which are in foreign languages, are published outside the United States. Other indexes that provide some access to dance are *Humanities Index* (see above) and *Music Index.*

See the National Endowment for the Arts under Theater, above.

GOVERNMENT
AGENCIES

ASSOCIATIONS

American Dance Guild
31 W. 21st Street, 3d floor
New York, NY 10010
(212) 627-3796
The membership of this organization, founded in 1956, includes teachers, performers, historians, critics, writers, and students in the field of dance, including ballet, modern, jazz, tap, and ethnological dance forms. Sponsors seminars and workshops, maintains a speakers bureau and a career counseling service, and publishes a newsletter.

Congress on Research in Dance
State University of New York
Department of Dance
Brockport, NY 14420
(716) 395-2590
The purpose of this organization is to gather and evaluate research on dance performed in the United States and abroad. It publishes a newsletter and also the semiannual *Dance Research Journal.*

LIBRARIES

The Chicago Public Library
Visual and Performing Arts Department
Harold Washington Library Center
400 S. State Street
Chicago, IL 60605
(312) 747-4800
Subject strengths include history, ballet, biography, and folk dance. Special supporting collections include the *Folk Dance Index* and the Dance Video Collection.

New York Public Library
Dance Collection
111 Amsterdam Avenue
New York, NY 10023
(212) 870-1657

Holdings include books, manuscripts, videotapes, oral history tapes, clippings, original stage and costume designs, photographs and photographic negatives, prints, posters, programs, and scrapbooks. Among the special collections are the American Ballet Theatre Papers and the collections of Agnes de Mille, Loie Fuller, Lucia Chase, and Ted Shawn.

LC SUBJECT HEADINGS

Dance is not a subject heading; *Dancing* is used instead. This may subdivide geographically, e.g., Dancing—United States. Headings for types of dance and dancing are also used:

Ballet
Folk dancing
Modern dance
Tap dancing

There are also headings for types of dancers, e.g., Ballet dancers.

Films and videotapes of dance are important tools for research. For a complete list, see *Dance Film and Video Guide.* Dance Horizons, 1991.

Lists 2,000 films and videotapes indexed by choreographer, composer, dance companies, dancers, directors, and subjects.

TRAVEL

See also: General Reference Sources

The figures on tourism, both domestic and worldwide, are staggering; it is the third-largest industry in the United States. Six million Americans earn their livings providing goods and services to travelers.

Travel research ranges from such theoretical questions as the economics or the sociology of travel to practical matters for the business traveler or the tourist.

GENERAL SOURCES OF INFORMATION

The Leisure Literature: A Guide to Sources in Leisure Studies, Fitness, Sports, and Travel. Edited by Nancy Herron. Libraries Unlimited, 1992.

Aimed at the researcher, not the tourist, this guide lists books, core journals, and statistical sources on the tourism industry.

Travel Industry World Yearbook; The Big Picture. Edited by Somerset R. Waters. Child & Waters, 516 Fifth Ave., New York, NY 10036. 1956– . Annual.

An annual summary with statistics on trends in the international and national tourism industry.

Traveler's Reading Guide: Ready-Made Reading Lists for the Armchair Traveler. 2d ed. Edited by Maggy Simony. Facts On File, 1993.

Lists nonfiction and fiction books and travel articles arranged by place. Especially useful for determining what travel guides are available for countries not covered by the better-known series, for its citations to the *New York Times* Sunday travel section articles, and for its recommendations of novels and other background reading.

Worldwide Travel Information Contact Book. 2d ed. Edited by Burkhard Herbote. Gale, 1992.

A country-by-country listing for tourists and business travelers of approximately 25,000 sources of information. You can write or call for free travel literature from all over the world. Contacts in more than 300 countries, provinces, regions, and states are included. Each entry lists address, phone, and fax and telex numbers when available. Similar coverage of just the United States is available in an inexpensive paperback, *The USA Travel Phone Book: A Quick Self-Help Guide to Essential Addresses and Telephone Numbers for Business and Vacation Travelers.* (Bon A Tirer, 1991).

The traveler also needs a good atlas (see Chapter 18, General Reference Sources, for suggestions) and a gazetteer that lists place names. *Cambridge World Gazetteer; A Geographical Dictionary* (also published as *Chamber's World Gazetteer*), edited by David Munro (Cambridge, 1990), is a good choice.

Guidebooks

Many of the best guidebooks are published in series. Each series defines its market. Here are capsule descriptions of some of the major series:

Access Guides. Access Press. Colorful graphics with many maps, floor plans, and isometric drawings of theaters, museums, transportation systems, and even supermarkets for such cities as London and Chicago.

Baedeker's Guides. Various publishers. Initiated in 1894, this longtime standard provides thorough descriptions and excellent pull-out maps in pocket-size volumes. Worldwide coverage.

Berkeley Guides. McKay. University of California student-compiled guides out to challenge the Harvard *Let's Go* series.

Blue Guides. Norton. Based on a French series, especially strong on history and culture, with detailed information on natural history (e.g., diagrams of snakebite marks in *Egypt*) and architecture.

Fielding. Morrow. Aimed at the typical American tourist. Heavy on accommodations, meals, and shopping.

Fodor's Guides. Fodor's Travel. Middle of the road; almost worldwide coverage, with more than 130 titles in the series.

Frommer. Prentice-Hall. Once a budget guide (. . . *on $5 a Day*) but now similar to Fielding and Fodor. Emphasizes hotels and restaurants; superficial treatment of sights.

Insight Guides. Houghton Mifflin. Notable for their coverage of Asia and the Pacific. Strong on culture; excellent color photos.

Knopf Guides. Alfred A. Knopf. Full color with historical sections, floor plans of landmark buildings, maps, and suggested itineraries.

Let's Go Guides (Harvard Student Agencies). St. Martin's. Focus on low-budget travel, especially good for Europe. Some practical information, but emphasizes historical background of areas treated.

Lonely Planet Survival Kits. Lonely Planet Publications. For the adventurous
independent traveler, "travelers who aren't going to Europe"; especially
good for Asia. Candid approach to the dangers and discomforts of travel
in some countries.

Michelin Guides: Red (auto) and Green (descriptions and accommodations). Michelin. More than twenty guides in English and fifteen more in
French provide detailed motoring information and finely drawn maps,
charts, and floor plans. With a few exceptions, coverage is limited to
Europe.

Mobil Travel Guides. Seven regional guides provide straightforward information on accommodations in the United States.

Passport's Illustrated Travel Guides from Thomas Cook. NTC Publishing. More
than two dozen guides to U.S. and foreign destinations for independent
travelers.

Wall Street Journal Guides to Business Travel. Fodor's Travel. Volumes on
Europe, the Pacific Rim, Canada, international cities.

For more thorough descriptions of guidebooks, see *Going Places; The
Guide to Travel Guides,* by Greg Hayes and Joan Wright. Harvard Common
Press/Gale, 1988. Trends and new titles in travel publishing are explored
every year in *Publishers Weekly* (e.g., four articles in the January 31, 1994
issue).

All of the following popular magazines carry articles on destinations, travel **PERIODICALS**
information, and a considerable amount of advertising, which in itself can **AND INDEXES**
be informative. All are indexed in *The Travel and Tourism Index,* below, as
well as in more popular indexes such as the *Readers' Guide.*

National Geographic Traveler. 1984– . Monthly.
Emphasizes U.S. travel, but has articles on foreign trips too.

Condé Nast Traveler. 1954– . Monthly.
For the affluent traveler, with tips on dining, entertaining, sports, the
arts.

Travel Holiday. 1901– . Monthly.
Focus is on the middle-class traveler.

Consumer Reports Travel Letter. 1985– . Monthly.
Provides unbiased evaluations; also reports on bargains.

Journal of Travel Research. 1962– . Quarterly.
For academic study. Indexed in *ABI Inform, Business Periodicals Index,*
and others.

The Travel and Tourism Index. 1984–   . Quarterly.

Published by Brigham Young University-Hawaii Campus and aimed at the travel researcher, this index covers more than forty periodicals. Titles indexed by subject include *Hungarian Travel Magazine, Cruise Travel, Tourism Management,* and *Travel Market Trends.*

ELECTRONIC SOURCES

OAG Electronic Edition Travel Service. Official Airline Guides. Updated daily.

Used by the travel industry, this online database is available through DIALOG, Knowledge Index (OAG), and, for an extra fee, CompuServe, Dow Jones News/Retrieval, Delphi, and GEnie. It contains airline schedules and fares for 400 airlines plus information on hotels worldwide. OAG can also be used to find out what movie will be shown on an overseas flight, to get arrival information for sixteen airports, to obtain frequent flyer information, and for such details about airports as parking rates, car rental agencies, and airline terminal locations. Flight information is also available in print form in two editions: *Official Airline Guide—North American Edition* (semimonthly) and *Official Airline Guide—Worldwide Edition* (monthly). The *Official Airline Guide Travel Planner and Hotel/Motel Redbook* is a print source for lodging information. Issued quarterly in three editions (North American, European, and Pacific), it contains, in addition to hotel/motel listings, airport maps, city maps, lists of embassies and consulates, time charts, and much more.

America Online, Prodigy, Delphi, GEnie, and CompuServe all offer, at no extra charge, EAASY SABRE, an airlines, hotel, and car rental reservation service. It is the consumer version of the American Airlines reservation system. Book reservations online with 315 airlines and get your tickets by mail, at the airport, or from your travel agent.

The above services all provide domestic and foreign weather reports for the traveler.

• Prodigy also has a travel columnist, a travel bulletin board, travel guides for a dozen large U.S. cities, plus the Mobil Travel Guide, which provides information on lodgings, restaurants, and things to do in 3,300 U.S. and Canadian destinations.

• CompuServe carries Department of State Advisories (as does the Internet) and Visa Advisors, and its Travel Forum has members in many foreign countries. About 200 to 300 messages a day are posted to the Travel Forum. In addition, the Travel Forum contains data libraries offering travel articles, hotel reviews, and Forum messages saved because of their usefulness to travelers.

• America Online has Hometown Event Boards on which participants can share information about restaurants, concerts, and other local events. Its Independent Traveler Boards cover U.S. and foreign travel.

Sony's Data Discman is a compact disc player about the size of a paperback that plays small CD-ROMs. Among CDs serving the traveler is *OAG Travel-Disc—North American Edition*, a stripped-down version of the *OAG Electronic Edition Travel Service*. It lists schedule information on 71,000 flights to more than 1,200 North American cities but does not give fares. Other Data Discman titles include *Frommer's Guide to America's Most Traveled Cities* (maps, hotels, restaurants, and sightseeing for five cities), *International Herald Tribune European Business Guide* (hotels, restaurants, executive services, and maps for thirty-two cities), *CIA World Factbook* (information on 249 countries from the Central Intelligence Agency), and *Passport's World Travel Translator* (words and phrases in nine other languages).

CIA World Factbook is available on CD-ROM (Quanta).

Countries of the World is a CD-ROM containing 100 country study books from the U.S. Army Area Handbook series (Bureau of Electronic Publishing).

Great Cities of the World is available on two discs, with information on ten cities on each. The first covers Bombay to Tokyo, the second, Berlin to Toronto.

The Internet has two travel news groups: **rec.travel** and **rec.travel.air.**

Electronic Bulletin Boards

- Boundary Waters BBS: Information for Northwoods recreation: **(218) 365-6907.**
- Worldwide Brochures BBS: A database of more than 9,000 free maps and travel brochures and booklets. To order items through the system, users pay a $12 membership fee: **(218) 847-3027.** For information, call (800) 852-6752.
- Consular Affairs Bulletin Board, which carries the U.S. Department of State's travel advisories: **(202) 647-9225.**

GOVERNMENT PUBLICATIONS

Department of the Interior. National Park Service.
    Various publications on the national parks, including visitors' guides, maps, and interpretive information. See the Government Printing Office's *Subject Bibliography #16* for a list of National Park Service handbooks.

Department of State. *Background Notes.*
    Issued for most countries, and revised every few years. Brief (six to twelve pages) descriptions of physical features, economy, population, political system, history, with "Travel Notes" and bibliography.

Department of State. *Your Trip Abroad.* 1992.

A pamphlet outlining passport and visa requirements, services overseas provided by the Bureau of Consular Affairs, immigration and customs procedures, and other advice.

Department of Health and Human Services. Centers for Disease Control. *Health Information for International Travel.* Annual.
   The authoritive source for medical regulations and advice worldwide.

Also see the Government Printing Office's *Subject Bibliography #303—Travel and Tourism.*

GOVERNMENT AGENCIES

Travel and Tourism Administration
Department of Commerce
14th St. between Constitution Ave. and E St. NW
Washington, DC 20230
(202) 377-3811
Maintains travel offices overseas to encourage foreign tourists to visit the United States. Assists the travel industry by collecting statistics.

Bureau of Consular Affairs
Department of State
2201 C St. NW
Washington, DC 20520
(202) 647-4000
Issues passports; protects the rights of American citizens abroad.

National Railroad Passenger Corp. (Amtrak)
60 Massachusetts Ave. NE
Washington, DC 20002
(202) 906-3860
Operates U.S. railroad passenger service.

Country, state, and city travel promotion offices are listed in *Worldwide Travel Information Contact Book,* cited above.

ASSOCIATIONS

American Automobile Association
1000 AAA Dr.
Heathrow, FL 32746-5063
(404) 444-7000
This federation of automobile clubs provides domestic and foreign travel services and emergency road service. Affiliates in every state and comparable organizations in many foreign countries.

American Society of Travel Agents
1101 King St.
Alexandria, VA 22314
(703) 739-2782
Most well-established travel agencies are members of this professional
organization and display its logo on their promotional materials.

Council on International Education Exchange
205 East 42d St.
New York, NY 10017
(212) 661-1414
Arranges foreign study programs and low-cost travel, and publishes three
useful directories: *Academic Year Abroad, Vacation Study Abroad,* and *Teaching Abroad.* Write for a free copy of its biannual magazine, *Student Travels.*

Elderhostel
80 Boylston St., Suite 400
Boston, MA 02116
(617) 426-7788 or (800) 733-9753
Domestic and foreign travel/study opportunities for seniors.

LIBRARIES

American Geographic Society Collection
University of Wisconsin, Milwaukee
2311 E. Hartford Ave., P. O. Box 399
Milwaukee, WI 53211
(414) 229-6282
One of the largest geography collections in the United States.

Travel Reference Center, Business Research Division
University of Colorado
Campus Box 420
Boulder, CO 80309
(303) 492-8227
Supports research on the travel industry; houses collection of international travel research studies.

National Geographic Society Library
16th and M Sts. NW
Washington, DC 20036
(202) 857-7787
Strong collections in geography, voyages, and travel.

Much travel information is found under the name of the destination, for example, Great Britain—Description and travel, or England—Description and travel, or Oxford—Description and travel.

Some other general headings are:

Air travel	Teenage travel programs
Bicycle touring	Tourist trade
Jet lag	Travel—Health aspects
Ocean travel	Travel agents
Pets and travel	Travel etiquette
Safaris	Travel photography

Abundant materials are available from foreign travel promotion agencies such as the Pacific Asia Travel Association, the European Travel Commission, and the Caribbean Tourism Association. Publicity materials are issued by airlines, resorts, cruise companies, and national/state tourist offices.

You can also rely on first-hand accounts by recently returned visitors. Or chat on an electronic bulletin board with local residents.

Newspapers and city magazines from the area of interest are available in larger public and academic libraries and on newsstands. *The New York Times* Sunday Travel section is the most complete of its kind.

More than thirty bookstores in the United States specialize in travel; Rand McNally, for example, has bookstores in ten cities. Some stores publish mail order catalogs, which can be very useful in locating all available titles of a travel series, identifying extremely specialized publications difficult to find elsewhere, and tracking down elusive maps. Here are a few examples, with approximate prices:

- The Complete Traveller, 199 Madison Ave., New York, NY 10016; (212) 685-9007. ($1).
- Phileas Fogg's Books and Maps for the Traveler, 87 Stanford Shopping Center, Palo Alto, CA 94304; (800) 533-3644. ($1–$5).
- Traveller's Bookstore Catalog, 22 W. 52d St., New York, NY 10019; (212) 664-0995. ($2).

51

VISUAL ARTS

See also: General Reference Sources, Film, Television

The visual arts include, but are not limited to, painting, drawing, design, architecture, prints, photography, video arts, and sculpture. The term *fine arts* is used to describe visual arts of high quality, primarily in painting, sculpture, and drawing.

This section has been designed to help you explore the complex and changing world of the visual arts. People—knowledgeable librarians and artists themselves—are often the best resource; but many printed, graphic, and electronic sources will help you find what you need on subjects as various as the folk art of the Ozarks, the photography of Cartier-Bresson, public sculpture in New York City, the video artist Nam June Paik, or neo-Dadaism.

Art Research Methods and Resources: A Guide to Finding Art Information. 3d ed. By Lois S. Jones. Kendall/Hunt, 1990.

GENERAL SOURCES OF INFORMATION

A combination of how-to-do art research and a list of more than 1,500 research tools, including electronic sources. Excellent for the beginning researcher.

Fine Arts: A Bibliographic Guide to Basic Reference Works, Histories, and Handbooks. 3d ed. By Donald Ehresmann. Libraries Unlimited, 1990.

Lists more than 2,000 works and supplies excellent annotations.

Guide to the Literature of Art History. By Etta Arntzen and Robert Rainwater. American Library Association, 1981.

This is the most complete bibliography on the topic, listing more than 4,000 titles.

Encyclopedia of World Art. 15 vols. McGraw-Hill, 1959.

Encyclopedia of World Art. Supplement I: *World Art in Our Time.* McGraw-Hill, 1983.

Encyclopedia of World Art. Supplement II: *New Discoveries and Perspectives in the World of Art.* Jack Heraty & Associates, 1987.

There is an abundance of textual and graphic information in these three essential volumes, though for recent movements and events you will need to consult more current sources, especially journals (see below). The encyclopedia covers art history from ancient times, major periods of art, movements and schools of thought, and artists famous and obscure. The supplements cover all time periods and update information in the basic set. The encyclopedia contains many illustrations.

The Oxford Companion to Twentieth Century Art. Edited by Harold Osborne. Oxford University Press, 1981 (reprinted with corrections 1988).

Contains short, clear, and concise articles, excellent bibliographies. Cross-references link movements and individual artists within those movements.

Individual Artists

"Every artist writes his own biography," wrote Havelock Ellis. In a sense, the story of the artist is to be found in his or her work; but if you are interested in the facts of an artist's life, an indispensable source of information on *contemporary* artists is the Contemporary Arts Series from St. James Press. This unique series includes:

Contemporary Architects. 2d ed. Edited by Ann L. Morgan. 1987.
Contemporary Artists. 3d ed. Edited by Colin Naylor. 1989.
Contemporary Designers. 2d ed. Edited by Colin Naylor. 1990.
Contemporary Photographers. 2d ed. Edited by Colin Naylor. 1988.

Each volume is international in scope and contains biographical information, bibliographies, artists' statements, and criticism. The many illustrations are in black and white.

Artist Biographies Master Index. Edited by Barbara McNeil. Gale Research, 1986.

Index to more than a quarter of a million short biographies of artists living and dead. The sources indexed include all the principal current and retrospective biographical dictionaries in the fine and applied arts. Includes entries for painters, sculptors, illustrators, designers, graphic artists, craftsmen, architects, photographers.

Who's Who in American Art. 21st ed. Bowker, 1994. Biennial. Also online with Dialog.

History of Art. By H. W. Jansen. 4th ed. By Anthony F. Janson. Abrams, 1992.

McGraw-Hill Dictionary of Art. Edited by Bernard S. Myers. McGraw-Hill, 1969.

Art Index. (CD-ROM) H. W. Wilson, 1984–   . Quarterly.
    Indexes about 250 American and international publications relating to all areas of the visual arts. An indispensable resource for the visual arts researcher. An annotated version on CD-ROM, *Wilson Art Abstracts,* will be released in 1995. Available online via Wilsonline and OCLC FirstSearch, 1984–   , and in print, 1930–   .

ArtBibliographies Modern. (Online) 1974–   . Semiannual.
    Available online via Dialog (File 56) and Knowledge Index (ARTS1). Contains abstracts of books, exhibition catalogs, and periodical articles dealing with the visual arts throughout the world from about 1800 to the present, but stressing the twentieth century. Also available in print from Clio Press, 1974–   .

Avery Index to Architectural Periodicals. (Online) RLIN, updated daily, and Dialog, updated semiannually.
    Compiled at the Avery Library of Architecture and Fine Arts at Columbia University, this database includes articles on architecture, decorative arts, furniture, landscape architecture, and housing. Also available in print as *Avery Architectural Index,* 2d ed. (G. K. Hall, 1973) plus supplements.

Art Literature International. (Online) 1973–   . Quarterly.
    This is the online version of *Bibliography of the History of Art: BHA,* published by the J. Paul Getty Museum for the College Art Association. *BHA* was formed in 1991 with the merger of *Répertoire International de la Littérature de l'Art* and *Répertoire d'Art et d'Archéologie* (1910–90). It is available via Dialog (File 191) and Knowledge Index (ARTS2). It covers books, dissertations, museum publications, periodical articles, and conference proceedings. Available in print, 1973–   , quarterly.

NewsBank Review of the Arts. (CD-ROM) NewsBank. 1983–   .
    Indexes reviews of art exhibitions from hundreds of American newspapers. The reviews are available on microfilm that accompanies the index.

SCIPIO (Sales Catalog Index Project On-Line). RLIN.
    Citations to more than 110,000 art sales catalogs from major auction houses in the United States and Europe.

CompuServe: The Grant-Making History of the Design Arts Program, National Endowment for the Arts (1967–   ), provides information on grants for public art and architecture from NEA, updated quarterly. CompuServe's Art Gallery Forum has scanned color images of paintings and other art works from around the world.

The Electronic Library of Art. (CD-ROM) Sony.

Covers painting, sculpture, and architecture. Features general surveys and in-depth studies of specific artists and periods with thousands of color images.

Philips Great Art Series on CD-I (Compact Disc-Interactive).

Makes information about art and full-color images available for viewing on a TV screen. Among the titles are *Art: Impressionism, Art: Renaissance of Florence,* and *Treasures of the Smithsonian.*

The Internet has many mailing lists of interest to artists and art historians. Some examples are:

ARTCRIT is a discussion forum on Bitnet open to anyone interested in the visual arts. Access via: **ARTCRIT%YORKVM1.BITNET@VM1. NODAK.EDU.**

CLAYART provides a forum for a discussion of issues in the field of ceramic arts/pottery. Access via: **LISTSERV@UKCC.uky.edu.**

The FINEART forum disseminates information on the use of computers in fine arts. Access via: **FINEART%ecs.umass.edu@RELAY.CS.NET.**

PERIODICALS   *American Artist.* 1937–   . Monthly.

For practicing artists, articles on art techniques and art as a business. Annual business supplement lists galleries, sales, grants.

Art Bulletin. 1912–   . Quarterly.

A leading scholarly art journal, published by the College Art Association. All reproductions are in black and white. CAA also publishes *Art Journal* (quarterly), every issue of which is built around a theme (e.g., Political Journals and Art, 1910–40). Contains reviews of books and exhibitions.

Art in America. 1913–   . Monthly.

Offers a comprehensive view of the contemporary American visual art scene in a format that is appealing to laypeople. It covers modern and older artists and art themes. Color and black and white illustrations, reviews of U.S. and foreign exhibitions, critical articles, news.

Artforum. 1962–   . 10 times/year.

The most modernist of the magazines listed here, with an international focus for the serious collector and curator of contemporary art. Contains color and black and white illustrations, pictures of original art works ("projects"), reviews of U.S. and foreign exhibitions, critical articles, opinion pieces.

ARTnews. 1902–   . 10 times/year.

Among the most accessible and popular of the journals covering contemporary American art. Contains color and black and white illustrations, news articles, critical articles, reviews of U.S. and foreign exhibitions and gallery shows, art market news.

The Artist's Magazine. 1984–   . Monthly.

For the practicing artist, articles on tools and techniques and on where and how to sell art.

Arts Magazine. 1926–   . 10 times/year.

Elegant, understated, modernist art magazine. Contains color and black and white illustrations, detailed review articles of American and foreign exhibitions, critical articles, news of the New York, Los Angeles, and Chicago art scenes. Publishing schedule has been somewhat erratic in recent years.

Smithsonian Studies in American Art. 1987–   . Quarterly.

Covers American art of all time periods. Articles are academic but accessible.

Most large museums publish a bulletin with scholarly articles on acquisitions and art from their own collections. The names of these publications can be found in the *Official Museum Directory* (annual). Among them are:

Museum Studies (Art Institute of Chicago)
Bulletin of the Cleveland Museum of Art
J. Paul Getty Museum Journal
Bulletin of the Metropolitan Museum of Art
Yale University Art Gallery Bulletin

Information Resources in the Arts: A Directory. Compiled by Lloyd W. Shipley. Library of Congress, 1986.

The United States has a thriving network of arts associations and organizations with an array of services connecting artist and audience. This comprehensive directory lists federal, state, and local government arts agencies,

GOVERNMENT PUBLICATIONS

national and regional arts services organizations, arts education programs, and international arts organizations. Each entry lists address and telephone number, areas of interest, holdings, publications, and information services.

ARTSREVIEW. National Endowment for the Arts. 1983–88.

This attractive quarterly magazine of the arts devoted each issue to a special theme. It ceased publication in 1988.

See also the Government Printing Office's *Subject Bibliography* #107—Art and Artists, #215—Architecture, and #72—Photography.

State and Local Government Publications

A world of information on the visual arts can be found in state and local government publications. For example:

The Arizona Commission on the Arts publishes the *Bi-Cultural Information Quarterly*.

The Chicago Office of Fine Arts publishes a quarterly newsletter, *Art Post*.

GOVERNMENT AGENCIES

Government agencies offer direct assistance as well as publications. The marriage between government and the arts is often stormy, but government at all levels continues to play a role in the creation and dissemination of art.

National Endowment for the Arts
Director of Public Information
1100 Pennsylvania Avenue NW
Washington, DC 20506
(202) 682-5400

The Endowment for the Arts was established to promote the dissemination of cultural resources, assist cultural institutions, support creativity, encourage preservation, and improve quality in the arts. It awards fellowships to artists and matching grants to arts organizations. Its library/information center, (202) 682-5485, contains information on all aspects of the arts, including arts and government, arts administration, cultural history, economics of the arts, and grants. Most materials are available through interlibrary loan.

The Office for Special Constituencies of the Endowment is devoted to making the arts more accessible to the handicapped, older adults, veterans, the hospitalized, and others.

National Endowment for the Humanities
1100 Pennsylvania Avenue NW
Washington, DC 20506
(202) 786-0438

While NEA (above) gives grants to practicing artists, NEH awards money to art critics and art historians for research.

Smithsonian Institution
1000 Jefferson Dr. SW
Washington, DC 20560
(202) 357-1300
Operates art museums (National Portrait Gallery, National Museum of American Art, National Museum of African Art) in Washington, D.C., and New York City.

Information on the arts that is special to a state and region can come from the arts commissions or councils of the individual states and other state-supported arts bodies. Many have libraries and/or information services. Examples include:

State Councils

California Arts Council (Sacramento)
New York State Council on the Arts (New York)
Ozark Folk Center (Mountain View, AR)
Texas Commission on the Arts (Austin)
At the local level, publicly supported bodies concerned with the arts can be located in the phone directory's Yellow Pages under such headings as Art Galleries, etc., Arts Organizations and Information, Art Museums, Museums. They are often unique sources of local information. Examples include:

Chicago Office of Fine Arts
East Bay Center for the Performing Arts (Richmond, CA)

American Art Directory. 54th ed. Bowker, 1992.
Lists more than 2,500 museums and libraries, 1,700 art schools, state arts councils, exhibition booking agencies, and more.

ASSOCIATIONS

American Federation of Arts
41 E. 65th Street
New York, NY 10021
(212) 988-7700
The AFA provides support to all types of museums in promoting appreciation of the arts. Its main activity is organizing traveling exhibits.

Alliance for Arts Education
JFK Center for the Performing Arts
Washington, DC 20566
(202) 416-8847
All sectors of education for the arts are members of the Alliance. Among its primary aims are the collection and dissemination of information about arts education.

Art Libraries Society of North America
3900 E. Timrod Street
Tucson, AZ 85711
(602) 881-8479

ARLIS is primarily an organization for art librarians. It publishes the quarterly *Art Documentation* and various subject guides and reference aids.

Arts and Business Council
130 E. 40th Street
New York, NY 10016
(212) 683-5555

Provides liaison between the business and arts communities. Sponsors Business Volunteers for the Arts, a program in which business executives contribute their skills to help nonprofit arts organizations.

College Art Association
275 7th Avenue
New York, NY 10001
(212) 691-1051

Members are artists, art historians, and museum directors and curators. Publishes several journals, such as *Art Journal* and *The Art Bulletin,* and directories of academic programs in the visual arts.

National Association for Artists' Organizations
1007 D Street NE
Washington, DC 20002
(202) 544-0660

An association of art centers. Provides technical assistance, maintains a library, publishes the *NAAO Directory* (see below).

National Art Education Association
1916 Association Drive
Reston, VA 22091
(703) 860-8000

A clearinghouse for information on art education, methods of instruction, and art materials.

Other organizations may concentrate on a particular type of art; art in a particular locality; or even the work of a particular artist. Use reference sources such as the *NAAO Directory* (2d ed.; National Association of Artists' Organizations, 1989) and the advice of a librarian to locate them.

Among the richest sources of visual arts knowledge and information are specialist libraries and the librarians who work in them. However, since not all these libraries are open to the public, you should call first.

Archives of American Art
Smithsonian Institution
Balcony, Room 3311
8th and G Sts., NW
Washington, DC 20560
(202) 357-2781

The national depository for primary research materials on American art, the Archives seeks to document the art world of the country as a whole. Most materials can be obtained, *in microform,* from regional archival offices through interlibrary loan.

Ryerson-Burnham Libraries
Art Institute of Chicago
Michigan at Adams
Chicago, IL 60603
(312) 443-3666

The Art Institute Libraries have special collections in architecture, Russian art, Japanese art, French impressionist art, Chicago art history.

Columbia University
Avery Architectural and Fine Arts Library
Avery Hall
New York, NY 10027
(212) 854-3501

The Avery is the most comprehensive architecture library in the United States. It contains a special collection of drawings and archival materials focusing on nineteenth- and twentieth-century American architecture.

Libraries of the Metropolitan Museum of Art
5th Avenue at 82nd Street
New York, NY 10028
(212) 879-5500

The chief library of the Metropolitan is the Thomas J. Watson Library. Special collections include American visual arts, ancient art, European painting, photography, and Native American art.

New York Public Library
The Research Libraries
Wallach Division of Art, Prints, & Photographs
5th Avenue at 42d Street
New York, NY 10018
(212) 340-0834
Special collections include art history, architectural design, nineteenth-century French and American art, contemporary European and American art.

The libraries of major universities have substantial collections in the arts, and most have specialist reference librarians who are able to help. For a directory of art libraries, as well as slide and photographic collections, see:

Directory of Art Libraries and Visual Resource Collections in North America. By Judith A. Hoffberg and Stanley W. Hess. Neal-Schuman, 1978.

LC SUBJECT HEADINGS The name of an artist can lead not only to materials about this figure but also to areas of the library containing materials about the artist's school and period. For example:

Matisse, Henri—Catalogs (meaning *catalogues raisonné*, descriptive catalogs of an artist's work)

Matisse, Henri—Criticism and interpretation

Matisse, Henri—Exhibitions (meaning exhibition catalogs)

Subject headings begin with the type of art (Painting, Sculpture, etc.) or type of artist (Painters, Sculptors, etc.), often followed by a geographic (e.g., France) or time (e.g., twentieth century) qualifier. The general heading *Art* is similarly subdivided. When these headings are followed by a comma and the adjectival form of a country name (Painting, French), they refer to paintings created in that country. When they are followed by dashes and the name of the country (Painting—France), they refer to paintings located in that country, regardless of where they were painted:

Painting, American [paintings by Americans]

Painting—U.S. [paintings in American museums]

Painting, Modern—19th century—France

Sculpture—African—Exhibitions

Handicrafts is the heading, not *Crafts*.

Pottery is used for ceramics as art, and *Ceramics* for ceramic technology.

Outsider art is particularly difficult to trace. The term itself is not used. Try *Primitivism in art, Folk art, Art brut,* and the outdated but still-used *Art and mental illness.* The last will get you to material on Outsider art as well as on art therapy, etc.

Art reproductions: Notice that in a cataloging record, after the pagination, there is often the note "ill.," denoting that the book has illustrations. Sometimes the note will read "ill. (some col.)," meaning that some of the illustrations are in color. University and museum libraries often have slide and/or picture collections. Ask a reference librarian if this source of art reproductions is available to you.

Art Information Center
280 Broadway, Suite 412
New York, NY 10007
(212) 227-0282
A clearinghouse for information on contemporary fine arts, it provides information to the public, as well as to artists and art professionals, on most aspects of the current arts scene. A major strength of the collection is a set of files on more than 65,000 living artists.

Franklin Furnace
112 Franklin Street
New York, NY 10013
(212) 925-4671
Specializes in artists' books (books created as works of art) and other nontraditional art works—postcards, audiotapes, broadsides, etc. Reference library in the field of avant-garde expressions and an archival collection of artists' books.

Art Hazards Information Center
5 Beekman Street, Suite 1030
New York, NY 10038
(212) 227-6220
Run by the Center for Safety in the Arts, this group will answer telephone and written inquiries on art hazards and art safety issues and will provide referrals. Publishes *Art Hazards News.*

National Center for Afro-American Artists
122 Elm Hill Avenue
Boston, MA 02121
(617) 442-8614
A museum and resource center for African-American artists. Its main goal is to promote cultural activities and to encourage African-American arts.

Association of Hispanic Arts
173 E. 116th Street, 2d Floor
New York, NY 10029
(212) 860-5445
The Association maintains a central information office and has a mailing list of currently active arts associations, individual artists, media sources, and funding sources.

52

WOMEN'S STUDIES

See also: *General Reference Sources, History, Literature, Sports*

The field of women's studies has exploded over the past few decades. More than 600 U.S. colleges now offer women's studies degrees, and feminist scholarship has altered the nature of traditional disciplines. Research on feminist topics is being conducted in departments of literature, history, psychology, and the other social sciences and humanities.

Today, reference sources within the traditional disciplines as well as specialized interdisciplinary sources guide the researcher through vast accumulations of information and scholarship.

Bear in mind, however, that since women's studies is an interdisciplinary endeavor, reliance on browsing in the library bookstacks isn't an adequate way of finding all relevant material. A University of Wisconsin study indicated that only 21.5 percent of the titles bought out of the women's studies budget fell in the Library of Congress call number range for "women and feminism" (HQ1101 to HQ2030). The remainder of the titles were found under many different call numbers. It's best to investigate thoroughly all likely subject headings.

The American Woman: A Status Report. Norton, 1987–   .

    This annual report, previously published with the subtitle "A Report in Depth," is compiled by the Women's Research and Education Institute, the research arm of the Congressional Caucus for Women's Issues. It reviews the previous year, surveying broad topics such as African-American families and women and affordable housing. An appendix presents a statistical portrait of contemporary women.

GENERAL SOURCES OF INFORMATION

Introduction to Library Research in Women's Studies. By Susan E. Searing. Westview Press, 1985.

The best, most thorough guide available for research on women. Hints on defining a research strategy and using a library are provided, along with an extensive annotated list of books.

United States Government Documents on Women, 1800–1990. 2 vols. By Mary Ellen Huls. Greenwood, 1993.

Lists more than 3,000 government publications pertaining to women. Volume 1 covers social issues; Volume 2 treats labor.

Women's Information Directory. Edited by Shawn Brennan. Gale, 1993.

This directory lists 6,000 organizations, institutions, programs, and publications concerned with women in the United States. Includes libraries, museums, women's studies programs, awards, videotapes, electronic sources, and others.

Women's Studies: A Guide to Information Sources. By Sarah Carter and Maureen Ritchie. McFarland, 1990.

Though compiled in Britain, this guide lists mostly American books and journals and updates the two core bibliographies in the entries that follow.

Women's Studies: A Recommended Core Bibliography. By Esther Stineman. Libraries Unlimited, 1979.

More than 1,700 titles are annotated.

Women's Studies: A Recommended Core Bibliography 1980–1985. By Catherine R. Loeb, Susan E. Searing, and Esther F. Stineman. Libraries Unlimited, 1987.

Describes more than 1,200 titles published in the five-year period following the 1979 edition. Some libraries may own a concise version of this book, also published in 1987.

Women's Studies Encyclopedia. 3 vols. Edited by Helen Tierney. Greenwood, 1989–91.

Volume 1: *Views from the Sciences*
Volume 2: *Literature, Arts, and Learning*
Volume 3: *History, Philosophy, and Religion*

Brief entries by women's studies scholars summarize research on such topics as comparable worth, fear of success, learned helplessness, math anxiety, lesbian literature, and supermarket romances. Most entries conclude with brief lists of further reading. A good place for beginning research on a topic.

Statistical Record of Women Worldwide. Edited by Linda Schmittroth. Gale, 1991.

Statistical Handbook on Women in America. Edited by Cynthia Taeuber. Oryx, 1991.

Though the first of these statistical handbooks is international in scope, both have extensive coverage of women in the United States. Historical tables, charts, and graphs, most of them taken from government publications, are provided.

Atlas of American Women. By Barbara Gimla Shortridge. Macmillan, 1987.

Women in the World: An International Atlas. By Joni Seager and Ann Olson. Simon & Schuster, 1986.

The Women's Atlas of the United States. By Anne Gibson and Timothy Fast. Facts On File, 1986.

These three atlases display statistical data visually.

Also see Electronic Sources below.

Also see Electronic Sources below.

PERIODICAL INDEXES

Women Studies Abstracts. Rush Publishing, 1972–   . Quarterly.

Selectively indexes about 300 popular and scholarly publications. Stronger representation of American periodicals.

Women's Studies Index. G. K. Hall, 1990–   . Annual.

Indexes eighty feminist periodicals, both scholarly and popular, including some not covered in *Women Studies Abstracts.*

Feminist Periodicals: A Current Listing of Contents. Office of the Women's Studies Librarian, University of Wisconsin, Madison, 1980–   . Quarterly.

Reproduces the title pages of more than 100 periodicals, from *Affilia: Journal of Women and Social Work* to the *Yale Journal of Law and Feminism.* This is an excellent way to keep up with what is being published currently, especially if the local library doesn't subscribe to many women's studies journals. Skim through each quarterly issue and order photocopies of relevant articles on interlibrary loan.

Other Indexes

Feminist research is fairly well represented in mainstream periodical indexes. For articles dealing with more radical feminist perspectives on health care, lesbianism, the media, and the like, see *Alternative Press Index* and *The Left Index.* For African-American and Latina publications, check *Index to Black Periodicals* and *Hispanic American Periodicals Index.*

Little in the way of specialized electronic databases has appeared specifically for women's studies. The *National Council for Research on Women Work-in-Progress Database* (NCRW) is available online through RLIN. Developed in collaboration with the Schlesinger Library (see below) and the Research Libraries Group, it is designed to include information about research projects in progress on women—books, articles, dissertations, planning documents, art, working papers, videotapes, software, and curricula. The database is also available in print from the NCRW as *WIP: A Directory of Work-In-Progress & Recent Publications*, 1992.

For more detailed guidance about online searching, see *Women Online: Research in Women's Studies Using Online Databases*, edited by Steven D. Atkinson and Judith Hudson (Haworth Press, 1990). Chapters treat online searching in the humanities, social sciences, biomedicine, business, news files, citation databases, reference sources, and national online bibliographic utilities such as OCLC and RLIN. Additional chapters cover lesbians, women of color, women in developing countries, women in sport, and women's studies curriculum materials online. Essays describe sample searches and search strategies and compare coverage of competing files.

Because of the interdisciplinary nature of the field, databases in many areas may be useful for research in women's studies. For example:

America: History and Life on Disc. (CD-ROM) ABC-Clio, 1982–   . Updated 3 times/year.
This most comprehensive index includes abstracts of periodical articles and citations to reviews and dissertations on the history and culture of the United States and Canada. Articles are abstracted from 2,100 serial publications in forty languages. Of these, 900 are published in North America. Also available online with Dialog (File 38) and Knowledge Index (file HIST1), 1964–   , updated quarterly. Available in print, ABC-Clio, 1964–   , updated five times a year. Issues 1–3 include indexes. Issue 4 includes abstracts and citations only. Issue 5, the annual index, includes cumulative subject and author indexes.

ERIC (Educational Resources Information Center), a service of the U.S. Department of Education, contains a great deal of information on the education of girls and women. The two ERIC databases are available on CD-ROM, online, and in print form with more than 750,000 citations to journal and report literature:
• *Current Index to Journals in Education (CIJE)*. Abstracts of articles from 750 education journals.
• *Resources in Education (RIE)*. Abstracts of hundreds of thousands of

research reports, including conference papers, curriculum materials, and other unpublished documents of interest to educators.

These files are available on CD-ROM from two companies and updated quarterly: *DIALOG OnDisc: ERIC.* UMI. 1966–   , and *ERIC on SilverPlatter,* 1966–   . These files are also online through CompuServe, Dialog, Knowledge Index (EDUC1), BRS, BRS/AfterDark, BRS Colleague, OCLC FirstSearch, 1966–   , updated monthly.

The print versions of *CIJE* (Oryx, 1969–   ) and *RIE* (U.S. Government Printing Office, 1966–   ) are updated monthly.

To search ERIC most efficiently, whether on CD-ROM, online, or in print, use the *Thesaurus of ERIC Descriptors* (12th ed., Oryx, 1990) to find the appropriate subject headings.

ERIC Microfiche Collection contains the full text of more than 300,000 educational documents indexed in *Resources in Education.* Collections are located at approximately 825 libraries and agencies and are open to the public. Call ACCESS ERIC for locations, (800) USE-ERIC.

PsycLIT. (CD-ROM) SilverPlatter, 1974–   . Quarterly.

Abstracts of articles from more than 1,300 psychology journals representing professional and scientific literature from fifty countries. Compiled by the American Psychological Association. Also available online as *PsycInfo,* 1967–   , with monthly updates. Available on BRS, BRS/AfterDark, BRS Colleague, Data-Star, Dialog (File 11), Knowledge Index (PSYC1), OCLC FirstSearch, 1967–   . Also available in print form as *Psychological Abstracts,* 1927–   , updated monthly.

Social Sciences Index. (CD-ROM) H. W. Wilson, 1983–   . Monthly.

Indexes by author and subject over 300 leading periodicals in the social sciences. As is true of all Wilsondisc products, it is possible to dial up the online file at no extra charge and find the latest citations. Also available in some libraries as *Social Sciences Index/Full Text* (1989–   , monthly) with the full text of the articles indexed on compact disc. An annotated version on CD-ROM, *Wilson Social Sciences Abstracts,* is due to be released in 1995. Online with Wilsonline and OCLC FirstSearch, 1983–   . Print version, *Social Sciences Index,* 1974–   , formerly *Social Sciences and Humanities Index,* 1965–74; *International Index,* 1907–65.

- WMST-L is the most general file for women's studies. To subscribe, send the following command: **LISTSERV@UMDD.UMD.EDU: subscribe WMST-L your name.** When you subscribe, you will receive instructions on obtaining a user guide that includes the commands for requesting files. To find out what files are available, send LISTSERV the command **INDEX WMST-L.** Women's studies course syllabi are contained in a

On the Internet

subdirectory; feminist film reviews are in another subdirectory. To find out what these subdirectories contain, use the command **INDEX SYLLABI** or **INDEX FILM.** Also includes information on conferences, job openings.

- FEMAIL: A moderated list "that exists to provide a shared communication channel for feminists around the world." **FEMAIL-REQUEST@ LUCERNE.ENG.SUN.COM.**
- GENDER: Devoted to "discussion of issues pertaining to the study of communication and gender." **COMSERV@VM.ECS.RPI.EDU.**
- WOMEN: A general-purpose list, intended to be a connection between all women's groups and areas of interest for women and their friends. **WOMEN-REQUEST@ATHENA.MIT.EDU.**
- Women's Online Network (WON): An electronic political group for women. Fee of $20/year. **CARMELA@ECHO.PANIX.COM** or telephone (212) 255-3839 for more information.

There are more specialized lists for feminist perspectives in various academic disciplines (psychology, economics, etc.). For example, MEDFEM-L is a discussion group sponsored by the Society for Medievalist Feminist Studies. To subscribe, send a message to **LISTSERV@INDYCMS. IUPUI.EDU.** FIST (Feminism in/and Science and Technology) is a forum for the discussion of critiques of science, how to create a feminist science, how to teach science. To subscribe, send a message to **FIST-REQUEST @HAMPSHIRE.EDU.**

PERIODICALS   *Ms.* 1990–   . Bimonthly.

Recently reborn as a reader-supported publication printed on matte-finish paper, *Ms.* now features fiction, poetry, news, and essays reflecting the essence of liberal feminism. It was originally published starting in 1972.

New Directions for Women. 1972–   . Bimonthly.

This feminist newspaper covers both national and international concerns.

off our backs: a women's news journal. 1970–   . Monthly.

One of the early radical feminist publications, *oob* is essential for information about international and domestic radical feminist politics, lesbian feminism, women prisoners, and the politics of race within women's movements. A complete run of *oob* provides good historical documentation of the feminist left.

Sage: A Scholarly Journal on Black Women. 1984–   . Semiannual.

An academic journal featuring black feminist scholarship.

Signs: Journal of Women in Culture and Society. 1975–   . Quarterly.
    Leading academic journal of women's studies scholarship; interdisciplinary.

The Women's Review of Books. 1983–   . 11 times/year.
    This monthly publication offers in-depth reviews of current scholarly and popular books in all fields by and about women and is an excellent way to keep up with what's being published. Read this and *Feminist Periodicals* (above) to keep current with books and periodical articles in women's studies.

Women and Business Ownership: An Annotated Bibliography. U.S. Department of Commerce, 1986.

**GOVERNMENT
PUBLICATIONS**

Women on the Job: Careers in the Electronic Media. U.S. Department of Labor, 1990.

A Working Woman's Guide to Her Job Rights. U.S. Department of Labor, 1988.

Why Women Don't Get Mammograms (And Why They Should). U.S. Department of Health and Human Services. Food and Drug Administration, 1988.

See also *Subject Bibliography* #111—Women, available from the Government Printing Office.

See also *United States Government Documents on Women, 1800–1990* (p. 489).

Women's Bureau
Department of Labor
200 Constitution Ave. NW
Washington, DC 20210
(202) 523-6611
    Responsible for formulating standards and policies that promote the welfare of wage-earning women, improve their working conditions, and advance their opportunities for employment. Ten regional offices.

**GOVERNMENT
AGENCIES**

Equal Employment Opportunity Commission
1801 L Street NW
Washington, DC 20509
(800) USA-EEOC

Charged with eliminating discrimination based on race, color, religion, national origin, age, or sex in all terms of employment. Regional offices.

Commission on Civil Rights
1121 Vermont Ave. NW
Washington, DC 20405
(202) 376-8177
Collects and studies information on discrimination or denial of the equal protection of the law because of race, color, religion, handicap, national origin, age, or sex. Regional offices.

ASSOCIATIONS

International Center for Research on Women
1717 Massachusetts Ave. NW, #501
Washington, DC 20036
(202) 797-0007
ICRW's purpose is to improve the productivity and income of women in the developing countries by providing technical assistance for development projects that integrate women into mainstream economic roles. Publishes books and technical reports addressing the social and economic status of women.

National Council for Research on Women
The Sara Delano Roosevelt Memorial House
47-49 E. 65th St.
New York, NY 10021
(212) 570-5001
A coalition of sixty-five U.S. centers for research on women, NCRW has links to thousands of scholars and professionals through such programs as the National Women's Caucuses in the Disciplines and Professional Associations and other women's networks here and abroad.

National Organization for Women
1000 16th St. NW
Washington, DC 20036
(202) 331-0066
Men and women who support "full equality for women in truly equal partnership with men" belong to NOW and its 800 local chapters. Promotes passage of the Equal Rights Amendment, engages in lobbying, and works to increase the number of women elected to political office. The separate NOW Legal Defense and Education Fund provides legal assistance to women and educates the public on gender discrimination.

National Women's Political Caucus
1275 K St. NW
Washington, DC 20005
(202) 898-1100

Supports increased political influence of women at local, state, and national levels. Provides multipartisan support for women candidates for elective office, raises such issues as comparable worth and women's reproductive rights in elections.

National Federation of Business and Professional Women's Clubs
2012 Massachusetts Ave. NW
Washington, DC 20036
(202) 293-1200

With 3,500 local groups, its purpose is to provide full participation, equal opportunities, and economic self-sufficiency for working women. Offers nationwide career and personal training seminars, lobbies Congress on issues affecting women. Its Business and Professional Women's Foundation is the research and education arm of the Federation and has a specialized library collection.

Arthur and Elizabeth Schlesinger Library on the History of
Women in America
Radcliffe College
Cambridge, MA 02138
(617) 495-8647

LIBRARIES

Since 1949, the Woman's Rights Collection, as it was known, has been collecting records of women in politics, government, reform, education, and the missions. Archive includes papers of Susan B. Anthony, Lucy Stone, Charlotte Perkins Gilman, Emma Goldman, Helen Keller, Betty Friedan, and others. Its Black Women's Oral History Project (available from Meckler on microfilm) features interviews with distinguished women writers, activists, and community leaders.

Sophia Smith Collection
Smith College
Northampton, MA 01063
(413) 584-2700

Begun in 1942 with collection priorities in the arts, education, humanities, health care, industry, the peace movement, the professions, science, sports, psychology, and activism/social reform.

University of Massachusetts Library
Amherst, MA 01003
(413) 545-0284
Comprehensive collection of materials by and about Elizabeth Cady
Stanton and Susan B. Anthony.

Women's Studies Collection
Northwestern University Library
Evanston, IL 60208
(708) 491-3635
Extensive holdings on the women's liberation movement in the United
States and Europe from 1960 to the present.

Bethune Museum-Archives
National Historic Site
1318 Vermont Ave. NW
Washington, DC 20005
(202) 332-1233
Museum and archives on black women's history. Distributes educational
and display materials.

**LC SUBJECT
HEADINGS**

In recent years, the Library of Congress has changed many subject headings
in the area of women's studies to make them conform with modern usage.
However, many libraries have not been able to change all their records for
older books, so you may still find some of the old headings, especially in
large university libraries. For example, until 1980 the term *Feminism* was
not a subject heading; readers were told to See Woman. Also, many head-
ings that began Women as (e.g., Women as accountants, Women as physi-
cians) are now direct, e.g., Women accountants, Women physicians.
    Here are some current headings:
Feminism
Women's rights
Women's studies
And subheadings under Women:
Women—Biography
Women—Crimes against
Women—Education
Women—Employment
Women—History
Women—Legal status, laws, etc.
Women—Social conditions
Headings for special groups of women may be direct or inverted:
Afro-American women

Irish-American women
Women, Deaf
Women, Pentecostal
Women, Jewish
There are also headings for women in specific occupations or avocations:
Women air pilots
Women authors
Women bodybuilders
Women engineers
Women in the performing arts
Women may be a subdivision of more general topics:
Latin American literature—Women authors
There are also topics particular to women's experience:
Abused wives
Gynecology
Adolescent mothers
For a comprehensive list of subject headings on this topic, see *Women in LC's Terms: A Thesaurus of Library of Congress Subject Headings Relating to Women.* By Ruth Dickstein, Victoria A. Mills, and Ellen J. Waite. Oryx Press, 1988.

Another guide to the confusing nomenclature of women's studies used in indexes is *A Women's Thesaurus: An Index of Language Used to Describe and Locate Information By and About Women,* edited by Mary Ellen S. Capek (Harper, 1987). The most useful feature of this book is its list of subject headings in a "rotated display" by keyword. It's possible, for example, to look up the word *rights* and get a list of all subject headings incorporating that word: abortion rights, equal rights, homemaker rights, maternity rights, name rights, parental rights, reproductive rights, etc.

Office of the Women's Studies Librarian-at-Large
University of Wisconsin System
Memorial Library
Madison, WI 53706
(608) 263-5754

SOURCES OF EXPERT ADVICE

Staff produce a biannual model acquisitions list, *New Books on Women and Feminism,* along with current topical Wisconsin Bibliographies in Women's Studies, the quarterly contents listing, *Feminist Periodicals* (see above), and the quarterly *Feminist Collections: Women's Studies Library Resources in Wisconsin,* which includes reports and reviews from Wisconsin and elsewhere.

53

WRITING

William Faulkner once remarked that a writer needs only "experience, observation, and imagination" and sometimes only one of the three. Perhaps he meant writers with his own bounty of inner resources and mastery of the language. For the rest of the crowd, even the most imaginative poets and novelists, the three traits eventually must be backed by research. Research extends experience; research supports observation; research gives language to the imagination.

Writers draw not only from the general and topical research tools cited throughout this guide, but also from resources on writing itself. Of the latter type, no end is in sight; some works treat the art of writing, some the business aspects, some both. Journalists and literary authors often produce writing guides; some of these are small masterpieces. Publishing practitioners such as editors produce other guides. Numerous aids come from Writers Digest Books, a specialized publisher.

As for research on words and language, writers use not only general sources but works as specialized as a handbook of phrases for authors of romance fiction.

GENERAL REFERENCE SOURCES AND MARKET GUIDES For general orientation, one of the best starting places is a savvy guide that has been polished and updated through four editions:

How to Get Happily Published. 4th ed. By Judith Appelbaum. HarperCollins, 1992.

Appelbaum shows how writers, rather than counting on luck, can acquire the skills to influence the destiny of their work, even as they hone their writing skills. Her advice is organized under: Getting the Words Right, A Foot in the Door, The Sale and Its Sequels, The Self-Publishing Option,

Money, and Spinoffs. A Resources section follows the same plan, recommending books, databases, magazines, newsletters, research centers, schools, organizations, and more.

Geared to writers of imaginative literature is this general research guide:

The Fiction Writer's Research Handbook. By Mona McCormick. Plume/New American Library, 1988.
Though the resources given here are only starters, McCormick is a reference librarian and author with a good sense of research strategies.

Although Appelbaum and others are optimistic about opportunities for writers, the novice must still travel a long road that often begins at the library. There, the first sources to examine are language-usage and style authorities, how-to writers' guides, and market directories. The directories are often kept behind the reference desk, available on request. One of the most all-around useful directories is an annual reference book known as *LMP:*

Literary Market Place; The Directory of the American Book Publishing Industry with Industry Yellow Pages. Bowker. Annual.
A tome of some 2,000 pages, *LMP* provides among its many offerings lists of: U.S. and Canadian book publishers, including some small presses, with major personnel and brief notes on the nature and size of the publisher's output; literary agents; book reviewers, exhibits, and clubs; word-processing services; literary associations, events, conferences, courses; writers' workshops; literary awards and grants; reference sources; and publicity contacts. Although not always the ultimate source for each category, it is the best directory overall.

Also kept behind the reference desk, owing to its popularity, is this market directory:

Writer's Market. Writer's Digest Books. Annual.
Provides good detail on some 4,000 publishing opportunities, large and small, general and specialized. Users should bear in mind that listings in *Writer's Market* draw even more manuscripts to the mountains already in each publishing house. One way to help move your manuscript beyond the "slush pile" is to address it to a personal contact at the publishing firm or to a specific editor (see *Insider's Guide to Book Editors, Publishers, and Literary Agents,* below).

The Writer's Handbook. Edited by Sylvia K. Burack. The Writer. Frequently updated.

Another popular source of market information, distinguished by its roughly 100 brief chapters of advice by successful writers. Covering many types of writing, the contributions may sometimes seem elementary to the experienced author; but even old pros will find new tips and worthy reminders. In the 1989 edition, Stephen King's eighth rule of twelve ("Everything You Need to Know About Writing Successfully—In Ten Minutes") stands out: "Ask yourself frequently, 'Am I having fun?' The answer needn't always be yes. But if it's always no, it's time for a new project or career."

The International Directory of Little Magazines and Small Presses. Edited by Len Fulton. Dustbooks. Annual.

Lively descriptions of some 5,000 markets available to unknown writers. Many of the publications offer their authors no more than a few complimentary copies and the experience of being published. Yet the small presses, more hospitable to new voices than mainstream publishers, have probably launched the majority of our established authors. Indexed by region and broad subject headings.

Directory of Poetry Publishers. Edited by Len Fulton. Dustbooks. Annual.

Some 2,000 markets, with more detailed information for poets than can be found in Fulton's *International Directory.* Regional and subject indexes.

Agents, Contracts, and Editors

Resources on literary agents and book editors give background and specific contacts for breaking into print with mainstream publishers. Some also offer business advice for those who have successfully crashed the gates.

How to Be Your Own Literary Agent: The Business of Getting Your Book Published. By Richard Curtis. Houghton Mifflin, 1984.

Curtis is forthright and amusing about what an agent can and cannot do for writers. His chapters on book publishing contracts are among the most lucid of those in the many guides available. Other fine discussions of contracts appear in Carol Meyer's *The Writer's Survival Manual* (Bantam, 1984), and *A Writer's Guide to Book Publishing* by Richard Balkan (New American Library-Dutton, 1981).

The following three guides list agencies, as does *Literary Market Place* (above):

Literary Agents of North America. 5th ed. Author Aid, 1993.

Detailed listings of some 900 agents.

Literary Agents: A Writer's Guide. Poets & Writers, 1992.

A popular listing.

ed. By Jeff Herman. Prima Publishing, 1992.

Frequently updated, this is perhaps the only guide that names the editors who acquire books at major publishing houses and explains what they seek. Herman also provides a descriptive list of agents.

Certain major principles emerge from research into the technique of writing. Most of these principles are articulated in a few enduring "classics." Among the titles that have become modern standards are:

TECHNIQUE AND INSPIRATION

The Elements of Style with Index. By William Strunk, Jr., and E. B. White. 3d ed. Macmillan, 1979.

The celebrated "little book" of Cornell professor William Strunk's composition rules and E. B. White's advice on style was first published in 1959. Though critics call some of the rules antiquated, millions of copies have been sold and continue to leap off the shelves. Experienced writers find a rereading practical and inspirational.

On Writing Well. 4th ed. revised and enlarged. By William Zinsser. Harper, 1990.

Treats the writing of nonfiction. Zinsser, in the tradition of Strunk and White, is an advocate and master of prose that works without laboring. Don't set out to "commit an act of literature," is good Zinsser advice.

Writing Fiction. 2d ed. By R. V. Cassill. Prentice-Hall, 1975.

A solid advisory from a respected writer.

The Art of Fiction: Notes on the Craft for Young Writers. By John Gardner. Random House paperback edition, 1991.

The teaching legacy of the late novelist and creative writing instructor.

Becoming a Writer. By Dorothea Brande. Jeremy Tarcher, 1981.

Brande's book was first published in 1934. In reissued editions, her advice and teachings have encouraged would-be fiction authors. She is particularly good on techniques for drawing on one's own inspiration.

If You Want to Write. By Brenda Ueland. Graywolf Press, 1987.

A writer and writing instructor, Ueland helped would-be authors value themselves and what they wanted to say, particularly in fiction. First published in 1938, her book has reestablished itself among writers in this reissued volume.

The following titles concentrate on liberating your creativity:

Writing Down the Bones. By Natalie Goldberg. Shambhala Publications, 1986.

A Zen-influenced, well-written approach to creative authorship by this popular workshop instructor.

Writing on Both Sides of the Brain; Breakthrough Techniques for People Who Write. By Henriette Anne Klauser. Harper San Francisco, 1987.

The right hemisphere of the brain creates; the left half edits. Blockage comes from trying to do both at once. Play first to set the words free, then work, Klauser advises.

WORD AND USAGE BOOKS

Words and their shades of meaning occupy much of the writer's research activity. To enrich and distinguish their work, to find a special word, or simply to enjoy language, they turn to a type of reference tool known loosely as "word books." Word books might include such common resources as a general thesaurus or a usage manual, as well as specialized collections of words and phrases:

American Usage and Style, the Consensus. By Roy H. Copperud. Von Nostrand Reinhold, 1979.

For thousands of problem words and phrases, Copperud does the work of riffling through the major usage books and dictionaries to come up with a consensus of expert opinion. He spices these brief summaries with his own informed commentary.

Harper Dictionary of Contemporary Usage. 2d ed. By William and Mary Morris. HarperCollins, 1992.

One of the usage guides consulted by Copperud, the dictionary is itself a consensus of opinion drawn from a large panel of language observers and writers. Though other guides cover more terms, this one offers some of the most entertaining commentary.

Roget's Thesaurus of Words and Phrases. Rev. ed. By Peter M. Roget. Putnam, 1989.

A profusion of words and phrases grouped by concept in a progressive order, with an index to every word. Roget's ingenious classification scheme of related and opposing words was first published in 1852 by Longman, still the British publisher. Today's Longman and Putnam editions represent more than 140 years of refinement. Contemporary word-processing programs usually include a "thesaurus," but such software versions may be no more than lists of synonyms. Roget's is a far richer source and one to savor and explore.

With Roget-like enthusiasm for word groupings, Glazier gathered contemporary words into some 75,000 listings under 800 categories and subcategories. Not only does Glazier group words logically and conceptually, but under everyday subjects he gathers long lists of everyday objects, such as types of hammers or luggage. This particularity, and the brief definitions appearing with most entries, are distinguishing strengths of the *Word Menu,* especially for writers seeking the exact word.

The New York Times Dictionary of Misunderstood, Misused, and Mispronounced Words. Rev. ed. Edited by Laurence Urdang. NAL-Dutton, 1987.

One of dozens of word-collection books to extend one's special-effects vocabulary as well as entertain. Urdang, a distinguished lexicographer and word watcher, writes in the introduction to this dictionary: "it is hoped that the haecceity of this enchiridion of arcane and recondite sesquipedalian items will appeal to the oniomania of an eximious Gemeinschaft. . . ."

Richard Lederer is another droll collector of words and phrases, with a special interest in "embarrassing, egregious, and excruciating" errors in English. He has collected these in *Anguished English: An Anthology of Accidental Assaults Upon Our Language* (Dell, 1989) and *More Anguished English* (Delacorte, 1993).

Concise Science Dictionary. 2d ed. Oxford, 1991.

Not intended as a word book, this lexicon of 7,000 entries can nevertheless freshen the vocabulary of humanists, and, of course, be directly useful to science writers. *Gluon, podzol, purple-headed sneezeweed,* and *nictitating membranes* are among the delights of science nomenclature.

Slang and Jargon books

Writers find lively means of expression in the lingo of subcultures, from Wall Street to Death Row. Among the standard slang dictionaries that include derivations are *Dictionary of Slang and Unconventional English,* edited by Eric Partridge (8th ed., Macmillan, 1985) and *New Dictionary of American Slang,* edited by Robert L. Chapman (HarperCollins, 1986). Although slang tends to date fast, writers find older dictionaries useful for period slang and for phrases that have acquired the charm of antiquity. For contemporary slang, however, some of the more recent general dictionaries are:

The Oxford Dictionary of Modern Slang. Edited by John Simpson and John Ayto. Oxford, 1992.

Draws on the twentieth-century slang in the *Oxford English Dictionary* (1989 edition) plus hundreds more words from *OED*'s unpublished files of mainly American, British, and Australian slang. Includes *dweeb, rad, tubu-lar,* and *homeboy,* as well as earlier *peachy-keen* slang.

The Random House Historical Dictionary of American Slang, Volume 1: A–G. By Jonathan E. Lighter. Random House, 1994.

More than 20,000 definitions with dated citations ranging from the Middle Ages to 1994. Volumes 2 (H–Q) and 3 (R–Z) are due in 1996 and 1997, respectively.

The Random House Thesaurus of Slang. By Esther Lewin and Albert E. Lewin. Random House, 1989.

Some 12,000 standard words are listed alphabetically; each is followed by contemporary slang equivalents. Slang terms total about 150,000.

Trash Cash, Fizzbos, and Flatliners. A Dictionary of Today's Words. By the American Heritage Dictionary Editors et al. Houghton Mifflin, 1993.

Brief definitions of about 12,000 selected terms, such as *spooged,* refer-ring to a teen hairstyle that sticks out straight or to the sides.

Some examples of specialized slang collections are:

Whistlin' Dixie: A Dictionary of Southern Expressions. By Robert Hendrickson. Facts On File, 1993.

High Steppers, Fallen Angels, and Lollipops: Wall Street Slang. By Kathleen Odean. Dodd, Mead, 1988.

The Book of Jargon; An Essential Guide to Medicalese, Legalese, Computerese, Basic Jock, and 21 Other Varieties of Today's Most Important Specialized Lan-guages. By Don Ethan Miller. Collier/Macmillan, 1982.

The Queens' Vernacular; A Gay Lexicon. By Bruce Rodgers. Straight Arrow Books, 1972.

The Language of Sexuality. By Alan Richter. McFarland, 1987.

Prison Slang. By William K. Bentley and James M. Cornbett. McFarland, 1992.

College Slang 101. By Connie Eble. Spectacle Lane Press (Georgetown, Conn.), 1989.

Every author must stop writing his/her sentences like this one, a poor solution to the problem of distracting readers by sexist or sex-specific language. Better choices and good ideas come from *The Handbook of Nonsexist Writing* by Casey Miller and Kate Swift (2d ed., HarperCollins, 1988) and Rosalie Maggio's *The Bias-Free Word Finder* (Beacon Press, 1992), among other such guides.

Style in the literary sense generally refers to a writer's distinctive voice and its development. In research writing, however, style means the conventions established for reporting one's findings and sources with precision, consistency, and clarity. The following are some of the major style manuals used by researchers in the United States:

The Chicago Manual of Style: For Authors, Editors, and Copywriters. 14th ed. Revised and expanded. University of Chicago, 1993.

First published in 1906, the *Chicago Manual* has evolved into an American standard for authors of academic papers and editors of learned journals and many other types of publications. Publishers of general-audience books often base their style requirements on this manual, especially the conventions for styling punctuation, capitalization, italics, and numbers.

The Random House Guide to Good Writing. By Mitchell Ivers. Random House, 1991.

Words Into Type. 3d ed. Edited by Marjorie E. Skillin, Robert M. Gay et al. Prentice-Hall, 1986.

A classic, authoritative compendium of style conventions for writers, manuscript editors, and production editors, with a distinguished grammar section and superb index.

A Manual for Writers of Term Papers, Theses, and Dissertations. 5th ed. By Kate Turabian. Revised and expanded by Bonnie Birtwhistle Honigsblum. University of Chicago, 1987.

Known as "Turabian," this spin-off of the *Chicago Manual* includes many more examples of applied style rules and emphasizes the reference process for students in academic institutions. A geared-down version is titled *Student's Guide for Writing College Papers* (3d ed., University of Chicago, 1976).

Other style manuals include those used by journalists, such as *The Associated Press Stylebook and Libel Manual: The Journalist's Bible* (rev. ed., Addison-Wesley, 1987) and *The New York Times Manual of Style and Usage* (Times Books, 1982).

Nonsexist
Language Books

**RESEARCH AND
STYLE MANUALS**
*(See also Chapter 2,
Style Manuals)*

Those who have long struggled to learn bibliographic style may sniff, but some word-processing and specialized software can do a large chunk of the job for you. You fill in the blanks, and the software formats your citations in the style of your choice. *Term Paper Writer* (International Educations) is one such program. *Pro-Cite* (Personal Bibliographic Software) formats bibliographies in any of eight styles and offers several other features, such as quick subject indexing and subject bibliographies. *Academic DataManager* (KarlMarx Software) and *EndNote: A Reference Database and Bibliography Maker* (Niles and Associates) offer four and eight styles respectively. Other software from these producers allows automatic transfer of bibliographic information from an electronic database to one's research bibliography, in a choice of styles.

Automated Footnotes and Bibliography

PERIODICALS

When consulting popular magazines for writers, remember that any writing "secrets" or markets they reveal are revealed simultaneously to tens of thousands of writers. Articles are uneven in authority; the most enduring basic advice might be found in standard books for writers. But magazines do update information on grants, workshops, and other opportunities, and provide some down-to-earth advice. These two established magazines are carried in almost all public libraries:

The Writer. 1887–   . Monthly.
Leans toward advice on how to write well in various categories.

Writer's Digest. 1920–   . Monthly.
Focused on how to write to sell.

Poets & Writers Magazine. 1972–   . Bimonthly.
An important tabloid periodical, offers generally thoughtful content for writers. Ranges from middle- to high-brow in its features. Poetry counts here. Strong on announcements of grants, awards, and workshops.

Other key periodicals for keeping up with the publishing world include:

Publishers Weekly. 1872–   . Weekly.
The trade journal of the U.S. publishing and bookselling industries. For the writer, *PW* offers fast reporting of trends and attitudes among publishers of general-audience books. Spring and fall announcement issues are snapshots of U.S. publishing output, house by house. Other writer-related features include reviews of selected forthcoming books, columns on literary agency activity, best-seller lists, and articles on legal issues.

Small Press. 1983–   . Quarterly.

Articles for and about small publishers provide insights for writers on the tastes and inclinations of these quality houses. Reviews small-press publications.

The New York Review of Books. 1963–   . 21 issues/year.

More than a book review, this newsprint journal provides a forum for leading intellectuals and literary figures to reflect on central issues in politics, the arts, science, and history. Reviews tend to be long and probing.

The New York Times Book Review. 1890–   . Weekly.

Influential reviews of current literature (including children's books), author profiles, lively reader correspondence, literary features, and the famous Best Sellers list. Covers some small and university presses as well as mainstream publishers.

Booklist. 1905–   . 22 issues/year.

Published by the American Library Association, this reviewing medium offers brisk evaluations of about 7,000 of the 45,000 books published each year in the United States. Only books recommended for various types of libraries are reviewed. Well organized for tracking new titles by category. Reviews include reference books and other media, such as videotapes and software.

WritePro, the Sol Stein Creative Writing Program. (Software) By Sol Stein. The WritePro Corp.

ELECTRONIC SOURCES

Author and lexicographer Stein is a pioneer in learn-to-write software programs. *Write Pro* offers prompting, mentoring, and tricks of the trade, especially for fiction writers.

Other writers' software, including such powerful grammar and usage checkers as *Right Writer* (RightSoft, Inc.) can be found under Word Processing in *Software Encyclopedia* (Bowker, annual; gives producers' addresses) and *Software Reviews on File* (Facts On File, monthly). However, as Arthur Plotnik cautions in his wry advisory, *Honk If You're a Writer* (Fireside/Simon & Schuster, 1992), "Software for writers can become a distraction, drawing too much attention to its own fun self. Do you want to play or write?"

Bulletin Boards

It may be just another way to avoid writing, but writers are exchanging ideas via bulletin boards on the consumer online services:
- Prodigy: The Arts Club features three BBS: Writing/Poetry, Writing/Prose, and Writing/Technique. Discussion is more or less at the begin-

ner-to-intermediate level, but reviewer Digby Diehl is available to answer questions about the publishing and reviewing worlds.

- America Online: Bulletin boards for fiction, nonfiction, and poetry are hosted within the Writers Club. Poetry and Fiction workshops offer scheduled chats (real-time interactive sessions). Writers can upload drafts of their materials to a reading library, from which others can download for reading and comment.
- GEnie offers a Writers Ink bulletin board.

On the Internet, professional and aspiring writers can join a Bitnet group discussing the art, craft, and business of writing and new opportunities for writers. Access via: **WRITERS%NDSUVM1.BITNET@VM1.NODAK.EDU.**

LC SUBJECT HEADINGS

Authorship (use this, not Writing)

Authorship—Style handbooks, manuals, etc.

Authorship—Marketing

Authorship—Style manuals

Book proposals

Children's literature—Technique

Creative writing

Crime writing

Fiction—Technique

Playwriting

Poetry—Authorship

Technical writing

Travel writing

ASSOCIATIONS

National Writers Club
1450 S. Havana, Suite 620
Aurora, CO 80012
(303) 751-7844

Offers full membership to published writers, associate memberships to anyone else; also home study courses, contests. Houses a 2,000-volume library on writing for its 4,000 members.

Authors Guild
330 W. 42d St.
New York, NY 10036
(212) 398-0838

National society of professional authors founded in 1921. Some 6,500 members. Provides information relevant to the contractual, business, and professional interests of writers along with advisory services and publications, surveys, and lobbying efforts. For membership requirements, request the "Précis" brochure.

PEN American Center
568 Broadway
New York, NY 10012
(212) 334-1660

Membership in PEN (which stands for poets, playwrights, editors, essayists, and novelists) is by invitation, but the 2,500-member organization is of interest to every writer for its support of intellectual freedom, the international flow of ideas, and literature in general. Among its varied activities is sponsorship of writing competitions for prisoners in the United States. About 100 autonomous PEN centers in some sixty nations are associated with PEN American Center.

American Society of Journalists and Authors
1801 Broadway, Suite 302
New York, NY 10036
(212) 997-0947
A select group of about 800 freelance writers of nonfiction magazine articles and books. Forum for issues and concerns. Develops codes of ethics.

International Women's Writing Guild
Box 810, Gracie Station
New York, NY 10028-0082
(212) 737-7536
Serves 6,000 members from twenty-four nations. Offers writing workshops, conferences, help with finding agents.

International Black Writers
P. O. Box 1030
Chicago, IL 60690
(312) 924-3818
Fosters new black writers. About 1,000 members; regional and local groups. Programs include awards, referrals, and events. Maintains a library.

Literary Market Place (above) and *Encyclopedia of Associations* (Gale) list writers' groups, including many specialized associations.

SPECIAL CONCERNS

Neither special libraries nor government publications and agencies are critical to research on writing itself; they are listed in other chapters of this guide for help in researching specific subject areas. Some public funding for literary activity comes from the National Endowment for the Humanities and state arts councils; these grant and fellowship offerings are announced in the writers' periodicals.

Some special concerns of writers are addressed by the resources noted below.

Legal Matters

Copyright, libel, and invasion of privacy are the three legal matters that most concern writers. By law a manuscript is copyrighted from the moment it is in tangible form, and the publishers will arrange for copyright registration before publication. In almost every instance, this is safe standard procedure. A book is usually copyrighted in the author's name rather than the publisher's. Although some not-for-profit publishers prefer to hold the copyright, authors can often insist on proprietary rights.

Of more general concern is the law as it affects copyrighted materials that you draw upon for your own work. The legal term that describes how much you can use and under what restrictions is *fair use.* You should do careful research on when and how to request permissions for copyrighted material.

Other sources of litigation are libel and invasion of privacy. The rules are complex and subject to the interpretation of the courts. This is another area where research into what you can and cannot publish is essential.

Among the many good legal reference sources for writers are the following (see also *The Associated Press Stylebook and Libel Manual* and the general writers' guides, above, and the discussion of copyright in Chapter 33, Law):

- *Circular One.* Copyright Office, Library of Congress, Washington, DC 20559, 1993. (202-707-3000.) Basic guide to copyright registration. Revised as changes in law and practice dictate.
- *A Writer's Guide to Copyright.* 2d ed., 1989, and the reprint, *Libel & Fiction.* From Poets & Writers, 72 Spring St., New York, NY 10012.
- *Writer's Lawyer: Essential Advice for Writers and Editors in All Media.* By Ronald Goldfarb and Gail E. Ross. Times Books, 1989.
- *Author Law and Strategies: A Legal Guide for the Working Writer.* By Brad Bunin and Peter Beren. Nolo Press, 1984.

Writing Courses   Check with your librarian for writing courses and workshops in the community. The following national guides, as well as *Literary Market Place* (above), provide basic information, updated by writers' periodicals:

AWP Official Guide to Writing Programs. Associated Writing Programs, Old Dominion University, Norfolk, VA 23529. Biennial.

A directory of writing programs at some 310 U.S. and Canadian institutions.

Guide to Writers Conferences: Writers Conferences, Workshops, Seminars, Residencies, Retreats, and Organizations. Edited by Dorlene V. Kaplan and Lawrence H. Caplan. ShawGuides, 1992.

Describes hundreds of programs.

Grants and Awards   In addition to the substantial, up-to-date listings in periodicals for writers and *Literary Market Place*, the following sources reveal the variety of competitive opportunities for writers:

Grants and Awards Available to American Writers. PEN American Center.
Issued every two years.

Awards, Honors & Prizes. 10th ed., 1993–94. Edited by Gita Siegman. Gale
Research, 1992.
   Briefly describes some 24,000 awards in two volumes. Volume 1 covers
the United States and Canada; Volume 2, foreign and international awards.
Use of the index will lead to hundreds of items of interest to writers.

*Publication Grants for Writers & Publishers: How to Find Them, Win Them, and
Manage Them.* Edited by Karin R. Park and Beth Luey. Oryx, 1991.
   Step-by-step advice on this type of proposal, from the publishers of
Directory of Grants in the Humanities (frequently updated) and other funding
resources.

Aspiring writers can find at least one guide for almost every writing spe-   **OTHER SOURCES**
cialty—juveniles, travel, mystery, romance, and so on. The large bookstores
or "superstores" generally have a better selection to examine than the
library does. Many smaller independent bookstores specialize in writers'
guides. For a vast list of current offerings, consult the library's *Books in Print*
subject volume under the heading *Authorship*.
   Free catalogs from the following sources feature a selection of materials:
Writer's Digest Books, 1507 Dana Ave., Cincinnati, OH 45207, (513) 531-
2222; Tools of the Trade—Books for Communicators, 3148-B Duke St.,
Alexandria, VA 22314-4523, (800) 827-8665; Poets & Writers, 72 Spring
St., New York, NY 10012, (212) 226-3586.

INDEX